Ethiopian Yearbook of International Law 2018

The Ethiopian Yearbook of International Law (EtYIL) is a peer-reviewed academic Yearbook that publishes scholarly works of the highest standard in the field of international law broadly defined, but with a focus on Ethiopia and the Horn of Africa region. International law presents both opportunities and challenges to developing countries; however, their role in the making of the law and the scholarly analysis and debate that informs and underpins its evolution remains marginal. By choosing Ethiopia as its geographical focus, this Yearbook aims to contribute towards filling this gap and the long-term goal of rebalancing the narrative of international law in a manner that better reflects the diversity of its actors and subjects. With this in mind, EtYIL welcomes contributions in all areas of international law and relations. Particular issues of interest to the Yearbook include sustainable development law, the law of international trade and investment, the peaceful settlement of disputes, the sharing and preservation of transboundary resources, regional integration, peace and security, humanitarian law and human rights, and regional and international institutions.

More information about this series at http://www.springer.com/series/15093

Zeray Yihdego • Melaku Geboye Desta •
Martha Belete Hailu
Editors

Ethiopian Yearbook of International Law 2018

In Pursuit of Peace and Prosperity

Springer

Editors
Zeray Yihdego
School of Law
University of Aberdeen
Aberdeen, UK

Melaku Geboye Desta
Faculty of Business and Law
De Montfort University
Leicester, UK

Martha Belete Hailu
Addis Ababa University
Addis Ababa, Ethiopia

ISSN 2522-5286 ISSN 2522-5294 (electronic)
Ethiopian Yearbook of International Law
ISBN 978-3-030-24077-6 ISBN 978-3-030-24078-3 (eBook)
https://doi.org/10.1007/978-3-030-24078-3

This Springer imprint is published by the registered company Springer Nature Switzerland AG.
The registered company address is: Gewerbestrasse 11, 6330 Cham, Switzerland

Contents

Part I
Introduction

In Pursuit of Peace and Prosperity through International Law

Zeray Yihdego, Melaku Geboye Desta, and Marta Belete Hailu

Abstract EtYIL 2018 comes at a time when multilateralism and its underpinning norms of international law and institutions are under siege. At the same time, in 2018, Africa stood out for upholding multilateralism and international law. From the adoption of the Agreement establishing the African Continental Free Trade Area (ACFTA) to the signing of a series of peace agreements that brought to an end two decades of hostilities between Eritrea and Ethiopia, 2018 was indeed a remarkable year for international law in Africa. EtYIL 2018 covers some of these issues with emphasis on the lessons learnt from the Eritrea-Ethiopia claims Commission decisions on *jus ad bellum*, *jus in bello*, evidentiary and procedural matters and the role of arbitration in upholding the international rule of law. New developments such as the lifting of United Nations Security Council sanctions against Eritrea and the aforementioned new agreements signed between Eritrea and Ethiopia have also been covered in this volume. The volume also devotes considerable attention to other legal issues including: the use and misuse of European patent law to the detriment of developing countries' legal interests, sharing transboundary resources, production sharing agreements on extractives between African countries and multinationals, evolving rules governing economic relations between Africa and its traditional partners relating to Brexit, contract-farming in the African cocoa (and its derivative chocolate) industry, the international Criminal Court and the extraterritorial application of human rights law from an African perspective, and the emerging challenge of cyber-attacks and the role of international law in tackling it. Such timely and pioneering articles authored by experts from Africa, Asia, Europe and North America not only bring new and diverse voices to international law discourse, they also contribute to the EtYIL's overarching goal of contributing to the effort to rebalance the narrative of international law.

Z. Yihdego (✉)
School of Law, University of Aberdeen, Aberdeen, UK
e-mail: zeray.yihdego@abdn.ac.uk

M. G. Desta
Faculty of Business and Law, De Montfort University, Leicester, UK

M. B. Hailu
Addis Ababa University, Addis Ababa, Ethiopia

Z. Yihdego et al. (eds.), *Ethiopian Yearbook of International Law 2018*, Ethiopian Yearbook of International Law 2018, https://doi.org/10.1007/978-3-030-24078-3_1

1 Background

Since its inaugural issue in 2016, the Ethiopian Yearbook of International Law (EtYIL) has dedicated itself to matters of international law that are of particular interest to the African continent in general and Ethiopia and the Horn in particular. In pursuit of its long-term goal of contributing towards rebalancing the narrative of international law, EtYIL has been systematic in its selection of issues, thorough and objective in its analysis, fearless in its conclusions, and challenging and provocative in its policy recommendations. We are pleased to report to our readers that this same approach is in full display in EtYIL 2018, our third volume in as many years.

EtYIL 2018 comes at a time when multilateralism and its underpinning norms of international law and institutions are under siege, when some of its traditional guardians have turned their focus and trust away from it in favour of raw power, leaving the future of the rules-based international order hanging in the balance. At the same time, in 2018, Africa stood out for upholding multilateralism and international law. From the adoption of the Agreement establishing the African Continental Free Trade Area (ACFTA), which promises to usher in a new era of rules-based regional and continental trade liberalisation and integration, to the signing of a series of peace agreements that brought to an end two-decades of hostilities between Eritrea and Ethiopia, 2018 was indeed a remarkable year for international law in Africa. EtYIL 2018 covers some of these issues in some depth, while others have been considered in EtYIL 2017 and no doubt will also be covered in future issues. EtYIL also devotes substantial effort to other international law issues of no less serious gravity to the region that have been with us for longer, such as legal issues related to sharing transboundary resources, evolving rules governing economic relations between Africa and its traditional partners, Africa's complicated relations with the International Criminal Court, and the issue of extraterritoriality in the context of human rights fall under this category. Finally, and for the first time in this series, we also look at the fast-emerging challenges of cyber-attacks and the role of international law in tackling it. The volume starts with articles, followed by book reviews, concluding with new international law instruments of regional significance along with brief commentaries and/or explanatory notes.

2 Highlights of the Contributions

2.1 *Articles*

The full articles section opens with a major contribution by Thomas R. Snider and Aishwarya Nair entitled '*Ten Years On: A Look at The Legacy of the Eritrea-Ethiopia Claims Commission*', which re-visits the Commission's decisions on claims over losses, damages and injury that arose out of the 1998–2000 armed conflict between the two neighbouring countries. After providing a background to the case and articulating the structures and procedures of the Commission, the article examines the legal contributions of the Commission on matters of *jus ad bellum*, *jus in bello*, evidentiary standards and the treatment of 'dual nationals'. The article further examines the practical contributions of the decision with respect to the development of mass-claims processing and identifies those approaches that could be beneficial to future commissions confronted with complex mass claims issues.

The second article, co-authored by Constantinos Yiallourides and Zeray Yihdego (of the editorial team) '*Disputed Territories and the Law on the Use of Force: Lessons from the Eritrea-Ethiopia Case*', follows almost naturally from the first, developing the *jus ad bellum* aspect of the decision of the same Eritrea-Ethiopia Claims Commission. After providing a historical and political context to the conflict itself, including the causes of the war and current developments in the relations between the two neighbouring states, the article examines the interface between *jus ad bellum* and the law of territories. The article then delves into the legal arguments presented by the parties, along with the merits of the findings of the Commission in light of relevant international case law and academic commentary. The authors articulate the lessons to be learnt from the case by the two countries and the international community at large in the fields of self-defence, the law of territories and the role of arbitral tribunals in upholding the international rule of law.

The third article, authored by Beka Melkamu, on '*Patenting Developing Countries' traditional knowledge as new invention*', looks into the legality of a patent right granted by the European Patent Office (EPO) to a Dutch company on the processing of teff, Ethiopia's staple grain whose actual processing has been perfected in Ethiopia through tradition built up over millennia. The article describes how knowledge of its gluten-free characteristics and reputation as a super-grain became known more widely around the world, which drove a Dutch company to use legally and morally questionable methods to secure patent rights over the processing of teff from the EPO, and how that threatened to deprive Ethiopia of any opportunities to export food items that are products of its traditional knowledge. After discussing the international law of patent rights and the teff patent claim from a comparative legal perspective, the article outlines the grounds for challenging the legality of the European patent over the processing of teff and articulates strategies for how to place the rights and legal interests of Ethiopian farmers on a firmer legal footing for the future.

The fourth article, authored by Götz Reichert, on '*International Water Cooperation in Europe: Lessons for the Nile Basin Countries?*', explores the implications of changing power constellations among upstream and downstream riparians, both as a challenge and an opportunity, to promote cooperation on the sharing and protection of Nile waters. The article starts with an examination of the efforts that have been made over the years to manage the sharing of European river basins, which provide some lessons for the Nile basin countries while still keeping in mind the differing historical and geographical contexts that would make direct replication difficult. The article concludes with an outline of the shifting paradigms, including from (a) coexistence to cooperation, (b) substantive to procedural, and (c) bilateral or trilateral to multilateral, and building trust through an international river commission and epistemic communities.

The fifth article, authored by John Paterson, on '*Production Sharing Agreements in Africa: Sovereignty and Relationality*' builds upon, and critiques, the article by Melaku Desta (of the editorial team) published in the maiden volume of this Yearbook on a related subject. The article begins with a summary of the relevant aspects of Desta's article, outlines regulatory and theoretical frameworks, which take into consideration the laws and practices of several African countries, including (a) state options for legal arrangements in the petroleum sector, (b) the dynamic risk matrix for oil and gas projects, (c) designing petroleum fiscal arrangements, (d) complexifying stabilisation by building in self-adjustment and by moving from freezing to economic equilibrium, and (e) introducing relationality in PSAs. This is then followed by proposed principles to guide renegotiations and the arbitral adaptation of relational contracts, thereby re-balancing state sovereignty and relationality.

The sixth article, authored by Lindsey Callahan, on '*Contract-Farming in Cocoa Value Chains in Africa: Possibilities and Challenges*', investigates the legal, socio-economic, human rights, environmental and equality aspects of the cocoa industry, which is a global multi-billion dollar industry, from a contract-farming business model perspective, and using Theo Chocolate (Democratic Republic of Congo), Divine Chocolate (Ghana), and Madécasse (Madagascar), as case studies. The article offers a detailed discussion of the nature of the cocoa value chain, including its derivative, the chocolate industry; it then moves to exploring the nature of contract-farming between smallholder farmers and multinational chocolate companies, and the challenges and prospects of contract-farming on cocoa production in terms, inter alia, of pricing arrangements, sustainable development, gender equality, research and knowledge generation.

The seventh article, authored by Joseph McMahon, on '*Africa post-Brexit in EU Development Cooperation Policy and UK Trade Policy*', explores the likely implications of Britain's exit from the EU (Brexit), the fate of the various Economic Partnership Agreements (EPAs) signed between the EU and African countries after Brexit, and the future of British and EU development cooperation policy towards Africa in the context of the United Nations Sustainable Development Goals (SDGs). The article commences with an introduction to the history of development cooperation between the EU and Africa and the legal and policy frameworks that govern such relations; it then devotes a great deal of attention to the future of EU cooperation policy and likely UK trade policy towards Africa post-Brexit. The Article, by way of conclusions, offers useful insights into the future of UK and EU development partnerships with Africa and the uncertainties therein.

The eighth article, authored by Enenu Okwori, on '*The Obligation of Due Diligence and Cyber-attacks*', examines the growing problem of cyber-attacks and the due diligence obligations of states to prevent such conduct against other states under international law. At the outset, the article articulates the challenge of cyber-attacks to both developed and developing countries. It then examines the nature of the due diligence obligation with reference to several fields of international law, including international environmental, humanitarian and human rights laws. This is followed by an in-depth examination of the application of a due diligence duty to cyber-attacks with a focus on such key issues as knowledge and foreseeability, risk of significant transboundary harm, and incompatibility of conduct with the rights of another State. After exploring the duties of transit countries in mitigating and preventing cyber-attacks, the article offers proposals to address the gaps in the law as a universal remedy.

2.2 Book Reviews

This section reviews two books that deal with different but related areas of public international law relevant to Africa. The first book, '*Extraterritorial Human Rights Obligations from an African Perspective*' (L. Chenwi and T. Soboka Bulta (eds.), Cambridge: Intersentia, 2018, 308 Pages), is reviewed by Cedric Ryngaert, who critically looks at socio-economic human rights from theoretical, doctrinal and practical perspectives. The reviewer concludes that the book is 'a carefully edited collection which forms a coherent whole', with individual contributions that are 'well-written and contain a wealth of doctrinal insights and empirical information'. Most notably, the reviewer stresses that 'the voices of the new generation of African (and Africa-minded) scholars who have contributed to this volume deserve a wide audience'.

The second book, '*Selective Enforcement and International Criminal Law: The International Criminal Court and Africa*' (James Nyawo, Intersentia 2017, 288 Pages), is reviewed by Chris Maina Peter, who begins his task with a quote from Archbishop Desmond Tutu's strongly-held and well-known view in support of the ICC and articulates and comments on four key areas of the book—Africa's initial love affair with the ICC, the Court's targeting of Africa, the exodus of African countries from the ICC, and the failure of unity and short-term interests of African states with respect to their responses to the ICC-Africa relationship. The review commends the book as an invaluable contribution to knowledge in international criminal justice and the workings of the ICC, and a must read for all interested in the field.

3 Current Decisions and Legal Instruments

This section reproduces important UN and other bilateral decisions and instruments concluded in 2018 along with short introductory notes. It is notable at the outset that, by documenting such international law instruments and decisions from or pertaining to the region, EtYIL aims to ensure that researchers and practitioners have access to a record of state practice from this part of the world, which is often either lacking or not given sufficient attention by scholars of international law. The first instrument, introduced by Melaku Geboye Desta (of the editorial team) on '*Peace Agreements between Ethiopia and Eritrea: Ending Two Decades of Hostilities – an Introductory Note',* provides a brief background to the war between the two neighbouring countries and summarises the two agreements signed between the leaders of the two countries to restore peaceful relations between them—the *Joint Declaration of Peace and Friendship* signed on 9 July 2018 in Asmara, Eritrea, and the *Agreement on Peace, Friendship and Comprehensive Cooperation Between the Federal Democratic Republic of Ethiopia and the State of Eritrea* signed on 16 September 2018 in Jeddah, Saudi Arabia. The introductory note also refers to the joint statement issued by the two leaders and their hosts following the July 2018 agreement. The note concludes by underlying the need to base this new chapter in the relations between the two countries on enduring principles and strong institutions. The two agreements and the statement are re-printed along this introductory note.

The second instrument, introduced by Nicole Hirt, is the '*UN Security Council Resolution 2444 (2018) and the Lifting of Sanctions against Eritrea*'. In her introduction, Hirt offers background commentary on the sanctions against Eritrea, their national and regional effects and implications, and the key considerations behind Resolution 2444 (2018) that led to the lifting of sanctions against Eritrea. The resolution is re-printed next to the commentary.

4 Conclusion

As can be seen from the highlights above, EtYIL 2018 contains a rich body of analysis on some of the most topical issues of international law of particular interest to Ethiopia and the Horn, but also to Africa and the rest of the world. In times like this when the most powerful members of the international community are turning against international law, developing countries need to learn lessons from their successes and challenges, reassert their faith in international law, and contribute to its preservation and further development. In the absence of international law, the powerful are likely to do what they wish while the less powerful will do what they must. International law itself has never been free of the disproportionate role of the powerful in its making and interpretation, but it is also clear that the imperfect international law we have today is far superior to the world some are imagining for us without it.

In concluding, let us seize this opportunity to invite contributions on matters of peace and security, development and investment, the respect of fundamental human rights, and regional and sub-regional integration aspects, that are of interest to Ethiopia, the Horn, the African continent and the developing world more generally. Finally, the successful completion of this volume, like the previous editions, would not have been possible without the dedication of our contributors, the full support of our external reviewers, the unreserved commitment of our assistant editors, Abubakri Yekini, Jasmin Hansohm and Emily Hirst, and our Springer colleagues; we thank you all for your hard work and dedication!

Part II
Articles

Ten Years on: A Look at the Legacy of the Eritrea-Ethiopia Claims Commission

Thomas R. Snider and Aishwarya Suresh Nair

Abstract This paper analyses the work of the Eritrea-Ethiopia Claims Commission, which was established in December 2000 to adjudicate claims for loss, damage and injury arising from violations of international law that occurred during the 1998–2000 conflict between Eritrea and Ethiopia. In particular, this paper critically considers some of the Commission's legal and practical innovations and attempts, from its analysis, to draw out some key lessons for future bodies that may have to work under similar situations with similar mandates. After providing contextual background on the conflict and the efforts to achieve a peaceful resolution of it in the first section, the second section of this paper describes the workings of the Commission. In the third section, the authors seek to critically analyse the legal and practical contributions of the Commission. The fourth section is devoted to considering the circumstances under which the constitution of such a body is appropriate. As part of this section, and with specific reference to the Ethiopia-Eritrea dispute, the paper weighs the strengths of such bodies against bodies with a purely fact-finding mandate. The fifth and final section then presents a summary of the key findings of the paper.

1 Introduction

In July 2018, Eritrea and Ethiopia formally announced the end of the "state of war" between the two nations through a Joint Declaration of Peace and Friendship.[1] This declaration came 18 years after the armed war between the two African states

[1]For a detailed review of recent agreements between Ethiopia and Eritrea, see Desta (this volume), pp. 261–268.

T. R. Snider (✉)
Al Tamimi and Company, Dubai, UAE
e-mail: t.snider@tamimi.com

A. S. Nair
National Law Institute University, Bhopal, India

Z. Yihdego et al. (eds.), *Ethiopian Yearbook of International Law 2018*, Ethiopian Yearbook of International Law 2018, https://doi.org/10.1007/978-3-030-24078-3_2

formally ended in December 2000. This paper considers some of the key determinations of the Eritrea-Ethiopia Claims Commission ("Claims Commission"), one of the formal bodies established in the aftermath of the conflict to adjudicate claims for loss, damage, or injury arising from violations of international law that occurred during the armed conflict. A decade since the Claims Commission issued its final awards July 2009, it is now an opportune moment to take a fresh look at the Claims Commission's work. The remainder of this section aims to set the backdrop for this discussion by providing a brief overview of the conflict between Eritrea and Ethiopia and the efforts that were made to negotiate an end to the conflict.

1.1 Brief Background to the Conflict

The armed conflict between Eritrea and Ethiopia commenced in May 1998 with an Eritrean attack on the Ethiopia-administered town of Badme. This conflict would claim more than 70,000 lives[2] and lead to the displacement of 1.2 million people[3] before finally ending in December 2000.

Almost from the start of the conflict, there was a persistent international diplomatic effort to end it. When the fighting first broke out in May 1998, the United States and Rwanda joined together as mediators in an attempt to resolve the conflict and proposed a cease-fire based on certain conditions.[4] In November 1998, these proposals were adopted by the Organisation of African Unity ("OAU") into a proposed Framework Agreement.[5] However, these proposals ultimately were not implemented because they could not invoke an equal interest from Eritrea and Ethiopia.

Eritrea and Ethiopia's eventual participation in "proximity talks" under the auspices of the OAU later in the conflict in May and June 2000 marked the beginning of the end of the hostilities. On June 18, 2000, Eritrea and Ethiopia signed the Cessation of Hostilities Agreement by which they committed themselves to a cease-fire and Ethiopia agreed to the redeployment of its forces back to areas under Ethiopian administration prior to May 1998.[6] In addition, the two states agreed to the deployment of a United Nations peacekeeping force of some 4200 troops, known as the UN Mission in Ethiopia and Eritrea ("UNMEE"), within a 25-kilometre-wide zone just inside Eritrea along the Ethiopian-Eritrean border, as it existed prior to May 1998.[7]

[2]Gray (2006), p. 703.

[3]UNSC (2000), para. 111.

[4]U.S. Department of State (1998).

[5]UNSC (1998).

[6]Agreement on Cessation of Hostilities, Eri.-Eth., 18 June 2000, 2138 U.N.T.S. 86, paras. 1, 9 ('Cessation Agreement').

[7]Paras. 2-3, 12, Cessation Agreement.

While the UN Security Council authorized the establishment and deployment of UNMEE, talks continued for the purpose of reaching a final peace agreement. This culminated in the signing of the Agreement Between the Government of the Federal Democratic Republic of Ethiopia and the Government of the State of Eritrea in Algiers on December 12, 2000 (the "Algiers Agreement").[8] Under the Algiers Agreement, Eritrea and Ethiopia agreed to the permanent termination of military hostilities and to refrain from the threat or use of force against each other.[9] As per the preamble to the Algiers Agreement, its goals included "[t]he resettlement of displaced persons, as well as rehabilitation and peace building in both countries."

The crux of this six-provision agreement lay in the identification of three institutional structures to assist the parties in their post-war cooperation. Article 3, with the object of determining the origin of the conflict, provided for an investigation by an independent, impartial body of "the incidents of May 6, 1998 and on any other incident prior to that date which could have contributed to a misunderstanding between the parties ... including the incidents of July and August 1997." Article 4 provided for the creation of the Eritrea-Ethiopia Boundary Commission ("Boundary Commission"), consisting of five members charged with delimiting and demarcating the border between the two states on the basis of the pertinent colonial treaties and applicable international law. Finally, Article 5 called for the creation of the Claims Commission to "address the negative socio-economic impact of the crisis on the civilian population" by deciding claims for war-related injuries.

Only the Boundary Commission and the Claims Commission were actually set up. This setback was, however, addressed to some extent by the Claims Commission, which, in the course of events, went on to consider the origins of the conflict, ultimately finding that Eritrea initiated the conflict through the unlawful use of military force, i.e., that Eritrea had violated the *jus ad bellum*.[10] Thus, between them, the Boundary Commission and Claims Commission acted as "complementary bodies"[11] to fulfil the objectives of the Algiers Agreement. The Boundary Commission was to look at the stated root cause of the dispute (i.e., the boundary) while the Claims Commission was to address the consequences of the conflict.

[8] Agreement, Eri.-Eth., 12 December 2000, 2138 U.N.T.S. 94, 40 I.L.M. 260 ('Algiers Agreement').

[9] Article 1, Algiers Agreement.

[10] See Partial Award, *Jus Ad Bellum*, Ethiopia's Claims 1-8 (19 December 2005), 45 I.L.M. 430 (2006) para. 3 ('Partial Award, Jus Ad Bellum').

[11] Greppi (2009), p. 61.

2 Overview of the Structure, Functions, and Procedure of the Claims Commission

The Claims Commission's mandate was set out in Article 5(1) of the Algiers Agreement as deciding "[t]hrough binding arbitration all claims for loss, damage or injury by one Government against the other, and by nationals (including both natural and juridical persons) of one party against the Government of the other party or entities owned or controlled by the other party...." The remainder of Article 5 detailed the procedural and structural aspects of the Claims Commission.

The Claims Commission was comprised of five arbitrators with two party-appointed arbitrators from each side. As per Article 5(3), the only requirement of the arbitrators was that they should not be nationals or permanent residents of either party. Eritrea's appointees to the Claims Commission were John Crook and Lucy Reed, while Ethiopia's appointees were Dean James Paul and George Aldrich. The four commissioners together appointed Professor Hans van Houtte as the president of the tribunal.[12]

Consistent with Article 5(5) of the Algiers Agreement, The Hague was designated as the seat of the arbitration; the entirety of the proceedings took place there. While the Algiers Agreement empowered the Claims Commission to employ professional, administrative, and clerical staff and retain consultants and experts for the completion of its work,[13] the Claims Commission opted to use the facilities and registry services of the Permanent Court of Arbitration ("PCA"). The PCA stored and catalogued the parties' pleadings and acted as an intermediary between the parties and the Claims Commission.[14] Outside of the services the PCA provided, all costs arising from the work of the Claims Commission were split equally between the two states.[15]

As required under Article 5(7) of the Algiers Agreement, the Claims Commission's Rules of Procedure were based on the PCA Optional Rules for Arbitrating Disputes Between Two States. However, the Algiers Agreement allowed the Claims Commission to exercise flexibility in determining particular procedures for handling claims and in modifying its own rules. Crucial additions to the Rules of Procedure were Chapter 2, which detailed the procedure for the individual consideration of claims, and Chapter 3, which, in furtherance of Article 5(10) of the Algiers Agreement, provided for a mass-claims procedure.

The Claims Commission was to decide claims resulting from violations of international law, but not claims arising from the "costs of actual military operations, preparation for them or the use of force" (e.g., the costs of weapons, equipment, and

[12]UNSC (2001), para. 2.

[13]Article 5(6), Algiers Agreement.

[14]Holtzmann and Kristjánsdóttir (2007), p. 308.

[15]Id. pp. 362–363.

other material required to fight the war) unless they involved violations of international humanitarian law ("IHL").[16] The law applicable to the determination of these substantive questions was only briefly touched upon in the Algiers Agreement[17] and was discussed more extensively under Article 19 of the Rules of Procedure. This provision broadly mirrors Article 38(1) of the Statute of the International Court of Justice but notably adds arbitral decisions as a subsidiary source of applicable law and also acknowledged the possibility of referencing national law.[18]

In compliance with the 1-year deadline for the submission of claims under the Algiers Agreement,[19] the parties filed a total of 41 claims with the Claims Commission in December 2001—Ethiopia filed a total of nine claims, while Eritrea filed a total of 32 claims. The claims brought by the two parties largely paralleled one another; the difference in numbers was merely a result of different methods of organisation of the claims. The parties' claims were organised by subject matter, geography, and, in some instances, by particular incidents. With respect to subject matter, claims were filed relating to the treatment of prisoners of war ('POWs'), treatment of enemy aliens and their property, expulsion of enemy aliens, harm to diplomats and diplomatic property, and aerial bombardment.

After receiving the parties' respective statements of defense in February 2002, the Claims Commission bifurcated the proceedings into a liability phase and a damages phase. Under the latter phase, the Claims Commission proceeded to assess the damages claimed by both parties stemming from the Commission's findings on liability. For this phase, the claims were organised into two groups. Group No. 1 claims consisted of the war-front claims, POW claims, displaced-person claims, and injuries arising from Ethiopia's *jus ad bellum* claim (i.e., Eritrea's unlawful use of military force in initiating the conflict), while Group No. 2 claims covered all residual claims.

The principal form of relief that the parties sought and the Commission granted was monetary compensation. The Commission noted that it did not "foreclose the possibility of providing other types of remedies . . . if the particular remedy [could] be shown to be in accordance with international practice, and if the Tribunal determine[d] that a particular remedy would be reasonable and appropriate in the circumstances."[20] However, the Commission did not deem restitution or other alternate types of remedies appropriate for any of its liability findings.

---

[16]Article 5(1), Algiers Agreement.

[17]Article 5(1), (13), Algiers Agreement.

[18]Article 19(2)(d), Eritrea-Ethiopia Claims Commission, Rules of Procedure (October 2001) ('Rules of Procedure').

[19]Article 5(8), Algiers Agreement.

[20]Eritrea-Ethiopia Claims Commission, Decision No. 3, Remedies (August 2001).

3 The Legal and Practical Contributions of the Claims Commission

The Claims Commission's contributions are manifold. This section aims to highlight and weigh some of the key ones. In doing so, the discussion proceeds in two categories: legal and practical. Each shall be considered in turn.

3.1 *Legal Contributions*

3.1.1 *Jus ad Bellum* Award

The Commission's Partial Award in respect of Ethiopia's *jus ad bellum* claim against Eritrea was a significant contribution to the development of international law. International legal decisions that have found a state responsible for unlawfully resorting to force have been scarce. While on paper it appears a simple task, in action, it is very complex to establish the facts necessary to establish such a claim as both parties will typically maintain that they acted in self-defense.[21] Therefore, the Partial Award will be a vital reference point for future disputes on the use of force in border disputes.[22] Under this claim, Ethiopia contended that Eritrea planned and carried out a series of unlawful armed attacks against it in violation of Article 2(4) of the UN Charter and customary international law and made this an element of all the other claims it submitted to the Claims Commission.[23] Eritrea denied these allegations and made three defensive assertions. The most important of these, for the purpose of this discussion, was the argument of self-defense. Eritrea asserted that it commenced combat operations against Ethiopia in May 1998 as a response to incursions by Ethiopian armed militia earlier that month that had ended in the alleged killing of eight Eritrean soldiers; Eritrea asserted that the combat operations it conducted were lawful measures of self-defense consistent with Article 51 of the UN Charter.

For self-defense to be permissible under the UN Charter, it is required that the party resorting to force have faced an armed attack.[24] In rejecting Eritrea's defense, the Claims Commission concluded that "[l]ocalized border encounters between small infantry units, even those involving the loss of life, do not constitute an armed attack for purposes of the Charter."[25] Although it did not refer to the International Court of Justice ('ICJ') ruling in the *Nicaragua* case, which laid

[21]Gray (2004), p. 97.

[22]Weeramantry (2009) p. 241.

[23]Partial Award, Jus Ad Bellum, para. 6.

[24]United Nations, Charter of the United Nations, October 24 1945, 1 UNTS XVI, Article 51('UN Charter').

[25]Partial Award, Jus Ad Bellum, para. 11.

down a similar standard,[26] and did not provide a detailed explanation of its decision, the award is significant because the exact ambit of armed attack under the UN Charter is uncertain.[27] In identifying the scale and the location of the conflict (with respect to the border), the Claims Commission helped clarify this ambit. The fact that the award was a unanimous one further cements the value of this finding.

It is important to note here that the value of this award has been often questioned on jurisdictional grounds[28]; the main argument is that the Claims Commission, through this award, had allegedly interfered with the competence of the two other bodies set up under the Algiers Agreement. However, these arguments were adequately considered and rejected by the Commission in the award itself. The Claims Commission noted that its own investigation extended beyond the ambit of a factual inquiry into the origins of the dispute—unlike the investigative body—and was primarily for the purpose of determining whether there had been a jus ad bellum violation.[29] Further, unlike the Boundary Commission which had to delimit and demarcate the border,[30] in determining the jus ad bellum violation, the Claims Commission had to ascertain whether Eritrean troops had crossed the de facto administrative boundary existing between the states at the time of the conflict. This latter decision would therefore have no effect on the boundary determined by the Boundary Commission.[31] Thus, the fundamental importance of this award should not be eclipsed by the criticisms regarding its alleged interference.[32]

3.1.2 Progress and Development of IHL and Customary International Law

With respect to IHL, the Claims Commission advanced the interpretation of various concepts, contributed to the strengthening and establishing the customary status of various IHL norms, and identified gaps in the existing framework of customary IHL.[33]

[26]ICJ, *Military and Paramilitary Activities in and against Nicaragua (Nicaragua v. United States)*, Merits, Judgement, (1986) ICJ Rep 14, para. 195.

[27]Randelzhofer (2002), p. 796.

[28]See for example, Gray (2006).

[29]Partial Award, Jus Ad Bellum, paras. 3–5.

[30]Article 4(2), Algiers Agreement.

[31]Partial Award, Jus Ad Bellum, para. 15.

[32]For a more detailed study of the Jus Ad Bellum Award, see Yiallourides and Yihdego (this volume), pp. 35–62.

[33]Kidane (2007), p. 86.

Advancing the Interpretation of IHL

The Claims Commission's Partial Award on Ethiopia's Central Front claim is a perfect illustration of how the Commission advanced the interpretation of IHL. This Award contributed to the interpretation and development of the precautionary principle expressed in Article 57 of Geneva Protocol I. Here, Ethiopia claimed that Eritrea had intentionally targeted a civilian neighbourhood in the city of Mekele as part of a three-part cluster bombing spread over some hours. Two of three of the bomb runs failed to come close to their intended targets. Eritrea blamed the civilian bombing on this failure and maintained that it had been an accident.

In its award, the Claims Commission found Eritrea liable despite its plea because Eritrea "had not taken all feasible precautions in the conduct of its air strikes."[34] More interestingly, the Claims Commission also seems to have drawn an adverse inference from Eritrea's failure to produce evidence indicating subsequent "changes to Eritrean training or doctrine aimed at avoiding possible recurrence of what happened."[35] It appears, therefore, that the Claims Commission would have considered the adoption of such measures as an extenuating circumstance[36]—a probability not envisioned under Article 57 of Geneva Protocol I.

Strengthening the Customary Status of IHL Norms

The Claims Commission also contributed to strengthening the customary status of IHL norms. The foremost example is the Commission's finding, placing reliance on other authorities, including the ICJ's Advisory Opinion in the Nuclear Weapons case, that the Geneva Conventions largely reflected customary international law.[37] This finding was crucial to ensure the application of the Conventions to the dispute as Eritrea did not accede to the Geneva Conventions until August 2000 and, therefore, would not otherwise have been bound by them as noted by both the Claims Commission[38] and the International Committee of the Red Cross ("ICRC").[39]

It was using this logic that the Commission found Article 57 of Protocol I, discussed above, applicable. In the words of the Commission, Article 57 reflected "a generally shared view . . . and the Commission considers [it] to express customary

[34]Partial Award, Central Front, Ethiopia's Claim 2 (28 April 2004), 43 I.L.M. 1275 (2004) para.112 (Partial Award, Ethiopia's Central Front Claim').

[35]Id. para. 111.

[36]Venturini (2009), p. 303.

[37]Partial Award, Prisoners of War, Eritrea's Claim No, 17 (1 July 2003), 42 I.L.M. 1083 (2003), para. 40 ('Partial Award, Eritrea's POW Claim').

[38]Id. para. 33.

[39]Id. Para. 34.

international humanitarian law."[40] In a similar vein, the Claims Commission noted that the power of the ICRC under Article 10 of Geneva Convention III to act as an external monitor of the conditions of detention of protected persons was "an essential part of the regime protecting POWs" and, although it was treaty-based, it incorporated "past practices that had a standing of their own in customary law."[41] Consequently, Eritrea was held responsible for refusing to permit ICRC delegates to visit the Ethiopian prisoners of war even for the time period during which Eritrea was not a party to the Geneva Conventions.

Establishing the Customary Status of IHL Norms

Since the Claims Commission found the Geneva Conventions to be largely reflective of customary international law, the Commission presumed the applicability of its provisions to the disputes. Therefore, if a party sought to argue that any provision of the Geneva Conventions was not part of customary law, the burden of proving this would fall on it.[42] The only instance of such an assertion before the Commission was Ethiopia's defence to an aerial bombardment claim from Eritrea. Ethiopia argued that Article 54 of Protocol I, which provides for the protection of objects indispensable to the survival of the civilian population, "was a new development in 1977 that had not become a part of customary IHL by the 1998-2000 war."[43] The Claims Commission found that the "compelling humanitarian nature" of Article 54 and its uniform acceptance by all parties to the protocol meant that Article 54 had acquired customary status despite the short period of time since its passing.[44]

Another example that falls within the scope of this discussion is the Claims Commission's comments on the obligations of belligerents to Prisoners of War ("POWs"). While most of the Commission's guidance reflected established customary IHL, the Commission also made some advancements to this corpus. For example, the Commission noted that the Detaining Power's obligation to conduct monthly examinations of POWs was recognised under customary international law.[45] While the obligation to provide POWs with adequate food, water, clothing, shelter, and medical attention is identified under customary IHL,[46] the obligation to conduct

[40] Partial Award, Western Front, Aerial Bombardment and Related Claims, Eritrea's Claims 1, 3, 5, 9–13, 14, 21, 25 & 26 (Dec. 19, 2005), 45 I.L.M. 396 (2006), para. 95 ('Partial Award, Eritrea's Western Front, Aerial Bombardment and Related Claims').

[41] Partial Award, Ethiopia's POW Claim, para. 61.

[42] Partial Award, Eritrea's POW Claim, para. 41.

[43] Partial Award, Eritrea's Western Front, Aerial Bombardment and Related Claims, para. 103.

[44] Id. paras. 104, 105.

[45] Partial Award, Prisoners of War, Ethiopia's Claim No. 4 (1 July 2003), 42 I.L.M. 1056 (2003) para. 120 ('Partial Award, Ethiopia's POW Claim').

[46] Henckaerts, Doswald-Beck (2005a) (Vol. 1), pp. 428–431.

monthly examinations per se is not. At the time of the passing of the award, only three countries provided for this duty in their military manuals.[47]

In both of these examples, the Claims Commission authoritatively established the customary status of IHL principles despite the lack of evidence of extensive state practice.

Identifying Lacunae in the Existing Framework

The Claims Commission also identified gaps in the existing framework of IHL. The Claims Commission's observations on the use of landmines is a particularly illuminating case worth considering under this section. The Claims Commission held that the Convention on the Prohibition or Restrictions on the Use of Certain Conventional Weapons, the Protocol on Prohibitions or Restrictions on the Use of Mines, Booby-Traps and Other Devices, and the Convention on the Prohibition of the Use, Stockpiling, Production and Transfer of Anti-Personnel Mines and on their Destruction had been concluded too recently and received treatment too varied to be accorded the status of customary international law. Consequently, as neither state was a party to any of these conventions, the Claims Commission held that the obligations found under them were not binding upon the states.[48] Having said that, the Claims Commission went on to emphasize the importance of the rapid development of international conventions restricting or prohibiting the future use of landmines.[49] This is significant because, by doing so, the Claims Commission clearly indicated that the existing restrictions on the use of landmines under customary law[50] were not sufficient to address the risk of their use to civilians.

3.1.3 Evidentiary Standards

The Claims Commission's Rules of Procedure offered only limited guidance on evidentiary matters. Consistent with international practice, these rules placed the burden of proof on the party that relied on a given fact.[51] Notwithstanding this, in certain limited circumstances, the Commission would accept an inability to bring forward evidence in support of a claim when that evidence was wholly within the control of the other party. In such cases, where the relevant evidence should have

[47]Henckaerts, Doswald-Beck (2005b) (Vol. 2), pp. 2778–2787.

[48]Partial Award, Central Front, Eritrea's Claims 2, 4, 6, 7, 8 & 22 (April 28, 2004), 43 I.L.M. 1249 (2004), para. 24.

[49]Partial Award, Ethiopia's Central Front Claim, para. 51.

[50]Id.

[51]Article 14(1), Rules of Procedure.

been readily available to the other party, a failure of that party to produce the evidence could result in an adverse inference against that party.[52]

The Rules of Procedure did not indicate the standard of proof that the two states were to meet; this was left to the Claims Commission's discretion. The Claims Commission concluded that the proper standard of proof had to be greater than the standard adopted in civil proceedings and yet less severe than the standard of proof suitable for criminal responsibility. Accordingly, the Claims Commission settled on a standard of "clear and convincing evidence," a relatively high standard of proof in a civil proceeding, as the proper standard of proof for a finding of liability.[53] The Claims Commission also required the parties to establish that violations occurred in a "frequent or pervasive" manner.[54]

In terms of proving the damages, the Claims Commission concluded that a lesser standard of proof was appropriate. Not only was the use of this standard "much less compelling for ... matters involved in assessing the monetary extent of injury" but also "would often – perhaps almost always – preclude any recovery" due to the difficulty in quantifying damages arising out of the war.[55] Despite this conclusion, the Claims Commission did not articulate a precise standard of proof for assessing the damages claims. Rather, it indicated that determining an appropriate amount of compensation for the violations of international law "involves questions of a different order, requiring exercises of judgment and approximation ... on the basis of the available evidence."[56]

Of the abovementioned aspects of the evidentiary standards that the Claims Commission laid down for itself, the use of the "frequent or pervasive" standard is worth studying in particular. This standard of proof was introduced by the Claims Commission in its partial award on Eritrea's Prisoner of War claims wherein it identified its task as the determination of liability for "serious violations of the law by the Parties ... that were frequent or pervasive and consequently affected significant numbers of victims."[57] The use of this standard led the Claims Commission to refuse to impute liability in cases of individual violations such as incidents of questionable disciplinary measures,[58] forced labour,[59] and forced separation of children from families.[60]

---

[52]Article 14(4), Rules of Procedure.

[53]Partial Award, Eritrea's POW Claim, para. 46; Partial Award, Ethiopia's POW Claim, para. 37.

[54]Partial Award, Ethiopia's POW Claim, para. 54.

[55]Final Award, Eritrea's Damages Claims, para. 36; Final Award, Ethiopia's Damages Claims, para. 36.

[56]Id.

[57]Partial Award, Eritrea's POW Claim, para. 56.

[58]Id. para. 81.

[59]Partial Award, Ethiopia's Central Front Claim, para. 66.

[60]Partial Award, Civilians Claims, Eritrea's Claims 15, 16, 23 & 27–32 (17 December 2004), 44 I.L.M. 601 (2005), para. 157 ('Partial Award, Eritrea's Civilians Claims').

However, the use of this standard must be understood in terms of the time and resources made available by the parties.[61] In the Claims Commission's words, its task was not to identify whether there had been violations; it was to identify whether there had been violations which warranted "the imposition of damages because they clearly endangered the lives and health of POWs in contravention of the basic policy of the Convention and customary international law."[62] In doing so, the Claims Commission was not condoning illegal acts that did not satisfy the standard—it was simply limiting the imposition of liability to more widespread cases.

Furthermore, this standard was not inflexible. It was, in at least three instances, amended.[63] For instance, the Claims Commission deliberately abandoned the standard when dealing with rape allegations. In finding the states liable for violations concerning rape, although there was no evidence of the use of rape or other sexual violence as an instrument of war, the Commission referred to the evidentiary challenges posed by the intrinsic character of the offense; the "heightened cultural sensitivities" and the "typically secretive and hence unwitnessed nature of rape" meant that evidence of frequent or pervasive rapes would be very difficult to obtain.[64] Therefore, in this case, the Commission simply looked for "clear and convincing evidence of several rapes in specific geographic areas under specific circumstances".[65]

While the imposition of this standard is not a perfect solution, it must be judged not as a standard to be applied by all international adjudicatory bodies but as a feasible solution for commissions strapped for time and capacity. In this sense, its success cannot be denied. Unfortunately, however, this standard has not received any further attention from international tribunals.

The Claims Commission's finding that, as a general matter, it was compelled to award some level of damages for the liability findings it made even if the evidence was inadequate is another important takeaway in this regard. The Commission noted in this regard that "when obligated to determine appropriate compensation, it must do so even if the process involves estimation, or even guesswork, within the range of possibilities indicated by the evidence."[66]

The Commission practically followed this finding over the course of the proceedings as well, for example, in relation to the claim forms used by Eritrea during the damages phase. These claim forms did not quantify the extent of injury or prove entitlement to the amounts claimed and were resultantly rejected by the Commission in their entirety.[67] Having rejected these claim forms—which essentially were

---

[61] Partial Award, Ethiopia's POW Claim, para. 6.

[62] Id. para. 88.

[63] Sommario (2009), p. 403.

[64] Partial Award, Ethiopia's Central Front Claim, para. 40.

[65] Id. para. 41.

[66] Final Award, Eritrea's Damages Claims, para. 37; Final Award, Ethiopia's Damages Claims, para. 37.

[67] Final Award, Eritrea's Damages Claims, paras. 66–67.

Eritrea's only support for these damages claims—the Commission observed that "[i]n a commercial arbitration between two private parties, this might warrant dismissal of a damages claim for failure of proof. The Commission is not prepared to take that step.... [T]here was widespread injury here. There were significant violations of international law causing harm to many individual victims. In such circumstances, it is not appropriate to dismiss the claim outright."[68] Therefore, the Commission sought to "develop a reasonable estimate of the losses resulting from the injuries it found, taking account of the likely population of the affected areas and estimates of the frequency and extent of loss."[69]

This situation inevitably brought the Claims Commission back to the need to "exercise . . . judgment and approximation" as discussed above. But this finding also articulates an important aspect of assessing damages for mass violations of international law: while inherent evidentiary difficulties often exist in proving damages, these difficulties typically cannot preclude compensation altogether.

All in all, it may be concluded that in addressing claims of state responsibility for violations of IHL, the Claims Commission has significantly contributed to the evidentiary standards to be applied by third parties in assessing these claims.[70]

3.1.4 Treatment of the Question of Dual Nationality

One of the most difficult adjudicatory challenges faced by the Claims Commission related to Eritrea's claims that Ethiopia's expulsion of persons of Eritrean origin at the start of the war amounted to an unlawful denationalization of these individuals.[71]

Ethiopia argued that the affected individuals had acquired Eritrean nationality under Eritrean and Ethiopian law. Proclamation No. 21/1992, issued by the Eritrean Provisional Government with regard to the referendum for Eritrea's independence in May 1993, limited participation in the referendum to persons having Eritrean citizenship.[72] Further, Ethiopia's own nationality law of 1930 provided that Ethiopian nationality is lost when a person acquires another nationality.[73] Ethiopia's position was, however, diluted by its continued treatment of these individuals as Ethiopian citizens after the referendum and up to the start of the war; referendum participants were shown to hold Ethiopian passports and other official documents aside from immovable property and business licenses in Ethiopia even after the referendum.[74]

---

[68] Id. para. 70.

[69] Id. para. 72.

[70] Klein (2004), p. 245.

[71] Partial Award, Eritrea's Civilians Claim, paras. 6, 7.

[72] Id. para. 41.

[73] Id. para. 43.

[74] Id. para. 46.

In resolving this issue, the Claims Commission could not look to international precedent because it had to resolve a unique question.[75] Typically, questions with regard to dual nationals assumed the dual nationality of the individual; what had to be determined was which nationality would be the relevant one for the purposes of deciding the dispute. In determining this, international tribunals were guided by the theory of dominant and effective nationality laid down in the Nottebohm decision[76] and since, widely adopted.[77] Here, however, the question was the reverse—whether the individuals in question did in fact hold dual nationalities. Therefore, the theory of dominant and effective nationality was of no use. Even in bringing these claims, Eritrea did not have to use this theory by virtue of Article 5(9) of the Algiers Agreement which provided that either State may "file claims on behalf of persons of Ethiopian or Eritrean origin who may not be its nationals."

In deciding this question, the Claims Commission weighed the legal effects of the Eritrean referendum against the post-referendum treatment of the affected individuals by the Ethiopian government. In doing so, the Claims Commission placed the "human dimensions" of the question of nationality[78] on par with the legal effects of the referendum. The Commission noted that the evidence before it suggested that it had been the intention neither of the referendum participants nor of the two governments to immediately sever ties of nationality with Ethiopia after participating in the referendum.[79] While both states had agreed that the such individuals who had "so far been enjoying Ethiopian citizenship should be made to choose and abide by their choice", they were to continue to enjoy Ethiopian citizenship until they had determined the rules governing their future economic relations.[80] In this context, the Commission concluded that the continued treatment of these individuals as Ethiopian nationals by the Ethiopian government, and especially the continued issuance of passports to these individuals, constituted an act of international significance which was sufficient to counter the legal effect of the referendum.

[75]Kidane (2007), p. 54.

[76]ICJ, *Nottebohm, Liechtenstein v Guatemala,* Preliminary Objection (Second phase), Judgment, [1955] ICJ Rep 4.

[77]See Brownlie (2003), p. 19.

[78]Partial Award, Eritrea's Civilians Claim, para. 50.

[79]Id. paras. 50, 52, 53.

[80]As per the formal Agreed Minute. See Id. para 52.

3.2 *Practical Contributions*

3.2.1 Development of Mass-Claims Processing

As noted above, the Algiers Agreement provided for a mass-claims procedure for the "expeditious resolution" of disputes.[81] Right from its inception, the Claims Commission raised the question of the mass-claims processing. In May 2001, the Claims Commission held a teleconference with the parties and computer and software experts regarding the possible development of a mass-claims system.[82] In August 2001, the Claims Commission issued five decisions on procedural issues, two of which laid some more groundwork for the mass-claims procedure.[83] The Claims Commission's Decision No. 2 "established" the mass-claims procedure under which five categories of claims[84] by persons could be filed for fixed-amount compensation using claim forms that were to be created by the Claims Commission. Decision No. 5 then provided that the fixed-amount compensation would be available, depending on the type of evidence available, in two tiers: USD 500 per individual national and USD 1500 per individual national. Consequently, the Rules of Procedure, adopted in October 2001, provided for the filing of both individual and mass claims. Chapter Three of the Rules of Procedure was devoted to the mass-claims procedure. Aside from outlining Decision No. 2 once again, Chapter Three discussed the manner of decision-making in relation to mass claims.[85]

In this regard, the Rules of Procedure provided that to prove a category of mass claims, the claimant state would have to prove that the alleged acts or omissions did occur, that such acts or omissions constituted a violation of international law, and that they were attributable to the other state.[86] If one or more of these determinations was not made or sufficiently proven, the Claims Commission would dismiss all claims in that sub-category.[87] However, if these determinations were proven, then the claims in that sub-category would be subject to random sampling of their evidence to ascertain the percentage of such claims for which the evidence was inadequate to establish the claim. The compensation for all claims in that compensation level of that sub-category would be automatically reduced by that percentage

---

[81]Article 5(10), Algiers Agreement; Final Award, Eritrea's Damages Claims, para. 70.

[82]UNSC (2001), para. 5.

[83]Eritrea-Ethiopia Claims Commission, Decision No. 2: Claims Categories, Forms and Procedures (Aug. 2001); Eritrea-Ethiopia Claims Commission ('Decision No. 2'), Decision No. 5: Multiple Claims in the Mass Claims Process, Fixed-Sum Compensation at the $500 and $1500 Levels, Multiplier for Household claims (Aug. 2001).

[84]Decision No. 2, §A.

[85]Article 32, Rules of Procedure.

[86]Article 32(1), Rules of Procedure.

[87]Article 32(2), Rules of Procedure.

in the award that the Claims Commission would finally issue for the sub-category of claims.[88]

As it turned out, however, neither party made use of the mass-claims procedure. Instead, all claims were filed under the individual claims procedure. Almost all the claims were filed as claims of the governments themselves although, to a very large degree, the claims reflected loss, damage, or injury sustained by Eritrean and Ethiopian nationals rather than the governments themselves. Only six of the claims filed by the Eritrean Government were "on behalf of" individual Eritrean nationals.[89]

While the 1-year deadline for the submission of all claims to the Claims Commission can be argued to have led to the abandonment of mass-claims processing, both states had in fact collected thousands of claim forms within the 1-year time period.[90] These claim forms were later used as evidence for inter-state claims by both Ethiopia[91] and Eritrea.[92] Commenting on the claim forms submitted by Ethiopia, the Claims Commission noted the "weaknesses" and the lack of supporting evidence.[93]

As per Decision No. 2, and as later reiterated by the Rules of Procedure, the duty to design the claim forms (or, in the case of the Rules of Procedure, to "approve" the claim forms used by the parties) had been specifically laid on the Claims Commission. Had the Claims Commission actually designed and circulated a model form to the parties at the outset, perhaps the inherent weaknesses in the forms could have been avoided or at least reduced.

Furthermore, even if the amount of time required to collect information and compile "strong" claim forms would have exceeded the 1-year period, the parties and the Claims Commission could have considered the possibility of extending the 1-year period under Article 5(8) of the Algiers Agreement for the mass claims alone. Although the Algiers Agreement does not provide for the extension of the filing deadline,[94] a consideration of the Claims Commission's decisions over claims barred by Article 5(8) indicates that the object was to avoid the introduction of late claims into the proceedings that may have prejudiced the opposite party.[95] Article 5(12), which states that the Claims Commission "shall *endeavour* to complete its work within three years," is a clear indication that the extension of the time-frame of the proceedings may be allowed if the adjudication process requires it. As the mass-claims procedure would be used by both parties, there would have been no fear of an

[88]Id.

[89]Murphy et al. (2013), p. 57.

[90]Murphy et al. (2013), pp. 88–89.

[91]Ethiopia used the forms in the Prisoner of War Proceedings. See Commission's characterisation of the forms in Partial Award, Eritrea's POW Claim, paras. 40–41.

[92]Eritrea used data from claim forms in the damages phase in an effort to quantify the loss of personal and business property. See Final Award, Eritrea's Damages Claims, para. 32.

[93]Partial Award, Eritrea's POW Claim, paras. 66–67.

[94]Article 5(8), Algiers Agreement provides that "[A]ll claims submitted to the Commission *shall* be filed no later than one year from the effective date of this agreement. . .".

[95]Murphy et al. (2013), p. 67.

unfair disadvantage to any one party. Thus, there is a strong probability that the deadline could have been extended for the purpose of filing the mass claims.

Although the mass-claims procedure was never put into motion, the procedure envisioned must be appreciated for advancing the existing mass-claims processing structures existent at the time. For example, compared to the United Nations Compensation Commission, the principal example of a mass-claims reparation program for war-related claims,[96] the method for determination of compensation was far more nuanced: the Claims Commission foresaw the possibility of limited evidence collection and provided a unique and fair solution to address this problem. This solution was tailored to meet the Claims Commission's own time and capability constraints and provided a viable model for commissions that had to work under similar conditions.

3.2.2 Prototype for Future Commissions

The Claims Commission may be likened to a prototype in that it provides valuable lessons for future commissions with similar mandates through both its successes and shortcomings.

In terms of shortcomings, the most obvious one is the lack of enforceability of the Claims Commission's awards on damages. In its final award on damages, the Commission awarded USD 161,445,000 to Eritrea[97] and USD 174,036,530 to Ethiopia.[98] However, to date, neither of these awards has been paid wholly or partly (so far as the authors are aware).

Thus, the requirement for an enforcement mechanism becomes the first lesson from the Claims Commission's work. A provision for the prompt payment of awards in the constituting agreement (in this case, Article 5(17) of the Algiers Agreement) is of limited use. Instead, the best way to ensure that the monetary awards are honoured would be to secure some funds from the involved states before the commencement of the proceedings, For example, each government might be expected to fund a bank account in a third country at a certain amount calculated to cover all or at least some portion of the claims against it, if those claims are shown to be valid.[99] The models of the Iran-US Claims Tribunal (where funds were obtained from government bank accounts frozen during the armed conflict) or the United Nations Compensation Commission (where Iraqi proceeds from the export of oil were used) provide different methods by which this can be done. Aside from ensuring that compensation will be paid, such an exercise has the additional value of providing the commission with a realistic estimate of the states' paying capacities, which will ensure that the awards rendered by the tribunals are also realistic. In a way, the Claims

[96]See generally, Houtte et al. (2008).

[97]Final Award, Eritrea's Damages Claims §XI.

[98]Id. §XII.

[99]Murphy et al. (2013), p. 409.

Commission's adjustment of damages to reflect Ethiopia's and Eritrea's economic status reflects this. On Ethiopia's damages claims against Eritrea, the Claims Commission noted that the total amount was "more than three times Eritrea's estimated total national product."[100]

The Claims Commission's treatment of compensation, as touched upon earlier, also provides a second and equally important lesson. The Algiers Agreement did not provide any directions on the use of compensation that may be received by either state. It was only during the proceedings that the Claims Commission brought up the issue. By a letter to the parties in 2006, the Claims Commission invited the states to inform it of "how they intend to ensure distribution of damages received to civilian victims, including presently available information on existing or anticipated structures and procedures for this purpose."[101] The governments responded to that request in their written pleadings on damages, after which the Claims Commission noted that "as to many claims on which it has found liability, it would probably be impossible, and certainly inordinately expensive, to attempt to identify the specific individuals who suffered injuries as a result of the various illegal acts committed against them."[102] With that in mind, the Claims Commission invited the governments to "consider further means by which, in the exercise of their discretion, regarding the use and disposition of damages that may be awarded to them, the humanitarian objectives of Article 5(1) can be best achieved."[103] To what extent the parties presented proposals of that type to the Claims Commission is not publicly known; if made, they were likely hindered in part by not knowing how much compensation the Claims Commission intended to award and by a political concern with crafting detailed relief programs that might never be undertaken if compensation was not actually paid.[104] In any case, the Claims Commission did not identify any such proposals in its final award, instead asserting its confidence that "the Parties will ensure that the .... funds received in respect of their claims will be used to provide relief to their civilian populations injured in the war."[105]

Given that the primary objective behind setting up the Claims Commission was to address "the negative socio-economic impact of the crisis on the civilian population,"[106] it made sense that the Commission sought a plan from the parties for the delivery of this compensation to the people. Without this, there was no guarantee that the compensation, if it had been paid by both states, would have been distributed for public relief programmes. As an illustration, consider the Claims Commission's parallel awards of USD 2,000,000 to both states "for failing to prevent the rape of

[100]Final Award, Ethiopia's Damages Claims, para. 18.

[101]Eritrea-Ethiopia Claims Commission, Decision No. 8, Relief to War Victims (27 July 2007), para. 2.

[102]Id. para. 5.

[103]Id. para. 6.

[104]Murphy et al. (2013), p. 408.

[105]Final Award, Eritrea's Damages Claims, §IX.

[106]Article 5(1), Algiers Agreement.

known and unknown victims in the towns of Senafe, Barentu and Teseney" with the "hope that Eritrea (and Ethiopia) [would] use the funds awarded to develop and support health programs for women and girls in the affected areas."[107] In the absence of any proposed plan for the distribution of this amount, in reality, if the states had in fact paid compensation, both states would have merely exchanged cheques for identical sums of money.[108] Thus, it is advisable that in the future, commissions (or other bodies with similar mandates) commence work only after receiving plans from the parties on the planned uses of any compensation received. Practical concerns in prematurely devising such plans can be addressed by requiring the parties to produce relief plans of different scales and requiring them to identify the level of compensation required for realising each alternative.

4 Claims Versus Fact-Finding Commissions

Although the previous section enumerates the many significant contributions of the Claims Commission, at a primary level, the Claims Commission ultimately faced difficulties in being able to address "the negative socio-economic impact of the crisis on the civilian population." This can be attributed to a problem-solution mismatch. In attempting to gain redressal for their primary problem (i.e., the effects of the war on the civilian population), the parties adopted a solution incongruous to their own financial circumstances. In such cases, the parties may instead be encouraged to adopt an alternative approach through the establishment of a fact-finding commission. While the purpose, legal bases, and actors of fact-finding may vary depending on the legal framework and authority applied to it,[109] the key characteristics of any fact-finding body include instituting and conducting an inquiry based upon consent (of states), examining factual or legal questions, and the making of non-binding (or binding) findings and recommendation.[110]

In the context of the Eritrea-Ethiopia dispute, Article 3 of the Algiers Agreement did in fact provide for the establishment of such a body "to determine the origins of the conflict" through the investigation of "the incidents of May 6, 1998 and on any other incident prior to that date which could have contributed to a misunderstanding between the parties regarding their common border."[111] The body was to be appointed by the Secretary-General of the OAU in consultation with the Secretary-General of the UN and the two states.[112] However, the body was never appointed by the OAU, and the states themselves did not call for its appointment.

---

[107]Final Award, Eritrea's Damages Claims, para. 239.

[108]Dybnis (2011), p. 273.

[109]Yihdego (2012), p. 6.

[110]Id. pp. 5–6.

[111]Article 3(1), Algiers Agreement.

[112]Article 3(2), Algiers Agreement.

According to one AU official, the issuance of an investigation report under Article 3 was deemed "not conducive" to the maintenance of peace between the two states.[113] This is a reasonable assertion to have made given the parties' own stances at the time. In November 1997, for example, the two states convened a Joint Border Commission. This body was unable to arrive at any decision due to the states' diametrically opposed views regarding their common boundary; "[b]orders defined by colonial treaties became the ultimate points of departure for the Eritreans while the Ethiopians appeared convinced that 'long-term administration of the border areas constituted ownership.'"[114] Once the war broke out, both states' official positions grew further entrenched. As per Eritrea, the crisis "was rooted in the violation by the Ethiopian government of Eritrea's colonial boundaries, and its decision to wilfully claim, as well as physically occupy, large swathes of Eritrean territory."[115] In stark contrast, Ethiopia's core position was that Eritrea was attempting "to resolve the border issue by force reneging from the process of peaceful settlement of the matter."[116] Thus, a final decision on the origins of the conflict may indeed have had the possibility to inflame tensions in either camp.

However, this justification for the non-establishment of the investigative body begins to unravel when the Claims Commission's decision on Ethiopia's *jus ad bellum* claim against Eritrea is considered. In determining in this award that Eritrea had violated the *jus ad bellum* in starting the war, the Claims Commission did, in fact, investigate the origins of the conflict. A closer look at the functions of the three bodies set up under the Algiers Agreement leads to the conclusion that, to some extent, the mandates of the Boundary Commission and Claims Commission would, in fact, have been dependent upon the rulings of the investigative body under Article 3 had it been set up. By determining the origins of the conflict, the investigative body would be looking into the "misunderstanding between parties regarding their common border" and would, therefore, be likely to pass comments on the actual boundary between both states. Thus, the report of this body may have also exerted some influence on the rulings of the Boundary Commission. Similarly, as there was no express preclusion of *jus ad bellum* claims before the Claims Commission, its rulings may have been influenced by the report of the investigative body. This reasoning, in turn, would require one to discredit the above assertion that the investigation report under Article 3 would not have been conducive to the maintenance of peace. The work of all three bodies was envisioned to deal with contentious areas that were not, *per se*, conducive of an air of cooperation. Thus, the setting aside of one of the three envisioned organs was not going to solve the issue.

This line of thinking leads to the second possible reason for the non-establishment of the investigative body: the conflation of the duties of the investigative body with those of the Claims Commission. Knowing that the origins of conflict could be

[113] Plaut (2005), p. 111.

[114] Lata (2003) p. 369, 380.

[115] Gilkes and Plaut (1999), pp. 21–22.

[116] Id. pp. 24–25.

investigated under the aegis of the Claims Commission, the parties were not concerned with the establishment of the investigative body under Article 3. To some extent, this approach presents a practical solution. Where the states involved intend to provide for the redressal of grievances arising from the conflict, a "claims" commission may serve as a useful means for promoting popular support for the final peace agreement by enabling the states to explain how, in a post-war setting, their grievances will be addressed. As the resolution of claims cannot always be reached as a part of the peace agreement, a claims commission is a method of "completing the contract in the future" by providing a mechanism for resolving the dispute over time. The commission, in this role, becomes an impartial forum for the resolution of the claims, ensuring that they are addressed gradually and do not fester as irritants in the governments' relations.[117]

However, to the extent that the states are unwilling or incapable of paying claim amounts, they may instead seek relief through a "fact-finding" commission such as the one provided for under Article 3. In such a situation, the establishment of a "claims" commission may foster a false sense of hope and divert considerable time and energy to a process of proving and quantifying injuries for which compensation is not forthcoming.[118] In contrast, in the words of the Claims Commission itself, an investigative body would be "helpful in promoting reconciliation and border delimitation. . . ."[119] As appropriate, a fact-finding commission could calibrate the timing of its work, i.e., expedite or slow down its work, to achieve an optimal resolution of the matters it is considering so as to not unduly interfere with any improvement of relations between the states involved.

Additionally, a fact-finding commission could better enable the creation of an historical record. Although the Claims Commission at times asserted that it was "charged with determining the truth,"[120] this was not the express mandate of the Claims Commission.[121] Unlike a claims commission that is charged with deciding cases placed before it, a fact-finding commission focuses on recording objective truths by sifting through all available information. Therefore, where the parties solely seek a neutral body that will provide a detailed accounting of a conflict and more clarity on their collective past, a fact-finding commission would likely be the better option.

---

[117] Murphy et al. (2013), p. 399.

[118] Murphy et al. (2013), p. 409.

[119] Partial Award, Jus Ad Bellum, para. 5.

[120] For example, see Partial Award, Central Front, Eritrea's Claims 2, 4, 6, 7, 8, and 22, para. 6 (Apr. 28, 2004), 43 I.L.M. 1249 (2004).

[121] Murphy et al. (2013), p. 404.

5 Conclusion

Over the course of this paper, the authors have sought to examine the various contributions of the Claims Commission to the existing framework for the determination of civil liability in cases of violation of IHL. In terms of purely legal developments, the Commission greatly contributed to the development of IHL concepts and customary IHL norms. Aside from this, the Commission also introduced new evidentiary standards for determining liability and damages and provided a creative solution for addressing the plight of individuals affected by the nationality laws of either state. In terms of practical contributions, the creation of the mass-claims processing system signifies the Commission's most important contribution. Although it was not actually put to use, the system was made to accommodate the limitations on evidence collection and time that the Commission faced.

The common thread through all these contributions is the Claims Commission's problem-solving approach. The Commission's primary objective was to address concerns most effectively and in the least amount of time. While this meant that the Commission could not always pay sufficient attention to the evidence at hand, or provide a detailed account of its own reasoning, the ingenuity and practical value of the solutions offered cannot be dismissed.

With the advantage of a retrospective vision, it is also clearer now that in the context of the Eritrea-Ethiopia dispute, a "claims" commission was of practically very limited use to the civilians in either state. However, even in its shortcomings as a vehicle of relief for the general populations, the Claims Commission imparts several lessons—including the appropriate conditions for the establishment of a "claims" commission and the necessary powers it must have in order to see its mandate through successfully.

Thus, the work of the Claims Commission serves as an invaluable guidebook for future tribunals and commissions with similar mandates working under similar constraints. It was the object of this paper to capture the legacy of the Commission as succinctly as possible. It is the authors' hope that through this paper, the Commission receives the recognition and appreciation that it truly deserves.

References

Books

Brownlie I (2003) Principles of public international law. Oxford University Press

Gilkes P, Plaut M (1999) War in the horn: the conflict between Eritrea and Ethiopia. Royal Institute of International Affairs, London

Gray C (2004) International law and the use of force, 2nd edn. Oxford University Press, Oxford

Henckaerts JM, Doswald-Beck L (eds) (2005a) Customary international humanitarian law, vol 1. Cambridge University Press

Henckaerts JM, Doswald-Beck L (eds) (2005b) Customary international humanitarian law, vol 2. Cambridge University Press
Holtzmann HM, Kristjánsdóttir E (eds) (2007) International mass claims processes: legal and practical perspectives. Oxford University Press
Houtte H, Delmartino B, Yi I (2008) Post-war restoration of property rights under international law, volume I: institutional features and substantive law. Cambridge University Press, Cambridge
Murphy S, Kidane W, Snider T (2013) Litigating war: mass civil injury and the Eritrea-Ethiopia claims commission. Oxford University Press, New York

Chapters in Books

Desta M (this volume) Peace agreements between Ethiopia and Eritrea: ending two decades of hostilities—an introductory note. In: Yihdego Z, Desta MG, Hailu MB (eds) Ethiopian Yearbook of International Law 2018: in pursuit of peace and prosperity. Springer, Cham, pp 261–268
Greppi E (2009) The 2000 Algiers Agreements. In: de Guttry A, Post H, Venturini G (eds) The 1998–2000 war between Eritrea and Ethiopia: an international legal perspective. TMC Asser Press, pp 55–77
Lata L (2003) The Ethiopia-Eritrea war. In: Boulden J (ed) Dealing with conflict in Africa: the United Nations and regional organizations. Palgrave Macmillan, New York, pp 153–184
Plaut M (2005) The conflict and its aftermath. In: Jacquin-Berdal D, Plaut M (eds) Unfinished business: Eritrea and Ethiopia at war. Red Sea Press
Randelzhofer A (2002) Article 51. In: Simma B (ed) The charter of the United Nations: a commentary, vol I. Oxford University Press, Oxford, pp 789–799
Sommario E (2009) State responsibility for violations of international humanitarian law in the work of the Eritrea-Ethiopia claims commission. In: de Guttry A, Post H, Venturini G (eds) The 1998–2000 war between Eritrea and Ethiopia: an international legal perspective. TMC Asser Press, pp 393–407
Venturini G (2009) International law and the conduct of military operations. In: de Guttry A, Post H, Venturini G (eds) The 1998–2000 war between Eritrea and Ethiopia: an international legal perspective. TMC Asser Press, pp 279–305
Weeramantry R (2009) International law as to the use of force. In: de Guttry A, Post H, Venturini G (eds) The 1998–2000 war between Eritrea and Ethiopia: an international legal perspective. TMC Asser Press, pp 227–242
Yiallourides C, Yihdego Z (this volume) Disputed territories and the law on the use of force: lessons from the Eritrea-Ethiopia case. In: Yihdego Z, Desta MG, Hailu MB (eds) Ethiopian Yearbook of International Law 2018: in pursuit of peace and prosperity. Springer, Cham, pp 35–62

Journal Articles

Dybnis A (2011) Was the Eritrea–Ethiopia claims commission merely a zero-sum game?: Exposing the limits of arbitration in resolving violent transnational conflict. Loyola Los Angeles Int Compet Law Rev 33:255–286
Gray C (2006) The Eritrea-Ethiopia claims commission oversteps its boundaries: a partial award? Eur J Int Law 17(4):699 721
Kidane W (2007) Civil liability for violations of international humanitarian law: the jurisprudence of the Eritrea-Ethiopia claims commission in The Hague. Wis Int Law J 25(1):23–87

Klein N (2004) State responsibility for international humanitarian law violations and the work of the Eritrea-Ethiopia claims commission so far. Germ Yearb Int Law 47:214–266

Yihdego Z (2012) The Gaza Mission: implications for international humanitarian law and UN fact finding. Melb J Int Law 13(1):6–59

UN Documents/Reports

UNSC (1998) Letter from the Permanent Representative of Ethiopia to the United Nations Addressed to the President of the Security Council (28 December 1998). U.N. Doc. S/1998/1223

UNSC (2000) Report of the Secretary-General on Ethiopia and Eritrea to the Security Council (27 June 2000). U.N. Doc. S/2000/643

UNSC (2001) Progress Report of the Secretary-General on Ethiopia and Eritrea (19 June 2001). U.N. Doc. S/2001/608

Official Statements

U.S. Department of State (1998) Press Statement, The Dispute Between Ethiopia and Eritrea (3 June 1998). https://1997-2001.state.gov/briefings/statements/1998/ps980603.html

Thomas R. Snider is a Partner and the Head of Arbitration at Al Tamimi and Company. Mr. Snider served as counsel for the Federal Democratic Republic of Ethiopia before the Eritrea-Ethiopia Claims Commission. All views expressed in this paper are solely those of Mr. Snider and his co-author and do not necessarily reflect the views of the Ethiopian Government or any other entity or individual.

Aishwarya Suresh Nair is a final year law student at the National Law Institute University, Bhopal, India.

Disputed Territories and the Law on the Use of Force: Lessons from the Eritrea-Ethiopia Case

Constantinos Yiallourides and Zeray Yihdego

Abstract On 19 December 2005, in its partial award, the Eritrea-Ethiopia Claims Commission found that Eritrea had acted in violation of the rules of international law on the use of force (*jus ad bellum*) in resorting to armed force to attack and occupy the disputed border town of Badme and surrounding areas, which were then under the administration of Ethiopia. In its award, the Claims Commission made a number of important findings which, taken with the Eritrea-Ethiopia Boundary Commission's 2002 decision on boundary delimitation, contribute towards informing and clarifying the substance of international law applicable to disputed territories and the legal obligations of states acting in those areas, especially where the use of force is engaged. This article examines the Claims Commission's *jus ad bellum* award and concentrates on three key issues: (a) the legality in international law of the resort to force as a means of gaining control over territory to which a state has (or believes that it has) a valid sovereign title; (b) the specific contours of self-defence in relation to territorial sovereignty claims, and (c) the legitimacy of dealing with use of force issues by arbitral tribunals. In September 2018, the leaders of the two countries signed a peace and friendship agreement, thus, setting course for a new era of peace and cooperation. The lessons that ought to be learnt by these two neighbouring countries and other states have been articulated as concluding remarks.

The authors would like to extend their thanks and appreciation to the participants of the University of Tokyo International Law Colloquium (Tadashi Mori, Kazuhiro Nakatani, Koji Teraya, Yurika Ishii and Kentaro Nishimoto) for their instructive comments and suggestions on earlier versions of this paper. Many thanks also to **Olivia Kirkbride**, Research Volunteer in Public International Law, British Institute of International and Comparative Law (BIICL) for her contribution to this paper. Any errors or omissions remain the authors' own.

C. Yiallourides
British Institute of International and Comparative Law (BIICL), London, UK
e-mail: c.yiallourides@BIICL.org

Z. Yihdego (✉)
University of Aberdeen, Aberdeen, UK
e-mail: Zeray.yihdego@abdn.ac.uk

Z. Yihdego et al. (eds.), *Ethiopian Yearbook of International Law 2018*, Ethiopian Yearbook of International Law 2018, https://doi.org/10.1007/978-3-030-24078-3_3

1 Introduction

Eritrea was part of the Aksumite Kingdom, the foundation of the ancient empire of Abyssinia, now the Ethiopian State, up until 1890, the year when Italy proclaimed Eritrea as its colony.[1] Despite the defeat of Italy by Ethiopia at Adowa in 1896, Eritrea remained in the hands of the Italians until 1941 when Britain took over and administered the territory as a United Nations (UN) trustee. Eritrea became part of Ethiopia in 1952 pursuant to General Assembly Resolution 390A(V).[2] It declared its independence in 1993 following a civil war that lasted almost 30 years.[3] Ethiopia (with current population about 105 million) and the newly-independent State of Eritrea (with current population about 5 million) enjoyed stable socio-economic and security relations until a number of border incidents erupted in 1998 near the town of Badme. These incidents led to the deployment of Eritrean armed forces to Badme and its environs which, in turn, triggered a declaration of self-defence by the Ethiopian Parliament on 13 May 1998.[4] A large-scale war between the two countries erupted inflicting devastating harm on both sides.[5] The Eritrea-Ethiopia Claims Commission was established subsequently to assess all claims for loss, damage or injury by one state against the other resulting from violations of international law. It concluded that Eritrea's action to forcibly reclaim Badme and other territories, which were then under the administration of Ethiopia, constituted a violation of Article 2 (4) of the UN Charter on the prohibition of the use of force.[6] As a consequence,

[1]The Kingdom of Aksum existed during the first seven (although others submit nine) centuries AD in Northern Ethiopia. Its rule and power influence encompassed modern Yemen, Somalia and Djibouti. It adopted Christianity in the fourth Century AD, introduced, and used its own language called *Ge'ez*. This ancient civilisation was a dominant trading empire in the Red Sea until the end of the ninth century, see Philipson (1988), pp. 1–55.

[2]General Assembly Resolution 390A(V) (2 December 1950) https://documents-dds-ny.un.org/doc/RESOLUTION/GEN/NR0/059/88/IMG/NR005988.pdf?OpenElement.

[3]On the history of the Ethiopian region see Marcus (2002) and Zewde (1998).

[4]The Declaration called upon Eritrea 'immediately' and 'unconditionally' to withdraw its army from Ethiopian controlled territories, 'Letter dated 20 December 2005 from the Charge d'affaires a.i. of the Permanent Mission of Ethiopia to the United Nations addressed to the President of the Security Council' 3 https://www.securitycouncilreport.org/atf/cf/%7B65BFCF9B-6D27-4E9C-8CD3-CF6E4FF96FF9%7D/EE%20S2005816.pdf.

[5]The war lasted 2 years and involved the deaths of 70,000 soldiers and the displacement of over a million civilians. Government spending had been diverted to the arms race. Drought and famine seriously aggravated the situation causing a large humanitarian crisis, Gray (2006), pp. 702–704; In addition, one of the consequences of this conflict was its spillover effect on the conflict in Somalia. Ethiopia and the UN accused Eritrea of supporting Al-Shabaab or other Islamises; Eritrea denied such accusations, see Yihdego (2007), pp. 666–676; see also Cliffe (1999), pp. 89–111.

[6]Eritrea-Ethiopia Claims Commission, Partial Award, *Jus ad Bellum*: Ethiopia's Claims 1–8 (19 December 2005). The Claims Commission was composed of Hans van Houtte (President), George H Aldrich, John R Crook, James C N Paul, and Lucy Reed. See Klein (2013).

Eritrea was liable to compensate Ethiopia for the damages caused by this violation of international law.[7]

In its award, the Claims Commission made a number of important findings which, taken with the Eritrea-Ethiopia Boundary Commission's 2002 decision on boundary delimitation, contribute towards informing and clarifying the substance of international law applicable to disputed territories and the legal obligations of states acting in those areas, especially where the use of force is engaged.

This article discusses the interplay between disputed territories and the law on the use of force by looking at how the Claims Commission applied the rules of *jus ad bellum* to the Eritrea-Ethiopia territorial dispute. It focuses on three main issues: (a) the legality in international law of the resort to force as a means of gaining control over territory to which a state has (or believes that it has) a valid sovereign title; (b) the specific contours of self-defence in relation to territorial sovereignty claims, and (c) the legitimacy of dealing with use of force issues by arbitral tribunals. The lessons that ought to be learnt by these two neighbouring countries, in the light of recent developments in the relations between them, and other states involved in disputes over territory are articulated as concluding observations.

1.1 Factual Background: Who Started the War and Why?

The two sides took different views as to who began the war in the first place.[8] The Ethiopian version was that the conflict erupted when Eritrean soldiers entered Ethiopian controlled territories without any legal justification and later attacked and occupied the border town of Badme and adjacent areas, all of which were controlled and administered at the time by Ethiopia. According to Ethiopia, Eritrea's action warranted a forcible counteraction in self-defence to regain control over the territory that Eritrea had managed to occupy.[9] On its part, Eritrea contended that Ethiopia was illegally occupying Badme and sought to correct this perceived injustice by reclaiming the territory by force.[10] This seemingly geographically-isolated border friction, which might have been caused by various other factors, discussed later in this piece, quickly escalated to a full-scale war between the two states.

After a series of offensives and counter-offensives involving the military forces of the two states that lasted for nearly 2 years and following the advancement of

[7]Ibid, para 16. For a detailed analysis of the Commission's decisions see Snider and Nair (this volume), pp. 11–34.

[8]For a detailed factual background to the Eritrean-Ethiopian armed conflict 1998–2000, see Gray (2006), pp. 700–704; Murphy et al. (2013), Ch 1; Murphy (2018), pp. 552–572; de Guttry et al. (2009), pp. 109–223.

[9]Eritrea-Ethiopia Claims Commission, Partial Award, *Jus ad Bellum*: Ethiopia's Claims 1–8 (19 December 2005); Murphy et al. (2013), p. 16.

[10]Murphy et al. (2013), p. 30.

Ethiopian troops to many parts of Eritrea, the two parties negotiated and concluded the 2000 Algiers Agreement which officially, but not in reality, ended the Eritrea-Ethiopia war.[11] Pursuant to the 2000 Algiers Agreement, the parties undertook to carry out four main tasks. First, to 'permanently terminate military hostilities' and respect humanitarian law in treating prisoners of war and civilians. Second, to investigate and determine the causes of the conflict. Third, to award damages for violations of international law. Fourth, to delimit and demarcate their boundaries on the basis of international law through the establishment of a Boundary Commission.[12]

The first task, to terminate hostilities and respect humanitarian law, largely succeeded.[13] The United Nations Mission in Ethiopia and Eritrea (UNMEE) was established pursuant to Security Council Resolution 1312/2000 with the mandate to monitor the cessation of hostilities until the delimitation and demarcation of the border are completed.[14] The Mission was terminated on 30 July 2008 by UNSC resolution 1827 because of the 'crippling restrictions imposed by Eritrea on UNMEE', amongst other reasons.[15]

The second commitment, to investigate the causes of the conflict, was never carried out.[16] However, the third and fourth components of the 2000 Algiers Agreement led to the decisions of the Boundary Commission and the Claims Commission.[17]

The Boundary Commission rendered its unanimous decision on delimitation on 13 April 2002.[18] It found that the colonial treaties concluded between Italy and Ethiopia in 1900, 1902 and 1908 determined the course of the boundary line between

[11] Art 1, 'Ethiopia/Eritrea Peace Agreement' (2000) https://peacemaker.un.org/sites/peacemaker.un.org/files/ER%20ET_001212_AgreementEritreaEthiopia.pdf; A situation of "no war, no peace" prevailed for the following years, see Woldemariam (2018), pp. 407–427.

[12] Ibid, Arts 3–5.

[13] For a detailed account, see Woldemariam (2018), pp. 407–427.

[14] S/RES/1312 (31 July 2000); see 'United Nations Mission on Ethiopia And Eritrea' https://unmee.unmissions.org/mandate.

[15] Ibid.

[16] Article 3 of the Algiers Agreement provided for the creation of an independent body tasked with the investigation of 'the origins of the conflict'. This body was never constituted by the UN Secretary-General, nor by either the Organisation of African Unity (OAU) or its successor, the African Union, see Gray (2006), p. 703; Murphy et al. (2013), p. 23; Murphy (2018), p. 557.

[17] Article 4 of the Algiers Agreement provided for the creation of a neutral Boundary Commission ('the Boundary Commission') charged with delimiting and demarcating the parties' land border in accordance with pertinent colonial treaties and applicable international law; Article 5 of the Algiers Agreement provided for the establishment of a neutral Claims Commission ('the Claims Commission') 'with the mandate to decide through binding arbitration all claims for loss, damage or injury by one State against the other resulting from violations of international law'.

[18] Eritrea-Ethiopia Boundary Commission, Decision Regarding Delimitation of the Border (13 April 2002) http://legal.un.org/riaa/cases/vol_XXV/83-195.pdf; UN Security Council, 'Special Report of the Secretary-General on Ethiopia and Eritrea' (15 December 2016) S/2006/992 https://reliefweb.int/sites/reliefweb.int/files/resources/10E68923496B29C049257252000457C4-Full_Report.pdf.

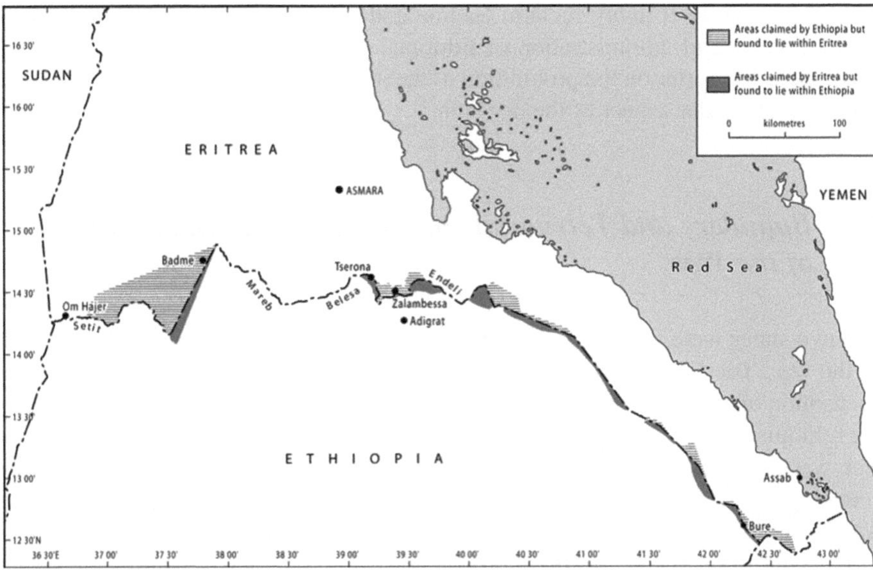

Fig. 1 Eritrea-Ethiopia Border Area. Source: T Lyons, 'Avoiding Conflict in the Horn of Africa U.S. Policy Toward Ethiopia and Eritrea' (Council on Foreign Relations, 2006). Copyrighted to International Boundaries Research Unit, Durham University, www.dur.ac.uk/ibru

the two states and awarded Badme to Eritrea [see Fig. 1], despite the fact that Ethiopia had exercised administrative authority over Badme for a considerable period of time.[19] According to the Boundary Commission, the evidence of Ethiopian administration of Badme and adjacent areas was 'not sufficiently clear in location, substantial in scope or extensive in time to displace the title of Eritrea that had crystallised as of 1935'.[20]

The Claims Commission dealt with various aspects of international law including with *jus in bello* (international humanitarian law (IHL)[21] and *jus ad bellum* (the rules of international law on the use of force).[22] The Claims Commission concluded that

[19]Murphy (2018), p. 553; Plaut (1999), p. 59; It has to be noted, however, that Badme was not the only contentious area of the boundary delimitation award. There were territories on other fronts of the border that have been awarded to Eritrea and Ethiopia that were also hotly contested by both parties. Clearly, Badme has become the flashpoint for legal, political, military, and purely symbolic reasons but was not the only point of disagreement with respect to the delimitation award.

[20]Eritrea-Ethiopia Boundary Commission, Decision Regarding Delimitation of the Border (13 April 2002) para 9.95.

[21]IHL is the branch of international law that regulates the behaviour of warring parties during armed conflict and aims to promote humanity, distinction between civilians and combatants and civilian and military targets, necessity and proportionality, amongst others, see Green (2008). See also Snider and Nair (this volume), pp. 11–34.

[22]In contrast to IHL, the law on the use of force prohibits the threat or use of force by a state against another state as a tool of national or international policy. The primary legal source of this field of law

Eritrea's action to forcibly reclaim Badme and other territories, which were then under the peaceful administration of Ethiopia, constituted a violation of Article 2 (4) of the UN Charter on the prohibition of the use of force.[23] The focus of this paper is on this particular aspect of the decision.

1.2 *Boundary and Territorial Questions Not the Only Cause of the War*

The two states were in fundamental disagreement as to the origins and deeper roots of the war. The Eritrean side focused on its territorial rights, particularly after the occupation of some Eritrean territories following the successful counter-offensive by the Ethiopian defence forces. Ethiopia, for its part, argued that the main cause of the war was the Eritrean aggression caused by a desire to dominate the Ethiopian economy, not Eritrea's desire to advance its territorial sovereignty claims. What was clear with respect to the pre-war events was that the two states were having serious and multifaceted confrontations around currency, movement of goods and businesses across their borders and on related policy issues that were of crucial importance to their national interests. It has to be mentioned that Ethiopia and Eritrea shared the same currency until a few months prior to the waging of the war, the Ethiopian *Birr.* When Eritrea introduced its own currency, the *Nakfa* in 1998, Ethiopia proposed the use of the US dollar as a medium of exchange, with which Eritrea was not happy. Such economic, monetary and trade issues were publicly stated as grounds of contention by officials and leaders of the two states, but less so boundary and territorial issues.[24] Some authors have suggested that the underlying roots of the conflict can be found in the Eritrean and Ethiopian divergent approaches to democracy, government, and state building and their competition for hegemonic control within the former Ethiopian polity, rather than a mere boundary dispute.[25]

---

is Article 2(4) of the UN Charter and customary international law. However, two key exceptions exist to the ban on the use of force: (a) the inherent right of states to self-defence when there is a prior armed attack launched against them as expressly recognised under Article 51 of the UN Charter and customary international law and; (b) a use of force authorised by the UN Security Council; for an analysis, see Gray (2018), Chapters 2 and 4.

[23]Eritrea-Ethiopia Claims Commission, Partial Award, *Jus ad Bellum*: Ethiopia's Claims 1–8 (19 December 2005). The Claims Commission was composed of Hans van Houtte (President), George H Aldrich, John R Crook, James C N Paul, and Lucy Reed.

[24]As Plaut and Gilkes (1999) explain:

> Occasional disputes did occur along the entire Ethiopian-Eritrean border after 1991. Most were local and small-scale. They were the sort of conflicts that frequently flare up along any ill-defined border which is straddled by farming communities. Low-level meetings between local officials took place in an attempt to resolve these matters, but when these failed the problems were referred upwards.

[25]Dias (2008), pp. 53–64; see also Gilkes and Barry (2005); Cliffe (1999).

However, when the war began between the two countries, the rhetoric and nature of the conflict shifted almost exclusively to boundary and territorial issues.

It may well be that the war had multiple causes, and coming up with a single primary cause would prove to be difficult. According to Lencho Lata:

> Picking the most pivotal one/ones from among the array of the conflict's stipulated causes also looks quite daunting. Border dispute, economic issues, the divergence of the ideologies of the groups ruling the two entities, differing visions and nature of state types, the contrast between democracy in one state and authoritarianism in the other, etc. are offered as some of the causes. But which one or ones is/are decisive, the resolution of which would pave the way for addressing all others?[26]

The interview given by the President of Eritrea with ERi-TV on 3 November 2018, aligns with such characterisation of the causes of the conflict. The first point President Afeworki made was that 'the Badme issue is an invention'; it was a cause neither for the war nor for the unfriendly relations between the two neighbouring countries.[27] The second point he made, which is more difficult to corroborate, is that the border and Badme issues were part of an international ploy (particularly by the United States) to 'corner' and 'sanction' Eritrea by inventing border issues with Yemen, Djibouti and later with Ethiopia.[28]

Leaving the merits of such assertions to political scientists, we would like to emphasise that the cause of the Eritrea-Ethiopia war was not merely boundary and territorial issues, although the incidents in and around the border town of Badme do seem to have triggered the devastating 1998–2000 war by escalating the tension and animosity over economic and political mis-trust between the two countries.[29]

The following section looks at the interplay between disputed territories and the law on the use of force in general before turning to the specific contours of the Eritrea-Ethiopia Claims Commission's award on *jus ad bellum*.

2 Disputed Territories and the Law on the Use of Force

Few issues have become the focus of such heated contestation, and conflict amongst states than the determination of disputed claims of territorial sovereignty and disputes over the determination of territorial boundaries (generically referred to in this paper as 'territorial disputes').[30] There are four key factors behind the escalation

---

[26]Lata (2003), p. 369.

[27]Interview with President Isaias Afwerki (3 November 2018) https://www.youtube.com/watch?v=FUWQG6XlEDo (rough translation from Tigrigna to English by author).

[28]Ibid.

[29]Ibid, p. 50.

[30]'A territorial dispute can be defined as a legal dispute between two or more States over the acquisition or attribution of territory (continental or island), or to the creation, location and effect of territorial boundaries', Yiallourides et al. (2018), pp. 3–4; On the distinction between 'boundary disputes', 'delimitation disputes', and 'territorial disputes' more broadly, see Prescott and Triggs

of territorial disputes; (a) strategic importance of the disputed land, (b) economic importance, (c) ethnic, cultural or religious reasons, and (d) unsettled border lines following inter-state conflict.[31] Geographical factors are vastly important in influencing the outbreak of territorial disputes, with studies revealing that disputes tend to escalate more frequently between contiguous countries; anxieties regarding security breaches are naturally higher between such states, and proximity also provides more ample opportunity for physical occupation of land.[32] As shown in this case study, moreover, other factors such as symbolic, economic and political factors might also play a role in causing territorial tensions and legal disputes.

In international law, sovereignty constitutes the ultimate authority over a territory.[33] Territorial boundaries define the spatial limits of a state's sovereignty, namely, those geographical areas over which sovereignty may be exercised to the exclusion of all other states.[34] The fundamental norms of sovereignty and territorial integrity enable a state with sovereignty over a given territory to act freely upon that territory and to prevent other states from acting upon it. The same norms protect the sovereign state from unilateral territorial incursions and violations of its territorial boundaries by other states.[35]

But what if that state's territorial boundaries are disputed by another state and there is no clear answer as to which state has sovereignty over the territory in question? In practice, states may disagree over the definition of the course of a land boundary (i.e. delimitation) or over the way it is positioned on the ground (i.e. demarcation).[36] At some point, the exact course of their boundary has to be settled for the territory in question to be attributed; until then the essential basis for the protection of sovereignty, namely a title to territory, remains obscure. This raises several important legal questions, the foremost of which and indeed the crux of the Eritrea-Ethiopia *jus ad bellum* case being: Can a state legitimately reclaim the disputed territory by force on the basis that it has a valid sovereignty title over that territory? Whichever way it is addressed, this question has far-reaching practical

(2008), pp. 138–140; Sharma (1997), pp. 21–28; Cukwurah (1967), p. 6; Hill (1945), p. 25; Thirlway (2018), p. 117.

[31]The Hague Centre for Strategic Studies, 'Pushing the Boundaries: Territorial Conflict in Today's World' (2015), p. 21.

[32]Diehl, 'Territorial Disputes' (2008), p. 2083.

[33]Besson defines sovereignty as the 'supreme authority within a territory' pursuant to which States can enjoy 'the plenitude of internal jurisdiction, their immunity from other States' own jurisdiction and their freedom from other States' intervention on their territory (Art. 2 (4) and (7) UN Charter), but also their equal rank to other sovereign States', Besson (2011), paras 1–2.

[34]'[O]ne of the essential elements of sovereignty is that it is to be exercised within territorial limits, and that, failing proof to the contrary, the territory is co-terminous with the Sovereignty', *North Atlantic Coast Fisheries Case* (1910), p. 948; see also Shaw (1986), pp. 1–11.

[35]*Island of Palmas Case* (1928), p. 829; Bernárdez (1987), pp. 487–494; Territorial integrity constitutes, according to the ICJ, 'an essential foundation of international relations' and 'an important part of the international legal order', *Corfu Channel* [1949] para 35; *Kosovo* Advisory Opinion [2010] 403.

[36]Yiallourides et al. (2018), pp. 3–4.

implications on a number of areas of international law, extending beyond the possibility of self-defence, to the possibility of countermeasures and the law relating to state responsibility.

3 The Eritrea-Ethiopia Claims Commission's Award on *jus ad bellum*

3.1 Legal Positions of the Parties

As mentioned earlier, the Eritrea-Ethiopia Claims Commission was established pursuant the 2000 Algiers Agreement which terminated the Eritrea-Ethiopia armed conflict.[37] During the proceedings, Ethiopia claimed that, beginning 12 May and throughout June 1998, Eritrea carried out a series of armed attacks against Ethiopian territory in violation of Article 2(4) of the UN Charter.[38] According to Ethiopia, Eritrea was responsible for initiating the conflict.[39]

Eritrea did not deny its forcible conduct but sought to justify it on the basis of self-defence, pursuant to Article 51 of the UN Charter.[40] Specifically, Eritrea put forward three alternative legal grounds to justify its actions. First, that Ethiopia was unlawfully occupying Eritrean territory in the area around Badme (citing the decision of the Eritrea-Ethiopia Boundary Commission of 13 April 2002 which awarded Badme to Eritrea) and therefore Eritrea was justified in using military force to defend its territory. In essence, Eritrea argued that because it was correct in May 1998 that Badme was part of Eritrea, it was justified in using force to seize Badme and expel Ethiopian troops.[41] Second, that Eritrea's action was in response to Ethiopia's 'forcible incursions' into Eritrean territory along the border area in early May 1988.[42] Third, that it was Ethiopia that had commenced the conflict by issuing a war declaration on 13 May 1998 and therefore Eritrea was permitted to use military force against Ethiopia.[43]

[37]Art 1, 'Ethiopia/Eritrea Peace Agreement' (2000).

[38]Ibid, paras 6–8.

[39]Murphy (2018), p. 563.

[40]Eritrea-Ethiopia Claims Commission, Partial Award, *Jus ad Bellum*: Ethiopia's Claims 1–8 (19 December 2005) para 9.

[41]Murphy (2018), p. 561.

[42]Whilst Eritrea claimed that the armed incidents occurred within Eritrean territory, Ethiopia asserted that they occurred within Ethiopian territory, Eritrea-Ethiopia Claims Commission, Partial Award, *Jus ad Bellum*: Ethiopia's Claims 1–8 (19 December 2005) para 9.

[43]Ibid, para 9.

3.2 Main Findings of the Claims Commission

The Claims Commission rejected Eritrea's arguments on self-defence. As regards Eritrea's first line of argument, that its forcible takeover of Badme and other areas was a lawful measure of self-defence because it was territory to which Eritrea had a valid claim, the Claims Commission held that 'self-defense cannot be invoked to settle territorial disputes'.[44] According to the Claims Commission, the boundary lacked demarcation and the parties clearly had differing interpretations as to the location of the border. But the existence of a disputed territory could not condone the illegality of Eritrea's recourse to military force.[45] It held that:

> [B]order disputes between States are so frequent that any exception to the prohibition of the threat or use of force for territory that is allegedly occupied unlawfully would create a large and dangerous hole in a fundamental rule of international law.[46]

In relation to Eritrea's second line of argument, that recourse to the use of force was lawful action in self-defence in response to Ethiopia's armed incursions into Eritrean territory in early May 1998, the Claims Commission found the requirements of self-defence had not been satisfied.

According to the Claims Commission, 'the predicate for a valid claim of self-defense under the UN Charter is that the party resorting to force has been subjected to an armed attack.'[47] Based on the evidence at hand, viewed in this particular context, the incidents that predated Eritrea's armed action along the border involved 'geographically limited clashes between small Eritrean and Ethiopian patrols along a remote, unmarked, and disputed border', which 'were not of a magnitude to constitute an armed attack by either state against the other within the meaning of Article 51 of the UN Charter'.[48] Moreover, Eritrea's use of force was directed at areas which were 'all either within undisputed Ethiopian territory or within territory that was peacefully administered by Ethiopia'.[49] Therefore, because there was no armed attack against Eritrea, its actions could not be justified as lawful self-defence under the UN Charter.[50] In addition, the Claims Commission noted that Eritrea had failed to report its use of force against Ethiopia on 12 May 1998 to the Security Council as a measure taken in self-defence, in accordance to the procedural requirements embodied in Article 51 of the Charter.[51]

As regards Eritrea's third line of argument, that Ethiopia was the first to declare war on Eritrea, the Claims Commission held that Ethiopia only declared that it

---

[44] Ibid, para 10.
[45] Ibid, para 10.
[46] Ibid, para 10.
[47] Ibid, para 11.
[48] Ibid, paras 11–12.
[49] Ibid, para 15.
[50] Ibid, para 13.
[51] Ibid, para 11.

'would not accept Eritrea's advances as a *fait accompli* and was determined to act in self-defense until the Eritrean forces withdrew or were compelled to leave the areas they had occupied'.[52] According to the Claims Commission, 'the essence of a declaration of war is an explicit affirmation of the existence of a state of war between belligerents'; Ethiopia's resolution was not, as Eritrea had asserted, a declaration of war.[53]

The Claims Commission concluded that Eritrea's action to attack and forcibly take control over Badme and adjacent areas, which were at that time under the peaceful administration of Ethiopia, constituted a violation of Article 2(4) of the UN Charter. As a consequence, Eritrea was liable to compensate Ethiopia for the damages caused by this violation of international law.[54]

The outcome of the *jus ad bellum* ruling may well be welcomed or criticised, depending on one's reasoning and justification. The verdict could be, and has been, criticised due to the sensitivity and speciality of the subject matter involved. Gray, at first, gave the benefit of the doubt to the substantive *jus ad bellum* decision of the tribunal as follows: 'It may be that the Claims Commission's decision on the merits was a sustainable one. It may be that Eritrea was, in fact, responsible for violations of Article 2(4) in 1998'.[55] However, she then questioned (a) the mandate of the tribunal on *jus ad bellum*, (b) the consistency of the award with the Boundary Commission decision 2002, and; (c) the expertise of members of the Claims Commission and the role of an arbitral tribunal on matters of the law on the use of force. Each of these points is dealt with below.[56]

First, the mandate of the Claims Commission, as expressly provided for in Article 5(1) of the Algiers Agreement, includes deciding 'through binding arbitration all claims for loss, damage or injury by one Government against the other... related to the conflict --resulting from violations of international humanitarian law... or other violations of international law'.[57] As Gray observes, however, the same article appears to put some limitation on the mandate of the Claims Commission: 'The Commission shall not hear claims arising from the cost of military operations, preparing for military operations, or the use of force, except to the extent that such claims involve violations of international humanitarian law'.[58] Moreover, the Algiers Agreement envisages the establishment of a separate body with the duty of determining 'the causes of the conflict'.[59] Eritrea challenged the jurisdiction of the Claims Commission based upon these two different sentences of Article 5 (1) which

[52]Ibid, para 17.

[53]Ibid, para 17.

[54]Ibid, para 16.

[55]Although the article also argues that the Commission 'did not give a satisfactory decision on the substantive law on the use of force', Gray (2006), pp. 721–722.

[56]Ibid.

[57]Article 5(1), 'Ethiopia/Eritrea Peace Agreement' (2000).

[58]Ibid.

[59]Art 3, ibid.

forms the basis for Gray's criticism that the Commission may have exceeded its mandate.

The Claims Commission rejected Eritrea's argument, noting that a factual inquiry into 'origins' and 'misunderstandings' is not the same as a determination of the *legal* claim advanced by Ethiopia, which concerned whether Eritrea's actions in May and June 1998 constituted a violation of the *jus ad bellum*. As the Commission saw it, determining 'the origins of the conflict and the nature of any misunderstandings about the border, had they been made by an impartial body anticipated by Article 3, could have been helpful in promoting reconciliation and border delimitation, but they certainly would not have answered the question of the legality of Eritrea's resort to force.' The factual inquiries to be undertaken by the two bodies were not the same, and only the Commission was empowered to determine whether one of the states violated the *jus ad bellum*.[60] Therefore, this rules out exceeding a mandate by the Claims commission over the issues of *jus ad bellum.*

However, as a second point, it might be asked whether arbitral tribunals should refrain from delivering a verdict on sensitive issues such as *jus ad bellum*, as a matter of judicial policy. One view may be that they should refrain from making bold decisions on issues of state responsibility for violation of Article 2(4) of the UN Charter in the interest of creating a non-confrontational environment in which the parties could move to a speedy implementation of the decision 'without opening a new phase of proceedings concerning the calculation of due compensation'.[61] The contrary view may see the verdict at issue or other similar decisions as exemplary and a neutral application of the law on the use of force by legal experts for several reasons. The first is that all institutions of international law, including international arbitral tribunals, must contribute to upholding the fundamentals of the international legal order—the ban on the use of force is among them. When a state breaches the rules of the international legal order, this should be followed by the determination of a breach either to stop the breach itself or remedy the injury sustained as a result of the breach. Despite the potentially negative effect of this approach, the message of such a practice sent to the parties of a dispute or other third states would contribute towards deterring future violations of a fundamental norm of international law.[62]

This issue was raised by Judge Robinson in his separate opinion in *Costa Rica v Nicaragua*.[63] In this case, Nicaragua occupied and deployed its troops in a territory which was under the administration of Costa Rica, but was also claimed by

[60]Ibid, 5.

[61]Milano and Papanicolopulu (2011), p. 593.

[62]According to Mikanagi (2018), p. 1034, finding a breach of the provisions of the UN Charter on the use of force and the peaceful settlement of disputes in relation to disputed territories contributes 'to the "rule of law" in the international community, or the rule-based international order, by encouraging the settlement of disputes based on international law.' It also 'discourage[s] States from resorting to military measures to resolve international disputes in their favour and thus contribute[s] to the maintenance of international peace and security, which is the most important purpose of the UN'.

[63]*Costa Rica v Nicaragua* (2015).

Nicaragua. Although the ICJ refrained from ruling on whether Nicaragua had used force in sending and deploying troops in the disputed territory, Judge Robinson provided a separate opinion on the issue, explaining that the hesitation on the part of international courts and tribunals to adjudicate on the issue of Article 2(4) in relation to disputed territories, is particularly problematic:

> If indeed a line of jurisprudence is developing in which the Court abstains from ruling on the merits of claims of the use of force in a disputed territory, this course is to be regretted. Disputed territories are one of the most sensitive categories of international relations and particularly prone to provoking the use of force by states. A judicial practice of ruling on the merits of every claim by a state that another state has breached Article 2 (4) of the United Nations Charter would be entirely consistent with, and supportive of the system established after World War II for the maintenance of international peace and security and the Court's role in that system.[64]

Another reason might be to do with the weaknesses of the UN Security Council to discharge its duties on matters of the use of force. The determination of a violation of *jus ad bellum* is a highly politicised business and the Council is often reluctant to determine a wrong-doing relating to this subject. Therefore, the ICJ and other international tribunals should undertake to fill this gap when they are mandated by states to resolve a dispute such as the one involving Eritrea and Ethiopia. Finally, such verdicts contribute to enhancing our understanding of the laws and their application, in this case on the convergence or supplementarity of *jus ad bellum* and the law of territory.

Second, the argument that 'the Claims Commission in the *jus ad bellum* case paid very little respect to the Delimitation Decision of the Boundary Commission' might appear plausible at the first glance from consistency perspective of resolving a dispute.[65] However, as this article shows, the norms prohibiting the use of force and the laws requiring respect for sovereignty and territorial integrity serve distinct functions; 'they reflect overlapping, but not identical, concerns'.[66] Most importantly, the mandates of the two Commissions were different, one was charged with delimiting the boundary between the two countries while the other with claims of loss or damage arising from violations of international law. Relying on the notion of consistency without due regard to questions of justice and *jus cogens* violations would have been a very serious mistake and miscarriage of international justice.

---

[64]*Costa Rica v Nicaragua (2015)* (Sep Op Judge Robinson) paras 43, 58–59; see also separate opinion of Judge Simma in *Iran v United States of America* (2003), para 327–328:

> [It is] regrettable that the Court has not mustered the courage of restating, and thus re-confirming, more fully fundamental principles of the law of the United Nations as well as customary international law (principles that in my view are of the nature of jus cogens) on the use of force, or rather the prohibition on armed force, in a context and at a time when such a reconfirmation is called for with the greatest urgency.

[65]Gray (2006), pp. 707–710.

[66]*Costa Rica v Nicaragua* (2015) (Sep Op Judge Robinson) para 39.

Third, and finally, the argument that the arbitrators' 'main area of expertise' is not in the 'field of *jus ad bellum*'[67] does not appear to be convincing given that they are all highly recognised scholars and practitioners of public international law with the capacity, skills and experience in determining legal claims that emanate from violations of international law, including matters involving the use of force.[68] As a result, they have dealt not only with *jus ad bellum* but also with *jus in bello* violations. If we accept the argument on expertise, should we also question and probe whether or not members of the Claims Commission have expertise in international humanitarian law and the law of territory? Not really. What the arbitrators did was to apply well-established rules of international law to the facts that are well-known and, to a large extent, uncontested by Eritrea. As examined in the following section, the Claims Commission looked at the basic question: Whether the use of force can be deployed as a means of regaining territorial rights under international law.

3.3 Jus ad bellum *Rules Are Applicable to Territorial Disputes*

The Eritrea-Ethiopia Claims Commission affirmed that the rules of international law on the use of force make no exception in respect of disputed territories. According to the Commission, recognising such an exception would significantly weaken the fundamental rule of international law prohibiting the use of force.[69] This finding was, in fact, re-stated in the *Guyana/Suriname* case of 2007.[70] In this case, Surinamese naval vessels boats had threatened Guyana's concessionaires operating an oil rig in the disputed areas to 'leave the area in 12 hours' or 'the consequences will be [theirs]'.[71] Suriname believed it had a valid claim to the area in question and, thus, that it had the right to forcibly expel the operators of the rig as part of legitimate law

[67]Gray (2006), p. 707.

[68]Hans van Houtte, the President of the Claims Commission, is Chair holder in public international law at Leuven University with strong practice in arbitration including as President of the Iran-US Claims Tribunal; Judge George H Aldrich, Professor of international (humanitarian) law at Leiden University is also experienced on matters of international law including as a member of the International Law Commission; John R Crook is a senior figure in the field of public international law including acting as president of the American Society of International law, Judge on NATO's Administrative Tribunal and advisor to the United States Government; James CN Paul was Professor of Law Emeritus and Dean of Rutgers School of Law-Newark in the United States with several books publications on public international law; and Lucy Reed, a renowned public international lawyer.

[69]Eritrea-Ethiopia Claims Commission, Partial Award, Jus ad Bellum: Ethiopia's Claims 1–8 (19 December 2005) para 10.

[70]*Guyana/Suriname* (Award) (2007).

[71]Ibid, paras 433, 445.

enforcement measures.[72] The arbitral tribunal found that the action by Surinamese Navy was more akin to a threat of force than a law enforcement activity.[73] While this is a law of the sea case, it is remarkable in that a threat of force by Suriname within the maritime area claimed by Suriname, also represented a breach of 2(4) of the UN Charter, which the *Guyana/Suriname* tribunal found remains applicable in the context of both territorial and maritime boundary disputes.[74]

That the prohibition of the use of force applies to disputed territories is also supported by state practice, as shown in the following indicative examples. The UN Security Council Resolutions 242 (1967) and 298 (1971), adopted by majority vote in response to the Israeli-Palestinian conflict, stressed the inadmissibility of acquiring territory by force whilst calling for the '[w]ithdrawal of Israel armed forces from territories occupied in the recent conflict' and '[t]ermination of all claims or states of belligerency'.[75] Moreover, the majority of the members of the Security Council strongly condemned Argentina's 1982 military invasion of the Falkland Islands, to recover them from the United Kingdom, whose territorial title over the Falklands Argentina rejected.[76] In relation to the military conflict in the former Yugoslavia, the UN Security Council also re-stated the inadmissibility of the alteration of international boundaries through the use of force.[77]

In connection to the armed conflict between Eritrea and Ethiopia along their disputed boundary, the Security Council passed Resolution 1177 (1998) expressing its 'grave concern at the conflict' and stressing that 'the use of armed force was not acceptable as a means of addressing territorial disputes or changing circumstances on the ground'.[78] In 1999, after the conflict escalated to a full-scale war, the Security Council, in Resolution 1227 (1999), condemned the recourse to force by Ethiopia and Eritrea and demanded an immediate end to the hostilities.[79] Therefore, it is clear that the use of force as a means of acquiring territory and settling international disputes, including disputes over territory, is contrary to international law.[80]

The Declaration on Friendly Relations emphasises that point in stipulating that:

---

[72]Ibid, para 433.

[73]Ibid, paras 433, 445.

[74]Ibid, paras 423, 483–484.

[75]Security Council Resolutions 242 (1967) (22 November 1967) and 298 (1971) (25 September 1971).

[76]Security Council Official Records S/PV 2345 (1 April 1982); Security Council Official Records S/PV 2346 (2 April 1982); Security Council Resolution 502 (3 April 1982) noted that the 'invasion on 1982 by armed forces of Argentina' and demanded Argentina to withdraw its forces from the Falklands; Security Council Resolution 505 (26 May 1982), noting 'with the deepest concern that the situation in the region of the Falkland Islands (Islas Malvinas) has seriously deteriorated'.

[77]Security Council Resolutions 752 (15 May 1992) and 757 (30 May 1992), 'no territorial gains or changes brought about by violence are acceptable'.

[78]Security Council Resolution 1177 (26 June 1998).

[79]Security Council Resolution 1227 (10 February 1999).

[80]Crawford (2006), pp. 131–132.

> Every State has the duty to refrain from the threat or use of force to violate the existing international boundaries of another State or as a means of solving international disputes, *including territorial disputes and problems concerning frontiers of States* [emphasis added].[81]

The threat or use of force by one state against another would not escape the scope of Article 2(4) of the UN Charter simply because they take place in, or are directed at, a disputed territory. As the Eritrea-Ethiopia Claims Commission and the *Guyana/ Suriname* tribunal respectively confirmed, the legal status of the territory in question (delimited or undelimited, demarcated or not clearly demarcated, disputed or not subject to a dispute) does not affect the characterisation of a certain conduct as a threat or use of force in the sense of Article 2(4) of the UN Charter.[82]

3.4 The Administrative **status quo** *Is Legally Protected Under* **jus ad bellum**

Another important aspect of the Eritrea-Ethiopia *jus ad bellum* award concerns the relationship between the prohibition on the use of force and the principles of sovereignty and territorial integrity. Article 2(4) of the UN Charter provides that member states shall refrain from the threat or use of force 'against the territorial integrity… of any State'.[83] As noted above, the principles of sovereignty and territorial integrity protect the legitimate holder of sovereignty title over a given territory from adverse or belligerent occupation, unilateral incursions, and violations of its land borders by other states. However, when that title of sovereignty is rejected by another state, or when the legal status and location of the border itself is unclear, the protection afforded by this principle is truly meaningful only after the dispute has been settled and the situation is characterised *ex-post facto* as an unlawful occupation or as a breach of that state's territorial integrity in contravention of international law.[84] If the essential basis for the protection of sovereignty, namely a title to territory, remains obscure and will not become clear until the dispute resolution process is completed, then the preservation of the factual situation on the ground becomes crucially important.

The Eritrea-Ethiopia *jus ad bellum* case shows that in the context of a disputed territory, where two or more states oppose each other's sovereignty claim, and where

---

[81]'Declaration on Principles of International Law concerning Friendly Relations and Co-operation among States in accordance with the Charter of the United Nations' 2625 (XXV) (24 October 1970).

[82]Eritrea-Ethiopia Claims Commission, Partial Award, *Jus ad Bellum*: Ethiopia's Claims 1–8 (19 December 2005) para 10; *Guyana v Suriname* (2007) para 423.

[83]The ICJ has repeatedly emphasised that the principle of territorial integrity is an important feature of the international legal order, see *Kosovo Advisory Opinion* (2010) para 80; *Costa Rica v Nicaragua* (Provisional Measures) (Order of 16 July 2013) paras 13–14.

[84]Milano and Papanicolopulu (2011), p. 589.

there is no clear answer as to which state holds title over that territory, what the law protects, pending the settlement of the dispute, is not so much the territorial integrity of the holder of a valid title in the disputed territory (which can be either of the two claimants), but rather the existing administrative *status quo* on the ground. Indeed, in 1998 Eritrea directed its armed attack at Badme and the surrounding area which were administered at the time by Ethiopia. In 2002, the Boundary Commission delimited the boundary, meaning that Badme subsequently fell within Eritrean territory.[85] The Eritrea-Ethiopia Claims Commission found that even if Eritrea was correct in May 1998 that it held a valid title of sovereignty over Badme, this could not condone the illegality of its resort to force against Ethiopia (i.e. the administering state).[86]

Seen from this angle, the factual reality on the ground forms the relevant baseline against which to test the application of *jus ad bellum* where the use of force is engaged in the context of a territorial dispute. The relevant exercise in any given situation is to ascertain which of the two claimants has crossed this baseline, in other words, which party was the first to disturb the existing territorial *status quo* on the ground, through the use of force.

That the factual reality on the ground is immune to unilateral modifications by force is also supported by relevant state practice. The Goan incident between India and Portugal is a good example in that regard. Armed disputes erupted between India and Portugal in 1961, over the disputed territory of Goa. Portugal had held Goa as an overseas territory since it was first acquired in 1510, however, following India's independence in 1947, India had been placing increasing pressure upon the Portuguese to release their claim over the country. Indo-Portuguese tensions increased from the mid-1950s onwards, and in November 1961 shots were fired at Indian fishing vessels passing near the Goan border, killing a passenger onboard. These tensions culminated in December 1961, when Indian troops were sent over the border into Goa, in order to seize control of the state. In the period leading up to the conflict, the UN urged both sides to negotiate peacefully and to avoid outright warfare, with the UK government also calling for restraint. The December dispute lasted less than 24 hours, with the significantly outnumbered Portuguese troops having withdrawn by December 19th. Third states including the United States and the United Kingdom outwardly condemned India's actions and the international press also criticised India's handling of the situation with the British Times indicating that Indian authorities had exaggerated the potential for 'anarchy and chaos'[87] in order to seize control. Conversely, India denied any breach of the UN Charter on the

---

[85]Eritrea-Ethiopia Boundary Commission, Decision Regarding Delimitation of the Border (13 April 2002); The Boundary Commission was composed of Professor Sir Elihu Lauterpacht (President), Prince Bola Adesumbo Ajibola, Professor Michael Reisman, Judge Stephen Schwebel, and Sir Arthur Watts.

[86]Eritrea-Ethiopia Claims Commission, Partial Award, *Jus ad Bellum*: Ethiopia's Claims 1–8 (19 December 2005) para 10.

[87]Keesing's Contemporary Archives, 'Indian Occupation of Portuguese Territories in India', (Volume 8, March 1962), 10.

basis that Portugal had itself breached the Charter in its 'repeat provocations', hence India's actions were justified.[88]

The Doklam incident, which took place in summer 2017 and saw India and China engaged in a 73-day stand-off along their shared border, is a similar example. The two countries have been involved in an unresolved dispute over the border since the Sino-Indian War of 1962, when repeat skirmishes in Aksai Chin culminated in full armed conflict. In 1967, military conflict broke out again with attacks on both sides at Nathu La in eastern-Sikkim and, in October 1975, four Indian soldiers were shot by Chinese military on the 'McMahon Line' between Tibet and Assam.[89] The 2017 incident was one of the most severe escalations over the past decade with India reacting against China's attempts to build a border road through the disputed area of Doklam which sits between China, the Indian State of Sikkim and Bhutan. The Bhutanese Government also rejected the road claiming that the construction breached existing agreements between China and Bhutan.

Third countries voiced concerns over the territory dispute; Australia, the United Kingdom and the United States all urged China and India to engage in peaceful negotiation, and the Indian Express reported Japanese Ambassador Hiramatsu's comments that the parties involved should 'not resort to unilateral attempts to change the status quo by force but resolve the dispute in a peaceful manner'[90] Although the face-off came to an end on 28 August 2017, tensions continue to simmer and each side persist in placing troops along the border. The vigorous reaction of third countries to the Doklam incident, however, supports the notion that the factual *status quo* continues to be advocated and protected in international law when it comes to disputed territories.

3.5 Force Cannot Be Used to Reclaim Territory

Another important lesson that can be drawn from the Eritrea-Ethiopia *jus ad bellum* award is that force cannot be used retroactively to correct situations of unlawful occupation of a territory, on grounds of self-defence. In essence, a state cannot legitimately invoke a right of self-defence to forcibly take control over a disputed area which is under the *de facto* control and administration of another state, even if it aimed at correcting a 'past injustice'.[91]

For an exercise of self-defence to be regarded as legitimate, three key requirements must be met: (a) self-defence can only be taken in response to 'an armed

[88]Ibid, 9.

[89]Keesing's Contemporary Archives, 'India-China: Indian Soldiers Killed in Border Incident' (30 January 1976).

[90]Roy (2017).

[91]Arend (1984), p. 102.

attack'[92]; (b) it must be directed against the state responsible for the attack (the state to whom the armed attack can be attributed)[93]; and (c) any act of self-defence must be carried out within the limits of necessity and proportionality.[94] Article 51 of the UN Charter sets out a further procedural requirement to report any measures taken in self-defence to the Security Council, along with the closely associated obligation to cease forcible actions when the Security Council has 'taken measures necessary to maintain international peace and security'.[95]

In the case of Eritrea and Ethiopia, the Claims Commission, after carefully examining the factual evidence presented before it, found that the conditions giving rise to the right of self-defence were not met. The Commission ultimately concluded that 'localised border encounters between small infantry units, even those involving the loss of life, do not constitute an armed attack' for the purposes of the UN Charter.[96] Hence, Eritrea had failed to establish that the minor skirmishes which had taken place between Eritrean and Ethiopian forces leading up to the Badme incident were sufficient to justify armed retaliation on Eritrea's part, on the grounds of self-defence; their actions were thus in violation of the UN Charter and constituted a breach of international law. Eritrea was also precluded from invoking the right to self-defence because it failed to comply with the requirement of reporting to the Security Council as required by Article 51 of the Charter.[97]

Moreover, the requirement that forcible action in self-defence only be exercised in response to an armed attack implies a condition of immediacy, namely that the action cannot be taken long after the armed attack has occurred.[98] The armed conflict between Argentina and Britain over the Falkland Islands is a useful reflection of this condition. On 2 April 1982, Argentina invaded and occupied the Falkland Islands which had been under Britain's control and administration since 1832. Argentina considered that because Britain had seized the territory by force in 1833, and given the lack of progress in diplomatic negotiations, it was justified in reclaiming the islands despite the intervening time.[99] The British government swiftly dispatched its

[92]An 'armed attack' is a type of aggression, as provided by UNGA Res 3314 (XXIX) (14 December 1974) on the Definition of Aggression.

[93]*Armed Activities on the Territory of the Congo* (2005) para 146.

[94]*Military and Paramilitary Activities in and against Nicaragua* (1986) paras 194, 237; *Legality of the Threat or Use of Nuclear Weapons* (Advisory Opinion) (1996) para 41.

[95]Art 51, UN Charter; In the *Nicaragua* case, the Court implied that when the use of force is governed by the UN Charter, failure to adhere to the reporting duty under the Charter carries irrevocable consequences for the invocation of the right of self-defence, *Military and Paramilitary Activities in and against Nicaragua* (1986) para 199.

[96]Eritrea-Ethiopia Claims Commission, Partial Award, *Jus ad Bellum*: Ethiopia's Claims 1–8 (19 December 2005) para 11.

[97]Ibid.

[98]Dinstein (2001), pp. 165–167.

[99]Prior to the invasion, General Galtieri, leader of the Argentine military government, told to President Reagan of the United States of America that the British had failed to relinquish sovereignty in 149 years and that 'time had run out', see 'Reagan, In a Phone Call, Tried to Deter

Royal Navy in the area and appealed to the Security Council to demand the immediate withdrawal of Argentine forces. The Security Council, by Resolution 502 of 3 April 1982, demanded that both governments immediately cease all hostilities and that Argentina immediately withdraw all its forces from the Falkland Islands.[100] The Resolution recognised the existence of a 'breach of the peace' as a result of the Argentine invasion and placed the onus on Argentina to withdraw, whilst calling upon both sides to pursue the peaceful settlement of this dispute. The British forces were able to dislodge Argentine forces from the Islands after 72 days of Argentine occupation. The two countries reached a de facto ceasefire in June 1982. The Falklands crisis of 1982 revealed the belief of the majority of the members of the Security Council that the use of force by Argentina to gain control over the Islands constituted an armed attack against the United Kingdom.[101] The latter, being the attacked State, acted legitimately in self-defence to protect its possession of the Islands.[102]

It should be noted that whilst forcible action in self-defence cannot be taken long after an armed attack on the disputed territory, delayed forcible action may still be legitimate if the lapse of time is warranted by the circumstances. For example, adequate time is usually required as the attacked State deliberates on or plans its next move, or if an attempt is first made to resolve the matter amicably via diplomatic means prior to resorting to self-defence but is persistently refuted by the latter.[103] However, as it was noted above, forcible action cannot be used to correct retroactively situations of perceived past injustice on grounds of self-defence.

The immediacy requirement and the existence of a territorial *status quo* to test the applicability of Article 2(4) have crucial implications for a dispossessed state's right to use forcible means to retake its territory. There are only two situations where a state which has lost a territory can forcibly reclaim it. The first situation is where there has been a UN Security Council's authorisation to use force. This is not done pursuant to the right of self-defence but instead the Security Council's power to maintain or restore international peace and security under Chapter VII of the UN Charter. One example is Security Council Resolution 678 which authorised UN Member States to use 'all necessary means' to uphold and implement resolution 660 to drive Iraq out of Kuwait following its invasion in 1990.[104]

Invasion' (*New York Times*, 3 April 1982) cited in Hassan (1982), pp. 54, 59; Security Council Official Records S/PV 2346 (2 April 1982) para 12.

[100]UN Security Council Res 502/1982 reproduced in (1982) 21 International Legal Materials 679.

[101]As evidenced by the widespread support (10 yes, 1 no and 4 abstentions) for Security Council Resolution 502/1982 demanding the 'immediate withdrawal of all Argentine forces from the Falkland Islands (Islas Malvinas)'.

[102]Greenwood (2012), p. 108; Waibel (2012), p. 1116.

[103]Dinstein (2001), pp. 212–213.

[104]UN Security Council Resolution 678 (29 November 1990); for other examples and analyses of the UN Security Council authorisation of the use of force, including Resolution 678, see, among others, Weston (1991), pp. 516, 517; Blokker (2000), p. 541; Blokker (2015), pp. 202–226.

The second situation is where a state is attacked and uses force in self-defence, pursuant to the requirements of Article 51 of the UN Charter, to protect the territory it administers. International law, as was seen above, protects the factual reality in existence on the ground, included in a disputed territory, when it comes to the use of military force. The immediacy requirement is of crucial importance here: if state A attacks neighbouring state B and occupies part of state B's territory and state B does not respond within a reasonable period of time, it loses the ability to rely on self-defence to retake its territory by force. The right to use force in self-defence cannot be reactivated at a later stage. Thus, unless the attacked state makes a forcible response which conforms to the requirements of self-defence within a reasonable time, it may be confronted with the newly established territorial *status quo* which it will be bound to respect[105] as far as waging war to change the situation is concerned.

The Russian swift take-over of Crimea presents a good case-study to test the extent and scope of the territorial *status quo* in its interaction with the right of self-defence. On 28 February 2014, Russian armed forces moved out of their naval base on the Black Sea and took over Crimea, triggering a crisis with Ukraine.[106] On 3 March 2014, at the UN Security Council, Ukraine claimed 16,000 Russian troops had entered Crimea.[107] Russia has put forward complex arguments under international law to attempt to justify its military action in Crimea and Eastern Ukraine, none of which is adequate to avoid the charge of aggression.[108] The Ukrainian acting Prime Minister, called upon Russia 'to immediately withdraw its troops, return to the place of deployment and stop provoking civil and military confrontation in Ukraine' and mobilized Ukrainian troops to counter Russian troops.[109] However, no counter-action was taken involving military force against Russian troops. On 15 March 2014, pro-Russian Crimean declared Crimea independent and on 18 March 2014, Russian President Vladimir Putin announced that Russia had annexed Crimea; Ukrainian troops withdrew from the peninsula one week later.[110]

Russian has, therefore, effectively occupied part of Ukraine's territory by force and has established its administration in there. A new factual reality has come into existence. This new factual reality on the ground forms the new administrative *status quo*. Ukraine did not militarily react at the time of the Russian attack and, therefore, may well have lost the ability to rely on self-defence at a later stage. Arguably, Ukraine, the dispossessed state, may not reactively take up arms and attack the area

[105]See Yiallourides et al. (2018), pp. 81–82.

[106]O'Connell (2018), p. 855.

[107]O'Connell (2018), p. 855.

[108]O'Connell (2018), p. 855; see also Daniel Wisehart, 'The Crisis in Ukraine and the Prohibition of the Use of Force: A Legal Basis for Russia's Intervention?' (*EJIL-talk!*, 4 March 2014) https://www.ejiltalk.org/the-crisis-in-ukraine-and-the-prohibition-of-the-use-of-force-a-legal-basis-for-russias-intervention/.

[109]Alison Smale and Steven Erlanger, 'Ukraine Mobilizes Reserve Troops, Threatening War' (New York Times, 1 March 2014) https://www.nytimes.com/2014/03/02/world/europe/ukraine.html.

[110]O'Connell (2018), pp. 855–856.

which Russian, the administering state, currently occupies, on the basis of self-defence. If Ukraine attempts to forcibly take-over Crimea, then Russia, as the current administrator of the occupied area, may well defend the territory by invoking self-defence against Ukraine, provided that the requirements of self-defence under Article 51 of the UN Charter are satisfied. How Russia established itself on the occupied territory and, how the new *status quo* came into existence does not affect its right to defend the territory in question against future attacks. In all, in view of the requirement that forcible action in self-defence must be 'temporally interwoven' with the armed incident triggering it, if Ukraine somehow obtained sufficient military power to try to take Crimea back from Russia by force, it may well not be legally permitted to do so considering the significant time that has elapsed since the Russian invasion and occupation of Crimea.[111]

However, Ukraine and third states, can still take countermeasures in response to Russia's internationally wrongful act—the annexation of territory by force.[112] Such countermeasures will be lawful provided that they comply with the substantive and procedural requirements laid down in the International Law Commission Draft Articles on Responsibility of States for Internationally Wrongful Acts. It is instructive that among the examples of continuing wrongful acts given by the International Law Commission is that of the 'unlawful occupation of part of the territory of another State or stationing armed forces in another State without its consent'.[113] So long as Russia's annexation persists, the internationally wrongful act will be continuing, and Ukraine, as well as third states, will be able to take or continue to take countermeasures against Russia.[114] Hence, while Ukraine may not resort to forcible means to reverse the situation and reclaim its territory, it can take lawful countermeasures or other lawful and peaceful action against Russia to compel the latter to cease its wrongful act. This example illustrates that, while international law protects the existing administrative *status quo* on the ground, it does not necessarily recognise this *status quo* as lawful; rather it recognises that an internationally wrongful act has been committed and empowers the dispossessed State to take non-forcible measures against the aggressor State in response. This is not withstanding the right of the people to external self-determination and a collective response and decision by the UN Security Council for example, which can include armed resistance or the authorisation of full-scale military force against occupiers, which are not within the scope of this article.

Clearly, this case-study is relevant to the Eritrea-Ethiopia *jus ad bellum* case as Eritrea tried to justify its use of military force *inter alia* based upon the prior control

---

[111]See Dinstein (2001), p. 219.

[112]Paddeu (2015); Milano (2004), p. 509; BBC, 'Ukraine Crisis: Russia and Sanctions' (19 December 2014) http://www.bbc.co.uk/news/world-europe-26672800; 'EU Sanctions Against Russia over Ukraine Crisis' https://europa.eu/newsroom/highlights/special-coverage/eu-sanctions-against-russia-over-ukraine-crisis_en.

[113]ILC Articles on State Responsibility 31, 60; see also Art 37 (point 4), ILC Articles on State Responsibility.

[114]For an account, see Tams (2005).

of its territory by Ethiopia, which was rightly rejected by the Claims Commission. However, the Crimea and Eritrea-Ethiopia cases have major differences, including the absence of prior aggression by Ethiopia against Eritrea, when the latter invaded Ethiopia in 1998. For this reason, therefore, the lapse of time argument made in relation to territorial occupation and self-defence will have to be applied with caution on a case-by-case basis, taking into consideration all relevant circumstances and applicable rules of international law.

3.6 A New Era of Peace and Cooperation on the Horizon

Almost 20 years after the end of the war, the political relations of Eritrea and Ethiopia have been characterised by a perpetual 'no war, no peace' stalemate with serious economic and security implications on both sides and the Horn of Africa at large.[115] However, after a change of leadership in Ethiopia in June 2018, the Ethiopian ruling party and the Government led by the newly elected Prime Minister took a fresh and unconditional peace offer to Eritrea, which was swiftly welcomed by Eritrea.[116] In a fairly short period of time, the two countries have begun to normalise their relations—including opening up their respective borders to their citizens (although the Zalambesa and Rama border corridors are partially closed shortly after their opening), commencing inter-state flights to, and from, both capitals and undertaking preparations for the use of Eritrean ports by Ethiopia and regulating trading relations of the two countries.

At the time of writing, the leaders of the two countries signed a peace and friendship agreement in Jeddah in the presence of UN Secretary-General António Guterres and King Salman of Saudi Arabia.[117] According to Addis Standard, an Ethiopian newspaper, the agreement considers 'the close bonds of geography, history, culture and religion between the two countries and their peoples', the need for 'Respecting each other's independence, sovereignty and territorial integrity' and affirming 'their commitment to the principles and purposes of the Charter of the United Nations'.[118] According to the same source, the two leaders agreed to, *inter alia*, end 'the state of war' and start 'a new era of peace, friendship and comprehensive cooperation. . .on the basis of complementarity and synergy'. This new era includes: (a) full implementation of 'the Eritrea-Ethiopia Boundary Commission's decision; (b) 'comprehensive cooperation' on matters of political, security, defence,

[115]For a discussion, see Woldemariam (2018), pp. 407–427.

[116]Gebrekidan (2018).

[117]Cornwell (2018).

[118]Agreement on Peace, Friendship and Comprehensive Cooperation Between the Federal Democratic Republic of Ethiopia and the State of Eritrea (18 September 2018) available at http://addisstandard.com/full-text-of-the-ethio-eritrea-agreement-signed-in-jeddah/. For specific provisions of the Agreement(s) accompanied by brief explanation see Desta (this volume), pp. 261–268; for lifting UN sanctions against Eritrea see Hirt (this volume), pp. 269–284.

economic and trade; (c) development of 'investment projects' and; (d) promotion of 'regional and global peace, security and cooperation'.[119]

These are very ambitious commitments, the specific details of which are not yet clear. While such developments should be welcomed, considering the contributions and reflections of others to this same volume on the many dimensions of the Eritrea-Ethiopia case and the way forward for the two East African neighbours, the final section of this article outlines the main lessons that ought to be learnt from the Claims Commission's *jus ad bellum* award in relation to disputes over territory.[120]

4 Lessons and Some Conclusions

First, rightly or wrongly, international law prioritises peace and border stability over justice. Where borders are unclear or the status of a territory is disputed, the law on the use of force takes its lead primarily from the factual reality on the ground. Although Ethiopia was administering territory belonging, in effect, to Eritrea, the Claims Commission made clear that Eritrea's forcible attempt to overturn Ethiopia's administration or occupation was an unlawful use of force in violation of Article 2 (4) of the UN Charter. Neither could such forcible attempt been accepted as self-defence in the absence of an armed attack against Eritrea. Force cannot be used to modify a border, however disputed, or to change the *status quo* on the ground. The administering state is legally permitted to use force to defend its administration over the disputed territory through an exercise of its right of self-defence.

Secondly, wars between countries can have various causes ranging from socio-economic and ideological matters to that of territorial claims. The Eritrea-Ethiopia case is clearly a good example of dealing with a devastating armed conflict caused by various factors but later painted in the guise of a boundary war. The latter may well have been used as a pretext for waging war despite being caused by other national, regional and international political rivalry. Whatever the causes of the war might have been, the resort to force as a means of advancing a territorial claim is outlawed by international law. The analysis contained in this piece affirms this bold conclusion from which the two Horn of Africa countries at issue, and others in the international community, should draw important lessons.

Thirdly, there is no question that the UN Security Council, or other regional organisations, are often charged with dealing with or facilitating the resolution of use of force-related disputes and situations. Given the political and practical limitations of such bodies in effectively and consistently responding to matters of the use of force and territorial disputes including claims of loss or damage arising from such

[119]Ibid.

[120]According to media reports, Ethiopia has started withdrawing its troops from Badme, 'Ethiopia Withdraws Troops from Contested Town (BBC World Service, 18 December 2018) https://www.bbc.co.uk/programmes/w172w23x1zrpc04.

events, it is important to recognise the role of international adjudicating bodies, such as arbitral tribunals, in applying the law, determining international responsibility and clarifying the laws under consideration. This should also be commended to promote and uphold international peace, stability and justice.

Finally, the aforementioned key points and the emerging positive relations between Ethiopia and Eritrea, which appear to go beyond resolving the border question, demonstrate that border wars are tremendously easy to start (it only takes a single border incident) but very hard to end and their implications are lasting and far-reaching on all sides. The two countries, and others, ought to learn hard lessons from the Eritrea-Ethiopia case and totally avoid military solutions to any territorial claims, interests or ambitions they might have, other than peacefully seeking beneficial cooperation in a spirit of understanding, good neighbourliness and good faith.

References

Accordance with International Law of the Unilateral Declaration of Independence in Respect of Kosovo (Advisory Opinion) [2010] ICJ Rep 403 [Kosovo Advisory Opinion].

Arend A (1984) The obligation to pursue peaceful settlement of international disputes during hostilities. Va J Int Law 24(1):97

Armed Activities on the Territory of the Congo (Congo v Uganda) (Judgment) [2005] ICJ Rep 168

Bernárdez S (1987) Territorial sovereignty. In: Encyclopedia of public international law, vol 10. North Holland, pp 487–494

Besson S (2011) Sovereignty. In: Max Planck encyclopedia of public international law (online edition, updated 2011)

Blokker N (2000) Is the authorisation authorised? Powers and practice of the UN Security Council to authorize the use of force by 'coalitions of the able and willing'. Eur J Int Law 11:541

Blokker N (2015) Outsourcing the use of force: towards more security council control of authorized operations? In: Weller M (ed) The Oxford handbook of the use of force in international law. Oxford University Press

Certain Activities Carried Out by Nicaragua in the Border Area (Costa Rica v Nicaragua); *Construction of a Road in Costa Rica along the San Juan River (Nicaragua v Costa Rica)* (Judgment) [2015] ICJ Rep 665.

Certain Activities carried out by Nicaragua in the Border Area (Costa Rica v Nicaragua); Construction of a Road in Costa Rica along the San Juan River (Nicaragua v Costa Rica) (Order of 16 July 2013) (Provisional Measures) [2013] ICJ Rep 275.

Cliffe L (1999) Regional dimensions of conflict in the horn of Africa. Third World Q 20(1):89–111

Corfu Channel (United Kingdom/Albania) (Judgment) (Merits) [1949] ICJ Rep 4

Cornwell A (2018) Ethiopian, Eritrean leaders sign peace agreement in Jeddah. Reuters, 16 September 2018

Crawford J (2006) The creation of states in international law, 2nd edn. Clarendon Press

Cukwurah A (1967) The settlement of boundary disputes in international law. Manchester University Press

'Declaration on Principles of International Law Concerning Friendly Relations and Cooperation Among States in Accordance with the Charter of the United Nations', UN General Assembly Resolution (UNGA) 2625 (XXV) (24 October 1970) reprinted in (1970) 9 International Legal Materials 1292 [Declaration on Friendly Relations]

Desta M (this volume) Peace agreements between Ethiopia and Eritrea: ending two decades of hostilities—an introductory note. In: Yihdego Z, Desta MG, Hailu MB (eds) Ethiopian

Yearbook of International Law 2018: in pursuit of peace and prosperity. Springer, Cham, pp 261–268

Dias A (2008) An inter-state war in the post-cold war era: Eritrea-Ethiopia (1998–2000). A thesis submitted for the degree of Doctor of Philosophy in International Relations, London School of Economics

Dinstein Y (2001) War, aggression and self-defence, 3rd edn. Cambridge University Press

Eritrea-Ethiopia Boundary Commission, Decision Regarding Delimitation of the Border (13 April 2002) XXV Reports of International Arbitral Awards 83-195

Eritrea-Ethiopia Claims Commission, Partial Award, *Jus ad Bellum*: Ethiopia's Claims 1-8 (19 December 2005) XXVI Reports of International Arbitral Awards 457-469

Gebrekidan S (2018) Ethiopia and Eritrea declare an end to their war. New York Times, 9 July 2018

Gilkes P, Barry T (2005) The war between Ethiopia and Eritrea: despite claims to the contrary, Ethiopia and Eritrea have been fighting not over a border but over rival hegemonic claims in the Horn of Africa and over "national pride" and "territorial integrity". Institute for Policy Studies, 11 October 2005. https://ips-dc.org/the_war_between_ethiopia_and_eritrea/

Gray C (2006) The Eritrea/Ethiopia claims commission oversteps its boundaries: a partial award? Eur J Int Law 17(4):699–721

Gray C (2018) International law and the use of force. Oxford University Press

Green L (2008) The contemporary law of armed conflict. Manchester University Press

Greenwood C (2012) In: Wolfrum R (ed) Self-defence, The Max Planck encyclopedia of public international law. Oxford University Press

Guyana/Suriname (Annex VII Tribunal) (Award) (2007) 47 International Law Reports 166

Hassan F (1982) The sovereignty dispute over the Falkland Islands. Va J Int Law 23(1):54, 59

Hill N (1945) Claims to territory in international law and relations. Oxford University Press

Hirt N (this volume) Commentary: UN Security Council Resolution 2444 (2018) and the lifting of sanctions against Eritrea: a commentary on domestic and regional perspectives. In: Yihdego Z, Desta MG, Hailu MB (eds) Ethiopian Yearbook of International Law 2018: in pursuit of peace and prosperity. Springer, Cham, pp 269–284

International Law Commission Draft Articles on Responsibility of States for Internationally Wrongful Acts, with commentaries (2001) 2(2) Yearbook of the International Law Commission 31, 60 [ILC Draft Articles on State Responsibility]

Island of Palmas Case (or Miangas) (United States v The Netherlands) (Award) (1928) II Reports of International Arbitral Awards 829

Klein N (2013) Claims Commission. In: Max Planck encyclopedia of public international law (online edition, updated 2013)

Lata L (2003) The Ethiopia-Eritrea War. Rev Afr Polit Econ 30(97):369–388

Legality of the Threat or Use of Nuclear Weapons (Advisory Opinion) [1996] ICJ Rep 226

Lyons T (2006) Avoiding conflict in the Horn of Africa U.S. policy toward Ethiopia and Eritrea. Council on Foreign Relations

Marcus H (2002) A history of Ethiopia. University of California Press

Mikanagi T (2018) Establishing a military presence in a disputed territory: interpretation of Article 2(3) and (4) of the UN Charter. 67(4):1021–1043

Milano E (2004) Territorial disputes, wrongful occupations and state responsibility: should the International Court of Justice go the extra mile? Law Pract Int Courts Tribunals 3:509

Milano E, Papanicolopulu I (2011) State responsibility in disputed areas on land and at Sea Heidelberg. J Int Law 71:587

Military and Paramilitary Activities in and against Nicaragua (Nicaragua v United States of America) (Judgment) [1986] ICJ Rep 14

Murphy SDD (2018) The Eritrean-Ethiopian War – 1998–2000. In: Ruys T, Corten O, Hofer A (eds) The use of force in international law: a case-based approach. Oxford University Press

Murphy SDD, Kidane W, Snider T (2013) Litigating war: mass civil injury and the Eritrea-Ethiopia Claims Commission. Oxford University Press

North Atlantic Coast Fisheries Case (Great Britain/United States of America) (Award) (1910) 4 American Journal of International Law 948
Novaci G (2009) The lines of tension in the Horn and the Ethiopia Eritrea case. In: de Guttry A et al (eds) The 1998–2000 war between Eritrea and Ethiopia: an international legal perspective. Acer Press, pp 109–223
O'Connell ME (2018) The crisis in Ukraine 2014. In: Corten O, Ruys T (eds) International law and the use of force: a case-based approach. Oxford University Press
Oil Platforms (Iran v United States of America) (Judgment) [2003] ICJ Rep 161
Paddeu F (2015) Countermeasures. In: Max Planck encyclopedia of public international law (Online edition, updated 2015)
'Peace Agreement' (Eritrea-Ethiopia) (signed and entered into force 12 December 2000). https://www.files.ethz.ch/isn/125337/1392_Algiers%20Agreement.pdf [the '*Algiers Agreement*']
Philipson D (1988) Ancient Ethiopia: Aksum, its predecessors and successors. British Museum Press, London
Plaut M (1999) The conflict and its aftermath. In: Gilkes P, Plaut M (eds) War in the Horn: the conflict between Eritrea and Ethiopia. Royal Institute of International Affairs
Plaut M, Gilkes P (1999) Conflict in the Horn: why Eritrea and Ethiopia are at war. Briefing Paper, Chatham House. https://reliefweb.int/report/eritrea/conflict-horn-why-eritrea-and-ethiopia-are-war
Prescott V, Triggs G (2008) International frontiers and boundaries. BRILL
Roy S (2017) Japan throws weight behind India and Bhutan, says no side should try to change status quo by force. The Indian Express, 19 August 2017
Sharma SP (1997) Territorial acquisition, disputes and international law. Springer
Shaw M (1986) Title to territory in Africa. Oxford, Clarendon Press
Snider T, Nair A (this volume) Ten years on: a look at the legacy of the Eritrea-Ethiopia Claims Commission. In: Yihdego Z, Desta MG, Hailu MB (eds) Ethiopian Yearbook of International Law 2018: in pursuit of peace and prosperity. Springer, Cham, pp 11–34
Tams C (2005) Enforcing obligations Erga Omnes in international law. Cambridge Studies in International and Comparative Law
Thirlway H (2018) Territorial disputes and their resolution in the recent jurisprudence of the International Court of Justice. Leiden J Int Law 31(1):117
UN Security Council, 'Special Report of the Secretary-General on Ethiopia and Eritrea' (15 December 2016) S/2006/992
Waibel M (2012) Falkland/Islas Malvinas. In: Wolfrum R (ed) The Max Planck encyclopedia of public international law. Oxford University Press
Weston B (1991) Security Council Resolution 678 and Persian Gulf Decision Making: precarious legitimacy. Am J Int Law 85
Woldemariam M (2018) "No war, no peace" in a region in flux: crisis, escalation, and possibility in the Eritrea-Ethiopia rivalry. J East Afr Stud 12(3):407–427
Yiallourides C, Gehring M, Gauci J-P (2018) The use of force in relation to sovereignty disputes over land territory. BIICL
Yihdego Z (2007) Ethiopia's military action against the Union of Islamic Courts and others in Somalia: some legal implications. Int Comp Law Q 56(4):666–676
Zewde B (ed) (1998) A short history of Ethiopia and the Horn. Addis Ababa University

Constantinos Yiallourides is the Arthur Watts Research Fellow on the International Law of Territorial Disputes at the British Institute of International and Comparative Law (BIICL), where he leads the Watts programme of research and events on maritime and territorial disputes, and JSPS Scholar in International Law and Public Policy at the University of Tokyo, Japan.

Zeray Yihdego holds a chair in Public International law, and is Co-director of the Centre for Constitutional and Public International Law at the University of Aberdeen.

Patenting Developing Countries' Traditional Knowledge As New Invention: An Examination of the Teff Processing Patent Claim by a Dutch Company and the Way Forward

Beka Melkamu Tesgera

Abstract Many agree that Teff originated in the highlands of Ethiopia. Teff is a gluten free grain that has a growing market in Europe and North America. This could potentially revolutionize the agriculturally led economy of Ethiopia. However, Ethiopia is unable to access the European gluten free market for now due to a patent granted by the European Patent Office (EPO) to a Dutch company called Health and Performance Food International (HPFI). The patent relates to the *Eragrostis* Teff flour and some Teff end products. This article will attempt to answer the question of whether the Teff patent right that was granted by the EPO under the European Patent Convention (EPC) meets patentability requirements. It also further discusses the role of traditional knowledge that is entangled with the processing of Teff. In addition, it explores which avenues or jurisdictions are more suitable to challenge the Teff patent in Europe. Finally, the article will suggest legal instruments that can be used to protect Teff and Teff products in the future.

1 Introduction

The controversy of the Teff patent started when a Dutch company named Soil and Crop Improvement (S&C) decided to breach the memorandum of understanding (MOU) that it had signed with the Ethiopian government and the technology transfer department of *Larenstein* University and applied for the Teff patent right in the Netherlands on July 22, 2003.[1] The MOU was signed on March 26, 2003 in order for S&C to develop and market Teff-based products to the global market.[2] However, since the MOU was not a legally binding agreement, the Ethiopian government

[1]Andersen and Winge (2012), p. 4.

[2]Andersen and Winge (2012), p. 116.

B. M. Tesgera (✉)
Independent Trade Law Consultant, Addis Ababa, Ethiopia

Z. Yihdego et al. (eds.), *Ethiopian Yearbook of International Law 2018*, Ethiopian Yearbook of International Law 2018, https://doi.org/10.1007/978-3-030-24078-3_4

negotiated for a legally binding new agreement, the Agreement on Access to, and Benefit Sharing from, Teff Genetic Resources ("Teff Agreement").[3] The Teff Agreement (TA) was signed on April 5, 2005 between the HPFI, i.e. (formerly S&C) and the Ethiopian government.[4]

The TA was focused on benefit sharing obtained from varieties of Teff originated from Ethiopia.[5] Although the Ethiopian government knew about the patent application, the understanding from the Ethiopian side was that the patent right would only cover the processing of Teff but not the variety of Teff itself and the traditional knowledge that is intertwined with the Teff production in Ethiopia.[6] In 2003, S&C received a Dutch patent that covered flour mixtures containing Teff flour and the Teff-end products. On January 10, 2007, the European Patent Office (EPO) granted the Teff process and product patent right to HPFI.[7] The patent is broad and covers the processing of Teff and its end products.

After 2 years of receiving the patent right, HPFI initiated a bankruptcy process in the Netherlands without giving any notice to the Ethiopian government. On August 4, 2009, HPFI was declared bankrupt by the Court of Assen, the Netherlands.[8] However, before being declared bankrupt, HPFI sold the Teff patent right on May 21, 2008 for Euro 60,000 to a partnership consisting of the HPFI directors.[9] Then, Ethiopian government terminated the TA officially on November 15, 2011.[10] The bankruptcy ruling means that HPFI does not legally exist and also does not own the Teff patent right. As a result, even if Ethiopia wants to share the benefits or seek monetary compensation based on the TA, legally it is impossible since the TA has been terminated. However, a clause in the Agreement provides that the termination of the TA "shall not affect the rights and obligations that were due accrue to either party prior to the effective date of the termination."[11]

In the meantime, the Teff patent benefited the "inventors" by protecting their claimed invention. Anyone who would like to sell processed Teff in Europe, must pay royalty to the "inventors". Currently, the patent is valid in Italy, Germany, Austria and the United Kingdom. However, in November 2018, the patent in the Netherlands was invalidated by the Court of The Hague due to lack of novelty or inventiveness following a dispute between Ancientgrain and Bakels.[12] Ancientgrain is the latest company, which owns the Teff patent and it is owned by the same

[3]Andersen and Winge (2012), p. 48.

[4]The Teff Agreement (2005).

[5]The Teff Agreement (2005).

[6]Andersen and Winge (2012), p. 54.

[7]EPO, Teff Patent (2005).

[8]Andersen and Winge (2012), p. 114.

[9]Andersen and Winge (2012), p. 114.

[10]Andersen and Winge (2012), p. 102.

[11]Teff Agreement (2005), Article 12.4.

[12]Ancientgrain v. Bakles, District Court The Hague, The Netherlands, 21 November 2018, Case No. ECLI:NL:RBDHA:2018:13960.

directors who founded S&C and HPFI. The patent owners seem to have deliberately created multiple companies and transfer rights between them in order to avoid responsibility. Currently, Germany and Italy are the leading markets for gluten free products in Europe.[13]

As a result of this broad patent right, it will be difficult for Ethiopia to access the European gluten-free market for processed Teff. In recent years, the demand for gluten-free foods in Europe has increased tremendously. According to Euromonitor, the gluten-free market globally was valued at around USD 3.5bn in 2016.[14] In 2017, Europe accounted for the major share of the global gluten-free food market and is expected to continue dominance in the upcoming years.[15] Accessing this huge market could have been a step forward in diversifying the Ethiopian economy and assisting the country in the fight to alleviate poverty by directly reaching approximately six million households that grow Teff in Ethiopia.[16]

For this reason, this article will attempt to answer the following questions: (1) whether the Teff patent right that was granted by the EPO under the European Patent Convention (EPC) meets the elements of patentability; (2) If it does not meet the elements of patentability, can it be invalidated and revoked; (3) If it is revocable, which institution or court has jurisdiction to hear the revocation proceedings; and (4) How can Ethiopia utilize and at the same time legally protect the traditional knowledge associated with the production of Teff and Teff products in the future.

This article has five parts. The first part will address what is patent right under the international law. The second part discusses the case of bio-piracy on Teff varieties and traditional knowledge (TK). The third part examines whether the Teff Patent meets the substantive requirements prescribed under the EPC and whether it can be revoked. The fourth part will analyse what avenues Ethiopia could use to secure revocation of the Teff patent. Finally, the paper explores the extent to which Ethiopia may use Geographical Indications (GI) as a tool that can protect its rights over Teff.

2 Patent Rights Under International Law: A Brief Overview

The main objective of patent is to promote creativity, innovation and extract economic values for such creativity. Patent rights encourage entrepreneurs to devote time and resources in creative endeavors in the expectation of supernormal profits through a monopolistic rights conferred on them regarding the commercial exploitation of their inventions.[17] This expectation would incentivize them to spend time

[13]Business Insider (2018).

[14]Financial Times (2017).

[15]Business Insider (2018).

[16]Agricultural Transformation Agency (2013).

[17]Schumpeter (1942), p. 132.

and money on innovation activities such as R&D.[18] If there is no protection for the creators, their invention might be imitated in a much lower cost or, in extreme cases, at zero cost.[19]

However, several economists question the link between patents and innovation. According to Michele Boldrin and David Levine, there is "weak or no evidence that strengthening patent regimes increases innovation".[20] Regardless, the international community has been protecting patent rights through national laws as well as regional and international treaties.

Although there are several international treaties on intellectual property rights (IPRs), this section only covers the Paris Convention for the Protection of Industrial Property (PC) and the Trade-Related Aspects of Intellectual Property Rights (TRIPS) under the World Trade Organization (WTO).

The PC[21] is the first truly global treaty that gives protection for industrialists with regards to their invention(s) through IPRs. The PC, which was adopted in 1883 applies to patents, trademarks, industrial designs, utility models, service marks, trade names, geographical indications (GI) and the repression of unfair competition.[22] Among the few common rules that the convention lays down, patent right is one of the most important one.

Article 4bis[23] underlines the core doctrine of territoriality—a notion that each state has exclusive powers over what happens within its territory. In addition, this article further expounds the principle that a "patent application in one country of the Union is examined and granted or denied independent of applications for patents for the same or related inventions filed in other countries within and without the Union".[24] In other words, the granting of a patent in one country does not mandate any other member country to grant a patent for the same invention.[25] Accordingly, this indicates that each jurisdiction has the right to grant or deny a patent for invention solely based on its national law.

Also, TRIPS is a comprehensive international treaty that introduced a global minimum standard for protecting and enforcing IPRs within the WTO. TRIPS was negotiated during the Uruguay Round of the General Agreement on Tariffs and

---

[18]Lopez (2009), p. 3.

[19]Arrow (1962), p. 622.

[20]Boldrin and Levine (2012), p. 15.

[21]The Paris Convention, concluded in 1883, was revised at Brussels in 1900, at Washington in 1911, at The Hague in 1925, at London in 1934, at Lisbon in 1958 and at Stockholm in 1967, and was amended in 1979.

[22]Summary of the Paris Convention for the Protection of Industrial Property (1883), http://www.wipo.int/treaties/en/ip/paris/summary_paris.html (accessed 15 January 2019).

[23]"bis" is a sequential Latin designation that is given to second proposed draft of an international legal instrument. *See* also Victor Conde (2004), p. 26.

[24]The Paris Convention (1883), Article 4bis.

[25]*Ibid.*

Trade (GATT) between 1986 and 1994.[26] The TRIPS agreement covers copyright, trademarks, geographical indications, patent rights and other IPRs. It has also a powerful enforcement mechanism under the dispute settlement mechanism of the WTO.[27]

From Article 27 to 34, the TRIPS Agreement sets out the obligations of Members with respect to standards concerning the availability, scope and use of patents. The TRIPS Agreement has incorporated the PC.[28] Article 27.1 of the TRIPS Agreement states, inter alia, that "... patents shall be available for any inventions,... provided that they are new, involve an inventive step and are capable of industrial application".[29] "These three substantive conditions are recognized as the basic tests of patentability in many countries' laws prior to the TRIPS Agreement.[30] In addition to these three tests of patentability, there is one other condition that is considered to be substantive: the disclosure of the invention."[31]

Ethiopia is neither a party to the Paris Convention nor the WTO/TRIPS. The next section discusses HPFI's patent claim on Teff processes and products.

3 The Teff Patent Claim from EU and Comparative Law and Practice Perspectives

The patent application on Teff Processing and Products was first filed in the Netherlands by S&C on July 22, 2004. A year after, HPFI filed a similar patent application with the EPO.[32] On March 24, 2006 the patent application was published internationally by the World Intellectual Property Organization (WIPO), under the Patent Cooperation Treaty.[33] On December 21, 2006, similar application was published in the USA.[34] On January 10, 2007 the EPO published the granting of the Teff Patent; EP 1 646 287 B1. HPFI B.V. is listed as the owner of the patent and Jans Roosjen as the inventor of the patent in the European Patent Specification published by EPO.[35]

[26] World Trade Organization, 'Introduction to TRIPS Agreement' Module I, page 3, https://www.wto.org/english/tratop_e/trips_e/ta_docs_e/modules1_e.pdf (accessed on 15 January 2019).

[27] TRIPS (1994), Article 64.

[28] TRIPS (1994), Article 2.1.

[29] TRIPS (1994), Article 27.1.

[30] World Trade Organization, 'Patents', Module V, page 3, https://www.wto.org/english/tratop_e/trips_e/ta_docs_e/modules5_e.pdf (accessed on 15 January 2019).

[31] *Ibid.*

[32] EPO, Teff Patent (2005), p. 2.

[33] Andersen and Winge (2012), p. 33.

[34] Andersen and Winge (2012), p. 68.

[35] EPO, Teff Patent (2005), p. 2.

The invention at issue covers 29 specific claims.[36] The patent covers both the combination of products and process claims. The claim stated that the invention relates to the flour of *Erarostis tef* and to products comprising this flour such as gluten-free food products and to methods for preparing these food products.[37] On the application, HPFI stated the benefits of Teff and emphasized how Teff is an attractive source of gluten-free flour. Also, it stated that the traditional way of using Teff flour causes problems on preparation of food products.[38] One example that was given by HPFI was the way in which wheat flour is mixed with Teff flour for preparation of *Injera,* which according to HPFI caused a problem of product instability, particularly in baked products.[39] In other cases, the product has an unattractive taste and/or structure.[40] The example that was given to demonstrate the problem of traditional way of preparing the Teff flour referred to the way Ethiopians prepare their staple food from Teff flour. Moreover, HPFI stated in its patent application that the traditional Teff flour has either too low or too high of a falling number to be processed into a good baking product.[41] Thus, as the claim goes, such problems led to HPFI's invention. Below is the summary of the three invention claims.

The first claim regarding the Teff Process and Product patent is related with the falling numbers[42] of the Teff flour. According to HPFI's patent application, the Teff flour with high falling numbers would not exhibit the above-mentioned problems. HPFI claims its invention provides the Teff flour's falling number at the moment of grinding at least 250, and most preferably at least 380 falling numbers.[43] According to the claims, in order for Teff flour to obtain at least 250 or more falling number, after harvesting, it has to go through an after-ripening process. This process leads us to the second claim of the invention of the Teff process and product patent.

The second claim of the patent relates to storage of the Teff grain. In order to achieve a high falling number of the Teff flour, HPFI claims that the Teff grain should be ground at least 4, preferably at least 5, and more preferably at least 8 weeks after harvesting.[44] As a result, storing the harvested grain for some time will increase the falling number of the Teff flour. The traditional Teff flour, which, according to

[36]EPO, Teff Patent (2005), p. 2.

[37]EPO, Teff Patent (2005), p. 3.

[38]EPO, Teff Patent (2005), p. 2.

[39]EPO, Teff Patent (2005), p. 2.

[40]EPO, Teff Patent (2005), p. 2.

[41]EPO, Teff Patent (2005), p. 3.

[42]"Falling numbers is an international standard of sprout measurement with the full name 'Hagberg Falling Number' which is widely used by the baking industry to indicate flour quality. The term refers to 'the amount of time it takes for the Hagberg steel ball in this sprout analysis tool to fall through a flour/water slurry that has been heated to release the starch from water".

[43]EPO, Teff Patent (2005), p. 3.

[44]EPO, Teff Patent (2005), p. 3.

the patent application is obtained by grinding the grain directly after the harvest, has low falling number.

The third claim of the patent is related to the grinding of the flour. According to the patent application, the traditional Teff flour is usually not ground fine enough. The flour according to the invention is preferably ground to a powder so fine that it can pass through a sieve with maximum pore size of 150 microns.[45] According to the claim of the invention, the grinding of the Teff can also be done according to conventional standard procedures for the preparation of flour. However, a pin-mill with integrated cooling is preferable.[46]

The Teff flour covered by the patent is gluten-free and is described as containing minimum values of iron, calcium and mineral binding substance. The patent claim also defines the composition of carbohydrates in the flour.[47] Furthermore, the patent claims cover dough and/or batter made from this flour, as well as a food product with such flour. The most daring and broad claim of the patent by far is claim 27. The claim clearly states that even unground Teff is covered as long as the unground grain belongs to Eragostis Teff and have a falling number ranging between 250 and 380.[48] Additionally, according to the claims, the Teff patent covers a method for baking a product, involving three steps: (a) preparing a dough or batter by mixing flour with a liquid and, optionally, a leavening agent; (b) kneading this dough into the desired shape; and (c) heating the dough for some time. Baked products prepared according to this method are also covered by the patent, as well as a food product or luxury food product prepared from unground Teff grain with a falling number of at least 250. Finally, the invention covers methods for binding a composition, preferably a pharmaceutical or cosmetic composition, of at least two components, involving mixing components with starch from flour produced according to the claims of the patent.[49]

Since HPFI arguably relied on the TK of the Ethiopian farmers in order to process its patent application in Europe, it is worth looking at the case of bio-piracy on Teff varieties and TK before moving into the substantive discussion on how to challenge the Teff patent under the EPC.

---

[45]EPO, Teff Patent (2005), p. 4. Micron is the measure of length most frequently used to describe tiny particle size.

[46]Andersen and Winge (2012), p. 53.

[47]EPO, Teff Patent (2005), p. 4.

[48]EPO, Teff Patent (2005), p. 5.

[49]Andersen and Winge (2012), p. 51.

3.1 *The Case of Bio-Piracy on Teff Varieties and Traditional Knowledge*

Although there is no officially agreed upon legal definition, scholars have attempted to define the term bio-piracy.[50] The term bio-piracy has been used to describe the ways corporations from the developed world use the genetic resources, TK of indigenous people and local communities of developing countries without compensating the source countries.[51] Bio-piracy may be defined as the misappropriation of TK of indigenous communities for the purpose of seeking exclusive patent ownership over the knowledge.[52] The most common type of bio-piracy is the exploitation of TK.[53] TK is defined "as a knowledge which is held by members of a distinct culture and/or sometimes acquired by means of inquiry peculiar to that culture, and concerning the culture itself or the local environment in which it exists."[54]

The two cases discussed below demonstrate how patenting bio-pirated TK leaves the owners of the TK without a benefit even though they are the source of the knowledge that kept the bio-diversity for centuries.

3.2 *Enola Beans*

In *re POD–NERS, L.L.C.*, the United States Federal Court of Appeals held that the patent that was granted for yellow beans (A.K.A Enola beans) was invalid as obvious.[55] The undisputed facts indicated that Mr. Larry Proctor bought a package of dry beans in Mexico that contained beans that had different types of colors including the yellow beans.[56] After spending 3 years selectively breeding some yellow beans from the package, Proctor named the line "Enola," obtained patent protection for the bean, the plant producing it, and the method for producing it.[57]

The procedural history of the case shows that the International Center for Tropical Agriculture requested for a third party re-examination to invalidate the claims of the patent. The Examiner rejected the claims of the patent as obvious since the "Enola plant and seed appeared to be genetically identical to the Azufrado Peruano, and that any variation between the two plants was likely only the result of environment conditions. The Board upheld the rejection, concluding that the Examiner

---

[50]Gervais (2005), pp. 141–178.

[51]Geoff and Tasmin (2008), p. 148.

[52]Stenton (2004), p. 30.

[53]Stenton (2004), p. 42.

[54]UNEP (1996).

[55]In *re POD–NERS, L.L.C*, United States Federal Court of Appeals, Judgment, p. 1, 2009.

[56]*In re POD–NERS, L.L.C* (2009) p. 2.

[57]*In re POD–NERS, L.L.C* (2009), p. 2.

established a prima facie case of obviousness and Proctor did not rebut the prima facie case."[58]

On review, the Court of Appeals stated that in "selecting and reproducing the yellow beans, the inventor did not create and use any new or unexpected techniques, but rather only followed the steps that one of ordinary skill would have done-planting the beans, harvesting the beans, and repeat the process." The court concluded that the claimed invention did not rise above the creativity of one of ordinary skill in the art of bean breeding. Thus, the patent was invalid for being non-obvious.

Although granting or revoking patent right is squarely territorial, an analogy may be drawn from Enola's case. While in Enola's case money is used to access the varieties of yellow beans, in Teff's case the TA and the Teff MOU are used to access the Teff varieties from Ethiopia. In 2003, *Debre Zeit Agricultural Research Centre* of Ethiopia sold 1440 kg of Teff seeds to *Larenstein University* for research and development purposes: 120 kg each of 12 specified Teff varieties according to the MOU.[59] More like the Elona case where the Mexican Azufrado Peruano beans were genetically identical to Enola, one can conclude that since the HPFI has been using the Teff varieties that were obtained from Ethiopia, the DNA finger print of the Teff could only be similar to the Ethiopian Teff. Thus, it is reasonable to conclude that HPFI Company has bio-pirated the Ethiopian Teff varieties without compensating Ethiopia. On the contrary, it is also possible for HPFI to argue that their patent covers only the Teff flour and Teff end products but not the Teff grain itself hence they have not pirated the bio-genetics of Teff.

3.3 *Pozol*

The case of *Pozol* patent is a good example to illustrate how TK has been exploited through bio-piracy. *Pozol* is a Mexican fermented drink created by the *Mayan* people centuries ago.[60] *Pozol* has antibacterial properties that enhance and protect human health. A Dutch corporation and the University of Minnesota extracted bacillus subtilis from *Pozol* to use as a natural inhibitor of unwanted flora in foods and feeds.[61] For extracting and isolating bacillus subtilis microorganism from Pozol, the entities were granted a patent right without compensating the *Mayan* Community for the invention of their ancestors. Consequently, critics argue that the patenting of the isolated microorganism, which is the active component, rather than the drink itself, constituted an exploitation of traditional knowledge.[62] Similarly, in Teff's case, storing Teff after harvesting and before grinding it in order to get the best baking

[58] *In re POD–NERS, L.L.C* (2009), p. 3.

[59] Andersen and Winge (2012), p. 39.

[60] DeGeer (2003), p. 9. *see also* Subbiah (2004), pp. 529 and 544.

[61] DeGeer (2003), p. 9.

[62] DeGeer (2003), p. 9.

quality of Teff has been traditionally known by Ethiopians for centuries. Thus, EPO's granting of Teff's patent right is based on exploiting the TK of Ethiopians without compensating for it. Next section covers patent rights under EPC.

3.4 The European Patent Convention and Its Application on Teff's Processing Patent

A patent is an exclusive right granted by a government office or an inter-governmental office acting for several countries to the owner of an invention.[63] Patents confer the right to prevent third parties from making, using or selling the invention without their owners' consent.[64] They are valid in individual countries usually for 20 years.[65] An inventor must file its patent application by following the right procedure to a patent office. Once the patent office conducted a proper examination of the documents filed and found out the invention is to be patentable then the patent will be granted to the inventor.[66] Patents are enforced mainly at the national level including patents granted by the EPO.[67]

3.4.1 EPC Substantive Provisions

In the EPC, the validation of a patent right can be challenged if the subject matter of an invention does not meet the elements of novelty, inventive step and industrial applicability.[68] Also, European patents shall not be granted "for plant or animal varieties or essentially biological processes for the production of plants or animals."[69] Before analyzing the elements of patentability under the EPC, first, it is important to understand what "invention" is under the EPC. According to *Pension Benefit Systems Partnership* case, within the meaning of Article 52 (1) an invention must have an implicit technical character.[70] In other words, for an invention to be patentable, the subject matter claimed must involve a "technical teaching", i.e. "an instruction addressed to a skilled person as to how to solve a particular technical

[63]WIPO, Fields of Intellectual Property Protection, p. 17, http://www.wipo.int/export/sites/www/about-ip/en/iprm/pdf/ch2.pdf (accessed January 18, 2019).

[64]WIPO, Fields of Intellectual Property Protection, p. 8.

[65]WIPO, Fields of Intellectual Property Protection, p. 13.

[66]WIPO, Fields of Intellectual Property Protection, p. 19.

[67]EPC, Article 64(3).

[68]EPC, Article 100 (a); and Article 52 (1).

[69]EPC, Article 53 (b).

[70]BOA, *Pension Benefit Systems Partnership,* Judgment, section 6, 2000. This case was tried in the European Patent Office- under Boards of Appeal (BOA). BOA is the first and final judicial instance in the procedures before the European Patent Office.

problem using particular technical means."[71] Thus, technical character is the key to determine whether a subject matter claimed meets the meaning of invention under Article 52 (1) of the EPC. Below is the discussion of the three elements under Article 52(1) of EPC that must be met in order for an invention to be patentable.

Novelty

The first requirement under Article 52(1) of the EPC is novelty. Unless an invention is new, it cannot be patented. The Board of Appeals (BOA) in the *Hoechst* case held that an invention is considered to be new if it does not form part of the state of the art.[72] In addition, the BOA stated that the purpose of Article 54 (1) of the EPC is to prevent the state of the art being patented again.[73] The state of the art is defined as "everything made available to the public by means of a written or oral description, by use, or in any other way, before the date of filing of the European patent application".[74] It is important to note that there is no restriction on the language or manner in which the relevant information was made available to the public.[75]

Under Article 54 (2) of the EPC, the state of the art is not left to written disclosure but also can be defined in any other way by which the technical subject matter was made available to the public.[76] Consequently, just because there were no written documents would not mean that there was no state of the art. This is because the state of the art could reside "solely in the relevant common general knowledge",[77] which, again, may or may not be in writing, i.e. in textbooks or the like, or be simply a part of the unwritten "mental furniture" of the notional "person skilled in the art".[78]

In order to assess the common general knowledge of skilled persons, the BOA identified three important aspects. First, the skilled person beyond having a general knowledge should know where to find such information for it to be common.[79] Second, the skilled person is not expected to do a thorough search for literature covering the whole state of the art.[80] Third, "the information found had to be unambiguous and usable in a direct and straightforward manner without doubts or

[71] *Ibid*; and Official Journal, European Patent Office (2007).

[72] BOA, *Hoechst*, Judgement, 1985.

[73] BOA, *Hoechst*, Judgement, 1985.

[74] EPC (1973), Article 54 (2).

[75] EPC (1973), Article 54 (2).

[76] BOA, *AgrEvo UK Limited*, Judgement, (1995), section 2.3, p. 10.

[77] *Common general knowledge of the person skilled in the art had been defined by the boards of appeal as being normally represented by encyclopaedias, textbooks, dictionaries and handbooks on the subject in question* (http://www.epo.org/law-practice/legal-texts/html/caselaw/2013/e/clr_i_c_1_6_1.htm) (accessed 7 March 2019).

[78] *AgrEvo, supra* note 43.

[79] BOA, *Sumitomo Rubber Industries Limited*, Judgement, (2000), p. 13.

[80] BOA, *Imperial Chemical Industries Ltd.*, Judgement, (2013), para 12, p. 11.

further investigation."[81] The "person skilled in the art" should be presumed to be a "skilled practitioner in the relevant field of technology, who is possessed of average knowledge and ability and is aware of what was common general knowledge in the art at the relevant date."

In the case of *Henkel*, the BOA held that if an inventor used information from the prior art[82] document in conjunction with the skilled person's common general knowledge which allowed him to practice the technical teaching, then the invention would lack novelty.[83] In order to determine whether an invention is new, it is important to define the prior art, the relevant part of that art and the content of the relevant art.

The BOA in different cases repeatedly held that if the subject matter of the invention is clearly and directly derived from the prior art, then the invention lacks novelty.[84] In other words, the subject matter should be inferred directly and unambiguously from a prior art document.[85] Moreover, "the disclosure is determined by what knowledge and understanding can and may be expected of the average skilled person in the technical field in question."[86] Therefore, after defining the prior art, one should compare the prior art with the invention in order to find if the invention is different from the prior art. If it is not different, then it lacks novelty.

Inventive Step

The second requirement under Article 52(1) of the EPC is an inventive step. According to Article 56, "an invention shall be considered as involving an inventive step if, having regard to the state of the art, it is not obvious to a person skilled in the art."[87] If the state of the art also includes documents within the meaning of Article 54 (3) these documents shall not be considered in deciding whether there has been an inventive step.[88] The issue of an inventive step will only arise when an invention is novel.[89]

The term obvious means an invention that merely follows plainly or logically from the prior art or that does not go beyond the normal progress of technology.[90] It is something which does not involve the exercise of any skill or ability beyond that to

[81]BOA, *Imperial Chemical Industries Ltd.*, Judgement, P. 11.

[82]BOA, *Henkel,* Judgement (2004), p. 2.

[83]BOA, *Henkel,* Judgement, (2004), p. 2.

[84]BOA, *Alcan International Limited*, Judgment, (1997), p. 25.

[85]BOA, *Kimberly-Clark Corporation*, Judgement, (2001), p. 8.

[86]BOA, *International Business Machines Corporation*, Judgement, (1998), p. 4.

[87]EPC (1973), Article 56.

[88]EPC (1973), Article 56.

[89]EPC (2016).

[90]EPC (2016).

be expected of the person skilled in the art.[91] If the claim of invention before the filing or prior date is something obvious to the person skilled in the art, then the claim is not valid since it lacks an inventive step.[92] Regarding inventive step, any published document related to knowledge of the subject matter before the filing or priority date is valid, if there is an inventive step in the claimed invention.[93] Therefore, if the invention is obvious to the person skilled in the art, then the claimed invention lacks an inventive step.

Industrial Application

The third requirement under Article 52(1) of the EPC is industrial application. If an invention can be made or used in any type of industry or even in agriculture, it shall be considered as susceptible of industrial application.[94] The word "industry" is understood in its broad sense as including any physical activity of technical character—an activity which belongs to practical arts but not the aesthetic arts[95] Because of this Article 57 of the EPC excludes very few inventions from being patented.

Finally, according to Article 138 (a) of the EPC, a European patent which has already been granted is revocable if the subject matter of the European patent is found not to be patentable under Articles 52 to 57.[96] In other words, if the invention does not meet the elements of novelty, inventive step or industrial applicability, then the patent is revocable.

3.5 *Does the Teff Patent Right Meet the Requirements of Article 52-57 of the EPC?*

3.5.1 Applying the Requirements to Teff Patent Right

The first step in evaluating whether a patent can be invalidated is to examine the claims of the invention to see if it meets the definition of invention. Although if we take the Teff patent for its face value, it might meet the definition of "technical character" since it explains that the claimed invention has tried to address what HPFI alleged to be a technical problem associated with the traditional Teff flour as traditionally used. The invention claimed to solve the problems of too low or too

[91]EPC (2016).

[92]EPC (2016).

[93]EPC (2016).

[94]EPC (1973), Article 57.

[95]EPC (1973), Article 57

[96]EPC (1973), Article 138 and 139.

high falling numbers associated with traditional Teff flour.[97] HPFI explained in its claims that storing Teff for some time after harvesting increases the falling number from 250 onwards, thereby resolving the alleged problem.[98] The other supposed technical problem that HPFI claimed to have resolved was the practice of mixing Teff flour with wheat flour which allegedly affected the shape and quality of the baked product in traditional Ethiopian practice.[99]

However, the claim for inventiveness in the patent application is entirely based on wrong and deliberately misleading premises. In a typical situation in Ethiopia, Teff is not ground right after harvest; instead it is stored for some time in a traditional storage unit called '*Gotera*'.[100] Ethiopian farmers practice this method of storing Teff because they know that Teff, unlike other grains, can be stored for a longer time without losing its moisture and quality.[101] In addition, the longer the Teff is kept in storage, the higher the price it fetches in Ethiopia.[102] Research shows that a falling number of flour obtained from 22 Ethiopian Teff varieties have numerical values ranging between 273 and 400.[103] Furthermore, Ethiopians prefer Teff without being mixed with wheat or with any other flour for that matter.[104] The only time Ethiopians mix Teff with wheat or any other grain is when they cannot afford having Teff on its own for cost reasons in terms of high market price. Thus, although the claimed invention might have a technical character, it was founded on false premises.

Second, the claimed invention lacks novelty. This is because the claimed state of the art by HPFI which is the storage of Teff after harvesting has already been made available to the public long before to the date of filing of the Teff patent through written materials such as books and research journals. Just to mention a few examples, the 2001 Food and Agriculture Organization of the United Nations (FAO) publication titled TEF Post-harvest Operations clearly explained different types of storages that are used to store Teff after harvest.[105] Teff has a high economic value as its grain can be kept for many years in, practically, any kind of storage facilities without being seriously damaged by common storage insect pests.[106]

Furthermore, storing Teff is a general common knowledge amongst those who are involved in cultivating and marketing Teff. In an interview by Fridtjof Nansens Institutt based in Norway regarding the common practices and knowledge of storing Teff in Ethiopia, all the interviewees who are farmers and researchers concluded that

[97]EPO, Teff Patent (2005), p. 2.

[98]EPO, Teff Patent (2005), p. 3.

[99]EPO, Teff Patent (2005), p. 2.

[100]Andersen and Winge (2012), p. 53.

[101]Andersen and Winge (2012), p. 53.

[102]Andersen and Winge (2012), p. 132.

[103]Andersen and Winge (2012), p. 52.

[104]Gamboa and van Ekris (2008), p. 329.

[105]Refera (2001), p. 37.

[106]Ketema (1997), p. 17.

storing Teff is a necessary part of the Teff process before grinding it.[107] Thus, since Teff farmers deal with Teff production regularly, the common knowledge standard should include the knowledge that the Ethiopian Teff farmers have.

So, here, the question should be whether the person having ordinary skill in the art could access this common knowledge without doing a thorough search and if the information found was not to be unambiguous and usable in a direct and straightforward manner without doubts or further investigation. HPFI must have known about the storage knowledge since they have spent a substantial amount of time in Ethiopia and have been adequately assisted by the farmers in order to observe the entire process of Teff since the beginning of this millennium. Moreover, HPFI's officials repeatedly mentioned that they have worked with small scale farmers in Ethiopia.[108] In addition, HPFI in its patent application mentioned one of Seyfu Ketema's research works regarding the benefits of Teff[109] which indicates that HPFI had access to publications of leading experts in Teff area.

As a result, HPFI cannot selectively ignore publications on Teff storages and the process of Teff's post-harvest steps in Ethiopia. Thus, it is reasonable to conclude that one cannot claim ignorance with regards to Teff storage within Ethiopia after harvest—especially a company such as HPFI that has a history of working with Ethiopian farmers and experts for quite a long time. Since this is a general knowledge on Teff, whoever has an interest in this area, will know about what Ethiopians do post Teff harvest without doing any thorough investigation. Additionally, they can easily use this information directly from Ethiopian traditional knowledge without doing further investigations. Therefore, since HPFI used this common knowledge, the claim of inventiveness in storing Teff clearly lacks novelty.

The other claim of the invention was increasing the falling number of the Teff flour. The invention claims that traditional Teff flour has either too low or too high falling numbers. As a result, the traditional Teff flour's quality is low for baking. However, this is factually incorrect since 22 Ethiopian Teff varieties have the falling-number values ranging between 273 and 400.[110] These falling numbers are higher than what HPFI stated as the minimum falling number required i.e. 250. Thus, these Teff varieties have met the minimum falling number requirement.

It is important to note that since the patent covers any Teff flour that is higher than 250 falling numbers, most of the Ethiopian Teff varieties fall in this category. As a result, it is fair to conclude that this invention covers the so called traditional Teff flour and the HPFI's Teff flour obtained as a result of the claimed invention. The supposed invention did not create anything new since there is no difference between the traditional Teff flour and the HPFI's Teff flour claimed in the patent application because both flours fall within the range of 250–380 of the same falling numbers as the invention claimed to achieve.

[107] Andersen and Winge (2012), p. 131.

[108] Andersen and Winge (2012), p. 109.

[109] EPO, Teff Patent (2005), p. 4.

[110] Andersen and Winge (2012), p. 52.

The above point is an indication that the patent claim is broad in scope and hinders the export of processed Teff from Ethiopia. It is also important to underline that the inventors copied the process of Teff from Ethiopia. In other words, processed Teff that originates from Ethiopia could only follow the process that is described in the Teff Patent since the process stated in the patent is similar to what is widely practiced in Ethiopia. Moreover, the patent is so broad that it even covers unground Teff as long as the unground grain belongs to Eragostis Teff and has a falling number ranging between 250 and 380.[111] According to the EPC Article 64 (2), "If the subject-matter of the European patent is a process, the protection conferred by the patent shall extend to the products directly obtained by such process."[112] In the Teff patent case, the patent does not only define the process but also covers products that are directly obtained from this processes.

However, others might argue that the scope of the Teff patent is narrow and only covers some types of Teff flour and some Teff end products. In addition, they could argue that patent right cannot give exclusive right over products that have been produced or process which have been used before the granting of the right hence the Teff patent right does not give the patentee the right to exclude firms from importing Teff into the Europe.

The other main part of the invention covers the issue of how the Teff flour should be ground. The flour according to HPFI's invention is preferably ground to a powder so fine that it can pass through a sieve with maximum pore size of 150 microns while the traditional Teff flour usually not ground fine enough. According to the claim of the invention, the grinding of the Teff can be done according to conventional standard procedures for the preparation of flour. But a pin-mill with integrated cooling is preferable.[113] The mention of grinding Teff flour through conventional standard or pin-mill does not have any direct bearing on the novelty of the Teff process and product invention. This is because the two procedures for making flour are not new. In sum, all the three claimed inventions lack novelty for the above-mentioned reasons.

Third, although one should not analyse the element of an inventive step when there is no novelty, assuming *arguendo* let us discusses the element of an inventive step. The three claimed inventions are obvious to any skilled person in the area of Teff process and products. The reason is because the claimed invention steps of storing Teff are already published in documents related to the Teff process and product patent before the filing date. Moreover, one could easily know about storage of Teff by simply observing the post Teff harvest practice of the person having ordinary skill in the art i.e. the Ethiopian farmers. The issues of falling numbers and fine dough did not follow any invention step since there were already existing Ethiopian Teff varieties that are within the falling numbers that the inventor claimed to create. Furthermore, the claimed invention did not go beyond the normal known

[111]EPO, Teff Patent (2005), p. 5.

[112]EPC (1973), Article 64(2).

[113]Andersen and Winge (2012), p. 53.

storage technique to add a progress of technology in this area. Therefore, since the invention is obvious to the person skilled in the area of Teff process and products, the claimed invention lacks an inventive step.

Fourth, if the Teff process and the product patent application pass the novelty and inventive step, then it might meet the element of industrial application. This is because the invention is used in the area of food production and it is susceptible to industrial application. Therefore, it meets the element of industrial application.

In conclusion, substantively the Teff process and product patent did not meet the elements of novelty as well as an inventive step. Thus, based on Article 138 (a) of the EPC, the Teff patent might be revoked since the claimed invention of storing Teff after harvest is not something new. In addition, the claimed inventions are obvious to any skilled person in the area of Teff process and products hence it does not meet the element of inventive step. Therefore, a court might find the Teff patent revocable. Next section discusses how USPTO handled the Teff patent application.

3.5.2 USPTO Rejected the Teff Patent Application

Although the USPTO is altogether a different jurisdiction, it is important to understand the reasons why it has rejected the Teff patent application. The patent application was rejected for lacking novelty, for being obvious and for subject matter exclusion.

First, the USPTO held that the claimed inventions were unpatentable since the invention "would have been obvious to one of ordinary skill in the art" as the inventive steps are naturally occurring attributes of Teff as gluten-free grain with naturally-determined nutritional content.[114] This is true because the average person in Teff production i.e. Ethiopian farmers would know that storing Teff is a widely practiced post-harvest technique in Ethiopia. Second, the USPTO stated that the claimed invention did not disclose any methods developed by applicant that enable falling number of the grain to achieve a specific value directly after being harvested.[115] Third, the claimed invention did not meet the element of novelty just because the applicants discovered properties of a known material.[116] The USPTO underlined in its decision that "If the product that is offered for sale inherently possesses each of the limitations of the claims, then the invention is on sale, whether or not the parties to the transaction recognize that the product possesses the claimed characteristics."[117] This means that Ethiopians from time in memorial have been preserving Teff the gluten-free grain with high falling number without using the technical term.

[114]USPTO, Processing of Teff Flour, Judgement, (2012), p. 22, 2012.

[115]USPTO (2012) p. 101.

[116]USPTO (2012), p. 22.

[117]USPTO (2012), p. 22.

The final blow for the applicant was that the USPTO rejection of the claim that Teff traditionally has been unsuitable for baking. The USPTO simply referred the applicants to look into Ethiopia's traditional Injera as it has been baked for centuries without any problem.[118] On 24 April 2013, the USPTO declared the application as "abandoned".[119] The next section will address which jurisdiction can be used to initiate the revocation process of the Teff patent in Europe.

3.5.3 EPC's Procedural Provisions

After a patent is granted by the EPO, there are procedural mechanisms one has to follow in order to file for revocation of the granted patent right.

The first step is to give a notice of opposition within 9 months of the publication of the mention of the grant of the European patent in the European Patent Bulletin.[120] The notice must have facts of the case, evidence and arguments in support of the ground for opposition.[121] However, since the publication date of the patent-10 January 2007, the 9-month period of notice had expired without Ethiopia using the opportunity to challenge the Teff patent right at the EPO.

The other way of challenging the patent is to take it to national courts. In *Roche v Primus,* the Court of Justice of the European Union (CJEU) stated that European patents are national rights that must be enforced nationally.[122] Moreover, concerning registration or validity of patents, Article 16 (4) of the Brussels I Regulation gives the national courts an exclusive jurisdiction.[123] The same principle has been repeated in *GAT v. LuK* and *Antriebstechnik v. Lamellen* that the validity of patent right might only be heard by the courts in the territory in which the patent is granted.[124] This means that the national courts have the authority to determine the validity of the European patents.

In Ethiopia's case, since the Teff patent that was granted by EPO is valid in Germany, Italy, the UK and Austria, the effort to invalidate the patent right must be filed in all the four nations and national courts.[125] The reason is because invalidation of a patent right in one jurisdiction or Member State does not mean invalidation in another jurisdiction since different national courts might have different interpretations regarding the registration or validity of a given patent right.

---

[118]USPTO (2012), p. 23.

[119]USPTO (2012), pp. 2–3.

[120]EPC (1973), Oppositions, Article 99.

[121]EPC (1973), Article 76(2)(c).

[122]CJEU, *Roche Nederland BV v Primus*, Judgement (C-539/03), 2006.

[123]European Union (2001), Brussels I Regulation, Article 16(4).

[124]CJEU, *GAT v. LuK,* Judgement (C-4/03), 2006; CJEU, *Antriebstechnik v. Lamellen,* Judgment (C-4/03), 2006.

[125]The Attorney General is given the greenlight to file a suit against the Dutch Company. See The Ethiopian Reporter (2018).

Although the patent law provisions are in most part harmonized within the EU, the member states have different procedural mechanisms and legal interpretations regarding the validation of a given patent right. In order to show the different procedural mechanism, below is the comparison between the German and the UK patent law regimes.

3.6 Germany

The legal system in Germany is a civil law system. This system does not follow the concept of *stare decisis*. This means that there is no concept of binding precedents. In practice, however, in most cases the lower courts follow the rulings of the higher courts decisions. Regarding patent law, the German Patent Act takes precedence over any other patent regulation.[126]

The German patent jurisdiction follows a bifurcated system. This means that the validation and infringement proceedings are handled in two different jurisdictions. Thus, invalidity cannot be used as a direct defence in infringement cases unless a defendant ask for a stay of the infringement proceedings. In addition, the regional and higher regional courts have exclusive jurisdiction over patent litigation matters such as infringement while the German Federal Patent Court has exclusive jurisdiction over first instance invalidity proceedings and the Federal High Courts of justice has exclusive jurisdiction over appeals.[127]

The German Patent Act (GPA) governs the grounds to invalidate a German or the German parts of European patent rights. The elements for invalidation are listed under GPA sections 21(1) and 22.[128] The first three elements are more or less similar to the EPC elements. These are novelty, inventive step and industrial applicability.

3.7 United Kingdom

The UK legal system is a common law system. In a common law system, there is a concept of binding precedents or *stare decisis*. Unlike the German patent litigation regime, in the UK there is no bifurcated system. Both patent infringement and invalidation cases can be heard in the Intellectual property Enterprise Court or the Patents Court. Moreover, invalidity can be used as a defence or counterclaim in patent infringement proceedings.[129]

[126]Kellenter et al. (2018).

[127]Kellenter et al. (2018).

[128]GPA (2017), Sections 21(1) and 22.

[129]Middlemiss and Balfour (2018).

Article 72(1) of the Patent Act (PA) states the grounds for revocation of a patent right. A court may revoke a patent for an invention on the application of any person if the invention is not a patentable invention.[130] Article 1(a)-(c) of the PA, clearly states that an invention should meet the following elements in order to be granted a patent right: (a) invention must be new; (b) involve inventive step; and (c) capable of industrial application.[131]

As seen above, the two jurisdictions have different procedural mechanism and legal structure for patent invalidation. This means filing for the same case in two different jurisdictions with different procedural mechanism. This will result in an expensive litigation battle for the Ethiopian government. Such patent litigations are also time consuming and could take a very long time to conclude. Moreover, in the case of Teff it requires hired patent law specialists in all the four jurisdictions where the Teff patent is valid at the moment. As a result, procedurally the revocation or invalidation process of the Teff patent will be an uphill task for the Ethiopian government. However, substantively, one could argue that since all the countries where the patent is valid are members of WTO and other key patent conventions such as the PC, most likely they have similar substantive elements to challenge the validation of given patent. For example, the ground for challenging patentability both in Germany and the UK are similar as it is stated above. Thus, Ethiopia could develop the same pleading in different languages by only adjusting to the different procedural mechanisms that are set out in the jurisdictions where the patent is challenged.

4 The Future for Teff Patent Right

Assuming that the Teff patent can be revoked, the next question would be what should Ethiopia do in order to protect its 'super grain' and benefit from the popularity that it has gained in the world's emerging gluten free market. The main goal for Ethiopia should be to protect the TK that is intertwined with the Teff production in Ethiopia. The reason is because the TK is the key factor in producing a Teff flour that is suitable for high quality baking or Teff-based end products. In order to protect Teff products and the TK that is associated with the process of producing such products, Ethiopia could use different legal instruments.

The first legal instrument could be a trademark. Article 15 of the TRIPs Agreement defines trademarks as "any sign, or any combination of signs, capable of distinguishing the goods or services of one undertaking from those of other undertakings shall be capable of constituting a trademark."[132] In addition, a trademark can

[130]PA (1977), Article 72(1) (a).
[131]PA (1977), Article 1(a)-(c).
[132]TRIPS (1994), Article 15.

be licensed to anyone, anywhere in the world, as it is connected to a specific enterprise and not to a particular place.[133]

In the past, Ethiopia opted to use trademark as a legal instrument to protect its premium coffee. Coffee is known to originate from Ethiopia.[134] From generation to another generation, TK was used in the process of producing arguably the best Arabica coffee in the world.[135] The Ethiopian government found it to be more practical to use trademark instead of setting up a national system of certification marks which would protect the coffee name as a GI since several varieties of coffee in Ethiopia are produced by an estimated 4 million smallholder farmers.[136] GI is a sign used on products that have a specific geographical origin and holds qualities or a reputation that are due to that origin.[137] Developing a certificate system for four million small-scale farmers would have been expensive. Also, since trademarks are not tied to a specific place and to methods and practices used to produce a product, Ethiopia could primarily focus on developing the reputation of its coffee quality without being limited to a particular place or processes. Ethiopia could actually introduce new technology to modernize methods and processes that could help to increase its coffee quality and add value.

Similarly, majority of Teff production in Ethiopia is produced by millions of smallholder farmers. Ethiopia could develop a trademark for its Teff products by designing brands that represent high quality. Trademark is a cheaper means to distinguish Ethiopian Teff products from others by getting trademark licenses in any part of the world without being linked with a specific geographical location. However, trademark also has its own limitations. The main limitation is that trademark licensing became acceptable where the licensor (the owner of the trademark) remained in control of the nature and quality of the goods or services sold in association with the trademark.[138] In the case of Teff, it might be difficult to do this because the owner of the trademark must control the quality and the entire process of production of the Teff flour and its end products.

The other legal instrument Ethiopia could use is GI. The TRIPS Agreement describes GIs as "indications which identify a good as originating in the territory of a member, or a region or locality in that territory, where a given quality, reputation or other characteristic of the good is essentially attributable to its geographical origin".[139] This definition works very well for the protection of agricultural products such as Teff that encompasses TK in the process of producing the Teff flour and

---

[133] WIPO, What is trade mark?, https://www.wipo.int/trademarks/en/ (accessed 18 January 2019).

[134] O'Kicki (2009), p. 328.

[135] IPRIA (2009), p. 6.

[136] International Food Policy Research Institute (2017).

[137] WIPO, Geographical Indication, https://www.wipo.int/geo_indications/en/ (accessed on 15 January 2019).

[138] WIPO, Trademark Licensing, p. 3, https://www.wipo.int/export/sites/www/sme/en/documents/pdf/ip_panorama_12_learning_points.pdf (accessed on 19 January 2019).

[139] TRIPS (1994), Article 22.

other end products which uniquely prints the reputation, quality and other characteristics of Teff. In Ethiopia there is a unique and more conservative post-harvest handling of Teff compared to developed countries where cosmetic qualities are often of critical importance.[140] For this reason one could argue that GI is better positioned to protect TK than trademarks as it covers methods and process of producing a specific agricultural product from a specific geographical origin.

However, it is important to state that in Ethiopia there is no specific law that directly protects GIs. Moreover, there is no specific definition of what a GI is and what it covers. Some claim that it is possible to protect GIs within the current trademark law of Ethiopia under Article 2 (1), i.e. collective trademarks.[141] Conversely, the collective trademarks will exclude most of the geographical names that could have been used to describe or indicate the origin of a product under agreements such as the TRIPS Agreement.[142] In addition, Article 6(1)(e) of the Trademark Registration and Protection Proclamation clearly states that a "trademark consisting exclusively of sings or indications which designate the kind, quality, quantity, intended purpose, value, geographical origin of goods or services, the time of production of the goods or rendering of the services, or other characteristics of the goods or services" are not protected as a collective trademarks under the Ethiopian trademarks law.[143] As a result, this will hinder producers of Teff products or any other agricultural product producers from distinguishing their GI products through their quality, reputation or other characteristics of goods that are attached to their geography.

As an agriculture-based economy, having a specific GI law will help Ethiopia to protect its diverse agricultural products. For example, Ethiopia is one of the top five producers and exporters of sesame in the world and the sesame comes mainly from a limited geographical areas in Ethiopia such as Wollega, Humera and Gonder.[144] Thus, those producers of sesame from these regions will benefit from having a specific GI law. Furthermore, if there is a legal protection for their agricultural products, it will encourage them to produce added value products rather than merely exporting the sesame itself. The same could be said when it comes to Teff. Therefore, by adding a specific protection of GI in the Ethiopian law, the whole agriculture sector benefits which by extension benefits the economy at large.

The other reason why Ethiopia should have a separate GI law from its collective trademark law is because Ethiopia would need to align its domestic law within the international IPRs laws and standards in order to access the international market without any legal barriers. Although Ethiopia has not yet ratified international treaties in the area of IPRs such as TRIPS and the PC, it is important to note that

---

[140]Lee (2018), p. 4.

[141]Hirko (2011), p. 27; *see also* Trademark Registration and Protection Proclamation (2006), Article 2(1).

[142]*Ibid.*

[143]The Trademark Registration and Protection Proclamation (2006), Article 6 (1) (e).

[144]Hirko (2011), p. 47, *see* also Biramo (2011), p. 1.

Ethiopia has been trying to join the WTO since 2003.[145] It is also important to underline that Europe requires reciprocity—this is to say that Europe will register and protect GIs associated with products from another country only if the other country gives equivalent GI protection to Europe GI products.[146] Having a domestic law that meets the standard of international law will be a good starting point and a foundation to further market Teff and other agricultural products in Europe, USA and other markets. However, having a sound domestic law on GI is not an end in itself because there are many more matters that needs to be settled besides having a comprehensive law. Below is the discussion of some of the actions that the government of Ethiopia should take in order to benefit from GI.

First, it is important to take into consideration whether the product for which GI protection is sought is commercially viable. This is because if they are not commercially viable, it will be hard to attract investors or producers to invest in these products.[147] Teff being a gluten-free grain, it has a huge market worldwide. In addition, the Ethiopian government has already done market assessment and planned to create the whole value chain starting from the farmers all the way up to the exporters of the end products.[148]

Second, it is important to define the exact boundaries of GI for Teff. Likewise, the Teff production process must be adequately described. This might be a difficult task to do in practice since some producers might feel left out from GI protection merely because they use different methods to produce the same type of grain even if they are from the same region.[149] Ethiopia already uses a grading system based on the International Organization for Standardization (ISO) standard to differentiate and classify the different categories of Teff based on their quality.[150] Regions such as Gojam, Gonder, Shewa, Wello and Wollega are the major Teff production areas.[151] However, it is also important to remember that Teff can be produced both in highlands and low lands of Ethiopia which cover much more area than the regions that are mentioned here. Therefore, the government of Ethiopia has a huge task to demarcate and define the exact boundaries of GI for Teff.

Third, most successful GIs have good links with commercial enterprises that market the products.[152] As a result, it is vital to create connections between Teff and these enterprises in order to dominate the gluten-free market. These enterprises might have stringent private standards that the producers must follow religiously.

[145]WTO, Ethiopia's effort in acceding to WTO is still in progress. *See* https://www.wto.org/english/thewto_e/acc_e/a1_ethiopia_e.htm (accessed 07 March 2019).

[146]USTR (2004), p. 6.

[147]Josling (2006), p. 25.

[148]The Reporter (2016), 'Ethiopia: Teff in the Global Trade' https://archiveenglish.thereporterethiopia.com/content/teff-global-trade (accessed 07 March 2019).

[149]Giovannucci et al. (2009), p. 22.

[150]Teff Specification (2001).

[151]Ketema (1997), p. 12.

[152]Giovannucci et al. (2009), p. 22.

This will mean extra cost to adapt their facilities, production methods, raw materials and overall organization to the specified standard that will need to be included in the designation application.

Although the above discussed actions do seem complicated, if GI is properly done, the advantage that will potentially bring to Ethiopia will be enormous. If Ethiopia introduces specific GI law, it can help to protect and preserve a traditional knowledge that is entangled with the production of Teff's final products. Moreover, it will enhance the confidence of both the domestic and the foreign investors to invest in GI products since they are locally protected. The trend of producing unique, reputable and quality GI products that meet the high standard of other jurisdictions will enhance institutional structure in the country. In other words, GI protection could bring institutional reforms to regions that produce GI products.

In sum, if there is a specific legal umbrella to protect GI products, and set up all the infrastructure required, Teff could be that GI product which could take the Ethiopian economy to another level.

5 Conclusions

The Teff patent right granted in Europe does not meet the substantive elements of the EPC i.e. the elements of novelty, inventive step and industrial applicability. The premises that the traditional Teff flour has low baking quality and usually mixed with wheat flour were unsubstantiated. This is because Ethiopians prefer Teff without being mixed with wheat or with any other flour for that matter. Also, research showed that the falling number of Teff flour obtained from 22 Ethiopian Teff varieties fall within the falling number that the invention claimed to achieve i.e. 250–380. Moreover, traditionally in Ethiopia Teff is not ground right after harvest but rather it was stored for some time in a traditional storage. The problem that the claimed invention tried to solve has already been solved by the Ethiopian traditional knowledge. Therefore, the claimed invention did not meet the elements of novelty as well as an inventive step.

Procedurally, the Ethiopian government will face a difficult task to take the Teff patent case to all national courts where the patents are valid. It will be very expensive for the Ethiopian government. The government should be strategic in picking which jurisdictions will have sympathy for the Teff case. In addition, it should take into consideration a market that has a bigger share for the gluten-free market.

Besides Ethiopia taking the Teff patent case to the national courts, it should also use different means to showcase how Ethiopia was unfairly locked out from accessing the Teff market in Europe due to the wrongfully granted patent right. Ethiopia should put more pressure on the patent owners to settle the issue by engaging different stakeholders in Europe. There should be a 360 campaign plan that engages consumers, civil societies, media and governments while simultaneously pushing the Teff patent case in the European national courts. Ethiopia could take a leaf out of its coffee trademark battle against Starbucks and adopt a similar method to intensify the process of revoking the Teff patent.

Finally, assuming that the Teff patent has been revoked, Ethiopia should protect Teff by using GI as a legal instrument. In order for this to happen, Ethiopia should amend its trademarks law and have a separate GI provision in itself. If the Ethiopian Teff has a GI protection, it will help to fetch much more money and dominate the gluten-free grain market since the consumers could trace back the sources of quality Teff from its origin, namely Ethiopia.

References

Agreement on access to, and benefit sharing from, Teff Genetic Resources, 2005

Agricultural Transformation Agency (2013) Working strategy for strengthening Ethiopia's Teff value chain, Agricultural Transformation Agency (ATA). http://www.ata.gov.et/download/. Accessed 25 May 2018

Andersen R, Winge T (2012) The access and benefit-sharing agreement on Teff genetic resources facts and lessons. Fridtjof Nansens Institutt. http://www.abs-initiative.info/fileadmin/media/Knowledge_Center/Pulications/FNI/FNI-R0612.pdf. Accessed 13 Apr 2018

Arrow K (1962) Economic welfare and the allocation of resources for invention. University Press, Princeton

Biramo H (2011) Export performance of oil-seeds and its determinants in Ethiopia. J Cereals and Oilseeds 2(1):1. Available online at http://www.academicjournals.org/jco. Accessed 8 Sep 2018

Boldrin M, Levine DK (2012) The case against patents. Federal Reserve Bank of St. Louis Research Division. https://research.stlouisfed.org/wp/2012/2012-035.pdf. Accessed 14 Jan 2019

Business Insider (2018) Gluten-free food: global market drivers, trends and opportunities analysis 2018–2026. https://markets.businessinsider.com/news/stocks/gluten-free-food-global-market-drivers-trends-and-opportunities-analysis-2018-2026-1027336470. Accessed 07 Mar 2019

DeGeer ME (2003) Bio-piracy: the appropriation of indigenous peoples' cultural knowledge. New Engl J Int Comp Law 9:719

European Parliament Directive (1998/44) The Legal Protection of Biotechnology Inventions

European Patent Convention (EPC) 1973

European Patent Convention Guidelines. http://www.epo.org/law-practice/legal-texts/html/guidelines/e/g_vii_1.htm. Accessed 07 Mar 2019

European Patent Office (EPO) (2005) Teff Patent number- EP 1 646 287 B

European Union (2001) Brussels I Regulation

Financial Times (2017) Healthy appetites drive jump in sales of gluten-free foods. https://www.ft.com/content/4ec0f2f2-2c0a-11e7-9ec8-168383da43b7. Accessed 12 Dec 2018

Gamboa PA, van Ekris L (2008) Survey on the nutritional and health aspects of Teff (Eragrostis Tef). http://educon.javeriana.edu.co/lagrotech/images/patricia_arguedas.pdf. Accessed 12 Apr 2018

Geoff T, Tasmin R (2008) A guide to international negotiations and rules on intellectual property, biodiversity and food security. Internal Development Research Center, Earth scan Publisher, London, p 148

German Patent Act (2017) Patent Act as published on 16 December 1989 (Federal Law Gazette 1981 I p. 1), as last amended by Article 4 of the Act of 8 October 2017 (Federal Law Gazette I p. 3546), Sections 21(1) and 22

Gervais D (2005) Traditional knowledge and intellectual property; a TRIPS compatible approach. Mich State Law Rev:141–178

Giovannucci D, Josling T, Kerr W, O'Connor B, Yeung MT (2009) Guide to geographical indications linking products and their origin. International Trade Center, Geneva
Hirko SB (2011) The legal protection of geographical indications in Ethiopia. Dissertation, Munich Intellectual Property Law Center, http://www.miplc.de/research/. Available at SSRN: http://ssrn.com/abstract=2135428. Accessed 09 Mar 2019
Intellectual Property Research Institute of Australia (IPRIA) (2009) Sidamo, A Teaching Case for WIPO. https://www.wipo.int/export/sites/www/academy/en/about/global_network/educational_materials/cs4_sidamo.pdf. Accessed 05 Jan 2019
International Food Policy Research Institute (2017) Ethiopia's Coffee farmers struggle to realize benefits from international markets. http://www.ifpri.org/blog/ethiopias-coffee-farmers-struggle-realize-benefits-international-markets. Accessed 19 Jan 2019
Josling T (2006) What's in a name? The economics, law, and politics of geographical indications for foods and beverages. Institute for International Integration Studies Discussion Paper No. 109. Trinity College, Dublin
Kellenter W, Migdal B, Mueller H (2018) Patent litigation in Germany: overview. Thomson Reuters, Eagan, Practical Law. https://uk.practicallaw.thomsonreuters.com/5-622-3450?transitionType=Default&contextData=(sc.Default)&firstPage=true&comp=pluk&bhcp=1. Accessed 26 July 2018
Ketema S (1997) Teff. Eragrostis tef (Zucc.) Trotter: promoting the conservation and use of underutilized and neglected crops. Institute of Plant Genetics and Crop Plant Research, Gatersleben/International Plant Genetic Resources Institute, Rome, p 17
Lee H (2018) Teff, a rising global crop: current status of Teff production and value chain. Institute for International Development Cooperation, Konkuk University, Seoul
Lopez A (2009) Innovation and appropriability, empirical evidence and research agenda. In: In the economics of intellectual property. Suggestions for further research in developing countries and countries with economies in transition
Memorandum of Understanding: Research & Development of International Markets for Teff-based products, 2003
Middlemiss S, Balfour L (2018) Patent litigation in the UK (England and Wales): overview. Thomson Reuters, Practical Law. https://uk.practicallaw.thomsonreuters.com/3-623-0277?transitionType=Default&contextData=(sc.Default). Accessed 26 July 218
O'Kicki M (2009) Lessons learned from Ethiopia's trademarking and licensing initiative: is the European Union's position on geographical indications really beneficial for developing nations?. Loyola University Chicago International Law Review. https://lawecommons.luc.edu/cgi/viewcontent.cgi?article=1044&context=lucilr. Accessed 05 Jan 2019
Refera A (2001) TEF post-harvest operations. Food and Agriculture Organization of the United Nations, Rome
Schumpeter JA (1942) Capitalism, socialism and democracy. Harper and Row, Manhattan
Stenton G (2004) Bio-piracy within the pharmaceutical industry: a stark illustration of how abusive, manipulative and perverse the patenting process can be towards countries of the South. Eur Intellect Property Rev 26:30
Subbiah S (2004) Reaping what they sow: the basmati rice controversy and strategies for protecting traditional knowledge. Boston Coll Int Comp Law Rev 27:529
Summary of the Paris Convention for the Protection of Industrial Property (1883). http://www.wipo.int/treaties/en/ip/paris/summary_paris.html. Accessed 15 Jan 2019
Teff Specification (2001) Federal Democratic Republic of Ethiopia Edict of Government. https://law.resource.org/pub/et/ibr/et.671.2001.pdf. Accessed 2 Aug 2018
The *Agreement* on Trade-Related Aspects of Intellectual Property Rights (*TRIPS*), 1994
The Ethiopian Reporter (2018) The Attorney general is given the greenlight to file a suit against the Dutch Company (2018). https://www.thereporterethiopia.com/article/attorney-general-sue-dutch-company-over-teff-patent. Accessed 20 June 2018
The Official Journal of the European Patent Office (2007). http://archive.epo.org/epo/pubs/oj007/08_07/special_edition_4_epc_2000_synoptic.pdf. Accessed 14 May 2018

The Paris Convention (1883)
The Reporter (2016) Ethiopia: Teff in the Global Trade. http://allafrica.com/stories/201506151943.html. Accessed 10 May 2018
Trademark Registration and Protection Proclamation No.501/2006.Federal Negarit Gazeta of the Federal Democratic Republic of Ethiopia, 12th Year, No.37, 2006
UNEP (1996) Traditional forest-related knowledge and the convention on biological diversity. https://www.cbd.int/doc/meetings/cop/cop-03/information/cop-03-inf-33-en.pdf. Accessed 18 Jan 2019
United States Patent and Trademark decision (2012) Processing of Teff Flour. https://globaldossier.uspto.gov/svc/doccontent/US/56537504.A/1-26-US%20%20105653750VP1%20/26/PDF, pp 2–3. Accessed 15 Jan 2019
USTR (2004) European Communities – protection of trademarks and geographical indications for agricultural products and foodstuffs. WTO Dispute Settlement, US submission. https://ustr.gov/sites/default/files/uploads/Countries%20Regions/africa/agreements/pdfs/dispute_settlement/ds174/asset_upload_file992_5560.pdf. Accessed 19 Jan 2019
Victor Conde H (2004) A handbook of international human rights terminology. University of Nebraska Press, Lincoln
WIPO Fields of Intellectual Property Protection. http://www.wipo.int/export/sites/www/about-ip/en/iprm/pdf/ch2.pdf. Accessed 18 Jan 2019
WIPO Frequently asked questions on Geographical Indication. https://www.wipo.int/geo_indications/en/faq_geographicalindications.html. Accessed 18 Jan 2019
WIPO Geographical Indication. https://www.wipo.int/geo_indications/en/. Accessed 15 Jan 2019
WIPO Introduction to TRIPS Agreement. https://www.wto.org/english/tratop_e/trips_e/ta_docs_e/modules1_e.pdf. Accessed 10 May 2018
WIPO Patents. https://www.wto.org/english/tratop_e/trips_e/ta_docs_e/modules5_e.pdf. Accessed 10 May 2018
WIPO Trademark Licensing. https://www.wipo.int/export/sites/www/sme/en/documents/pdf/ip_panorama_12_learning_points.pdf. Accessed 19 Jan 2019
WIPO What is Trademark. https://www.wipo.int/trademarks/en/. Accessed 18 Jan 2019

Beka Melkamu Tesgera is an independent trade, investment and competition law consultant covering the Eastern Africa Region. He has an LLM degree from the University of Barcelona in International Economic Law and Policy. He also received a Doctor of Law (J.D.) from Handong International Law School-South Korea in American Law, International Public Law and International Private Law. Beka also has B.A. in communication from Daystar University, Kenya.

International Water Cooperation in Europe: Lessons for the Nile Basin Countries?

Götz Reichert

Abstract The construction of the "Grand Ethiopian Renaissance Dam" (GERD) could be a catalyst for a general paradigm shift in relations between the countries of the Nile basin. Changing power constellations between upstream and downstream riparians not only challenge long-standing claims to the river's water resources, but also offer the opportunity to establish a truly basin-wide legal framework for the resolution of water disputes or even for the common management of the Nile for the mutual benefit of all riparians. In this respect, contemporary international water law offers valuable guidance for the development of substantive and procedural rules. Furthermore, experiences made in transboundary river basins in other regions of the world could provide inspiration to Nile riparians to devise their own solutions tailored to their specific needs. To this end, this article explores efforts made by riparians in European river basins—failures and successes alike—to solve their water-related conflicts. On this basis, it is suggested that some essential "lessons learned" in Europe are useful for fostering international water cooperation between the riparian countries of the Nile basin.

1 Introduction

The Nile—at over 6600 km the world's longest river and a basin shared by eleven riparian countries—has always been a lifeline for the people living along its banks. Population growth and economic development give rise to an ever increasing use of the river's resources. In a largely arid region, conflicts over competing water uses are bound to occur. Since ancient times, the downstream riparians Egypt and Sudan have used the Nile's waters intensively. In recent years, however, upstream riparians—such as Ethiopia, Kenya, Uganda and Tanzania—have demanded a greater share of the water resources. Even today, Egypt and Sudan reject such claims by invoking "historic and established rights" based on international treaties dating back

G. Reichert (✉)
Centre for European Policy, Freiburg, Germany

Z. Yihdego et al. (eds.), *Ethiopian Yearbook of International Law 2018*, Ethiopian Yearbook of International Law 2018, https://doi.org/10.1007/978-3-030-24078-3_5

to the colonial era.[1] Despite several recent attempts to intensify international cooperation, no legal framework comprising all Nile riparian countries has yet been established.[2]

In this respect, the construction of the "Grand Ethiopian Renaissance Dam" (GERD)[3] on the Blue Nile in Ethiopia close to the Sudanese border could be a catalyst for a general paradigm shift[4] in relations between the riparians of the Nile. When completed, the GERD will have the potential to generate approximately 6450 megawatts of electricity.[5] While potential positive and negative impacts of the GERD on the different riparians is a matter of political disputes and scientific discussions,[6] it is evident that the growing use of the waters of the Blue Nile by Ethiopia will fundamentally change long-standing power constellations between the upstream and downstream riparians concerned. It is not surprising, therefore, that the commencement of the GERD's construction has sparked severe tensions especially between Egypt and Ethiopia.[7]

Increasing water demand in general, and the construction of the GERD in particular poses a challenge to all riparians in the Nile basin, forcing them to rethink and perhaps alter traditional perceptions and legal positions, thereby also offering them the golden opportunity to develop a basin-wide legal framework for the resolution of water disputes and perhaps even for the common management of the shared resource for their mutual benefit. Given the vital interests at stake and the long history of conflict over the Nile's waters, it is evident that such an endeavor will be anything but an easy task. The good news, however, is that the riparians of the Nile will not have to completely reinvent the wheel. After all, options and solutions already offered by current international water law for the resolution of water-related conflicts can provide valuable guidance to them. Furthermore, experiences made in transboundary river basins in other regions of the world, which have contributed to the development of international water law, may provide useful inspiration to the Nile riparians.

To this end, I would like to make a contribution by exploring some efforts made by riparians in European river basins—failures and successes alike—to solve their water-related conflicts which could provide some lessons for the Nile basin countries. Obviously, there are profound differences between the relevant climatic,

---

[1]Salman (2017a), pp. 3 et seq. and p. 21.

[2]Salman (2017a), pp. 10 et seq.

[3]For a comprehensive discussion of the GERD from the perspectives of law, political science, economics and hydrology *see generally* Yihdego et al. (2017).

[4]Salman (2017b), pp. 42 and 57.

[5]Ezega News (2017) Ethiopian Renaissance Dam Generation Capacity Revised Up to 6450 MW (25 February 2017), www.ezega.com/News/NewsDetails/3978/Ethiopian-Renaissance-Dam-Generation-Capacity-Revised-Up-to-6-450MW (this and the following links were last accessed on 3 March 2019).

[6]*See generally* Yihdego et al. (2017).

[7]Lazarus (2018) Is Ethiopia Taking Control of the River Nile? CNN (21 October 2018), https://edition.cnn.com/2018/10/19/africa/ethiopia-new-dam-threatens-egypts-water/index.html.

hydrologic, geographic, socio-economic and political conditions in Africa and Europe in general and the respective river basins in particular. Most strikingly, while water conflicts in Africa, including in the Nile basin, arise mostly over questions of water quantity prompted by competition over scares resources, the focus in Europe has mainly[8] been—for at least the past half century[9]—on water quality and environmental protection. Nevertheless, one can argue that European experiences on international water conflicts also provide some "lessons learned" which might also be helpful to the Nile riparians in order to devise solutions tailored to their specific needs for the peaceful resolution of water disputes which already exist or which will emerge as water demand continues to grow in the future.

In the following, I will briefly sketch out the history and present challenges of international water conflicts in the Nile basin (part 2). Then, typical international water conflicts in European river basins will be illustrated using the example of the Rhine (part 3). On this basis, essential substantive and procedural features of international water law in Europe (part 4) and the respective normative influence of the water legislation of the European Union (part 5) will be described. In conclusion (part 6), I will suggest some essential "lessons learned" by riparians of transboundary river basins in Europe which might be useful for fostering international water cooperation between the riparian countries of the Nile basin.

2 International Water Conflicts in the Nile Basin: History and Present Challenges

International treaties on the Nile which were concluded in the colonial era continue to be a source of dispute between riparians even today.[10] In 1929, an agreement concluded by Britain on behalf of its colonies of Kenya, Uganda and Tanganyika (today's Tanzania), as well as the Sudan, on the one hand, and Egypt on the other hand (*1929 Britain/Egypt Agreement*[11]) stipulates a right of veto for Egypt regarding potentially detrimental water uses of the respective upstream riparians.[12] In 1959,

[8]Especially in the arid regions of Southern Europe, however, transboundary conflicts—for example between Spain and Portugal—over water quantity are a matter of concern. *See, e.g.,* Burgen (2017) Tagus river at risk of drying up completely. The Guardian (14 August 2017), https://www.theguardian.com/environment/2017/aug/14/tagus-river-at-risk-of-drying-up-completely. In this respect *see also* Agreement on Cooperation for the Protection and Sustainable Use of the Waters of the Spanish-Portuguese Hydrographic Basins between Spain and Portugal, signed in Albufeira on 30 November 1998, in force 17 January 2000, 2099 UNTS 275.

[9]It remains to be seen to which extent the increase of both aridity and floods due to climate change will intensify international conflicts over water quantity on the European continent.

[10]For the following *see generally* Salman (2017a), p. 19 et seq.

[11]Exchange of Notes between the United Kingdom and Egypt in regard to the Uses of Waters of the River Nile for Irrigation Purposes, 7 May 1929, 93 LNTS 44.

[12]Paragraph 4(ii) 1929 Britain Egypt/Agreement.

Egypt and Sudan concluded an agreement "for the Full Utilization of the Nile Waters" (*1959 Egypt/Sudan Agreement*[13]) which established the total annual flow of the Nile measured at Aswan as 84 billion cubic meters (BCM), and allocated 55.5 BCM to Egypt and 18.5 BCM to Sudan. The remaining 10 BCM represent the annual evaporation and seepage losses at the large reservoir of the High Aswan Dam in southern Egypt and northern Sudan. While Egypt and Sudan recognised the claims of other upstream riparian states to a share of the Nile waters, they reserved to themselves the ultimate decision in this respect. In order to justify this allocation and the claimed veto power, both downstream riparians invoke "historic and established rights" to the waters of the Nile. The other riparians, however, totally reject the 1959 Egypt/Sudan Agreement. They argue that they are not parties to the agreement and have never accepted it. Furthermore, they consider the claims of Egypt and Sudan to the entire flow of the Nile as an infringement of their rights under international law for a reasonable and equitable share of the Nile waters.

Subsequent bilateral agreements concluded by Ethiopia with Sudan in 1991, and with Egypt in 1993, however, indicate a general recognition by both downstream riparians of Ethiopia's right to the Nile waters.[14] Another major step towards cooperation amongst Nile countries was the *Nile Basin Initiative (NBI)*.[15] The NBI was established in 1999 under the auspices, *inter alia*, of the World Bank and the United Nations Development Programme (UNDP) by the ministers for water resources of the Nile riparians as an intergovernmental organisation. It was intended to foster cooperation between all Nile riparians "to achieve sustainable socio-economic development through equitable utilization of, and benefit from, the common Nile Basin water resources." Its ultimate objective is to serve as a transitional arrangement for the development of a legal instrument. Negotiations on the *Nile Basin Cooperative Framework Agreement (CFA)*, however, proved to be cumbersome and lengthy, especially since Egypt and Sudan insisted on their claims of "acquired uses and rights" of the Nile waters.[16] Finally, only five of today's eleven Nile basin states—the upstream riparians Burundi, Ethiopia, Kenya, Tanzania, Uganda and Rwanda—signed the CFA in 2010 and 2011. The CFA codifies the two fundamental principles of international water[17]: the right of all riparians to the "equitable utilization" of the Nile water resources and the requirement to take all appropriate measures to prevent significant harm to other riparian countries. Furthermore, the CFA includes provisions for the protection, use, conservation and development of the Nile Basin. The CFA further aspires to establish a permanent Nile Basin Commission that would replace the NBI as clearly anticipated in Part III of the Treaty. While the CFA is intended as *the* basin-wide legal instrument for the

[13]Agreement between the United Arab Republic and the Republic of Sudan for the Full Utilization of Nile Waters, 8 November 159, 453 UNTS 51.

[14]*See* Salman (2017a), p. 22 et seq.

[15]*See* Salman (2017a), p. 25 et seq.

[16]*See* Salman (2017a), p. 26.

[17]*See infra* Sect. 4.2.

regulation of the use and protection of the Nile, significant differences continue to hinder all riparians to become parties to the agreement.[18]

Another source of tension especially between Egypt and Sudan on one side, and Ethiopia on the other side was/is the construction of the GERD on the Blue Nile.[19] From the first announcement of the plan regarding the construction of the GERD in April 2011, Egypt and Sudan opposed the dam, claiming it to be an infringement of their "historic and established rights" to the waters of the Nile. In December 2011, however, the three countries managed to agree on the establishment of an international panel of experts to assess the impact of the GERD on the Blue Nile. Furthermore, Sudan announced in December 2013 that it supports the GERD. Finally, in March 2015 the three riparian countries concluded the *Agreement on Declaration of Principles on the GERD* (DoP)[20] by which Egypt and Sudan recognised explicitly the rights of Ethiopia to the Nile waters.

Both the CFA and the DoP are indicators of a paradigm shift which is underway in the relations between the riparians of the Nile and which has the potential to overcome the persisting obstacles to basin-wide cooperation on the use and protection of the Nile between all riparians. Given the increasing pressure of growing demand for the various uses of the Nile waters, the upstream and downstream riparians now have to continue to strive for ways to cooperate more closely for the peaceful resolution of their water disputes and perhaps even for the common management of the Nile for mutual benefit. Contemporary international water law offers valuable guidance for the development of substantive and procedural rules. In this respect, the experience of riparians in European river basins to solve their water-related conflicts will be examined in the following part.

3 International Water Conflicts in Europe: The Example of the Rhine[21]

There are over 75 transboundary river basins in Europe.[22] The Danube is Europe's largest, and with 19 riparian states sharing the river's drainage area it is also the world's most international transboundary river basin. In Europe it is followed by the catchment of the river Rhine with nine riparians.[23] With the growing industrial, municipal and agricultural uses of freshwater resources after World War II, the potential for conflict between riparian states increased considerably. The most famous example of an international water dispute in Europe from the point of

[18]*See* Salman (2017a), p. 27 et seq.

[19]For the following *see* Salman (2017a), p. 30 et seq.

[20]*See generally* Salman (2017a).

[21]This part is based on Reichert (2016), pp. 7–12.

[22]Zamparutti (2012), p. 6.

[23]Vogel et al. (2012), p. 158.

view of international law is the ICJ case concerning the *Gabčíkovo-Nagymaros Project* on the Danube.[24] For the purposes of this article, however, a closer look at the development in the Rhine basin promises deeper insight into innovative approaches towards dealing with international water conflicts which could be also applied in regions outside Europe. To this end, the following examples concerning the Rhine serve to illustrate typical features of water disputes between riparians in Europe as well as to describe early attempts for solutions, respective failures, "lessons learned" and successes. While predominantly focused on water quality, these cases feature essentially the same "upstream-downstream" conflict structure that is at the heart of conflicts over water quantity in the Nile basin in general and over the potential impact of the GERD in particular.

3.1 International Commission for the Protection of the Rhine (ICPR)

As Europe recovered economically in the period following World War II, the river Rhine became notorious as "Europe's most romantic sewer"[25] as it was polluted by wastewater discharges from industrial plants and households. As early as 1950, the Netherlands—which as a downstream riparian situated at the river's estuary into the North Sea suffered considerably from transboundary water pollution, resulting, e.g., in highly toxic sediments in the port of Rotterdam—initiated the establishment of the *International Commission for the Protection of the Rhine (ICPR).*[26] The ICPR, which until today coordinates international protection efforts concerning the river's main stream, was formalised in 1963 through an agreement between France, Germany, Luxembourg, the Netherlands and Switzerland.[27] Until the mid 1970s, however, the activities of the ICPR did not yield any significant progress in solving pollution problems caused by discharges of salt and other substances into the river.[28] In 1976, the five member countries of the ICPR and the then-European Economic Community (EEC) attempted to make their cooperation more effective by concluding the *Convention for the Protection of the Rhine River Against Pollution by Chlorides* (1976 Rhine Chlorides Convention)[29] and the *Convention for the Protection of the Rhine River Against Chemical Pollution* (1976 Rhine Chemical Convention).[30]

---

[24]ICJ, *Gabčíkovo-Nagymaros Project (Hungary v. Slovakia)*, Judgment, 1997 ICJ Rep 7. *See generally*, e.g., Steck and Eckstein (1997), pp. 41–50; Sands (1998), pp. 103–107.

[25]Nollkaemper (1996), p. 153.

[26]International Commission on the Protection of the Rhine, https://www.iksr.org/en/.

[27]Signed in Berne on 29 April 1963, in force 1 May 1965, 994 UNTS 3.

[28]Lammers (1984), p. 175; Birnie et al. (2009), p. 573.

[29]Signed in Bonn on 3 December 1976, in force 5 July 1985, 1404 UNTS 90.

[30]Signed in Bonn on 3 December 1976, in force 1 February 1979, 1124 UNTS 375.

3.2 The Chloride Arbitration

The 1976 Rhine Chlorides Convention was intended to limit the river's salinisation caused by discharges originating from potassium exploitation in the French region of Alsace,[31] which caused severe tensions especially between the Netherlands and France. The Convention's aim was "to improve progressively the quality of the waters of the Rhine so that at the German-Netherlands border the chloride ion content will not be greater than 200 mg/l."[32] With regard to financial burden-sharing for reduction measures on chloride discharges, the Convention provided for the distribution of the total cost of 132 million French francs between France (30%), Germany (30%), the Netherlands (34%) and Switzerland (6%).[33] However, environmental concerns in France over plans to inject saltwater into groundwater bodies in order to reduce discharges into the Rhine itself made the ratification process very cumbersome.[34] Therefore, the Convention entered into force as late as 1985 after intense diplomatic communication between the parties.[35]

Nevertheless, the conflict between France and the Netherlands continued, resulting in a compromise over a modified concept regulated in an *Additional Protocol* to the 1976 Rhine Chlorides Convention in 1991[36] which provided for further measures by both France and the Netherlands[37] and was accompanied by provisions on the allocation of the respective costs and on payment arrangements.[38] Subsequently, however, the Netherlands claimed the reimbursement of payments on grounds that France had only partially fulfilled its obligations under the 1991 Additional Protocol. The dispute was referred to arbitration under the rules of the Permanent Court of Arbitration in The Hague. Years later, in 2004 the arbitral tribunal held that France was obliged to reimburse the Netherlands for payments made for inadequate French efforts to reduce chloride discharges into the Rhine.[39]

---

[31] For the negotiation and ratification process of the 1976 Rhine Chlorides Convention with a focus on its economic background *see* Bernauer (1995), pp. 369–390.

[32] Preamble recital 4 1976 Rhine Chlorides Convention.

[33] Article 7(2) 1976 Rhine Chlorides Convention.

[34] de Villeneuve (1996), pp. 447–448.

[35] Exchanges of letters constituting an amendment to the 1976 Rhine Chemical Convention, dated at Neuilly on 29 April 1983, at Bonn on 4 May 1983, at The Hague on 4 May 1983, at Luxembourg on 13 May 1983 and at Berne on 13 May 1983, 1404 UNTS 99.

[36] Additional Protocol to the 1976 Rhine Chlorides Convention, concluded at Brussels on 25 September 1991, 1840 UNTS 372.

[37] 1991 Additional Protocol to the 1976 Rhine Chlorides Convention.

[38] Article 4 in conjunction with Annex III 1991 Additional Protocol to the 1976 Rhine Chlorides Convention.

[39] Case Concerning the Auditing of Accounts between the Kingdom of the Netherlands and the French Republic Pursuant to the Additional Protocol of 25 September 1991 to the Convention of the Rhine Against Pollution by Chlorides of 3 December 1976, Arbitral Award of 12 March 2004, 25 RIAA 267. *See* Boisson de Chazournes (2008), pp. 1–15; Salman (2006), pp. 5–6.

3.3 The Sandoz Chemical Spill

The 1976 Rhine Chemical Convention was intended to fight transboundary water pollution caused by especially detrimental chemical substances. It obliged its parties to eliminate pollution in the surface waters of the Rhine by certain "dangerous substances" specified in a "black list", which were to be chosen on the basis of their toxicity, persistence and bioaccumulation.[40] The Convention provided for an obligatory scheme of prior authorisation of discharges of "black list" substances by setting "emission standards" for maximum admissible "emission limit values" in the form of "concentration limits." The latter was proposed by the ICPR and adopted by unanimous approval of all parties to the Convention.[41] Less dangerous pollutants pursuant to a "grey list" had to be reduced by national programmes.[42] Furthermore, in case of "a sudden considerable increase" of listed substances or "of an accident which could seriously threaten the quality of Rhine water," all parties were obliged to notify the ICPR and the potentially affected countries "without delay."[43]

It soon became apparent, however, that the 1976 Rhine Chemical Convention was "a regulatory failure."[44] Especially the provisions on the adoption of detailed concentration limits for "black list" substances within the institutional framework of the ICPR, which required unanimous approval by all parties to the Convention for each single substance, turned out to be ineffective. The respective negotiation and ratification processes governed by international law were too cumbersome and lengthy to appropriately reflect ecological requirements and technological progress.[45] Predominantly due to this formalistic approach—accompanied by a general lack of political will—concentration limits were set only for a few substances. Furthermore, the few emission limit values which were actually set soon proved to be technically outdated and—given the increasing discharge of ever new detrimental substances—inadequate to combat the overall chemical pollution of the Rhine effectively.[46]

On 1 November 1986, the shortcomings of the 1976 Rhine Chemical Convention in general and its accident notification system in particular became most apparent: Firefighting operations at a warehouse of the Sandoz chemical company near Basel, Switzerland, washed over 20 tons of chemicals into the river. In the following days, the poisonous mix severely damaged the Rhine's aquatic ecosystem for hundreds of kilometers downstream, thereby extinguishing almost its entire eel population and threatening the water supply of thousands of households in cities along its banks as

---

[40] Article 1(a) in conjunction with Annex I 1976 Rhine Chemical Convention.

[41] Articles 3, 4, 5 and 14 1976 Rhine Chemical Convention.

[42] Articles 1(b), 3, 4 and 6 1976 Rhine Chemical Convention.

[43] Article 11 1976 Rhine Chemical Convention.

[44] Nollkaemper (1996), p. 155.

[45] Reichert (2005), p. 141.

[46] Lammers (1984), p. 196; de Villeneuve (1996), p. 450.

far as the Netherlands. Major economic damage was inflicted on the fishing, agriculture, industry and tourism sectors.[47]

3.4 The 1987 Rhine Action Programme and the 1991 Master Plan "Salmon 2000"[48]

The Sandoz Chemical Spill was a shock for the general public which generated enormous pressure on the public authorities of the Rhine riparians to take action. Less than a year after the accident, on 1 October 1987, the countries represented in the ICPR adopted the *Rhine Action Programme*, which was designed to restore the ecological integrity of the river by achieving the following targets by the year 2000[49]: (1) species that had become extinct in the Rhine, such as the salmon, should return; (2) the extraction of water for drinking should continue to be possible; and (3) the pollutant contents of river sediments should be reduced. With regard to point source pollution by industry and municipalities, the Rhine Action Programme set three deadlines for the attainment of its targets[50]: By 1989, the ICPR had to identify 45 "priority substances," to take stock of their sources and amount of inputs and to submit proposals for their reduction. This required the implementation of reduction measures in industrial production and municipal wastewater treatment plants. By 1995, discharges of priority substances were to be reduced by 50%. Based on interim results, additional measures were to be implemented until the final deadline of 2000, including the prohibition of dangerous substances in order to attain the water quality objectives. Furthermore, the parties to the ICPR agreed on a list of measures aimed at the prevention of accidents by securing industrial plants along the Rhine. In case of an accidental spill of dangerous substances into the Rhine, all Rhine riparians had to be informed immediately.[51]

On the basis of the 1987 Rhine Action Programme, in 1991 the ICPR drafted the *Ecological Master Plan for the Rhine "Salmon 2000"* which aimed at the ecological rehabilitation of the river's main stream through the protection of its riverbed, banks, alluvial land and tributaries.[52] The species of salmon was chosen *pars pro toto* as an indicator for the effectiveness of protection measures not only with a view to protecting the species itself, but with a broader focus on the Rhine's entire aquatic ecosystem ranging from the Alps to the North Sea. Furthermore, following severe floods along the Rhine in 1993 and 1995, the ICPR also adopted an *Action Plan on Floods* in 1998. In order to the minimise the danger of severe inundations in densely

[47]*See generally* Schwabach (1989).

[48]This section is based on Reichert (2016), pp. 12–14.

[49]ICPR (2003), pp. 5–7.

[50]*Ibid.*, p. 9.

[51]*Ibid.*, p. 19.

[52]Wieriks (1998), pp. 127–128.

populated areas downstream especially in Germany and the Netherlands, the Action Plan provided for the protection of alluvial land and for the creation of additional floodplains, including upstream in Switzerland and France.[53]

By and large, the 1987 Rhine Action Programme and the subsequent programmes developed on this basis turned out to be a success.[54] By the year 2000, the water of the Rhine had become cleaner, accidental spills were less frequent and salmon had returned to the river. While nitrate inputs, especially from agriculture, remained a problem, discharges of detrimental substances by industry and municipalities into the river were reduced considerably. Inputs of most priority substances diminished by over 70% or in some cases were no longer measurable. At first glance, this successful restoration of the ecological integrity of the Rhine may be surprising. In contrast to the 1976 Rhine Chemical Convention and the 1976 Rhine Chlorides Convention, the Rhine Action Programme, the Master Plan "Salmon 2000" and the Action Plan on Floods were not international treaties, but merely legally non-binding declarations of intent by the Rhine riparians. Furthermore, they contained comparatively general objectives and principles, the concrete implementation of which was left to the national authorities of the participating riparian countries. Nevertheless, they soon proved to be more effective than their legally-binding predecessors. So, what made the difference?

First, the experience of the Sandoz Spill generated strong public pressure and political support in all riparian countries for the programmes, which compensated for their lack of legal clout.[55] With regard to the substantial aspects of the new approach, the focus shifted away from ad-hoc attempts to solve specific, narrowly defined conflicts over antagonistic interests between upstream and downstream riparians on discharges of certain substances towards the holistic—and common—target of restoring and protecting the ecosystem of the Rhine as a whole. Choosing the salmon—a species which by nature needs to travel through the entire stream of the Rhine from the North Sea to the Alps—as an indicator for the effectiveness of the measures for the restoration of the Rhine's aquatic ecosystem set a visible goal and served as a powerful symbol which could be easily communicated to the general public and also created motivation for action.

Second, this newly defined overall objective was accompanied by a profound change in the procedural approach. While the 1976 Rhine Chemical Convention provided for the legally binding adoption of strict emission limit values through cumbersome formal ratification processes governed by international law, the more informal Rhine Action Programme set general, but verifiable objectives to be achieved within a certain timeframe and allowed for their flexible operationalisation through specific measures to be continuously developed within the ICPR and further specified by the Rhine riparian countries. Progress was monitored and reported regularly to the ICPR, enabling fact-based stocktaking, the detection of

---

[53] ICPR (2003), p. 7.

[54] *Ibid.*, pp. 8–9, 16 and 26.

[55] For the following *see* Irmer (1998), pp. 113–119.

shortcomings and the swift adaptation of measures in order to attain the targets. This programme implementation with its built-in learning-process was facilitated by the joint efforts of over 150 experts. The secretariat of the ICPR coordinated their meetings, informed the general public and established contacts with industry, municipalities and environmental NGOs. Over time, expertise was built within public administrations and the economic sector, mutual trust among representatives of the riparian states grew, and public support for the common goal and implementation measures was established.

4 Essential Features of International Water Law in Europe

4.1 The 1992 UNECE Water Convention

The Sandoz Spill was a "watershed" not only for international cooperation concerning the Rhine, but also for international water law in Europe in general. The positive experience of the Rhine riparians within the ICPR provided useful insights for the further development of new international water agreements and the establishment of river commissions in European river basins. This development was reinforced by a general paradigm shift in environmental policy from limited protection efforts towards the "integrated" management of natural resources under the overall *leitmotif* of "sustainability"[56] which was promoted on the global level, e.g., in the *1992 Dublin Statement on Water and Sustainable Development*[57] or *Chapter 18 of Agenda 21*[58] adopted at the United Nations Conference on Environment and Development (UNCED) held in Rio de Janeiro in 1992. In a nutshell,[59] in order to be "sustainable"—ecologically effective, economically efficient and socially appropriate—the regulation of domestic as well as transboundary freshwater resources needs to be based on the ecological characteristics of the freshwater body and its entire ecosystem. Surface water and groundwater as well as qualitative and quantitative aspects are to be managed in an integrated manner throughout the natural catchment area and irrespective of administrative or national boundaries. Such a holistic approach requires taking into account all relevant factors within decision-making processes, which must therefore be based on the continuous collection, evaluation and communication of information. To this end, all affected stakeholders—including

[56] *See generally* Reichert (2016), pp. 15–21.

[57] The Dublin Statement on Water and Development, International Conference on Water and the Environment, Dublin, Ireland, 26–31 January 1992, http://www.wmo.int/pages/prog/hwrp/documents/english/icwedece.html.

[58] Agenda 21, United Nations Conference on Environment and Development, Rio de Janeiro, Brazil, 3–14 June 1992, UN Doc. A/CONF/151/26 (Vol. II), http://www.un.org/documents/ga/conf151/aconf15126-2.htm.

[59] *See generally* Reichert (2016), pp. 20–21.

riparian states and their public authorities, water users and the general public—need to be given the opportunity to be heard within decision-making processes.

A major driving force for the promotion of sustainable and integrated water resources management in a transboundary context has been the *Convention on the Protection and Use of Transboundary Watercourses and International Lakes* of 1992 (1992 UNECE Water Convention),[60] which was originally developed as a regional framework convention for European and Central Asian countries under the auspices of the United Nations Economic Commission for Europe (UNECE).[61] In 2016, the 1992 UNECE Water Convention was "globalised" by opening it to all members of the United Nations.[62] Today, it has over 40 parties, including the EU and most of its Member States, Albania, Liechtenstein, Switzerland, countries of the former Republic of Yugoslavia, Russia, Belarus, the Ukraine, Azerbaijan, Kazakhstan, Turkmenistan and Uzbekistan.[63] Together with its *1999 Protocol on Water and Health*,[64] the *2003 Protocol on Civil Liability and Compensation for Damage Caused by the Transboundary Effects of Industrial Accidents on Transboundary Waters*[65] and a vast number of accompanying soft law instruments (recommendations, guidelines, assessment reports, etc.),[66] the 1992 UNECE Water Convention serves as a catalyst for the further development of international water law in Europe and beyond. It does not directly apply to specific water bodies but provides conceptual guidance for the design and further development of international cooperation on the protection and use of specific transboundary freshwater resources. Its elaborate institutional set-up[67]—which comprises a Bureau, regular Meetings of the Parties, an Implementation Committee, a Legal Board, various expert working groups and task forces, and permanent staff provided by the UNECE secretariat—enables the 1992 UNECE Water Convention to assist parties in its implementation.

In line with its character as a framework convention, the 1992 UNECE Water Convention obliges its parties to "enter into bilateral or multilateral agreements or

---

[60]Signed in Helsinki on 17 March 1992, in force 6 October 1996, 1936 UNTS 269. *See generally* Reichert (2016), pp. 21–24.

[61]*See* UNECE website, http://www.unece.org/env/water/.

[62]*See* UNECE Press Release of 13 October 2015, http://www.unece.org/info/media/presscurrent-press-h/environment/2015/ukraine-paves-the-way-for-globalising-the-water-convention/doc.html; *see generally* Trombitcaia and Koeppel (2015).

[63]*See* United Nations Treaty Collection website, https://treaties.un.org/pages/showDetails.aspx?objid=0800000280044685.

[64]Protocol on Water and Health to the 1992 Convention on the Protection and Use of Transboundary Watercourses and International Lakes, signed in London on 17 June 1999, in force 4 August 2005, 38 ILM 1708 (1999).

[65]Protocol on Civil Liability and Compensation for Damage Caused by the Transboundary Effects of Industrial Accidents on Transboundary Waters to the 1992 Convention on the Protection and Use of Transboundary Watercourses and International Lakes and to the 1992 Convention on the Transboundary Effects of Industrial Accidents, signed in Kiev on 21 May 2003, not in force, http://www.unece.org/env/civil-liability/welcome.html.

[66]*See* http://www.unece.org/env/water/publications/pub.html.

[67]Articles 17–19 1992 UNECE Water Convention.

other arrangements, where these do not yet exist, or adapt existing ones, where necessary to eliminate the contradictions with the basic principles of this Convention [...]."[68] Consequently, a considerable number of international agreements regulating specific river basins has been concluded, e.g., regarding the Danube (1994),[69] the Oder (1996)[70] and the Rhine (1999).[71] Riparians in these and other transboundary basins in Europe and beyond adapt the provisions of the 1992 UNECE Water Convention to the specific conditions of the respective water bodies. This process has made international water law in Europe increasingly coherent. In the following parts, its essential substantive and procedural features will be outlined.

4.2 Substantive Features[72]

In line with the 1992 UNECE Water Convention, international agreements on specific transboundary freshwater resources in Europe have followed the overall *leitmotif* of sustainability.[73] Following a holistic approach, their geographical scope is not limited to the mere water body of the relevant river or lake itself, but encompasses the "catchment area," "drainage basin" or "watershed"[74] with the respective surface waters and groundwater,[75] as well as the interconnected aquatic and terrestrial ecosystems. Based on an ecosystem-oriented interpretation[76] of the "no-harm rule," which is well-established in customary international water law,[77] the central obligation of riparian states is to prevent, control and reduce any "transboundary impact" on shared freshwater resources.[78] This is broadly defined

[68]Article 9(1) 1992 UNECE Water Convention.

[69]Convention on Cooperation for the Protection and Sustainable Use of the Danube (1994 Danbube Convention), signed in Sofia on 29 June 1994, in force 22 October 1998, 1997 O.J. (L 342) 19.

[70]Convention on the International Commission for the Protection of the Oder (1996 Oder Convention), signed in Wroclaw on 11 April 1996, in force 26 April 1999, 1998 O.J. (C 316) 6.

[71]Convention on the Protection of the Rhine (1999 Rhine Convention), signed in Berne on 12 April 1999, in force 16 November 2000, 2000 O.J. (L 289) 31.

[72]This section is based on Reichert (2016), pp. 30–35.

[73]*E.g.,* articles 2(5)(c) and 3(1)(i) 1992 UNECE Water Convention; article 2(1), (2) and (5) 1994 Danube Convention; articles 3(1) and 4(1)(g) 1999 Rhine Convention.

[74]*E.g.,* articles 2(6) and 9(2) 1992 UNECE Water Convention; articles 1(b) and 2(1) 1994 Danube Convention; article 2(a)-(e) 1999 Rhine Convention.

[75]*E.g.,* article 1(1) 1992 UNECE Water Convention; article 2(1) 1994 Danube Convention; article 2 (1) 1999 Rhine Convention.

[76]*See* Tanzi and Kolliopoulos (2015).

[77]*E.g.,* article 7 1997 United Nations Convention on the Non-navigational Uses of International Watercourses (1997 UN Watercourses Convention), adopted by the UN General Assembly and opened for signature in New York on 21 May 1997, in force 17 August 2014, 36 ILM 700 (1997).

[78]*E.g.,* articles 2(1)-(2) and 3 1992 UNECE Water Convention; articles 1(c), 2(2), 3(2), 5 and 6 1994 Danube Convention.

in article 1(2) 1992 UNECE Water Convention as "any significant adverse effect on the environment [. . .] caused by a human activity [and having] effects on human health and safety, flora, fauna, soil, air, water, climate, landscape and historical monuments or other physical structures or the interaction among these factors; [. . .] on the cultural heritage or socio-economic conditions resulting from alterations to those factors." The "no-harm rule" is often explicitly accompanied by the principle of cooperation[79] and the principle of equitable utilisation[80] of shared freshwater resources between riparian states. In order to operationalise these obligations, states have to apply a wide spectrum of measures,[81] e.g., the prior authorisation and subsequent control of waste-water discharges by industrial plants[82] or the purification of waste-water by municipalities before its release into the environment.[83]

4.3 Procedural Features

4.3.1 Information, Notification, Consultation and Negotiation[84]

A prerequisite for the implementation of the substantive measures for the holistic, integrated protection and management of freshwater resources is the permanent monitoring of the aquatic environment in order to collect and assess comprehensive, accurate and up-to-date information on its status.[85] In the case of transboundary water bodies, the riparian countries affected need to cooperate closely in order to develop a common understanding of problems, harmonise assessment methods, and share information on the common resource and respective measures.[86] Pursuant to the 1992 UNECE Water Convention, the sharing of information may encompass, *inter alia*, data on conditions of the shared aquatic environment; emissions and monitoring data; measures to prevent, control and reduce transboundary impacts; permits or regulations for waste-water discharges; experience gained in the application and operation of measures; the results of research and development.[87] In this

---

[79] *E.g.*, articles 2(6) and 9 1992 UNECE Water Convention; article 2(2) 1994 Danube Convention; article 1(1)-(2) 1996 Oder Convention. *See* Wouters and Leb (2015), pp. 285–295.

[80] *E.g.*, articles 5 and 6 1997 UN Watercourses Convention; article 2(2)(c) 1992 UNECE Water Convention; articles 2(1) and 6 1994 Danube Convention. *See* McIntyre (2015), pp. 146–159.

[81] Article 3(1)-(3) 1992 UNECE Water Convention.

[82] *E.g.*, article 7(5)(b) 1994 Danube Convention.

[83] *E.g.*, article 7(1) 1994 Danube Convention.

[84] This section is based on Reichert (2016), pp. 30–32.

[85] *E.g.*, articles 4 and 11 1992 UNECE Water Convention; article 9 1994 Danube Convention; article 2(1)(d) and (f) 1996 Oder Convention.

[86] *E.g.*, article 6 1992 UNECE Water Convention; articles 4(b) and 12 1994 Danube Convention; article 2(1)(k) 1996 Oder Convention. *See* Lipponen and Kauppi (2015), pp. 251–267.

[87] Article 13(1)-(2) 1992 UNECE Water Convention.

respect, the 1992 UNECE Water Convention[88] also requires riparian states to inform the general public on the conditions of transboundary waters and on measures to prevent, control and reduce the transboundary impact.[89] The duty to exchange information between riparian states also comprises the well-established obligation of customary international water law[90] to notify other riparians of planned measures or projects with potentially significant transboundary effects. In the event of sudden critical situations—such as accidental spills of hazardous substances, floods or droughts—riparian states are obliged to inform each other immediately of potential transboundary impacts[91] and provide mutual assistance upon request.[92] As a preventive measure, riparians are encouraged to set up warning and alarm systems.[93] In the case of conflicts on transboundary impacts, riparians are bound to comply with the general procedural obligations to consult[94] and to seek peaceful solutions through negotiations or other means of dispute settlement.[95]

4.3.2 Institutionalised Cooperation: International River Commissions[96]

As the successful cooperation within the ICPR framework following the Sandoz Spill has shown, international cooperation on transboundary freshwater resources can profit considerably from a stable institutional framework, within which riparian states can fulfill their respective procedural obligations on a permanent basis. To this end, the 1992 UNECE Water Convention requires the establishment of so-called "joint bodies,"[97] defined as "any bilateral or multilateral commission or other appropriate institutional arrangements for cooperation between Riparian Parties."[98] Subsequently, riparian states in Europe have set up such "joint bodies" for the protection of shared water bodies in various basins, including the Danube,[99]

[88] Article 16 1992 UNECE Water Convention. *See* Vykhryst (2015), pp. 268–282.

[89] *E.g.*, article 14 1994 Danube Convention; article 8(4) 1999 Rhine Convention.

[90] E.g., articles 12 and 18 1997 UN Watercourses Convention.

[91] *E.g.*, article 28(1)-(3) 1997 UN Watercourses Convention; article 14 first sentence 1992 UNECE Water Convention; article 16(3)-(4) 1994 Danube Convention; article 5(6) 1999 Rhine Convention.

[92] Article 15 1992 UNECE Water Convention; article 17 1994 Danube Convention.

[93] *E.g.*, article 28(4) 1997 UN Watercourses Convention; article 14 1992 UNECE Water Convention.

[94] *E.g.*, articles 17 and 24 1997 UN Watercourses Convention; article 10 1992 UNECE Water Convention; articles 4(a) and 11 1994 Danube Convention.

[95] *E.g.*, article 33 1997 UN Watercourses Convention; article 22 1992 UNECE Water Convention; article 24 1994 Danube Convention.

[96] This section is based on Reichert (2016), pp. 32–35.

[97] Article 9(2) 1992 UNECE Water Convention.

[98] Article 1(5) 1992 UNECE Water Convention.

[99] International Commission for the Protection of the Danube River, http://www.icpdr.org/main.

Meuse,[100] Scheldt,[101] Oder,[102] and Sava.[103] According to the 1992 UNECE Water Convention, the manifold tasks of international river commissions should, *inter alia*, encompass[104] the collection, compilation and evaluation of data in order to identify pollution sources likely to have a transboundary impact; the elaboration of joint monitoring programmes concerning water quality and quantity; the development of inventories and exchange of information on pollution sources; the evaluation of the effectiveness of control programmes; the development of joint programmes for the reduction of pollution; the establishment of warning and alarm procedures; and the exchange of information on existing and planned uses of water and related installations likely to result in a transboundary impact.

The organisational structure of "joint bodies" typically comprises a commission, various expert groups and a secretariat.[105] A commission usually consists of representatives of the participating parties who take decisions by consensus.[106] It can be supported by permanent or *ad hoc* expert groups for the provision of advice on specific scientific, technical or legal issues. A permanent secretariat may be entrusted with administrative tasks. While decisions of international river commissions are normally merely non-binding proposals or recommendations,[107] they nevertheless exert considerable influence on the development of international cooperation in a specific basin.

5 The Normative Influence of EU Water Law[108]

When dealing with the essential substantive and procedural features of today's international water law in Europe, one must also be aware of the defining normative influence of the water legislation of the European Union (EU). Since its adoption in 2000, the EU Water Framework Directive (WFD)[109] in combination with other EU

[100]International Commission for the Protection of the Meuse River, http://www.cipm-icbm.be.

[101]International Scheldt Commission, http://www.isc-cie.org.

[102]International Commission for the Protection of the Oder Against Pollution, http://www.mkoo.pl.

[103]International Sava River Basin Commission, http://www.savacommission.org.

[104]Article 9(2) 1992 UNECE Water Convention.

[105]*E.g.*, article 18 and Annex IV 1994 Danube Convention; articles 6–12 1999 Rhine Convention; article 5 2002 Meuse Convention.

[106]*E.g.*, article 10(1) 1999 Rhine Convention; article 5(4) first sentence 2002 Meuse Convention. For a "four-fifths" majority voting in exceptional cases *see* article 5(1) third sentence Annex IV 1994 Danube Convention.

[107]*E.g.*, article 11(1) 1999 Rhine Convention; article 5(4) 2002 Meuse Convention. For legally binding effects of decisions *see* article 5(2) Annex IV 1994 Danube Convention.

[108]For a detailed discussion of EU water law and its normative influence on international water law in Europe *see* Reichert (2016), pp. 35–103.

[109]Directive of the European Parliament and of the Council of 23 October 2000 establishing a framework for Community action in the field of water policy, 2000 O.J. (L 327) 1.

legislative acts has shaped not only the national water legislation of EU member states but also their international relations regarding transboundary freshwater resources. The normative clout of the WFD in this respect[110] arises from the far-reaching legislative competences of the EU for environmental protection[111]; the direct binding effect[112] of EU legislative acts[113] on EU member states; the primacy of EU law over the national laws of EU member states[114]; the powers of both the European Commission[115] and the Court of Justice of the European Union (CJEU)[116] for respective compliance and enforcement measures[117]; and the legal capacity of the EU to become a contracting party to international water agreements.[118]

The WFD aims at "maintaining and improving the aquatic environment" in the EU.[119] Its regulatory purposes comprise, *inter alia*, the protection of surface waters and groundwater[120] along with the interconnected terrestrial ecosystems and wetlands,[121] the promotion of sustainable water use,[122] and the mitigation of floods and droughts.[123] With regard to international water cooperation, the WFD is intends to contribute to achieving the objectives of international agreements on freshwater resources.[124]

---

[110] *See* Reichert (2016), pp. 35–44.

[111] Article 191–193 of the Treaty on the Functioning of the European Union (TFEU). *See* Consolidated Version of the TFEU, signed in Rome on 25 March 1957, in force 1 January 1958, 2012 O.J. (C 326) 47, last amended by the Treaty of Lisbon, signed in Lisbon on 13 December 2007, in force 1 December 2009, 2007 O.J. (C 306) 1, 2007 O.J. (C 306) 1.

[112] Court of Justice, judgment of 5 February 1963, *N.V. Algemene Transport- en Expeditie Onderneming van Gend & Loos v. Nederlandse Administratie der Belastingen*, C-26/62, EU: C:1963:1, 1963 E.C.R. 1(12-13).

[113] Article 288 TFEU.

[114] Declaration No 17 concerning primacy, annexed to the Final Act of the Intergovernmental Conference which adopted the Treaty of Lisbon, signed on 13 December 2007, in force 1 December 2009, 2012 O.J. (C 326) 346, explicitly referring to the established case law of the Court of Justice, e.g., judgment of 15 July 1964, *Flaminio Costa v. E.N.E.L.*, C-6/64, EU:C:1964:66, 1964 E.C.R. 585(593), and judgment of 9 March 1978, *Amministrazione delle Finanze dello Stato v. Simmenthal S.p.A.*, C-106/77, EU:C:1978:49, 1978 E.C.R. 629.

[115] Article 17(1) second and third sentence of the Treaty on European Union (TEU). *See* Consolidated Version of the TEU, signed in Maastricht on 7 February 1992, in force 1 November 1993, 2012 O.J. (C 326) 13, last amended by the Treaty of Lisbon, signed in Lisbon on 13 December 2007, in force 1 December 2009, 2007 O.J. (C 306) 1.

[116] Article 19(1) second sentence TEU.

[117] Articles 259 and 260 TFEU.

[118] Article 191(4) and article 216 TFEU.

[119] Preamble recital 19 WFD.

[120] Article 2(2) and (4)-(7) WFD.

[121] Article 1(a) WFD.

[122] Article 1(b) WFD.

[123] Article 1(e) WFD.

[124] Article 1 fourth indent WFD.

To realise the purposes of the WFD, EU member states must achieve specific "environmental objectives" regarding the ecological status of surface water,[125] groundwater[126] and "protected areas."[127] These environmental objectives are to be pursued within administrative units called "river basin districts" (RBDs).[128] A transboundary river basin which covers the territory of more than one EU member state has to be assigned to an "international RBD."[129] Consequently, EU member states sharing an international RBD are obliged to coordinate the implementation of the WFD.[130] In transboundary river basins extending beyond the territory of the EU, such as the Danube and the Rhine, EU member states must at least "endeavour" to "establish appropriate coordination" with third countries "with the aim of achieving the objectives" of the WFD throughout the international RBD.[131] By pursuing basin-wide coordination both among EU member states and with third countries, the WFD aims "to contribute to the implementation" of the obligations of the EU "under international conventions on water protection and management," expressly those pursuant to the 1992 UNECE Water Convention "and any succeeding agreements on its application."[132] In order to implement the WFD within each RBD, the EU member states designated a "competent authority"[133] which could be an existing "national or international body."[134] With regard to transboundary RBDs, the WFD expressly allows the designation of "existing structures stemming from international agreements."[135] Accordingly, a river basin commission established under international water law can be entrusted with the task of implementing the requirements of EU water law. In this way, the WFD creates a legal nexus between EU water law and international water law which has enabled the gradual development of a "multidimensional regime" for the management and protection of transboundary freshwater resources in Europe.[136]

EU member states are obliged to ensure that for each RBD, or for the portion of an international RBD lying within its territory, an integrated "programme of measures"[137] is drawn up in order to achieve the environmental objectives of the WFD.[138] In order to make the programme of measures in each RBD operational,

[125]Article 4(1)(a) WFD.

[126]Article 4(1)(b) WFD.

[127]Article 4(1)(c) WFD.

[128]Article 2(15) WFD.

[129]Article 3(3) WFD.

[130]Aricle 3(4) WFD.

[131]Aricle 3(5) WFD.

[132]Preamble recital 35 third sentence WFD.

[133]Article 3(2), (3) and (7) *in conjunction with* articles 2(16) and 24(1) WFD.

[134]Article 3(6) WFD.

[135]Article 3(4) WFD.

[136]Reichert (2016), pp. 2–3, 4–6, 91–97 and 100–103.

[137]*Ibid.*, pp. 77–80.

[138]Preample recital 26 and article 11(1) WFD.

all relevant information must be compiled in a "river basin management plan" (RBMP). In the case of an international RBD entirely within the EU, the EU member states concerned have to ensure coordination with the aim of producing a single "international RBMP."[139] For an international RBD extending beyond the EU, the EU member states concerned must at least "endeavour" to produce a single RBMP together with the third countries concerned.[140] In this way, the international RBMPs developed within the institutional framework of international river commissions transpose the substantive and procedural provisions of EU water law into international water law. Therefore, international RBMPs are the central interface of the multidimensional regime for the management and protection of transboundary freshwater resources in Europe.

Since the entry into force of the WFD in 2000, EU water law has exerted a formative influence on international water law in Europe.[141] The WFD is explicitly referred to in subsequent international water conventions such as the 2002 Sava Agreement.[142] The contracting parties to international water conventions, e.g., on the Danube[143] and the Rhine[144] have repeatedly declared their commitment to the implementation of the WFD via international RBMPs. By 2012, out of 105 transboundary river basins (75 basins and 30 sub-basins) identified in Europe, ten had developed international RBMPs, and a further 47 international RBMPs were planned.[145] By the end of 2015, new international RBMPs[146] had been adopted, *inter alia*, for the Danube[147] and the Rhine.[148]

---

[139] Article 13(2) WFD.

[140] Article 13(3) WFD.

[141] *See* Reichert (2016), pp. 91–97.

[142] Article 3(2) Framework Agreement on the Sava River Basin between Bosnia and Herzegovina, Croatia, Slovenia and the Federal Republic of Yugoslavia (2002 Sava Agreement), signed in Kranjska Gora on 3 December 2002, in force 29 December 2004, 2366 UNTS 479.

[143] Danube Declarations adopted at the Ministerial Meetings of the ICPDR on 13 December 2004, on 16 February 2010, and on 9 February 2016, www.icpdr.org/main/publications/legal-documents.

[144] Ministerial Declarations adopted by all riparians of the Rhine basin at the Conferences of Rhine Ministers on 29 January 2001, on 18 October 2007, and on 28 October 2013, www.iksr.org/en/international-cooperation/conferences-of-ministers/.

[145] Vogel et al. (2012), p. 169.

[146] For an overview of international RBMPs and the status of implementation of the WFD in EU member states *see* http://ec.europa.eu/environment/water/participation/mapmc/map.htm.

[147] ICPDR (2015), Danube River Basin District Management Plan – Update 2015, www.icpdr.org/main/activities-projects/river-basin-management-plan-update-2015.

[148] ICPR (2015), Second Internationally Coordinated Management Plan for the International River Basin District of the Rhine – Part A = Overriding Part, www.iksr.org/en/water-framework-directive/river-basin-management-plan-2015/.

6 Conclusion: European Lessons for the Nile Basin Countries?

By and large, the multidimensional regime for the protection and management of transboundary freshwater resources in Europe has been successful in fostering international cooperation between riparian states. With regard to this remarkable development, two questions are of special interest: (1) What are important factors that made the difference compared to earlier attempts to solve international water conflicts, e.g., in the Rhine basin prior to the Sandoz Spill? (2) What lessons can be learned from European experiences which might also provide useful insights and fruitful inspiration for international cooperation between riparian states in the Nile basin? Both questions, however, could raise caveats:

With regard to the first question, one should bear in mind that factors fostering international cooperation in general and regarding shared freshwater resources in particular are not predominantly legal in nature. Strong political will for cooperation, shared perceptions and concurrence of interests between riparians, as well as favourable economic and social conditions play a pivotal role.[149] On the other hand, the development of the legal regime for international water cooperation in Europe shows that substantive and procedural legal provisions can play a helpful supporting role in facilitating successful international cooperation between riparian states.

With regard to the second question on useful insights from the European experience for international cooperation in the Nile basin, one could argue that the European Union provides such favourable and incomparable conditions for international cooperation in general and for the protection and management of transboundary water resources in particular that no valuable conclusions can be derived from these specific circumstances for the resolution of international water conflicts in other regions of the world. Indeed, the degree of political, economic and legal integration between EU member states is exceptional. On the other hand, at least in the beginning, the conflict structure in most European transboundary basins was similar to other international disputes between riparian states of the Nile: The archetypal upstream-downstream constellation between riparian states was the defining characteristic of water conflicts, for example, caused by transboundary salinisation and other water pollution of the Rhine. Given this similarity, it is worthwhile to identify some essential factors which contributed to the development of close and successful international cooperation on shared freshwater resources in Europe.

[149] Bernauer (2002), p. 2.

6.1 *Shifting the Paradigm: From Coexistence to Cooperation*

6.1.1 The Paradigm of Coexistence

Until the Sandoz Spill in 1986, international water law in Europe in general and with regard to the Rhine in particular was characterised by ad-hoc attempts to solve specific, narrowly defined conflicts over antagonistic interests between upstream and downstream riparians on discharges of certain substances. Such upstream-downstream conflicts on transboundary rivers are least conducive to cooperation.[150] In political and economic terms, this conflict constellation is "asymmetrical" in the sense that the upstream riparian is in a more powerful position compared to downstream riparians. Due to its geographical advantage, an upstream riparian can, at least in theory, unilaterally impose or "externalise" the "cost" of its water use—e.g., by minimising the water quantity through extraction or impairing the water quality through pollution—on the downstream riparians.

Early discussions at the cradle of international water law clearly reflected the respective antagonistic interests of upstream and downstream riparians. The "law of the strongest" was at the core of the infamous "Harmon doctrine" which was propagated by U.S. attorney general *Judson Harmon* in 1895 in a water conflict between the U.S. as the upstream riparian and Mexico as the downstream riparian concerning the Rio Grande: "The fundamental principle of international law is the absolute sovereignty of every nation, against all others, within its own territory. [...] The fact that the Rio Grande lacks sufficient water to permit its use by inhabitants of both countries does not entitle Mexico to impose restrictions on the United States which would hamper the development of the latter's territory or deprive its inhabitants of an advantage with which nature had endowed them and which is situated entirely within its territory. To admit such a right would be completely contrary to the principle that the United States exercises full sovereignty over its natural territory."[151] Also derived from the claim of "full sovereignty" is the opposing principle of "absolute territorial integrity" which protects the interests of downstream riparians. It was formulated by *Max Huber* in 1907 on the occasion of a water conflict between Swiss cantons as follows: "[No State is allowed to] divert water to the detriment of one or more other States entitled to use [a transboundary] river, to interrupt its course, or to artificially increase or reduce its flow."[152] Although riparian states have repeatedly invoked the principles of absolute territorial sovereignty (e.g. India with regard to the Indus[153]) or absolute territorial integrity (e.g. Egypt with regard to the Nile[154]), they usually did not maintain this position. Even the

[150]Bernauer (2002), p. 6.

[151]Official Opinions of the US Attorney General, Volume XXI (1898), p. 274. *See generally* McCaffrey (2007), p. 76.

[152]Huber (1906), p. 160.

[153]*See* Salman and Uprety (2002), p. 41.

[154]*See* Ule (1998), p. 125.

U.S.-Mexico water conflict, which led to the formulation of the Harmon doctrine, was finally settled through a treaty. Both principles are not recognised under international law. They exclude each other in their respective claims to absoluteness and—within a legal system based on the equal sovereignty of states—inevitably require relativisation through mutual restriction.

In this respect, today's international water law provides two basic substantive principles in order to balance competing interests of riparians. First, the principle of "equitable utilisation"—which is well established under customary international water law and codified by article 5 of the 1997 UN Watercourses Convention[155]—stipulates that all riparians to a transboundary river, lake or aquifer are entitled to participate in its use. It is based on the idea that the right of a riparian state to exercise territorial sovereignty over that part of a transboundary freshwater body situated within its territory also includes the obligation to respect the equal sovereignty of other riparian states and to enable them to make appropriate use of the common resource. At the core of the principle of "equitable utilisation" is a comprehensive balancing or weighing process regarding the various interests of the riparian states which, in principle, requires that all relevant facts and circumstances of the individual case be taken into account. In this respect, article 6(2) of the 1997 UN Watercourses Convention provides an extensive—albeit non-exhaustive—list of potential weighing criteria which, *inter alia*, also includes "existing and potential uses of the watercourse." Second, international water law—e.g., article 7 of the 1997 UN Watercourses Convention—also recognises the prohibition of significant transboundary harm. According to this "no-harm rule," riparians are not allowed to perform or permit any water-related activities on their territory that would lead to "significant" damage to other riparians and thereby violate their territorial integrity. Obviously, downstream riparians can be harmed by impacts originating in the territory of upstream riparians, e.g., by the construction of dams decreasing water quantity or through pollution causing the deterioration of water quality. It is not widely realised, however, that upstream riparians can also be harmed "by the potential foreclosure of their future use of water, caused by the prior use, and the claiming of rights to such water by the downstream riparians."[156] Furthermore, what constitutes "significant" damage or harm is a question prone to diverging interpretation.

Given the respective ambiguities, it is more than questionable whether on an abstract level a general determination of the relationship between the principle of equitable utilisation and the no-harm rule is possible at all. Furthermore, a perceived dichotomy of the two basic principles of international water law in the form of an antagonistic, mutually exclusive understanding of the principle of equitable utilisation—as often claimed by upstream riparians—and the no-harm rule—as

[155]United Nations Convention on the Non-navigational Uses of International Watercourses (1997 UN Watercourses Convention), adopted by the UN General Assembly and opened for signature in New York on 21 May 1997, in force 17 August 2014, 36 ILM 700 (1997).

[156]Salman (2019), p. 116.

often propagated by downstream riparians—can only lead to a legal impasse. Therefore, the relationship between both principles must be clarified and reconciled in each individual case.[157] Consequently, both substantive principles of international water law provide in themselves only limited guidance for the resolution of international water conflicts. They must be further specified and also supplemented by additional procedural obligations regarding the exchange of information, notification, consultation and negotiation. Such elaborate sets of substantive and procedural rules on international water law issues facilitate the balancing of competing interests of upstream and downstream riparians, thereby enabling them to coexist. Therefore, they might be characterised as being governed by a "paradigm of coexistence." Both global framework water conventions which are open to all members of the United Nations—the 1997 UN Watercourses Convention and the 1992 UNECE Water Convention—offer such sets of model regulations which can be very helpful, also for the riparian states of the Nile, as they design their legal relationships in terms of shared freshwater resources.

One practical example for negotiated substantive and procedural rules on a shared water body are the aforementioned efforts of the riparians of the Rhine to solve their water conflicts within the framework of the ICPR since the early 1950s and also by the 1976 Rhine Chlorides Convention and the 1976 Rhine Chemical Convention. However, as the Sandoz Spill in 1986 clearly demonstrated, these legally-binding attempts proved to be inadequate and inferior to the more informal 1987 Rhine Action Programme and subsequent programmes. Therefore, the question arises as to what made the difference.

6.1.2 The Paradigm of Cooperation

In essence, the Sandoz Spill prompted the Rhine riparians to shift the paradigm of their efforts to resolve their water conflicts from one of coexistence to one of cooperation. A major driving force for this development was the strong public pressure and political support in all riparian countries for the new programmes which compensated for their lack of legal clout.[158] With regard to substantive aspects of the new approach, the focus shifted away from ad-hoc attempts to solve specific, narrowly defined conflicts over antagonistic interests between upstream and downstream riparians regarding discharges of certain substances, to establish instead the holistic goal of restoring and protecting the ecosystem of the Rhine as a whole. Most importantly, protecting and managing the Rhine ecosystem following the emerging *leitmotif* of sustainability was a *common* target shared by all riparians. Perceiving the Rhine ecosystem as a "public good"[159] enabled a shift from the mere balancing of coexisting interests to a more intensive stage of cooperation. Pursuing

[157] ILA (2004), p. 21.

[158] For the following *see also* Irmer (1998), pp. 113–119.

[159] Bernauer (2002), p. 8.

this ambitious aim was supported through the choice of salmon—a species which by nature needs to travel through the entire stream of the Rhine from the North Sea to the Alps—as an indicator for the effectiveness of the measures for the restoration of the Rhine's aquatic ecosystem. It set a visible goal and powerful symbol[160] which motivated the riparian states to intensify their efforts, provided prestige benefits for success, encouraged further cooperation and could also be easily communicated to the general public.

Similarly, the Nile riparians in general and those affected by the GERD in particular could shift their focus away from attempts only to solve narrowly defined conflicts towards the common management of the shared river and its resources as a whole, based upon the key principles, procedures and institutional mechanisms considered above. This could also include the identification of common projects—such as power generation, irrigation, flood control or environmental protection—and the sharing of their benefits. Successful benefit sharing could, over time, create a sense of community amongst Nile basin countries.

6.2 Changing the Focus: From Substantive to Procedural Regulations

The paradigm shift in the relations between the riparians of the Rhine characterised by a redefined substantive objective and common goal was accompanied by a profound change in the procedural approach. While the 1976 Rhine Chemical Convention provided for the legally binding adoption of strict emission limit values through cumbersome formal ratification processes governed by international law, the more informal 1987 Rhine Action Programme set general, but verifiable objectives to be achieved within a certain timeframe and allowed for their flexible operationalisation through specific measures to be continuously developed within the ICPR and further specified by the Rhine riparian countries. Progress was monitored and reported regularly to the ICPR, enabling fact-based stocktaking, the detection of shortcomings and the swift adaptation of goals and measures.

From this, two main conclusions can be drawn which could also be applied to future cooperation between the Nile basin countries: First, it is essential that riparians collect and share all relevant information regarding the problems they seek to solve. In this respect, international water law has developed model sets of procedural regulations—as codified, e.g., by the 1997 UN Watercourses Convention,[161] the 1992 UNECE Water Convention[162] and the CFA itself[163]—which facilitate the collection and exchange of information between riparian states. Second, successful

[160]Durth (1996), p. 311; Bernauer (2002), p. 14.

[161]*E.g.*, article 9, 11–15 1997 UN Watercourses Convention.

[162]*E.g.*, article 6, 9 and 11 1992 UNECE Water Convention.

[163]Article 3 CFA.

cooperation is facilitated through a gradual and flexible approach[164] which allows riparians over time to learn as much as possible about the problems they are attempting to address by gathering and analysing information, to develop and negotiate appropriate measures, and to be able to adjust them if necessary.

6.3 *Building Trust: International River Commissions and "Epistemic Communities"*

The implementation of the Rhine action programmes with its built-in learning-process was facilitated by the joint efforts of over 150 experts. The secretariat of the ICPR coordinated their meetings, informed the general public and established contacts with industry, municipalities and environmental NGOs. Over time, expertise was built within public administrations and public support for common goals and implementation measures was established.

Over the decades, international river commissions such as the ICPR for the management and protection of freshwater resources have served riparian states in many European basins as international *fora* for the collection and exchange of information as well as for notification, consultation, negotiation and conflict resolution.[165] This institutionalisation of international cooperation can over a long period of time facilitate the gradual creation of knowledge and the development of expertise and experience based on long-lasting, stable working relationships across disciplines, hierarchies and borders. As such, they have the potential to function as focal points for "epistemic communities," which may be defined as interdisciplinary networks of experts—government officials, scientists, economists, lawyers, etc.—in a specific issue area. These expert networks can gradually develop and share common values, causal beliefs, patterns of reasoning and policy approaches in order to pursue common objectives.[166] They can be very instrumental for drawing up appropriate and robust solutions for water-related problems, for learning from regulatory failures and for reacting expeditiously to new challenges. In this respect, the example of international cooperation on the Rhine within the ICPR following the Sandoz Spill has demonstrated that cooperative and flexible approaches based on expertise can be more successful than conflict-focused ad-hoc attempts to adopt legally binding regulations for a limited number of problems through contentious negotiation processes and lengthy ratification procedures. Therefore, the Nile basin countries are strongly advised to establish a robust institutional framework to facilitate their cooperation either by realising the establishment of the Nile River

[164]Bernauer (2002), p. 16.

[165]*See* Reichert (2016), p. 98.

[166]*See generally* Haas (1992), p. 3. For a discussion of "epistemic communities" in the specific context of international cooperation on transboundary freshwater resources *see* Brunnée and Toope (1997), pp. 34–35.

Basin Commission stipulated in Part III of the CFA or by negotiating and creating a new legal framework to that effect.

Most importantly, such institutionalised cooperation in the form of international river commissions accompanied by "epistemic communities" is essential for gradually building mutual understanding and trust among all actors involved, most importantly between the representatives of the riparian states concerned. Ultimately, a minimum of good faith and mutual trust is the *conditio sine qua non* for successful and sustainable cooperation of riparians sharing transboundary freshwater resources in all regions of the earth. Given their long history of water conflicts, this is especially true for the riparians of the Nile.

References

Bernauer T (1995) The international financing of environmental protection: lessons from the efforts to protect the river Rhine against Chloride Pollution. Environ Politics 4:369–390

Bernauer T (2002) Explaining success and failure in international river management. Aquat Sci 64:1–19

Birnie P, Boyle A, Regdwell C (2009) International environmental law & the environment. Oxford University Press, Oxford

Boisson de Chazournes L (2008) The Rhine Chlorides arbitration concerning the auditing of accounts (Netherlands – France): its contribution to international law. In: Permanent Court of Arbitration (ed) The Rhine Chlorides arbitration concerning the auditing of accounts (Netherlands-France): Award of 2004. T.M.C. Asser Press, Den Haag, pp 1–15

Brunnée J, Toope S (1997) Environmental security and freshwater resources: ecosystem regime building. Am J Int Law 91:26–59

Burgen S (2017) Tagus river at risk of drying up completely. The Guardian (14 August 2017). https://www.theguardian.com/environment/2017/aug/14/tagus-river-at-risk-of-drying-up-completely

de Villeneuve C (1996) Western Europe's Artery: The Rhine. Nat Resour J 36:441–454

Durth R (1996) Grenzüberschreitende Umweltprobleme und regionale Integration: Zur politischen Ökonomie von Oberlauf-Unterlauf-Problemen an internationalen Flüssen. Nomos-Verlagsgesellschaft, Baden-Baden

Ezega News (2017) Ethiopian Renaissance Dam Generation Capacity Revised Up to 6,450 MW, (25 February 2017). www.ezega.com/News/NewsDetails/3978/Ethiopian-Renaissance-Dam-Generation-Capacity-Revised-Up-to-6-450MW

Haas P (1992) Epistemic communities and international policy coordination. Int Organ 46:1–35

Huber M (1906) Ein Beitrag zur Lehre von der Gebietshoheit an Grenzflüssen, Zeitschrift für Völkerrecht und Bundesstaatsrecht 1:29-52 and 1:159-217

ICPDR (2015) Danube River Basin District Management Plan – Update 2015

ICPR (2003) Upstream – Outcome of the Rhine Action Programme

ICPR (2015) Second internationally coordinated management plan for the International River Basin District of the Rhine – Part A = Overriding Part

International Law Association (2004) Berlin Conference 2004 – Water Resources. https://slidelegend.com/international-law-association-international-water-law-project59da87aa1723dd355399be23.html

Irmer H (1998) Prerequisites for effective river Basin Management – the case of the river Rhine. In: Landsberg-Uczciwek M, Adriaanse M, Enderlein R (eds) The international conference on management of transboundary waters in Europe – 22–25 September 1997. Mrzeżyno, Warsaw, pp 113–119

Lammers J (1984) Pollution of international watercourses – a search for substantive rules and principles of law. Martinus Nijhoff, Boston

Lazarus S (2018) Is Ethiopia taking control of the river Nile? CNN (21 October 2018). https://edition.cnn.com/2018/10/19/africa/ethiopia-new-dam-threatens-egypts-water/index.html

Lipponen A, Kauppi L (2015) Monitoring and assessment and the duty of cooperation under the water convention: exchange of information among the riparian parties. In: Tanzi A et al (eds) The UNECE convention on the protection and use of transboundary watercourses and international lakes: its contribution on international water cooperation. Brill Nijhoff, Leiden, pp 251–267

McCaffrey S (2007) The law of international watercourses. Oxford University Press, Oxford

McIntyre O (2015) The principle of equitable and reasonable utilisation. In: Tanzi et al (eds) The UNECE convention on the protection and use of transboundary watercourses and international lakes: its contribution on international water cooperation. Brill Nijhoff, Leiden, pp 146–159

Nollkaemper A (1996) The river Rhine: from equal apportionment to ecosystem protection. Rev Eur Commun Int Environ Law 5:152–160

Reichert G (2005) Der nachhaltige Schutz grenzübergreifender Gewässer in Europa – Die Entstehung eines völker- und europarechtlichen Umweltregimes. Duncker & Humblot, Berlin

Reichert G (2016) Transboundary water cooperation in Europe – a successful multidimensional regime? Brill Res Perspect Int Water Law 1:1–111. Brill Nijhoff, Leiden

Salman S (2006) International water disputes: a new breed of claims, claimants, and settlement institutions. Water Int 31:2–11

Salman S (2017a) The Nile basin cooperative framework agreement – disentangling the Gordian Knot. In: Yihdego Z, Rieu-Clarke A, Cascão A (eds) The Grand Ethiopian Renaissance Dam and the Nile basin – implications for transboundary water cooperation. Routledge, London, pp 18–40

Salman S (2017b) Agreement on declaration of principles on the GERD – levelling the Nile basin playing field. In: Yihdego Z, Rieu-Clarke A, Cascão A (eds) The Grand Ethiopian Renaissance Dam and the Nile basin – implications for transboundary water cooperation. Routledge, London, pp 41–60

Salman S (2019) The obligation not to cause significant harm. In: Boisson de Chazournes L et al (eds) The United Nations Convention on the law of the non-navigational uses of international watercourse – a commentary. Oxford University Press, Oxford, pp 95–122

Salman S, Uprety K (2002) Conflict and cooperation on South Asia's international rivers: a legal perspective. Brill Nijhoff, Leiden

Sands P (1998) Watercourses, environment and the international court of justice: the Gabcikovo-Nagymaros Case. In: Salman S, Boisson de Chazournes L (eds) International Watercourses: Enhancing Cooperation and Managing Conflict – Proceedings of a World Bank Seminar, World Bank Technical Paper No 414, Washington D.C., pp 103–107

Schwabach A (1989) The Sandoz Spill: the failure of international law to protect the Rhine from pollution. Ecol Law Q 16:443–480

Steck S, Eckstein G (1997) Of solemn oaths and obligations: the environmental impact of the ICJ's decision in the case concerning the Gabčíkovo-Nagymaros Project. YIEL 8:41–50

Tanzi A, Kolliopoulos A (2015) The no-harm rule. In: Tanzi et al (eds) The UNECE convention on the protection and use of transboundary watercourses and international lakes: its contribution on international water cooperation. Brill Nijhoff, Leiden, pp 133–145

Trombitcaia I, Koeppel S (2015) From a regional towards a global instrument – the 2003 amendment to the UNECE Water Convention. In: Tanzi A et al (eds) The UNECE convention on the protection and use of transboundary watercourses and international lakes: its contribution on international water cooperation. Brill Nijhoff, Leiden, pp 15–31

Ule C (1998) Das Recht am Wasser – Dargestellt am Beispiel des Nils. Nomos Verlagsgesellschaft, Baden-Baden

Vogel B et al (2012) Part V: international coordination. In: WRc plc (ed) Comparative study of pressures and measures in the major river basin management plans, pp 145–176

Vykhryst S (2015) Public information and participation under the water convention. In: Tanzi et al (eds) The UNECE convention on the protection and use of transboundary watercourses and international lakes: its contribution on international water cooperation. Brill Nijhoff, Leiden, pp 268–282

Wieriks J (1998) Prerequisites for effective river basin management – the case of the river Rhine. In: Landsberg-Uczciwek M, Adriaanse M, Enderlein R (eds) The international conference on management of transboundary waters in Europe – 22–25 September 1997. Mrzeżyno, Warsaw, pp 121–134

Wouters P, Leb C (2015) The duty to cooperate in international law – examining the contribution of the UN water conventions to facilitating transboundary water cooperation. In: Tanzi et al (eds) The UNECE convention on the protection and use of transboundary watercourses and international lakes: its contribution on international water cooperation. Brill Nijhoff, Leiden, pp 285–295

Yihdego Z, Rieu-Clarke A, Cascão A (2017) The Grand Ethiopian Renaissance Dam and the Nile basin – implications for transboundary water cooperation. Routledge, London

Zamparutti T (2012) Part I: overview. In: WRc plc (ed) Comparative study of pressures and measures in the major river basin management plans, pp 1–51

Götz Reichert is Head of the Department on Environment, Energy, Climate and Transport at the Centre for European Policy, Freiburg, Germany; and formerly Legal Consultant for the World Bank.

Production Sharing Agreements in Africa: Sovereignty and Relationality

John Paterson

Abstract This paper considers Desta's critique of how contracts in the extractive industries involving host nations in Sub-Saharan Africa and international companies have been drafted and adjudicated. It first sets out the options that the state has in setting out a legal framework for the development of its hydrocarbon sector before going on to examine the dynamic risk matrix that characterises oil and gas projects. It then sets out the principles underpinning the design of fiscal systems for upstream oil and gas. With these foundations laid, the paper goes on to complexify the understanding of stabilisation in modern state-investor contracts, first, in terms of self-adjustment mechanisms and, secondly, in terms of the shift towards economic equilibrium clauses. It then examines the extent to which these contracts are best understood as relational in nature and concludes by proposing the development of principles to guide arbitral adjustment of contract terms based on this observation.

1 Introduction

In his paper "Competition for Natural Resources and International Investment Law: Perspectives from Africa", which appeared in the first issue of the *Ethiopian Yearbook of International Law*, Melaku Geboye Desta raises important questions about the way in which contracts in the extractive industries involving host nations in Sub-Saharan Africa and international companies have been drafted and adjudicated. Noting the challenge to sovereignty inherent in these arrangements both in terms of legislative jurisdiction (involving such phenomena as the internationalisation of contracts and the use of stabilisation clauses) and of judicial jurisdiction (involving international arbitration in place of domestic courts), Desta concludes that African nations can push back against this situation by adopting a

J. Paterson (✉)
School of Law, University of Aberdeen, Aberdeen, UK
e-mail: j.paterson@abdn.ac.uk

Z. Yihdego et al. (eds.), *Ethiopian Yearbook of International Law 2018*, Ethiopian Yearbook of International Law 2018, https://doi.org/10.1007/978-3-030-24078-3_6

common approach to the review, termination and renegotiation of such contracts.[1] As tough as such suggestions may sound to lawyers in other jurisdictions,[2] there is certainly evidence that there is an appetite for such a strong stance, for example, in the form of recent Tanzanian legislation which explicitly empowers the legislature to review both new and existing natural resource contracts and, where it finds that they contain "unconscionable" terms, to "advise" the government to commence renegotiation in order to rectify the situation.[3] The term "advise" turns out to be inaccurate, however, as the statute goes on to oblige the government to serve notice of intention to renegotiate within 30 days, and such renegotiation, unless extended by mutual agreement, must be completed within 90 days of the service of the notice.[4] In the event that the other party does not agree to renegotiate or there is a failure to agree to new terms, the statute provides that the "unconscionable. . .terms shall cease to have effect and shall. . .be treated as having been expunged".[5] Bargaining in the shadow of the law writ large! Lest there be any doubting the serious intent behind this legislation, one need only consider the approach of the Tanzanian government to the mining company Acacia in recent times. Such toughness undoubtedly holds an appeal in the context of the history of the relations between African countries and international companies that Desta so compellingly presents in his paper, but there must be a question as to whether it may equally have a chilling effect on foreign investment which may not necessarily be in the best interests of the countries concerned.[6] In this context, an argument may be made for a different approach to the development of the contractual relations between host states and investors that emphasises the mutuality of interest that exists and that seeks to achieve long-term stability to the benefit of both parties. It is, of course, by no means the case that the argument developed in this paper is inevitably an alternative to that set out by Desta. Rather, the approach outlined here could very much inform the common approach he is looking for with a view to bolstering the position of host nations in Sub-Saharan Africa and it is very much in this spirit that this paper proceeds.

The paper first of all sets out the options that the state has in setting out a legal framework for the development of its hydrocarbon sector before going on to examine the dynamic risk matrix that characterises oil and gas projects. It then sets out the principles underpinning the design of fiscal systems for upstream oil and gas. With these foundations laid, the paper goes on in the following two sections to

[1]Desta (2016).

[2]From the perspective of the investor, the challenges to sovereignty can be characterised to the contrary as "pillars of security". See Alexander (2010), p. 1 who refers to the right to monetise a discovery, the right to stability and the right to enforceable international arbitration.

[3]The Natural Wealth and Resources Contracts (Review and Re-Negotiation of Unconscionable Terms) Act 2017, s. 5.

[4]Ibid., s. 6.

[5]Ibid. s. 7.

[6]Halabi (2011), for example, is more concerned about the imbalance between the interests of host states and investors in the context of bilateral investment treaties, finding that investment contracts, by contrast, more often manifest the hallmarks of efficient contracting.

complexify the understanding of stabilisation in modern state-investor contracts, firstly, in terms of self-adjustment mechanisms and, secondly, in terms of the shift towards economic equilibrium clauses. Then, drawing on the work of Ian Macneil, it examines the extent to which these contracts are best understood as *relational* in nature rather than *discrete*. It notes that the particular features of hydrocarbon projects require contracts between states and oil companies to reflect certain issues if they are to have a realistic prospect of enduring to the mutual benefit of both parties, including: the need to preserve the relationship between state actor and contractor over the long term; flexibility to cope with complexity and uncertainty generated by the dynamic risk matrix in the context of the decades-long duration; recognition of the importance of reciprocity and of a cooperative stance on the part of both parties; and recognition of the link with wider social considerations. Insofar as that is the case, production sharing agreements reveal themselves to be perhaps the paradigm case of the relational contract. This has consequences for the way in which the parties to such contracts (and especially their lawyers) should understand them in general, and how they should react in the context of disputes in particular. Noting the increasing trend to "stabilise" such contracts by means of negotiated economic balancing clauses linked to an arbitral backstop, the paper concludes by proposing the development of principles to guide arbitral adjustment of contract terms based on this observation of inherent relationality. In this last respect, the paper very much seeks to respond to Desta's proposal for a common approach to the review of such contracts.

2 State Options for Legal Arrangements in the Petroleum Sector

In order to understand the problems that arise in the context of relations between international extractive companies and host nations, it is important first of all to consider the options that are open to state actors in terms of regularising the relationship between the parties concerned. The argument that follows focuses on hydrocarbons, but can be applied *mutatis mutandis* to contracts relating to mineral resources also.

When a state suspects that it may have hydrocarbons within onshore or offshore sedimentary basins, it must first of all decide whether it wishes to proceed to explore for those resources by itself (or at least using indigenous commercial capacity) or whether it would be appropriate to involve foreign commercial actors. Almost inevitably, because it is a frontier hydrocarbon province, it is unlikely that the country will possess the necessary technical expertise itself (either in state or indigenous commercial organs) and, as such, foreign involvement will be required.

It is then a question of deciding how that involvement will be achieved and broadly speaking there are three key models that states are able to choose from.[7]

First of all, they may adopt a licence and taxation approach in which foreign companies are issued with licences to explore for hydrocarbons and, in the event that they are successful, to develop and produce them. Payments may be made by the companies in respect of the issue of the licence and royalties may be payable from the start of production, but the substantial return of value to the state under this model will only come when oil and gas are produced and sold *and* when the companies concerned earn profits.[8]

Secondly, the state may adopt a Production Sharing Agreement (PSA) approach in which it enters into contracts with foreign companies which, similar to a licence, permit the companies to explore for and, if successful, to develop and produce oil and gas. Such contracts differ from licences in respect of the means by which value generated by successful developments will be returned to the state. Whereas under the licence this occurs substantially via the taxation of the operator's profits, in the case of the PSA, as the name suggests, the state derives value principally by receiving a share of the oil and gas produced (or the equivalent in cash where the operator is required to dispose of the hydrocarbons on the state's behalf), albeit that it may equally receive income via fees, royalties and bonuses. The precise means by which the share allocated to the state will be calculated will vary from contract to contract (and will occupy more of our attention below for reasons that will become apparent), but in essence it will be an agreed portion of so-called "profit" oil or gas that remains in any accounting period after "cost" oil has been allocated to the contractor to reimburse it for the money it has expended in exploration, development and production.[9]

Crucially, whether the state opts for the licence and tax model or the PSA model, the risk that no hydrocarbons will be found lies with the foreign commercial party. In other words, if after millions of dollars have been spent in seismic survey and exploratory drilling nothing has been discovered, then the cost will be borne by the licensee or the contractor respectively. This risk in no small measure explains why oil companies expect to make a relatively high return on their investment in the event that they are successful.

There is a third option open to the state, however, namely the use of service contracts. In this case, the state retains the services of foreign companies to carry out specific tasks and pays them a fee for the provision of those services. In this case, were the state to contract for the services of companies to provide seismic survey and exploratory drilling, the risk of failure would lie with the state.

It is accordingly not difficult to see why, in the case of developing countries entering oil and gas for the first time, the use of risk as opposed to non-risk contracts will be more attractive. That basic choice having been made, however, it then

[7]For further details see, for example, Taverne (2008) pp. 255ff.

[8]The UK, for example, uses such an approach. For a discussion, see Gordon (2018).

[9]For a discussion of this approach, see Taverne (1996a, b), pp. 158ff.

remains to explain why, almost without exception (Gambia employs a licensing approach), Sub-Saharan African countries have opted for PSAs as opposed to licences—a choice reflected almost uniformly by developing countries in other regions of the world also. Economists have pointed out that it is ultimately possible to derive the same value under each model over the life of a project,[10] so there must be another reason for the choice. No doubt individual cases will reveal specific rationales, but the following may well account for the choice in many cases. Whereas in the case of licence regimes, ownership in the produced hydrocarbons passes at the wellhead—after all, the licensee must be able to sell the product if any taxable profits are to be generated—in the case of PSAs, ownership passes at a point stipulated in the contract (usually the point at which export occurs)[11] and the state receives from the outset a share of "profit" oil and gas whether or not the contractor is yet generating profits. In other words, there is more of a sense of the state being in control of its own natural resources under the PSA model (whether that impression is reflective of reality or not) and the state receives value earlier in that model than under a licence regime, which may of course be an important consideration for a developing country.

Whatever the precise reasons for the choice of the PSA model in Sub-Saharan African countries, the fact that this contractual form is the norm does raise the sorts of issues which Desta has correctly identified as potentially problematical by posing a threat to sovereignty in terms of both legislative and judicial jurisdiction. But it is then a question of understanding *why* international oil companies do stipulate for internationalisation of contracts, stabilisation clauses and international arbitration. The first and third of these stipulations may, of course, be explained by nervousness (justified or not) on the part of international investors that in many jurisdictions may not benefit from judicial independence and may equally feel that judges (at least in the early years) may lack the specialist knowledge required to adjudicate on disputes arising from petroleum contracts.[12] The issue of stabilisation, however, is more complex. As Desta points out, contractors in the case of PSAs have traditionally sought to minimise the risk of state actors adversely affecting their investments during the lifetime of a project by seeking to freeze the applicable law as at the effective date of the contract.[13] Law students encountering this phenomenon for the first time react in precisely the same way as the citizens of countries whose governments have agreed to such arrangements: they are astonished that international companies would attempt to curtail the sovereignty of state actors in this way and perhaps even more surprised that the latter have actually accepted to be so curtailed. Desta's dismay at such arrangements is surely entirely understandable and widely shared.[14]

[10]Johnson (1994), p. 39.

[11]Taverne (2008).

[12]For an up-to-date overview of the situation, see Finizio (2017).

[13]Desta (2016), pp. 137ff. See also Maniruzzaman (2008), pp. 122ff.

[14]See, for example, Daniel and Sunley (2010).

It may be responded, however, that understanding the stabilisation of contracts on the basis purely of classical freezing clauses is to ignore the fact that it has over recent decades become a much more sophisticated concept, characterised both by a desire to build self-adjustment into PSAs and by a recognition that in the context of complex long-term agreements it will be impossible to foresee all future contingencies such that renegotiation may well become necessary. It is nevertheless the case that even this increased sophistication does not mean that the tension that exists between state and investor in the context of PSAs is thereby dissipated and that Desta's concerns are misplaced. A long-term upward trend in the number of arbitrations under such contracts in step with increases in oil prices[15] would appear to question the ability of sophisticated stabilisation mechanisms to remove worries either that states are failing to derive fair value or that contractors are being denied a legitimate "upside". Insofar as this is the case, it would not be unreasonable to assume that even if we broadened Desta's definition of stabilisation to include self-adjustment and renegotiation, his concerns with the challenge to sovereignty would remain. This paper argues, however, that in complexifying Desta's understanding of stabilisation to include recognition of the desire to ensure ongoing economic equilibrium through, firstly, self-adjustment mechanisms and, secondly, renegotiation arrangements, we actually gain a richer appreciation of the inherent nature of these contracts which in turn leads us away from an *adversarial* position and towards a *relational* one. This in turn has consequences for the way in which the parties to such contracts understand their efforts to enhance stabilisation and for the way in which arbitral tribunals deal with disputes. Before going on to examine these economic equilibrium aspects of modern stabilisation arrangements, it is necessary to examine, firstly, the risks that petroleum agreements must respond to and, secondly, the principles that underpin the design of petroleum fiscal systems if the interests of the parties are to be protected and promoted in a mutually beneficial way.

3 Oil and Gas Projects: The Dynamic Risk Matrix

That the oil industries successes are so visible goes some way to explaining why its failures are less so. Colourful maps of numerous oil and gas fields across the world's sedimentary basins and of the attendant production and transportation infrastructure can give the impression that this is an industry that requires no more than adequate capital to have access to the riches lying beneath the ground or the seabed. The truth is somewhat different. Finding oil and gas is not simply expensive, but also technically challenging: "The reality of oil and gas exploration worldwide is that despite best efforts, companies are going to be drilling 60–70% non commercial wells."[16] The substances involved are volatile and potentially polluting—and also of

[15]Stevens et al. (2013), p. 48.

[16]Kunjan (2016).

very considerable economic and political importance. There is, accordingly, much that can go wrong as well as potential success to be enjoyed. The range of risks confronting the international oil company contemplating bidding for acreage in a developing country may be conveniently listed under the following headings[17]:

geological	seismic survey reveals no prospectivity or wells drilled are either dry or reveal only uncommercial deposits or a commercial reservoir does not perform as anticipated
natural	a project is adversely affected by natural disaster
technical	equipment failures result in loss, damage and liability
managerial	a reservoir is damaged by poor decision making or poor implementation of good decision making
commercial	a discovery that is economically viable at current or envisaged prices at the point when the decision to develop is taken becomes marginal or uneconomic in the context of unanticipated low prices
financial	the viability of a project is adversely affected by movements in interest rates
currency	the viability of a project is adversely affected by movements in exchange rates

Insofar as the PSA is, as has been said above, a risk contract, the companies will be bearing all the costs. As such they must take action to minimise or mitigate these risks to the greatest practicable extent. Natural, technical and managerial risks can be managed, for example, by means of insurance.[18] Commercial, financial and currency risks may be managed, for example, by means of a hedging strategy using derivative financial instruments.[19] Geological risk, however, is not amenable to such techniques meaning that oil companies typically respond by:

- investing in a range of projects in different parts of the world with a view to compensating for problems encountered in one place with success in others[20];
- operating individual projects on the basis of joint ventures, sharing both risk and reward with co-venturers[21]; and
- looking for a significant return beyond normal commercial rates to compensate them for the scale of the risk taken on.[22]

Responses 1 and 2 may be explained in terms of the common sense approach of avoiding having "all the eggs in one basket", while response 3 reflects the fact that a PSA, as a risk contract, offers no guaranteed return of any money whatsoever for the work done in the exploration phase.

[17]For a discussion, see Nolan and Thurber (2010). See also Wälde (1994), pp. 5ff.

[18]See Allen and Aitken (2018).

[19]See Sas (1992), Kolb (1996), pp. 73ff; McDonald (2009), pp. 20ff.

[20]Nolan and Thurber (2010), pp. 15ff.

[21]See Styles (2018).

[22]See Carmalt (2017) pp. 3–23.

So far, of course, this discussion of risk has assumed that the counterparty to the agreement, the host state, is a neutral and static factor in the equation, which is by no means the case. A host state, uncertain whether there are hydrocarbons in the basin or, if there are, whether they exist in commercial quantities, but needful of the technical and/or financial resources of the international companies, may feel compelled to enhance its attractiveness to such investors who will be expected to spend significant time, money and effort in exploration without any guarantee that such expenditure will be compensated (as a consequence of geological risk, discussed above). The terms and conditions on offer at an early stage may, therefore, be extremely attractive to foreign companies, promising advantageous cost recovery arrangements and generous fiscal arrangements. In the event that significant commercial discoveries are made, however, it is not difficult to see that what appeared to be necessary to attract investment can in due course come to seem like unwarranted generosity to foreign companies at the expense of more deserving domestic needs.[23] In such circumstances, fiscal arrangements may be changed in order to rebalance returns from hydrocarbon extraction to the greater advantage of the state.[24] From the point of view of the companies, however, this appears to be moving the goalposts after the game has started and indicates a failure by governments to appreciate the extent to which oil companies must, out of necessity operate globally in order to offset the risk of failure in one place with successes in others—that is, response 1 above.

In short, in addition to the other risks listed above, oil companies also confront *political* risk, that is, the possibility that the counterparty to the PSA, precisely because it is not simply another commercial actor, but rather a sovereign power, may adversely affect the economic value of the contract to the companies by changing the general law, specifically but not exclusively as it relates to fiscal matters. It is precisely this risk which the stabilisation clause, discussed below, is designed to respond to. In order to understand more fully the source of this political risk, however, it is necessary next to consider the issues at stake in the design of a state's petroleum fiscal arrangements.

4 Designing Petroleum Fiscal Arrangements

As regards the taxation of upstream petroleum operations, the state is concerned to ensure that it puts in place a fiscal regime that both achieves an appropriate return from the state for development of its depleting natural resources and attracts the foreign investment that, as has been seen, is usually required to explore for and

[23]Bearing in mind also that these concerns often exist in a broader context of heightened, but perhaps misplaced, public expectations regarding the benefits the industry will bring. For a discussion, see Kakonge (2011).

[24]The so-called obsolescing bargain. See Vernon (1971), pp. 46ff. See also Pate (2009).

produce those resources. The companies bringing that investment are concerned to ensure that the fiscal regime permits them to make a return on their investment that appropriately reflects the risk they have taken on in entering into a PSA with no guarantee that they will be successful and thus no guarantee that their exploration costs will be recovered.

State and investor thus clearly have a mutual interest in a stable long-term relationship which avoids unnecessary disputes, but they equally both want to ensure that they extract maximum value from a petroleum project. There is a difference, however, between the maximum that could be extracted, all else equal, and the maximum that can be extracted without provoking the other party to protest in one way or another. Whilst, given the range of uncertainties and risks involved in such projects and their potentially long duration, these must inevitably be seen as incomplete contracts (perhaps even as the paradigm case of incompleteness) the aim of the drafters must be to achieve documents which are as robust as possible across a range of eventualities throughout the decades they are expected to endure. It may, therefore, appear harsh to say so, but the extent to which one party is perceived by the other to be enjoying an undue advantage at any given moment may be read as indicative of an arrangement that is deficient in some respect.

Broadly speaking, it is desirable from the point of view of both states and investors to have fiscal arrangements which are flexible, neutral and stable.[25] Flexibility in this context refers to the system's ability to ensure an appropriate return to the state under a wide range of price and production scenarios. Whereas an inflexible system which allows windfall profits to the investor as production and prices rise appears desirable from the perspective of the commercial actor, the probability that this will provoke a dispute in due course means that flexibility is also in the interest of the investor, provided it can be reassured as to an adequate rate of return on investment and a level of reward commensurate with the risk taken on in the first place. Neutrality in the context of petroleum fiscal systems refers to the extent to which petroleum projects which are regarded as profitable before taxation are still profitable after taxation is applied. It is clearly not desirable from the state's perspective to have a fiscal regime which discourages investment because it adversely affects the profitability of projects that would otherwise go ahead. Generally speaking, it is easier for systems which focus on the taxation of profits (for example, corporation tax) to achieve neutrality than those which focus on the taxation of output (for example, royalties charged per barrel of production). Finally, stability in this context refers to the quality of a fiscal regime which is either fixed or which changes only in pre-determined or otherwise predictable ways. From the point of view of the investor, stability makes it easier to rank a project compared to others given the range of other uncertainties which are faced in terms of such issues as geological and price risks. While one way of achieving stability is by means of a stabilisation clause of the sort that Desta is most concerned about, as mentioned above and discussed further below, it is also the case that a well-designed fiscal

[25]For a fuller discussion, see Tordo (2007), pp. 13–15.

regime can achieve the sort of stability that commercial actors desire in terms of relative certainty about rate of return on investment, whilst also accommodating the state's legitimate desire for flexibility in the face of, for example, variable and uncertain production levels and prices.

In short, a regime which is flexible, neutral and stable is best placed to meet the overlapping but not always coincident interests and objectives of state and investor.

The precise details of a fiscal regime are also dependent on a range of factors specific to the state in question and its position in relation to other states seeking to attract hydrocarbon investments. Thus, as mentioned above, a state new to hydrocarbons with uncertain and unproved prospectivity may feel the need to offer more favourable terms. Similarly, where political risk is perceived to be high, incentives in the form of a lighter tax burden may be required. In short, it will always be a matter for the state of seeking to measure its attractiveness compared to other opportunities for investors internationally and adjusting fiscal terms accordingly.

With these considerations behind us, we can now go on to look at those aspects of modern PSAs which we have suggested represent a more adequately complex understanding of stabilisation than is conveyed by a focus on the early practice of freezing clauses. The paper turns in the next section to examine efforts to introduce self-adjustment mechanisms into contracts and thereafter to the practice of including renegotiation clauses—both of which may be seen as seeking to ensure the ongoing economic equilibrium of the agreement.

5 Complexifying Stabilisation: Building in Self-Adjustment

In order to meet the requirements of flexibility, neutrality and stability, it is obviously desirable for the fiscal arrangements to be clearly established at the outset so that both parties may see clearly what value they will derive in a range of future scenarios. This is actually easier to achieve in a PSA system than in a licence and tax regime. In the latter, the only tools available to the state are to change the rate of taxation in response to new circumstances (notably increases in production level and in price are those that tend to be seen as creating the impetus for change) and perhaps in the extreme to add entirely new taxes to those already existing.[26] This leads to considerable uncertainty, as it is entirely unforeseeable what levels of taxation or what new taxes may be introduced in response to any given higher level of production or higher price—or indeed whether those higher rates or new taxes will be removed or disapplied in the event of lower production or reduced prices in the future. By contrast, it is a relatively straightforward matter in the context of a PSA to build in sliding-scale arrangements which adjust the proportion of profit oil and gas going to each party depending on predetermined production and/or price bands.

[26]For a discussion of the use of these tools in the context of the UKCS, see Kemp and Stephen (2018).

Insofar as the objective of this approach is to link the division of profit oil and gas between the parties to the contractor's profitability, more sophisticated PSAs tend to replace the price and production bands with those related to so-called R-Factors or to some measure of return on investment. The R-Factor is simply a calculation of the ratio of costs to income, albeit that the precise formula used in any given case may be quite complex as the drafters seek to achieve the most sensitive measure of profitability. Measures of return on investment are distinguished by their ability to incorporate the time value of money. These self-adjusting approaches have the advantage that they are sensitive (albeit to varying degrees) to changes in oil price as well as to the specific characteristics of individual reservoirs and are therefore attractive both to governments and to contractors.[27]

Whereas Desta focuses on the freezing clause variant of stabilisation, it is instructive to look at a range of PSAs (both model contracts and, where available, signed agreements[28]) from a variety of African jurisdictions to get a sense of the extent to which self-adjustment is built-in and thus to see whether the situation is as problematical as he suggests. In this regard, one contract stands out to the extent that it was the subject of a high-profile arbitration, the details of which were widely publicised, namely the Ugandan PSAs from 2007.[29] Albeit that the point in contention in that case related to whether capital gains tax was payable by the original contractor on a transfer of interest, the dispute exposed to public view the limitations of the contracts to the extent that while they included a sliding scale approach to the division of profit oil based on production levels, they lacked any means to achieve similar self-adjustment based on price.[30] A review of other African PSAs reveals that Uganda was by no means alone. The contract Mauritania signed for Bloc 1 in 1999 includes a production sharing clause very similar to the Ugandan one, insofar as it operates a basic sliding scale focused only on production levels,[31] and this approach was still evident in the contract the country signed for Bloc 25 in 2007.[32] The same

[27]For a discussion, see Bindemann (1999). See also Johnston and Johnston (2015), pp. 12–14.

[28]Historically, despite the fact that PSAs essentially set out potentially the most important fiscal terms relevant to a given country and could thus be easily argued to be of paramount public interest, such contracts were frequently treated as confidential. Today, notably under the impetus of the Extractive Industries Transparency Initiative, more and more countries are beginning to make them public as a matter of course. Insofar as signing up to the EITI is a voluntary arrangement and at the time of writing disclosure of licence and contract terms is not mandatory for implementing countries, the situation is by no means yet as good as could be. See EITI Standard 2016, Requirement 2.4. https://eiti.org/document/standard#r2-4.

[29]For a critique, see Platform (2010). See also Global Witness (2014).

[30]A draft version of the PSA between the Government of the Republic of Uganda and Heritage Oil and Gas Ltd. has been made available on the OpenOil website at https://repository.openoil.net/wiki/Uganda_Block-3A_dd20070123_PSA.

[31]Contrat de Partage de Production entre la République Islamique de Mauritanie et Dana Petroleum (E & P) Limited et Hardman Petroleum (Mauritania) Pty Ltd. et Elixir Corporation Pty Ltd., 1999, Bloc 1, Article 10.3.

[32]Contrat de Partage de Production d'Hydrocarbures entre La République Islamique de Mauritanie et Blue Chip Energy S.A sur le Bloc 25 du Bassin Cotier, Février 2007, Article 10.3.

may be said for the model contract from Madagascar in 2007,[33] the contracts signed by Gabon for the Etame area in 1995[34] and the Diaba Licence in 2006,[35] and for the model contract from Equatorial Guinea dated 2006. It should be noted, however, that the last-mentioned utilises accumulated production,[36] an approach mirrored in the contract signed by the Democratic Republic of Congo for Bloc III in 2010.[37] Straightforward production-based profit oil sharing is also a feature of Guinea's contract with US Oil Corporation in 2002,[38] and its contract with SCS Corporation in 2006.[39] Note, however, that, intriguingly, earlier signed contracts from Equatorial Guinea contain more sophisticated production sharing arrangements based on the contractor's rate of return,[40] whilst later contracts in Mauritania have moved on from the simple production-based sliding scale approach to one based on a more sophisticated R-factor approach.[41] The Nigerian model PSA from 2005 similarly uses an R-factor approach to the profit oil split and includes the possibility that the state oil company can take action to modify the calculation in the event of prolonged periods of low oil prices so as to increase its share—an approach very much in the state's favour rather than the contractor's.[42] The Libyan model contract from 2006 determines the contractor's share of profit oil by essentially applying two sliding scales, one focused on production levels, the other on the cumulative value of the production, thus generating a division that is sensitive to price levels,[43] an approach that is also evident in the contract signed by Libya in relation to Area 47 in the previous year.[44] The Angolan model contract from 2007 achieves the division of profit oil on

[33]Republic of Madagascar, Model Production Sharing Contract, Offshore and Onshore versions, 2007, Article 24.2.

[34]Exploration and Production Sharing Contract between the Republic of Gabon and Vaalco Gabon (Etame) Inc., Etame, 7 July 1995, Article 25.

[35]Exploration and Production Sharing Contract between the Gabonese Republic and Total Gabon, Diana Licence, 13 December 2006, Article 25.

[36]The Republic of Equatorial Guinea, Model Production Sharing Contract, 2006, Article 7.2.

[37]Contrat de Partage de Production conclu entre la Rėpublique Democratique du Congo et South Africa Congo Oil (Pty) Ltd. et la Congolaise des Hydrocarbures, Bloc III du Graben Albertine, 26 May 2010.

[38]Royalty and Production Sharing Agreement between the Republic of Guinea and USOil Corporation, 2002, Article 13.

[39]Hydrocarbon Production Sharing Agreement between the Republic of Guinea and SCS Corporation, 22 September 2006, Article 13.

[40]For example, Production Sharing Contract between the Republic of Equatorial Guinea and Triton Equatorial Guinea, Inc. For Block F, 26 March 1997.

[41]For example, see Exploration and Production Contract between the Islamic Republic of Mauritania and Kosmos Energy Mauritania Ltd. in relation to C12, 2012.

[42]Federal Republic of Nigeria, Model Production Sharing Contract for 2005 Bid Round, Clause 9.1.

[43]Great Socialist People's Libyan Arab Jamahiriya, Model Exploration and Production Sharing Agreement, 2006, Article 12.

[44]Exploration and Production Sharing Agreement between National Oil Corporation and Verenex Energy Area 47 Libya Limited and Medco International Ventures Limited, Contract Area 47, 12 March 2005.

the basis of a sliding scale where the bands are related to the contractor's rate of return, again implying a price-sensitive approach.[45] This approach is evident in contracts signed for Block 5/06 in 2006[46] and for Block 20/11 in 2011.[47] By contrast, the Liberian model contract from 2007 utilises a similar approach to Uganda's insofar as it divides profit oil purely on the basis of a sliding scale related to production levels,[48] and this approach is evident in the contract signed for Offshore Block 13 in 2005[49] and in the restated and amended contract for the same block signed in 2008.[50] At first sight, the Kenyan model contract from 2008 appears to adopt a similarly unsophisticated approach insofar as the basic approach is that profit oil is divided on the basis of production levels. The relevant clause also includes, however, protection for the government in the case of high oil prices by providing for a so-called "second tier" allocation to the government in the event that the price rises above $50/barrel.[51] This approach, which involves calculating a cash payment to address what are explicitly referred to as "windfall profits", is adopted, for example, in the contract signed for Block 2B in 2008.[52] The situation is similar with the Tanzanian model contract from 2008 where at first sight there appears only to be a production-based sliding scale,[53] but elsewhere in the agreement there is a provision for an additional profit tax based on the contractor's real rate of return.[54] This approach is, indeed, already evident in the contract signed for the Songo Songo gas field in 2001.[55] The Ghanaian model contract from 2008 allocates profit oil on the basis of a very complex formula for the calculation of the contractor's rate of return,[56] an approach that is already evident in the earlier contracts, such as that

[45]Sonangol, Model Production Sharing Contract, December 2007, Article 12.

[46]Production Sharing Agreement between Sonangol EP and Vaalco Angola (Kwanza) Inc., Sonangol Pesquisa e Produção SA, Interoil Exploration and Production SA in the Area of Block 5/06, 1 November 2006, Article 12.

[47]Production Sharing Agreement between Sonangol EP and CIE Angola Block 20 Ltd., Sonangol Pesquisa e Produção SA, BP Exploration Angola (Kwanza Benguela) Limited, China Sonangol International Holding Limited in the Area of Block 20/11, 20 December 2011, Article 12.

[48]Republic of Liberia, Model Production Sharing Contract, October 2007, Article 16.

[49]Production Sharing Contract between National Oil Company of Liberia (NOCAL) and Broadway Consolidated PLC, Offshore Block 13, 31 May 2005, Article 16.

[50]Restated and Amended Production Sharing Contract between The Republic of Liberia by and through the National Oil Company of Liberia and ExxonMobil Exploration and Production Liberia Limited and Canadian Overseas Petroleum (Bermuda) Limited, Offshore Block 13, 8 March 2008.

[51]Republic of Kenya, Model Production Sharing Contract, 2008, Clause 27.

[52]Production Sharing Agreement between the Government of the Republic of Kenya and Lion Petroleum Inc. relating to Block 2B, 17 September 2008.

[53]Government of the United Republic of Tanzania, Model Production Sharing Agreement, October 2008, Article 11.

[54]Government of the United Republic of Tanzania, Model Production Sharing Agreement, October 2008, Article 15.

[55]Production Sharing Agreement relating to the Songo Songo Gas Field between the Government of the United Republic of Tanzania and PanAfrican Energy Tanzania Limited, 11 October 2001.

[56]Ghana National Petroleum Corporation, Model Petroleum Agreement of Ghana, 2008, Article 10.

signed for the West Cape Three Points Block in 2004.[57] The Mozambique model contract from 2010 uses a sliding scale based on an R-factor calculation,[58] an approach that is already evident in the contract signed for the Rovuma onshore area in 2007.[59] The contract signed by Cameroon in respect of the Ndian River area in 2006 uses an R-factor sliding scale,[60] as does the model contract from Sao Tome and Principe from 2010,[61] and the contact signed by Chad in 2011 in respect of the Chari Ouest Dosea area,[62] while the Egyptian model contract from 2010 uses two sliding scales, one related to production levels and the other to price.[63] In view of the general trend evident above towards more sophisticated self-adjustment mechanisms, it is perhaps not surprising to find that relatively old PSAs signed by Benin in 1997 use straightforward production-based sliding scales,[64] but that the more recent Ethiopian model contract from 2011[65] and the contracts signed by Senegal in 2012[66] similarly contain no protection for the state in relation to high prices is less easy to understand.[67] This is especially the case given that, as early as 1994, Congo had a contract which, although based on a very simple production-related division of profit oil, also contained a provision which ensured that that the state took the lion's

---

[57]Petroleum Agreement among the Republic of Ghana, Ghana National Petroleum Corporation, Kosmos Energy Ghana HC and the EO Group in respect of the West Cape Three Points Block, 22 July, 2004, Article 10.

[58]Republic of Mozambique, Model Exploration and Production Concession Contract, 4th Bidding Round, May 2010, Article 9.10.

[59]Contrato de Concessão e Produção entre o Governo da República de Moçambique e Artumas Moçambique Petróleos Limitada e Empressa Nacional de Hidrocarbonetos EP para Área "Onshore" do Bloco do Rovuma, 18 April 2007, Artigo 9.

[60]Production Sharing Contract between the Republic of Cameroon and Kosmos Energy Cameroon HC, Ndian River, 2006, Article 13.

[61]Democratic Republic of Sao Tome and Principe, Exclusive Economic Zone Model Production Sharing Contract, March 2010, Clause 10.1(d).

[62]Contrat de Partage de Production, entre la République de Tchad et Griffiths Energy (Chad) Ltd., 19 January 2011, Article 42.

[63]Arab Republic of Egypt, English Model Concession Agreement for Petroleum Exploration and Exploitation, 2010, Article VII.

[64]Production Sharing Contract between Benin and Addax Petroleum Benin Limited and Abacan Resources (Benin) Limited, Offshore Block 4, 1 February 1997, as disclosed in Form 10-KSB, Annual Report Pursuant to Section 13 or 15(D) of the Securities Exchange Act of 1934 for the Fiscal Year ended December 31, 1998 Commission File Number 33-99978, Abacan Resource Corporation.

[65]Federal Democratic Republic of Ethiopia, Model Petroleum Production Sharing Agreement, 26 August 2011, Section 7.2.

[66]For example, Hydrocarbon Exploration and Production Sharing Contract between the Republic of Senegal and Petro-Tim Limited and Petrosen, Cayar Offshore Profond, 17 January 2012, Article 22.

[67]In the absence of any specific insight into the negotiations in these cases, one can only speculate as to why Ethiopia and Benin join Uganda in continuing to use relatively unsophisticated profit oil arrangements at such a late stage. It is, however, one of the frustrations of the oil and gas lawyer that mistakes made by other countries are sometimes repeated by those entering the field at a later date when it would have been a relatively simple matter to avoid them if proper advice had been sought.

share of any profit derived from the sale of oil for a price above $22 per barrel[68]—a provision that also appears in a contract signed a decade later.[69]

In short, even if there are a number of contracts in this set drawn from across the continent over the past twenty or so years which have minimal self-adjustment related only to production levels, there is plenty of evidence of African jurisdictions utilising much more sophisticated self-adjustment tools—and it is notable that *all* of the contracts considered include at least *some* degree of self-adjustment.

6 Complexifying Stabilisation: From Freezing to Economic Equilibrium

Recognising, nevertheless, that no matter how sophisticated the self-adjustment mechanism employed by a PSA might be, these are complex, long-term agreements and as such must be regarded as inevitably incomplete. It is then a question of moving on to consider just what sort of further arrangement might be made to seek to ensure that the relationship between the parties endures in a mutually beneficial way notwithstanding that the contract as agreed, including its self-adjustment arrangements, has, as it were, run out of road.[70]

At one extreme, of course, lies the classic freezing stabilisation clause highlighted by Desta. With the knowledge we now have of the context and content of the PSA, we can see that this attempts to protect the contractor come what may at the expense of the state. However much the state may want, indeed need, to adjust the terms of

[68]Contrat de Partage de Production entre la République de Congo et Elf Congo SA et la Societé Nationale de Recherche et Exploitation Pétrolières, Haute-Mer Nkossa, 21 April 1994, Article 8.

[69]Contrat de Partage de Production entre la République de Congo et Total E&P Congo, Haute-Mer C, 7 January 2004, Article 8.

[70]It is sometimes contended that this step is not inevitable inasmuch as things tend to happen differently in developed countries. Whilst it is generally true that stabilization clauses are a feature of petroleum arrangements in developing rather than developed countries, as observed by Erkan (2010), there is at least one recent exception in the UK which may point to the direction of travel in the later stages of the development of a hydrocarbon basin. This exception relates to the Decommissioning Relief Deed by which the Treasury guarantees the current value of decommissioning allowances under the fiscal regime by agreeing contractually to compensate an operator in the event that a future parliament legislates to reduce the value of those allowances or even to remove them altogether (see Aldersey-Williams 2018, p. 447). Quite what would happen were such a parliament also to take a dim view of the Treasury's pre-emptive efforts to negate the effects of its actions raises constitutional questions beyond the scope of this paper. Equally, whilst it is also generally true that developed countries do not tend to negotiate petroleum contract or licence terms, as observed by Cameron (2006), preferring to offer standardized terms, even a country like the UK has been open to the idea of a bespoke licence. It is also important to realise that some of the industry allowances to be found in general tax legislation in the UK are there only as a result of lobbying by operators who claim to be unable to develop marginal discoveries without some form of tax relief. The format of the negotiation may be different in developed countries, but it is not absent.

the contract or to pass legislation to mitigate the deleterious effects of the contract arising from unforeseen changed circumstances, the clause attempts to block its efforts and to leave it regretting the agreement it has entered into.[71] The knowledge we now have, however, also reveals that this clause fails the tests set out above for a mutually beneficial petroleum fiscal regime. It is not flexible, inasmuch as it requires one party to suffer in the event of price movements beyond those envisaged by any self-adjustment mechanism that are to its disadvantage, and to that extent it is also not stable, inasmuch as the rigid protection of the contractor is at the expense of the exposure of the state. These observations no doubt help to explain why, when subject to the consideration of arbitral tribunals, classic freezing clauses have not operated as those stipulating for them would have imagined. While the key published arbitral tribunal decisions dealing with stabilisation clauses have been concerned with expropriations rather than lesser regulatory or fiscal interventions, they may be interpreted as indicating that while even a freezing clause cannot rule out future legislative or regulatory action it could provide grounds for compensation insofar as it adversely affected the contractor.[72] Concern has been expressed, however, that this approach may have a chilling effect on the ability of poorer countries to take forward legitimate reforms of, for example, health, safety and environmental law and regulation where the presence of a freezing clause would lead to their being faced with potentially costly payments to affected contractors.[73]

Nevertheless, recognising the likely limitations of such clauses from the point of view of the contractor, practice in respect of stabilisation clauses in PSAs has evolved away from the classic freezing approach and towards an approach that aims instead to preserve the economic equilibrium of the contract. Whilst most academic commentary on such clauses tends to focus on the shift away from freezing, this development can perhaps best be understood as a continuation of the progressive enhancement of self-adjustment arrangements in the profit oil and gas sharing elements of PSAs. The advantage of such an approach is that it reflects the reality of the situation of both the commercial and the state party in the event that things develop in such a way that one or other is adversely affected to the extent that, had such circumstances been foreseen, they would have fundamentally altered the willingness of that party to sign the contract on the agreed terms.

Economic equilibrium clauses have been identified as falling in practice into three categories[74]: stipulated economic balancing (SEB); non-specific economic

---

[71]The clause we have been discussing so far is generally referred to as a stabilisation clause *stricto sensu*. A variation of the clause may seek to insulate the contract from any material adverse effect of existing or later laws, thus freezing the contract rather than the surrounding law, by prohibiting unilateral changes and requiring mutual consent. Such a stabilisation clause is sometimes referred to as an *intangibilité* clause. These two versions are sometimes referred to as classic stabilisation clauses. See Maniruzzaman (2008), pp. 122ff.

[72]For example, *Government of Kuwait v Aminoil* 1982.

[73]See especially, Shemberg (2009). See also, Cotula (2008) For a discussion, see Maniruzzaman (2008), pp. 156–157.

[74]I draw here on the categories suggested by Maniruzzaman (2008), pp. 127–132.

balancing (NSEB); and negotiated economic balancing (NEB). The aim in each case is both to allow legitimate subsequent legislative and regulatory action by the state while re-establishing the value of the economic balance that existed when the contract became effective. The SEB operates so as to amend the contract automatically in a specified manner should a stipulated triggering event come to pass, such as a modification of the tax law.[75] The NSEB stipulates that the contract will be amended automatically to re-establish economic equilibrium should a triggering event come to pass, but does not specify how this will be achieved. Finally, the NEB, as its name suggests, calls for the parties to agree to the amendments required to re-establish economic equilibrium in the event of a triggering event. Strictly speaking, the NEB could be further subdivided, as a clause which envisages a negotiation to re-establish a previous balance may genuinely seek to re-balance the positions of the state and contractor, or it may be specifically included to return only the contractor to its previous position.[76]

Recalling that one of the most contentious African disputes involving PSAs was that involving the Ugandan contracts from 2007, it is instructive to see what those instruments contained in relation to stabilisation. While it is not identified as such, but rather forms part of Article 33 headed "Applicable Law", there can be no doubt that Article 33.2 is a stabilisation clause.[77] It reads as follows:

> If, following the Effective Date, there is any change, or series of changes, in the laws or regulations of Uganda which materially reduces the economic benefits derived or to be derived by Licensee hereunder, Licensee may notify the Government accordingly and thereafter the Parties shall meet to negotiate in good faith and agree upon, the necessary modifications to this Agreement to restore Licensee to substantially the same overall economic position as prevailed hereunder prior to such change(s). In the event that the Parties are unable to agree that Licensee's economic benefits have been materially affected, and/or are unable to agree on the modifications required to restore Licensee to the same economic position as prevailed prior to such change, within ninety (90) days of the receipt of the notice referred to hereinabove, then either Party may refer the matter for determination pursuant to paragraph 26.1 [that is, by arbitration].

From the foregoing discussion of stabilisation clauses, it is possible to see quite clearly, firstly, that Article 33.2 is an economic equilibrium clause rather than a classic freezing clause; secondly, that among the varieties of economic equilibrium clause, it is a Negotiated Economic Balancing clause; and, thirdly, that among NEBs it is focused specifically on the position of the contractor rather than that of both parties.

[75]Indeed, an argument can be made that the self-adjustment mechanisms discussed above, such as sliding scale elements in profit sharing clauses, are varieties of stipulated economic balancing.

[76]It is a question whether returning the contractor to its original position must by definition so return the state actor also if we are genuinely talking about equilibrium or whether the latter variant rather sees the "negotiation" as something more akin to a zero-sum game.

[77]The clause at the heart of the dispute in *Amoco International Finance Corp. v Iran* was similarly headed "Applicable Law" and was found *not* to be a stabilisation clause, but that clause expressly protected the contractor only from the "provision of any current laws and regulations which may be...inconsistent with" it. See the discussion in Maniruzzaman (2007), p. 24.

Having looked at the production sharing arrangements of a series of PSAs for African states in the previous section, it is instructive to consider the stabilisation clauses, if any, in those same agreements—to what extent are the contentious Ugandan PSAs in line or out of step with equivalent contracts in other African states? Generally speaking, it may be said that the older agreements either lack a stabilisation clause or have a classic clause, whilst more modern agreements have stabilisation clauses in broadly similar terms to that in the Ugandan PSAs, that is, Negotiated Economic Balancing clauses. Thus, the model contract from Libya dated 2006 lacks a stabilisation clause,[78] while the older model contract from Mauritania, which dates from 1994, includes a classic stabilisation clause,[79] as does the Senegalese contract from 2012.[80] On the other hand, the Nigerian Model PSA dating from 2005 includes a Negotiated Economic Balancing Clause recognising the interests of both parties,[81] as does the Angolan model contract from 2007,[82] and the Liberian model contract from the same year. The last-mentioned, in addition to recognising the interests of both parties, also stipulates expressly that no party can see its benefits reduced as a result of any adjustment.[83] The Kenyan model contract

[78]Great Socialist People's Libyan Arab Jamahiriya, Model Exploration and Production Sharing Agreement, 2006.

[79]"The Contractor shall not be subject to any legislative provision which would give rise to an aggravation, whether directly or indirectly, in the charges and obligations arising from this Contract and from the legislation and regulations in force on the date of signing this Contract, unless as mutually agreed upon by the Parties." Islamic Republic of Mauritania, Model Production Sharing Contract, 1994, Unofficial English Translation, Article 27.3 (Applicable Law and Stability of Conditions).

[80]"No provision may be applied to the Contractor the purpose of which is to directly or as a consequence thereof increase the charges and obligations deriving from the systems mentioned in Chapter 7 of the Oil Code, as these systems are defined by the legislation and the regulations in effect as of the date this Contract is signed, without prior agreement of the Parties." Hydrocarbon Exploration and Production Sharing Contract between the Republic of Senegal and Petro-Tim Limited and Petrosen, note 66, Article 33.3.

[81]"If at any time or from time to time there should be a change in legislation or regulations which materially affects the commercial benefits afforded the Parties under this Contract, the Parties will consult each other and shall agree to such amendments to this Contract as are necessary to restore as near as practicable such commercial benefits which existed under the Contract as of the Effective Date." Federal Republic of Nigeria, Model Production Sharing Contract for 2005 Bid Round, Clause 27.3 (Changes in Legislation).

[82]"Without prejudice to other rights and obligations of the Parties under the Agreement, in the event that any change in the provisions of any Law, decree or regulation in force in the Republic of Angola occurs subsequent to the signing of this Agreement which adversely affects the obligations, rights and benefits hereunder, then the Parties shall agree on amendments to the Agreement to be submitted to the competent authorities for approval, so as to restore such rights, obligations and forecasted benefits." Sonangol, Model Production Sharing Contract, December 2007, Article 37 (2) (Double Taxation and Change of Circumstances). Note that insofar as this contract is designed to be entered into by the state oil company rather than the government, Sonangol can only undertake to present any agreed alterations for approval to the competent authorities.

[83]"In the event of changes in circumstances from those existing at the Effective Date, that have a material effect on the terms of this Agreement, either NOCAL [the state company] or the Contractor

also has a stabilisation clause which similarly recognises the interests of both parties,[84] as does that found in the Ethiopian model contract.[85] There is a similarly modern approach in the Mozambican contracts, where the relevant clause envisages renegotiation in the event of changes in legislation creating "a material adverse effect to the economic benefits of the Concessionaire or to the Government", albeit that it mysteriously later mentions restoring the economic benefits only of the Concessionaire.[86]

shall at the request of the other consult together. If it is established that such Profound Changes in Circumstances have occurred, then the Parties shall effect such changes in or clarifications to this Agreement that they agree are necessary. The Parties shall meet in good faith to make the necessary revisions and adjustments to the Agreement in order to maintain such expected economic benefits to each of the Parties, provided that the economic benefits to the Parties shall not be reduced as a result of exercising the terms of this article". Republic of Liberia, Model Production Sharing Contract, October 2007, Article 36.3 (Stability of Conditions).

[84]"If after the effective date of this contract the economic benefits of a party are substantially affected by the promulgation of new laws and regulations, or of any amendments to the applicable laws and regulations of Kenya, the parties shall agree to make the necessary adjustments to the relevant provisions of this contract, observing the principle of the mutual economic benefits of the parties." Republic of Kenya, Model Production Sharing Contract, 2008, Clause 40(3) (Governing Law).

[85]"In the event that after the Effective Date of this Agreement the economic benefits to be derived by a Party from the Petroleum Operations under this Agreement are substantially affected by the promulgation of new laws and regulations or of any amendments to the applicable laws and regulations of Ethiopia and if the affected Party so requests, the Parties shall agree to make the necessary adjustments to the relevant provisions of this Agreement, in order to ensure that the affected Party is restored to the same economic condition it would have been in if such change in the applicable laws had not taken place." Federal Democratic Republic of Ethiopia, Model Petroleum Production Sharing Agreement, 26 August 2011, Section 16.1.3 (Governing Law).

[86]"In the event of changes in Petroleum legislation or in other Mozambican legislation affecting Petroleum Operations that may, individually or in the aggregate, create a material adverse effect to the economic benefits *of the Concessionaire or to the Government* in terms of this EPC, the Parties shall, as soon as possible after any of the above-mentioned situations occur, meet to verify and agree on the changes, in all cases, that may be required to the EPC in order to restore, as closely as possible, the economic benefits that *the Concessionaire* would have derived if the change in the legislation had not been effected." Republic of Mozambique, notes 58 and 59, Article 27.13 (emphasis added).

The model contract from Sao Tome and Principe is more unequivocally focused on the interests of the contractor,[87] as is that from Egypt[88] and from Cameroon.[89] The Chadian contract signed in 2011 is interesting insofar as it includes what at first sight looks like a standard negotiated economic balancing clause recognising the interests of both parties, but which on closer inspection is weighted very much in favour of the contractor insofar as, if after the specified period of renegotiation no agreement has been reached, the changes to the law which provoked the renegotiation shall not apply to the contract.[90]

In surveying such contracts entered into by African countries, there are two which stand out because they appear at first sight to take a traditional approach to stabilisation before revealing a more modern approach. Thus, the Mauritanian contract from 2012 contains a freezing clause, but one which significantly includes a carve-out for changes to safety, environmental and employment law.[91] The Ghanaian Model Petroleum Agreement[92] is similarly interesting because it combines

[87]"If at any time or from time to time, there is a change in legislation or regulations which materially affect the commercial benefit afforded to the Contractor under this Contract, the Parties will consult each other and shall agree to such amendments to this Contract as are necessary to restore as near as practicable such commercial benefits which existed under this Contract as of the Effective Date." Democratic Republic of Sao Tome and Principe, Exclusive Economic Zone Model Production Sharing Contract, March 2010, Clause 27(2) (Review/Re-negotiation of Contract and Fiscal Terms).

[88]"In case of changes in existing legislation or regulations applicable to the conduct of Exploration, Development and production of Petroleum, which take place after the Effective Date, and which significantly affect the economic interest of this Agreement to the detriment of CONTRACTOR or which imposes on CONTRACTOR an obligation to remit to the A.R.E. [Government] the proceeds from sales of CONTRACTOR's Petroleum, CONTRACTOR shall notify GANOPE [the State Company] of the subject legislative or regulatory measure and also the consequent effects upon issuing legislation or regulation which impact on the stabilization. In such case, the Parties shall negotiate possible modifications to this Agreement designed to restore the economic balance thereof which existed on the Effective Date. The Parties shall use their best efforts to agree on amendments to this Agreement within ninety (90) days from aforesaid notice. These amendments to this Agreement shall not in any event diminish or increase the rights and obligations of CONTRACTOR as these were agreed on the Effective Date. In case of the parties' failure to solve the disputes, Article XXIV of this Agreement shall be applied." Arab Republic of Egypt, Model Concession Agreement for Petroleum Exploration and Exploitation, 2010, Article XIX (Stabilization).

[89]Republic of Cameroon, note 60, Article 29.

[90]République de Tchad, Note 62, Article 56.2.

[91]"No legislative or regulatory provision occurring after the Effective Date of the Contract may be applied to the Contractor which would have as a direct or an indirect effect to diminish the rights of the Contractor or to increase his obligations under this Contract and the legislation and regulations in force upon the Effective Date of this Contract, without the prior agreement of the Parties... However, it is agreed that the Contractor cannot, with reference to the preceding paragraph, oppose the application of the legislative and regulatory provisions which are generally applicable, adopted after the Effective Date of the Contract, in the matter of safety of persons and of protection of the environment or employment law." Islamic Republic of Mauritania, note 41, Article 26.3.

[92]Ghana National Petroleum Corporation, Model Petroleum Agreement of Ghana, 2008.

a classic freezing clause[93] with an NEB which accommodates the possibility that any party may be concerned that the economic equilibrium of the contract has been adversely affected.[94]

There are, however, some exceptions to the general position stated above among the African model PSAs reviewed so far. Firstly, the 2006 Model PSA from Equatorial Guinea mentions "Article 25 Applicable Law and Stabilization" in its table of contents, but within the body of the document only Applicable Law is discussed in Article 25—a potential contractor may nevertheless infer from this that the state would be open to negotiation of a stabilisation clause.[95] The Madagascan onshore and offshore model Production Sharing Contracts dating from 2007 contain no stabilisation clause, but do include "*Faits de Prince*" (acts of state) in the definition of *force majeure*, perhaps offering some protection for a contractor against more extreme government intervention.[96] The Congolese contract from 1994 contains no stabilisation clause, nor any other provision that might offer similar comfort to the contractor,[97] and the situation is similar in the Equatorial Guinean contract. In the Gabonese contracts considered above, the state offers a guarantee of stability without referring any dispute on this issue explicitly to the dispute resolution provisions—albeit that in each case the clause dealing with the application of the contract stresses the mutuality inherent in it and the need for cooperation between the parties.[98] The Tanzanian 2008 Model PSA contains no stabilisation clause[99] and in view of the new legislation mentioned in the introduction to this paper it is questionable whether any such clause would survive the test of unconscionability.

What this brief survey demonstrates is that the characterisation of stabilisation in Desta's paper is at best only partially correct and, where it is, this would have to be regarded as exceptional. Does this mean, then, that Desta's concerns with the

[93]"As of the Effective Date of this Agreement and throughout its Term, the State guarantees Contractor the stability of the terms and conditions of this Agreement as well as the fiscal and contractual framework hereof specifically including those terms and conditions and that framework that are based upon or subject to the provisions of the laws and regulations of Ghana (and any interpretations thereof)". Ibid, Article 26.2.

[94]"Where a Party considers that a significant change in the circumstances prevailing at the time the Agreement was entered into, has occurred affecting the economic balance of the Agreement, the Party affected hereby shall notify the other Parties in writing of the claimed change with a statement of how the claimed change has affected the relations between the Parties... The other Parties shall indicate in writing their reaction to such representation within a period of three (3) months of receipt of such notification and if such significant changes are established by the Parties to have occurred, the Parties shall meet to engage in negotiations and shall effect such changes in, or rectification of, these provisions as they may agree are necessary." Ibid, Article 26.3 and 26.4.

[95]The Republic of Equatorial Guinea, Model Production Sharing Contract, 2006.

[96]Republic of Madagascar, Model Production Sharing Contract, Offshore and Onshore versions, 2007, Article 39(3)(d).

[97]République de Congo, note 68.

[98]Republic of Gabon, notes 34 and 35, Article 13.

[99]Government of the United Republic of Tanzania, Model Production Sharing Agreement, October 2008.

challenge to sovereignty offered by stabilisation is more illusory than real? I would be inclined to say no. Even where disputes do not become public or where contracts have been signed in recent years in states where the industry is as yet at an early stage of development, there can be no gainsaying the passions that PSAs can give rise to. Whereas, as we saw earlier, the PSA has historically been favoured over the licence and tax alternative precisely because it sees the state (1) take possession of physical hydrocarbons, (2) derive value from successful projects earlier and (3) generally convey an impression of greater control over the foreign companies, it is not unusual for lingering doubts to remain that the government will lack the knowledge and experience either to negotiate the strongest deal or to hold the contractor to account in the long term or both.[100] As such, PSAs, even as a contractual form, are not infrequently the subject of quite strongly worded political attacks,[101] no matter how sophisticated the self-adjustment and the stabilisation clauses may be. In addition to fears about the abilities of government to reign in the industry, of course, are concerns about another of the challenges to sovereignty articulated by Desta, namely the removal of disputes from the jurisdiction of domestic courts and their treatment by international arbitral tribunals.[102] The idea that foreigners (even those chosen by the state) may pronounce on disputes relating to, in many cases, the most valuable sector of the domestic economy is not an easy one to accept. Nor is it always easy to persuade critics that the record of tribunals indicates something other than bias to commercial actors, but rather, in the main, a genuine attempt to give effect to the agreement the parties have entered into, albeit that circumstances have now caused the initial warmth of the relationship to cool.[103]

But these observations, added to those discussed earlier regarding the prevalence of self-adjustment in PSAs as well as the demonstrable evolution away from freezing clauses and towards negotiated economic equilibrium clauses, serve importantly to highlight the fact that, however acrimonious relations between the parties to a PSA may become and however intense the media and political criticism of the contractual form may be, these must surely be understood not as *discrete* contracts but rather as *relational* contracts to employ Ian Macneil's terminology.

---

[100]It is worth noting that concerns on the part of government that it is the junior partner in such negotiations are not confined to developing countries. Tony Benn, Secretary of State for Energy in the late 1970s, states in an explanatory note in his diary: 'Some oil companies are comparable in strength and wealth to national governments...As Secretary of State, I learned that relations between governments and oil companies were much like treaty negotiations' Benn (1990), p. 3.

[101]For a discussion of the situation in Russia in the 1990s in this regard, see Konoplyanik (2003). For a discussion of concerns relating to the impact of stabilisation clauses on the ability of host governments to protect human rights, see Sikka (2011).

[102]Desta (2016), pp. 140–141.

[103]See the extensive discussion in Maniruzzaman (2008), pp. 138ff.

7 Relationality in PSAs

Recalling the realities of oil and gas projects discussed previously, it is clear that these arrangements must reflect certain issues if they are to have a realistic prospect of enduring to the mutual benefit of both parties. Among these may be mentioned: the need to preserve the relationship between state actor and contractor over the long term; flexibility to cope with complexity and uncertainty generated by the dynamic risk matrix in the context of the decades-long duration; recognition of the importance of reciprocity and of a cooperative stance on the part of both parties; and recognition of the link with wider social considerations. In many respects, these considerations map almost exactly on to the key features of Ian Macneil's influential theory of relational contracting. Indeed, one might make a strong argument that PSAs are almost the paradigm case of the relational contract[104]—or, to use Macneil's characterization, that they lie at one end of the spectrum which runs from discrete at one end to relational at the other.[105] Insofar as that is true, it becomes important to understand how we best understand the nature of the obligation that is created by the contract between state and commercial parties in the context of the particular circumstances that characterise the oil and gas industry. How should an arbitral tribunal respond when confronted with a dispute that essentially arises because one party is not claiming *force majeure* but rather economic impossibility?[106] It is easy to resort in such circumstances to the safe haven that is signposted *pacta sunt servanda*. What could be simpler? What could be more in line with the pre-eminent concern with legal certainty? But, equally, what might be less realistic in the context of contracts so imbued with incompleteness? In those circumstances, the attraction of *pacta sunt servanda* must compete with the allure of *rebus sic stantibus*. Nor is this to make a radical proposal. The features discussed above in relation to PSAs are less and less unique, to the point where, at the IBA Arbitration day in Buenos Aires in April 2018, they were highlighted as increasingly common:

> we see more and more complex long-term relational contracts which include arbitration clauses. Because these contracts are structured to last for many years, sometimes decades, they become more vulnerable to technological, political and/or economic changes which may substantially affect the parties' rights and even disrupt the contract's economic equilibrium. Were that to happen, the possibility to restore that equilibrium through adjudication becomes crucial.[107]

The idea that arbitrators could adapt contracts in such circumstances is, of course, not uncontroversial, nor is the controversy new.[108] But the evidence would seem to

---

[104]Given this observation, it is surprising that the link has not been more widely made. Only one example appears in the literature, as far as I am aware, in relation to contracts for diamond mining. See Bernstein (1992).

[105]Macneil (1983), p. 342.

[106]For a discussion see, Saliba (2001).

[107]Bordacahar (2018).

[108]See Berger (2003) and Gotanda (2003).

suggest that the need to think more systematically about how it could operate in practice is becoming more pressing. Quoting again from the report of the IBA Arbitration Day in April 2018:

> the IBA debate revealed a feeling among practitioners that whether expressly or impliedly, or directly or indirectly, arbitrators frequently adapt contracts to meet the needs and intentions of disputing parties, and by doing so, they contribute to the rule of law. Were the tribunal not to do this, the dispute resolution procedure would not be fully effective. Our comfort level with arbitrators acting in this manner is reflected in the express hardship or re-negotiation clauses which have become a common feature of modern contracts that establish complex and long-term arrangements. As a general matter, the prevailing view seemed to be that we should not be too cautious to grant and/or accept that arbitrators have powers to fill gaps and adapt contracts, but we should demand that arbitrators be extremely cautious while making use of them.[109]

The question then is how we might recognise the need for arbitrators to be able to adapt contracts that we now understand to be inherently relational, whilst providing reassurance in respect of the concerns expressed by Desta. Two observations might be made in this respect. Firstly, it is surely the case that the very recognition of the relational nature of such contracts in itself offers reassurance for those concerned that the legitimate interests of the state are put at risk in the context of agreements characterised by stabilisation agreements. Realising that stabilisation in modern contracts is substantially about building in self-adjustment arrangements explicitly designed to maintain economic equilibrium reveals the extent to which such agreements can now more adequately protect the state's interests as well as those of the commercial actor, both in terms of ensuring a fair return of value in the long term and in terms of avoiding disputes that are costly in terms of money and of the relationship between the parties. Secondly, whilst arbitrators faced with the need to adapt a relational contract may look to a variety of sources for guidance (including the *lex arbitri*, the *lex causae* and the terms of the contract—especially the extent to which self-adjustment and renegotiation are explicitly envisaged), there is surely an opportunity to develop a set of principles of broad application and either explicitly incorporated by reference into new contracts or agreed to by parties in dispute at the point of arbitration. Such a set of principles would in a certain sense bridge the gap between *pacta sunt servanda* and *rebus sic stantibus* to the extent that they would be an acknowledgement of the inevitably incomplete character of relational contracts. Equally importantly, however, they would serve as an acknowledgement that the adaptive response to such incompleteness cannot be unbounded if we are to ensure that such contracts fulfil their prime objective of maintaining a mutually beneficial relationship between the parties in the long term. In this regard, it might be suggested that an argument that diverged from Desta's critique of Production Sharing Agreements by pointing to the need to complexify the understanding of stabilisation in the context of modern agreements returns to meet his analysis again by proposing that if African nations are indeed to take collective action with regard to such contracts, then it might most fruitfully be in the development of principles

[109]Ibid.

which could guide the arbitral adaptation of PSAs properly understood as relational contracts.

8 Conclusion: Towards Principles to Guide Renegotiations and the Arbitral Adaptation of Relational Contracts

The development of such principles would be a matter for the governments concerned in conjunction with other interested parties. In terms of sources of inspiration, the work of relational contract theorists such as Ian Macneil and Stewart Macaulay will, of course, be important. Discussing the former in this regard, the latter had the following to say:

> McNeil's work demands anyone who thinks seriously about contract doctrine confront the reality of long-term continuing relations. These relations can involve trust and joint effort for common, or at least consistent, and goals. These relationships can also involve power and expectation where the dominated party continues in the relationship because it is the best of a bad set of options open. But one thing is clear: if we are concerned with real expectations, that is, with reasonable reliance and good-faith, then we cannot be satisfied with only formal written documents.[110]

But in addition to the insights that might be drawn from the theoretical literature, it is surely also the case that, as has been suggested above, the evolving practice of drafting and managing PSAs could also provide an indication of the sorts of overarching principles to which arbitrators could fruitfully be directed to guide the adaptation of PSAs where renegotiation efforts have been unsuccessful. In this regard, the draft Guiding Principles for Durable Extractive Contracts produced by the OECD,[111] though they do not explicitly refer to the concept of relationality, are full of references to concepts that would be familiar to that school of thought. For example, Guiding Principle II reads:

> Durable extractive contracts are anchored in a transparent quality long-term relationship and operational partnership between host governments, investors and communities, to fulfil agreed and understood objectives based on shared and realistic expectations that are managed throughout the lifecycle of the project.

Guiding Principle III states, inter alia, that "Durable extractive contracts balance the legitimate interests of host governments, investors, and communities", while Guiding Principle IV reads, inter alia, "Durable extractive contracts seek to maximise overall value, including economic, social and environmental outcomes to be drawn from the development of the host country's resources". Guiding Principle V states that "Durable extractive contracts are negotiated and based on continuing sharing of key financial and technical data to build a common understanding of the

[110] Macaulay (1999).

[111] OECD Development Centre, Guiding Principles for Durable Extractive Contracts, Advanced Draft, available at: https://www.oecd.org/dev/Guiding-Principles-public-consultation.pdf.

performance and of the main risks and opportunities of the project throughout its life-cycle", while Guiding Principle VIII states that "Durable extractive contracts are underpinned by a fiscal system that provides for a fair sharing of economic rent between the investor and the host government, taking into consideration the risks and potential rewards." These draft principles are thus clearly consistent with the idea that PSAs are relational contracts. It must, of course, be acknowledged, that the impulse behind the development of the principles is explicitly to "to provide guidance for the content and negotiation of mutually beneficial, sustainable and therefore enduring extractive contracts and thus *reduce or eliminate the risk of disputes and renegotiation of contract terms* over time" [emphasis added]. Equally, Guiding Principle VIII also states that "A regime with automatic adjustments for the government take to prevailing market conditions (variable with commodity price, production volume, resource quality, or project profitability) *reduces the incentives for either party to seek re-negotiations of terms*" [emphasis added]. It is suggested, however, firstly, that recognition of the degree of incompleteness inherent in PSAs means that we should be open to the idea that renegotiation and disputes can never be ruled out even in the context of the most carefully drafted contract and, secondly, that by no means all existing PSAs have been drafted with such insights in mind. Accordingly, there would appear to be good reason to think in terms of the extent to which these principles aimed at negotiation and drafting could just as usefully inform parties involved in the renegotiation of existing agreements and, importantly, arbitrators faced with the need to adapt contracts in the context of disputes where there is a risk to the continuing viability of a mutually beneficial long-term relationship between state and commercial actors. In such circumstances, it is surely also the case that arbitral awards would be regarded as more broadly acceptable and indeed legitimate to the extent that contractual adaptations may be explained in terms of reference to widely acknowledged guiding principles—especially if these have been actively developed by the very African governments who have most at stake in these contracts. Recognising relationality in this way allows us to respect sovereignty in a way that ensures that the balance of interests inherent in PSAs is maintained to the mutual benefit of investors and states. In concluding this discussion, it is worth also bearing in mind that in addition to all the well-known risks and uncertainties facing the governments and companies involved in the search for and production of hydrocarbons, they must now also face the prospect that the value of existing investments and the commercial viability of new discoveries will be affected by climate change concerns. Accordingly, there are scenarios in which some existing and potential production will be preferred on the basis of the differential environmental impact of the production itself[112]—to say nothing of the increasing likelihood, especially within the multi-decade duration of a hydrocarbon project, that some will not be produced at all. The impact of these emerging, but inevitable, considerations on existing and potential contracts is yet to be fully felt.

[112]See Masnadi et al. (2018).

References

Aldersey-Williams J (2018) Decommissioning security. In: Gordon G, Paterson J, Usenmez E (eds) UK oil and gas law: current practice and emerging trends – volume II commercial and contract law issues. Edinburgh University Press, Edinburgh, pp 435–449

Alexander FA (2010) Security of Investment Considerations under PSCs and other Government Petroleum Contracts. Legal Education Society of Alberta. http://www.lesaonline.org/samples/11_32_13_p1.pdf. Accessed 6 Feb 2019

Allen J, Aitken S (2018) Finance, security and insolvency in the upstream oil and gas sector. In: Gordon G, Paterson J, Usenmez E (eds) UK oil and gas law: current practice and emerging trends – volume II commercial and contract law issues. Edinburgh University Press, Edinburgh, pp 331–367

Benn T (1990) Conflicts of interest: diaries 1977–80. Hutchinson, London

Berger KP (2003) Renegotiation and adaptation of international investment contracts: the role of contract drafters and arbitrators. Vanderbilt J Transnational Law 36:1347

Bernstein L (1992) Opting out of the legal system: extralegal contractual relations in the diamond industry. J Leg Stud XXI:115–157

Bindemann K (1999) Production sharing agreements, an economic analysis. Oxford Institute for Energy Studies, WPM 24

Bordacahar J (2018) The rule of law as created by arbitrators: an update on the discussions at the recent IBA arbitration day in Buenos Aires. Kluwer Arbitration Blog, 8 April 2018. http://arbitrationblog.kluwerarbitration.com/2018/04/08/iba-buenos-aires-report/. Visited 6 Feb 2019

Cameron P (2006) Stabilisation in investment contracts and changes of rules in host countries: tools for oil & gas investors. Association of International Petroleum Negotiators

Carmalt SW (2017) The economics of oil. Springer, pp 3–24

Cotula L (2008) Regulatory takings, stabilization clauses and sustainable development. Paper submitted to 7th OECD Global Forum on International Investment

Daniel P, Sunley E (2010) Contractual assurances of fiscal stability. In: Daniel P, Keen M, McPherson C (eds) The taxation of petroleum and minerals: principles, problems and practice. Routledge, Abingdon, pp 405–424

Desta MG (2016) Competition for natural resources and international investment law: perspectives from Africa. Ethiopian Yearb Int Law 1:117

Erkan M (2010) International energy investment law: stability through contractual clauses. Walters Kluwer Law & Business, Dordrecht

Finizio SP (2017) Energy Arbitration in Africa. Global Arbitration Review. 20 April 2017. https://globalarbitrationreview.com/insight/the-middle-eastern-and-african-arbitration-review-2017/1139822/energy-arbitration-in-africa. Visited 6 Feb 2019

Global Witness (2014) A good deal better? Uganda's secret oil contracts explained. Global Witness Limited, London

Gordon G (2018) Petroleum licensing. In: Gordon G, Paterson J, Usenmez E (eds) UK oil and gas law: current practice and emerging trends – volume I resource management and regulatory law. Edinburgh University Press, Edinburgh, pp 81–131

Gotanda JY (2003) Renegotiation and adaptation clauses in investment contracts, revisited. Vanderbilt J Transnational Law 36:1461

Halabi SF (2011) Efficient contracting between foreign investors and host states: evidence from stabilization clauses. Northwest J Int Law Bus 31:261

Johnson D (1994) International petroleum fiscal systems and production sharing contracts. Pennwell, Tulsa

Johnston D, Johnston D (2015) Fundamental petroleum fiscal considerations. Oxford Institute for Energy Studies, Oxford

Kakonge JO (2011) Challenges of managing expectations of newly emerging oil and gas producers of the south. J World Energy Law Bus 4(2):124–135

Kemp A, Stephen L (2018) Rejuvenating activity in the North Sea oil and gas industry: the role of tax incentives in context. In: Gordon G, Paterson J, Usenmez E (eds) UK oil and gas law: current practice and emerging trends – volume I resource management and regulatory law. Edinburgh University Press, Edinburgh, pp 14–41

Kolb RW (1996) Financial derivatives, 2nd edn. Blackwell Business, Cambridge

Konoplyanik A (2003) The fight against PSAs in Russia: who is to benefit and why not the state? Int Energy Law Tax Rev 10:277–286

Kunjan B (2016) Exploration chance of success predictions - statistical concepts and realities, ASEG-PESA-AIG 2016. https://www.researchgate.net/publication/314274552_Exploration_Chance_of_Success_Predictions_-_Statistical_Concepts_and_Realities. Visited 4 July 2019

Macaulay S (1999) Relational contracts floating on a sea of custom? Thoughts about the ideas of Ian Macneil and Lisa Bernstein. Northwest Univ Law Rev 94:775–804

Macneil I (1983) Values in contract: internal and external. Northwest Univ Law Rev 78:340

Maniruzzaman AFM (2007) Drafting stabilization clauses in international energy contracts: some pitfalls for the unwary. Int Energy Law Tax Rev 2:23–26

Maniruzzaman AFM (2008) The pursuit of stability in international energy investment contracts: a critical appraisal of the emerging trends. J World Energy Law Bus 1(2):121–157

Masnadi MS et al (2018) Global carbon intensity of crude oil production. Science 36:851–853

McDonald RL (2009) Fundamentals of derivatives markets. Pearson/Addison Wesley, Boston & London

Nolan PA, Thurber MC (2010) On the State's choice of oil company, risk management and the frontier of the petroleum industry. Program on Energy and Sustainable Development, Stanford. Working Paper no.99, December 2010

Pate TJ (2009) Evaluating stabilization clauses in Venezuela's strategic association agreements for heavy-crude extraction in the Orinoco Belt: the return of a forgotten risk reduction mechanism for the petroleum industry. Univ Miami Inter-American Law Rev 40:347

Platform (2010) Contracts Curse: Uganda's oil agreements place profit before people, February 2010. Available at http://platformlondon.org/wp-content/uploads/2012/01/Contracts-Curse-Uganda-Platform-CSCO.pdf. Visited 6 Feb 2019

Saliba AT (2001) Rebus sic stantibus: a comparative survey. Murdoch Univ Electron J Law 8(3)

Sas B (1992) Legal aspects of risk management in energy markets. Pet Econ Energy Law Suppl, 59:50–59

Shemberg A (2009) Stabilization clauses and human rights. IFC

Sikka P (2011) Accounting for human rights: the challenge of globalization and foreign investment agreements. Crit Perspect Account 22(8):811–827

Stevens P, Kooroshy J, Lahn G, Lee B (2013) Conflict and coexistence in the extractive industries. Chatham House, London

Styles SC (2018) Joint operating agreements. In: Gordon G, Paterson J, Usenmez E (eds) UK oil and gas law: current practice and emerging trends – volume II commercial and contract law issues. Edinburgh University Press, Edinburgh, pp 15–73

Taverne B (1996a) Production sharing agreements in principle and practice. In: David MR (ed) Upstream oil and gas agreements. Sweet and Maxwell, London

Taverne B (1996b) Cooperative agreements in the extractive petroleum industry. Kluwer Law International, London

Taverne B (2008) Petroleum, industry and governments: a study of the involvement of industry and governments in the production and use of petroleum, 2nd edn. Wolters Kluwer Law & Business, Austin

Tordo S (2007) Fiscal Systems for Hydrocarbons: Design Issues. World Bank Working Paper no. 123

Vernon R (1971) Sovereignty at Bay: the multinational spread of US enterprises. Basic Books, New York

Wälde TW (1994) Stabilising International Investment Commitments: International Law versus Contract Interpretation. CPMLP Professional Paper, No. PP13

John Paterson is Professor of Law at the University of Aberdeen and one of the founders of the Centre for Energy Law there. He is one of the co-editors of *UK Oil and Gas Law: Current Practice and Emerging Trends* (3rd ed.) (2 vols.) Edinburgh University Press, 2018, and co-ordinates Aberdeen's involvement in the North Sea Energy Law Programme. In the past year, he has held visiting posts at the National University of Singapore and the Chinese University of Hong Kong.

Contract-Farming in Cocoa Value Chains in Africa: Possibilities and Challenges

Lindsey Callahan

Abstract The cocoa industry is a global multi-billion dollar industry that faces numerous challenges at the farm production level. Cocoa is largely grown by smallholder farmers in equatorial Africa, who experience poverty, declining productivity, volatile prices and lack of funding for investment, as well as human rights and environmental issues. Contract-farming is a value chain model that has been proposed to address many of the challenges faced by cocoa farmers. This paper provides an overview of the cocoa industry, including past and current initiatives to address issues and inequities in the cocoa market, and an overview of current research on contract-farming of cocoa, including an examination of three chocolate companies that source cocoa from Africa using a contract-farming business model: Theo Chocolate (Democratic Republic of Congo), Divine Chocolate (Ghana), and Madécasse (Madagascar). This research finds that contract-farming does offer cocoa farmers the opportunity to receive a higher price point for cocoa, and is more beneficial than industry sustainability programmes. There are however significant gaps in the research into contract-farming. It is not clear how contract-farming impacts sustainable economic development in the longer term, even when farmers obtain a higher price point for cocoa. Contract-farming may increase risks associated with land tenure insecurity, marginalization of women, and crop monoculture; even so, contract-farming can be carried out in a way that mitigates these risks.

1 Introduction

The cocoa industry, including the cocoa derivative, chocolate, is a global multi-billion dollar industry. Despite continuing high demand for cocoa-derived products, the cocoa industry is currently facing many challenges at the farm level, including low productivity due to declining soil and tree fertility, pests and disease, limited knowledge of modern farming techniques, and limited access to finances for investment. These challenges hinder the economic development of the communities of

L. Callahan (✉)
University of Washington School of Law, Seattle, WA, USA

Z. Yihdego et al. (eds.), *Ethiopian Yearbook of International Law 2018*, Ethiopian Yearbook of International Law 2018, https://doi.org/10.1007/978-3-030-24078-3_7

smallholder farmers most often engaged in cocoa farming, as well as the sustainability of the cocoa industry. Further, the impact of challenges facing the cocoa industry extend far beyond the industry itself—cocoa is largely farmed by smallholder farmers in equatorial developing countries. The challenges facing the cocoa industry impact national economies that largely depend on agricultural exports. Agricultural contracts are increasingly being put forward as a value chain model with the potential to increase agricultural production while at the same time improving the livelihoods of smallholder farmers. Agricultural contracts offer risks and potential rewards for both the producer and the buyer of cocoa. Whether contract-farming could help solve some of the issues found in the cocoa industry in Africa depend on a number of factors that the current research literature does not adequately consider, including risks associated with tenure insecurity, marginalization of women, and crop monoculture. These risks, if not sufficiently addressed, pose a serious challenge to the broader implementation of contract-farming, and any potential positive impact thereof. Nevertheless, the potential for contract-farming to improve the livelihoods of smallholder farmers, and in turn, to improve the sustainability of the cocoa industry, make it a value chain model worth exploring for the cocoa industry and concerned governments alike.

First, this paper provides an overview of the cocoa industry, and the many challenges facing the cocoa industry today. Second, this paper provides an overview of contract-farming, which has been proposed as a value chain model for overcoming some of the challenges found in agricultural markets generally. Third, this paper looks specifically at examples of contract-farming being adopted as a value chain model for cocoa in Africa, by examining three studies that have been conducted, and by looking at three chocolate businesses sourcing cocoa from Africa. Finally, this paper concludes by, first, highlighting what is known about the potential for contract-farming in the cocoa value chain, and, second, addressing the limits of what is known. Contract-farming enables a higher price point and greater price stability for cocoa farmers; however, challenges remain for the implementation of contract-farming to have a positive impact on smallholder cocoa farmers in Africa and on the sustainability of the global cocoa value chain.

2 Overview of the Cocoa Industry

Cocoa, or more specifically, the *Theobroma cacao* tree, is indigenous to the Amazonian Basin.[1] It spread throughout South and Central America over thousands of years, likely through human intervention.[2] It is there that it became a cultivated crop, both for consumption of the pulp, and consumption of the seeds or beans which are

[1] Young (2007).

[2] *Id.*

made into chocolate.[3] Following the Spanish conquest of Central America, cocoa made its way via the trade routes to the west coast of Africa.[4] Cocoa cultivation was introduced in Africa in 1822, but it was not until 1879, when cocoa was introduced in what is now Ghana, that its cultivation in Africa took off.[5] Today, most of the world's cocoa harvest comes from Africa. For the 2013–2014 crop year, it is estimated that 73% of global production came from Africa.[6] The two countries leading production in Africa are Cote d'Ivoire and Ghana,[7] but cocoa is grown and harvested across equatorial Africa.

Broadly speaking, the cocoa global value chain can be broken down into five segments: (1) production by farmers, (2) sourcing and marketing, (3) processing, (4) manufacturing and distribution, and (5) retailing to consumers. Production generally involves smallholder farmers who grow and take care of the trees, harvest the pods, and ferment and dry the beans. Sourcing and marketing generally is carried about by an in-country broker who sources, cleans, and trades the beans. Processing entails roasting and grinding the beans, and producing semi-finished cocoa products, such as powder, butter, or liquor, which are used to make chocolate. Manufacturing and distribution involves turning the semi-finished cocoa products into finished chocolate-based products. Finally, retailing to consumers involves packaging, commercial marketing, and retailing of chocolate products.[8]

Cocoa is a labour-intensive crop, and the producers of cocoa are typically smallholder farmers. *Theobroma cacao* trees typically bear pods in their fifth year, and are productive for 25–30 years.[9] The trees generally produce cocoa pods twice a year.[10] When the pods ripen, they are harvested manually by cutting the pods from the trunk of the tree, usually with a blade.[11] The cocoa beans and pulp are removed from the pods, and allowed to ferment for 3–7 days.[12] Following fermentation, the beans are dried in the sun for 5–10 days.[13] After the cocoa beans are dried, they are ready for the market. Notably, smallholder farms account for 80–90% of global

[3] *Id.*

[4] *Id.*

[5] *Id.*

[6] Gayi and Tsowou (2015).

[7] *Id.*; *see also* Kroeger et al., Forest- and Climate-Smart Cocoa in Côte D'Ivoire and Ghana: Aligning Stakeholders to Support Smallholders in Deforestation-Free Cocoa 12 (World Bank).

[8] *Id.* at 10–13.

[9] *Id.* at 10.

[10] *Id.*

[11] *Id.*

[12] *Id.* at 11.

[13] *Id.*

cocoa production, and the typical farm size in Africa is two to four hectares.[14] Cocoa farms are typically a family enterprise.[15]

Generally, an in-country broker will purchase the cocoa beans from the farmers, inspect and grade the cocoa beans and prepare them for shipment, then trade them to a processing company.[16] The cocoa beans are almost universally transported out of Africa to more industrially developed countries for processing. The cocoa trading and processing market is dominated by just three companies: Berry Callebaut AG, Cargill, and Archer Daniels Midland Company (ADM). In 2013, these companies traded and ground 50–60% of the world's cocoa production.[17]

Once the cocoa is processed into semi-finished cocoa products, it is then sold to chocolate manufacturers. The manufacturers and retailers of chocolate are generally large multinational corporations, amongst the largest companies in the world. Specifically, the chocolate industry is dominated by a few chocolate companies: Mars Inc., Mondelez International, Nestlé SA, Meiji Holdings Co. Limited (Japan), Ferrero Group, Hershey Foods Corp. (US), and Arcor (Argentina).[18] In 2014, these companies made up approximately 40% of the market share for chocolate.[19] These companies and the brands they represent are household names in much of the world. Nevertheless, there are chocolate companies aside from "Big Chocolate" that carve out niches within the market.

The cocoa industry in Africa faces a number of issues that threaten its long-term viability and sustainability. African cocoa farms face declining soil and tree fertility, pests, and disease.[20] Cocoa farming has very low profitability and is associated with poor living standards for cocoa farmers.[21] As a result, young people do not consider cocoa farming a viable business or life choice, and the younger generation is not farming cocoa. They are shifting to more profitable crops, or more lucrative off-farm activities, or leaving farming altogether to migrate to cities.[22] As a result, the average age of a cocoa farmer in West Africa is 50 years old.[23] This is particularly shocking

[14] *Id.* at 10.

[15] Better Cocoa, Nestlé Cocoa Plan, http://www.nestlecocoaplan.com/better-cocoa/ (last visited May 26, 2018).

[16] *Id.*

[17] Gayi and Tsowou (2015), p. 14.

[18] *Id.* at 15.

[19] *Id.*

[20] Wessel and Quist-Wessel (2015).

[21] *Id.* at 2.

[22] *Id. See also* Flick, *Ageing cocoa farmers pose risk for Ghana industry*, Financial Times, https://www.ft.com/content/d9cb0d1c-26e7-11e5-bd83-71cb60e8f08c (last visited June 1, 2018).

[23] This is a widely cited statistic in materials on cocoa farming, *see, e.g.*, Cocoa, Fairtrade, https://www.fairtrade.org.uk/Farmers-and-Workers/Cocoa (last visited June 1, 2018); however, it is not clear where this statistic originated. The average age of a Ghanaian cocoa farmer is stated to be 55 years old, *see* Flick, *supra* note 22. One study found Nigerian farmers to mostly be over 60 years old: Wessel and Quist-Wessel (2015), p. 3.

in light of the fact that the average life expectancy in Ghana and Cote d'Ivoire is 63 and 54, respectively.[24] For men, it is 62 and 52, respectively.[25]

At the farm level, cocoa farms are experiencing low and declining productivity.[26] The low price that farmers receive for cocoa disincentivises them from investing in their farms or improving quality, because they may not recoup their investment.[27] Farmers have insufficient access to inputs, including planting material and fertilizer.[28] They have insecure land tenure, which leads to lower investment, difficulty in accessing credit, and can be a barrier to crop diversification and reforestation.[29] They have limited access to finance.[30] When there are banks that will lend money to smallholder cocoa farmers, they are perceived as being high risk, and the loans are subject to high interest rates.[31] Smallholder farmers have limited knowledge of modern agricultural techniques and farm management skills.[32] More issues are on the horizon: due to *theobroma cacao* trees' sensitivity, cocoa farms are particularly susceptible to climate change.[33]

The world market is stacked against cocoa farmers who, despite bearing all the risks of production, have the fewest resources in the global value chain to cope with market volatility. The world market price for cocoa is highly volatile. For example, between September 2016 and February 2017, it lost a third of its value, falling from $3000 per ton to $1900 per ton.[34] While this was an extreme loss in value, wide fluctuations are normal in the cocoa market.[35] Further, high market concentration in the cocoa global value chain reduces farmers to "price takers". The markets for cocoa export, cocoa processing, and chocolate production in the value chain are highly concentrated, both at country and global levels.[36] While this market concentration allows companies to benefit from economies of scale, the cost savings are not

[24] Life expectancy at birth, total (years), World Bank, https://data.worldbank.org/indicator/SP.DYN.LE00.IN (last visited May 25, 2018).

[25] Life expectancy at birth, men (years), World Bank, https://data.worldbank.org/indicator/SP.DYN.LE00.MA.IN (last visited May 25, 2018).

[26] Kroeger et al. at 14–16.

[27] What makes Theo different?, Theo Chocolate, https://www.theochocolate.com/blog/what-makes-theo-different/ (last visited May 26, 2018).

[28] Kroeger et al. at 18.

[29] ABVV/Horval et al. (2018).

[30] Kroeger et al. at 19.

[31] *Id.*

[32] *Id.* at 17.

[33] *Id.* at 14–16.

[34] ABVV/Horval et al. (2018), p. 7.

[35] *See* Monthly Review of the Market, ICCO, https://www.icco.org/statistics/monthly-review-of-the-market.html (last visited May 31, 2018).

[36] Gayi and Tsowou (2015), p. 18.

passed on to farmers.[37] This market concentration increases the bargaining power of traders and processors, to the detriment of smallholder farmers.[38]

In addition to the poverty created by this market dynamic, the end result has been negative for the environment and human rights as well. Cocoa farming has resulted in extensive deforestation, particularly in West Africa, driven by lack of government enforcement of environmentally protected areas and also lack of interest by companies in the sources of the cocoa supply.[39] Additionally, as a result of systemic poverty and lack of infrastructure in cocoa farming areas, the level of child labour in the cocoa farming sector is high.[40]

Broadly speaking, these issues impact the cocoa industry in two ways: first, they threaten the long-term environmental sustainability of cocoa farming; and second, they threaten the long-term sustainability of the production-side of the cocoa market, specifically, the viability of smallholder farming of cocoa. The net effect is the impoverishment of cocoa farmers and their communities, and in turn, the underdevelopment of national economies that depend upon cocoa.

There have been a number of international, governmental, and industry-wide initiatives to address some of the issues being experienced across the cocoa industry, including the International Cocoa Organization, national marketing boards, the World Cocoa Foundation, and the International Cocoa Initiative. The International Cocoa Organization (ICCO) was founded in 1973, following the United Nations International Cocoa Conference, to address the inequities in the cocoa industry, recognizing that international coordination was necessary to help address some of the negative consequences of market forces.[41] Its membership is made up of cocoa-producing and cocoa-consuming countries, with 51 member states.[42] The ICCO is tasked with implementing seven international agreements. Significantly, the 2010 Agreement (the most recent of the agreements) established a specific mandate for working toward a sustainable world cocoa economy and founded a consultative board.[43] The consultative board, which serves an advisory role, consists of experts on the cocoa sector from the private sector and civil society.[44]

The governments of Cote d'Ivoire and Ghana established cocoa marketing boards. Ghana's marketing board, known as the Ghana Cocoa Board or COCOBOD,

---

[37] *Id.*

[38] *Id.*

[39] ABVV/Horval et al. (2018), p. 18; *see also* Higonnet et al. (2017).

[40] ABVV/Horval et al. (2018), p. 16; *see also* Tulane University School of Public Health and Tropical Medicine (2015).

[41] About the International Cocoa Organization, International Cocoa Organization, https://www.icco.org/about-us/about-the-icco.html (last visited May 26, 2018); *and* International Cocoa Agreement, 1972, art. 1, Oct. 21, 1972, 882 U.N.T.S. 12652.

[42] *Id.*; *see* Membership of the International Cocoa Organization, International Cocoa Organization, https://www.icco.org/about-us/membership-of-the-icco.html (last visited May 26, 2018).

[43] *Id.*

[44] *Id.*

was established early on, in 1947.[45] Cote d'Ivoire's marketing board, known as Conseil du Café-Cocoa, was established more recently, in 2011.[46] Cote d'Ivoire and Ghana's marketing boards are governmental bodies that set domestic prices for cocoa, as well as carry out related research into quality, disease, and pest issues.[47] They set their respective prices for cocoa based on forecasts for production and sales, exchange rates, and forward sales.[48] Their setting of prices brings greater stability to price levels for Cote d'Ivoirian and Ghanaian cocoa farmers. Cote d'Ivoire and Ghana are increasingly cooperating in price setting.[49]

More recently, there has been a push for the business community to take a more active role. Cocoa processing companies and chocolate companies have responded both with non-profit initiatives, such as the World Cocoa Foundation and International Cocoa Initiative, and with corporate initiatives and strategies. The World Cocoa Foundation (WCF) is a non-profit organization that promotes sustainability in the cocoa sector. It is a membership-based organization, with members including cocoa and chocolate manufacturers, processors, and companies worldwide.[50] WCF's main initiative, CocoaAction, launched in 2014. CocoaAction is a voluntary, industry-wide strategy for cocoa companies to work with the government and stakeholders in Ghana and Code d'Ivoire on issues of cocoa sustainability.[51] CocoaAction participants include Berry Callebaut, Cargill, Ferrero, Hershey, Mars, Mondelez, Nestlé, and Olam.[52] CocoaAction's vision is "a sustainable and thriving cocoa sector—where farmers prosper, cocoa-growing communities are empowered, human rights are respected, and the environment in conserved."[53] Because CocoaAction is in its early stages, its efforts have so far focused on data collection, in order to establish a baseline for future monitoring and evaluation.[54]

The International Cocoa Initiative (ICI) was started in 2002 in an effort to address child labour on cocoa farms.[55] Its founding was the result of an agreement by cocoa and chocolate industry representatives, known as the "Harkin Engel Protocol", in

[45] About Us, COCOBOD, https://cocobod.gh/aboutus.php (last visited May 30, 2018).

[46] Statuts & Objectifs du Conseil du Café-Cacao, Le Conseil Du Café-Cocoa, http://www.conseilcafecacao.ci/index.php?option=com_content&view=article&id=112&Itemid=186 (last visited May 30, 2018).

[47] Objectives and Functions of the Board, COCOBOD, https://cocobod.gh/Objectives_Functions_Board.php (last visited May 30, 2018).

[48] Vigneri and Kolavalli (2017).

[49] ABVV/Horval et al. (2018), p. 27.

[50] Vision & Mission, World Cocoa Foundation, http://www.worldcocoafoundation.org/about-wcf/history-mission/ (last visited May 26, 2018).

[51] World Cocoa Foundation, CocoaAction Annual Report 2016: Learning As We Grow: Putting CocoaAction Into Practice (2016).

[52] *Id.*

[53] *Id.*

[54] *Id.*

[55] About Us, International Cocoa Initiative, http://www.cocoainitiative.org/about-ici/about-us/ (last visited May 26, 2018).

which the cocoa and chocolate industry collectively agreed to implement the International Labour Organization's "Convention concerning the Prohibition and Immediate Action for the Elimination of the Worst Forms of Child Labor".[56] ICI's board members from the industry include Berry Callebaut, Cargill, Ecom, Ferrero, Hershey's, Mars, Mondelez, Nestlé, Olam, and Touton.[57] The ICI currently works in 75 communities in Ghana and Cote d'Ivoire.[58] In cocoa producing communities, ICI carries out trainings and helps communities to produce and implement plans to reduce child labour.[59]

Likewise, the main cocoa processors have their own sustainability initiatives and publish annual sustainability reports. Berry Callebaut's "Forever Chocolate" strategy, launched in 2016, aims to, by 2025, eradicate child labour from the supply chain, lift more than 500,000 cocoa farmers out of poverty, become "carbon and forest positive," and have 100% sustainable ingredients in all their products.[60] Cargill's "Cocoa Promise" strategy, launched in 2012, aims to "achieve measurable, positive impacts for farmer and community livelihoods" by investing in farmer development, with focus on inputs; farmer training; access to services, such as education, health, and nutrition; and by working with, and empowering, farmer organizations. Cargill links their "Cocoa Promise" goals with the SDGs and aim to achieve their goals by 2030.[61] ADM publishes an annual corporate sustainability report. Their 2016 report broadly discusses the company's contributions to the Sustainable Development Goals (SDGs); corporate policies, including their environmental policy and human rights policy; and includes an independent third-party audit. The report also discusses ADM's external commitments, including as a signatory to the United Nations Global Compact and International Trade Commission's Trade for Sustainable Development Principles. The report does not specifically mention cocoa, but this is not necessarily surprising—ADM is one of the world's largest agricultural processor and food ingredient companies, and cocoa is just one crop amongst many within their operations.[62]

---

[56]Harkin-Engel Protocol, International Cocoa Initiative, http://www.cocoainitiative.org/knowledge-centre-post/harkin-engel-protocol/ (last visited May 26, 2018).

[57]Industry Members, International Cocoa Initiative, http://www.cocoainitiative.org/about-ici/our-partners/industry-members/ (last visited May 26, 2018).

[58]About Us, International Cocoa Initiative, http://www.cocoainitiative.org/about-ici/about-us/ (last visited May 26, 2018).

[59]Our Work: Community Level, International Cocoa Initiative, https://cocoainitiative.org/our-work/our-work/community-level/ (last visited May 26, 2018).

[60]Press Release, Barry Callebaut, "Forever Chocolate": Berry Callebaut targets 100% sustainable chocolate by 2025 (Nov. 28, 2016), *available at* https://www.barry-callebaut.com/news/2016/11/forever-chocolate-barry-callebaut-targets-100-sustainable-chocolate-2025.

[61]Sustainable Cocoa: Evolving the Cargill Cocoa Promise, Cargill, https://www.cargill.com/sustainability/cocoa/sustainable-cocoa (last visited May 28, 2018); *see also* Cargill, The 2016/2107 Cargill Cocoa Promise Global Summary Report (2017), *available at* https://www.cargill.com/doc/1432099950824/cargill-cocoa-promise-report-2016-17.pdf.

[62]Archer Daniels Midland, ADM 2016 Corporate Sustainability Report (2016), *available at* https://www.adm.com/sustainability.

The companies that dominate the chocolate industry also have independent sustainability initiatives and reporting. For example, Mars has its "Sustainable in a Generation Plan," which utilizes certification schemes and focuses on farm productivity.[63] Mondelez International's "Cocoa Life" is the programme through which it provides funding to WCF and ICI.[64] Nestlé's "Cocoa Plan" involves providing farmers with hardier, higher yield plants; training in agricultural practices; and addressing child labour, including by building schools.[65] Hershey's Corporate Social Responsibility Report 2016 advertises its "Learn to Grow" agricultural training and empowerment programme, which trains farmers in improving their yields as well as in entrepreneurship.[66] Hershey, Ferrero, and Mars have committed to sourcing 100% of their cocoa from certified sources by 2020; whereas Nestlé and Mondelez have focused on their own sustainability programmes rather than on certification.[67] Mondelez has announced that it is transitioning away from certified cocoa and sourcing all cocoa exclusively from its "Cocoa Life" programme.[68]

Certification schemes are another method for addressing issues in the cocoa industry. Certification schemes work by setting standards for farmers to improve farming practices, auditing farmer organizations to determine whether the standards were met, and labelling end-products to signal to consumers what products have met the standards. Farmers then earn a premium price for meeting certification standards.[69] There are two main certification schemes in the cocoa industry: Rainforest Alliance and Fairtrade.[70] Rainforest Alliance and Fairtrade operate differently when it comes to the premium farmers receive. For Rainforest Alliance, there is no fixed premium, so the farmer and buyer negotiate the premium on top of the market price. Fairtrade guarantees both a fixed minimum price and a fixed premium on top of the minimum price.[71]

---

[63]Cocoa: Caring for the future of cocoa, Mars, http://www.mars.com/global/sustainable-in-a-generation/our-approach-to-sustainability/raw-materials/cocoa (last visited May 28, 2018).

[64]Cocoa Life, Mondelez International, https://www.cocoalife.org/ (last visited May 28, 2018).

[65]Nestlé Cocoa Plan, Nestlé Cocoa Plan, http://www.nestlecocoaplan.com/ (last visited May 28, 2018).

[66]*See* Hershey, 2016 Hershey CSR Report (2016), *available at* https://www.thehersheycompany.com/content/dam/corporate-us/documents/csr-reports/2016-hershey-csr-report-detail.pdf.

[67]Nieburg, *Fair game: how effective is cocoa certification?*, Confectionary News.com, Dec. 21, 2017.

[68]*Id.*

[69]*See* Cocoa Certifications, Cargill, https://www.cargill.com/sustainability/cocoa/cocoa-certifications (last visited May 28, 2018) for a good brief synopsis on certification schemes.

[70]UTZ was a third certification scheme, and the dominant one in the cocoa industry. In January 2018, UTZ and the Rainforest Alliance merged, and now both operate as the Rainforest Alliance. *The Rainforest Alliance and UTZ To Merge, Forming New, Stronger Organization*, The Rainforest Alliance, Jun. 6, 2017, *available at* https://www.rainforest-alliance.org/articles/rainforest-alliance-utz-merger.

[71]Nieburg, *supra* note 67.

What is clear from the many approaches and initiatives to address inequities in the cocoa value chain is that the problems are not new. The same dynamics that existed 45 years ago, when the international community came together to form the ICCO, still dominate the cocoa industry today. In more recent decades, there has been a shift from these problems being within the exclusive realm of international organizations and governments, to also being within the realm of the business community. Cocoa processors and chocolate manufacturers have taken on a stronger role in addressing these problems. What is equally clear, though, is that the many approaches and initiatives have failed to solve the problems. While these efforts are still on-going, it is unlikely that the underlying problems will be entirely solved by corporate social responsibility programmes and certification schemes. To be sure, these corporate efforts are to be commended; however, corporations are ultimately taking a piecemeal approach to address a systemic issue.

3 Overview of Contract-Farming

Contract-farming has been proposed and promoted as an institutional arrangement with the potential to improve smallholder farmer livelihoods in developing countries.[72] To this end, the World Bank, the Food and Agriculture Organization of the United Nations, and UNIDROIT have all published numerous guides in recent years.[73] Behind the push for contract-farming is the idea that it has the potential to solve a number of problems associated with agricultural value chains from a development standpoint, with a mutually beneficial solution for both farmers and buyers, as well as recognition of the fact that contract-farming is increasingly being used in practice, especially in developing countries.[74]

Contract-farming, at its most basic, is a form of vertical integration between farmers and buyers (such as exporters, processors, and retailers).[75] More specifically, contract-farming is defined as:

> a particular form of supply chain governance adopted by firms to secure access to agricultural products ... meeting desired quantity, quality, location and timing specifications. Contracting is an intermediate mode of coordination, whereby the conditions of exchange are specifically set among transaction partners by some form of legally enforceable, binding agreement. The specifications can be more or less detailed, covering provisions regarding

[72]World Bank, World Development Report 2008: Agriculture for Development 127, 241 (2008).

[73]*See* Contract Farming Resource Centre, FAO, http://www.fao.org/in-action/contract-farming/en/ (last visited May 31, 2018).

[74]What is Contract Farming?, Contract Farming Resource Centre, FAO, http://www.fao.org/in-action/contract-farming/background/en/ (last visited May 31, 2018).

[75]Oya (2012).

production technology, price discovery, and risk sharing and other product and transaction attributes.[76]

Thus, contract-farming can be understood as covering a wide range of organizational arrangements that fall between spot purchasing at one end of the spectrum and complete vertical integration at the other end of the spectrum. Contract-farming is typically characterized by three attributes: first, a legally enforceable agreement between a farmer and a buyer, with terms and conditions for the future sale of a crop; second, the buyer agreeing to provide inputs to the farmer, such as seed plants, fertilizer, and technical assistance; and third, the farmer agreeing to meet certain specifications required by the buyer, such as farming organically or meeting requirements for a certification scheme.[77]

Contract-farming offers both farmers and buyers certain benefits. For farmers, it can mitigate risk, facilitate investment and training, and provide access to credit. For buyers, it can also mitigate risks, as well as reduce costs, and give them a stronger role in farming. First, it can mitigate risk for smallholder farmers, who generally assume all of the risks of production. Contract-farming allows farmers to better predict who their buyer will be, the timing of the purchase, and the price they will receive. Contracts can even provide a safety net in the event of crop failure. Greater predictability allows farmers to better plan, budget, prioritize, and invest.[78] Second, contract-farming can enable access to investment and services that smallholder farmers may not otherwise be able to gain access to, including inputs such as seeds and fertilizer; technology; skills training; and access to credit.[79] Contracts often include provision of inputs and production services to the farmer on credit through advances from the buyer.[80] Contracts can also be used as collateral to obtain loans from commercial banks or government agencies.[81] Finally, contract-farming can open up new markets for small farmers that might otherwise be unavailable to them.[82]

On the buyer's side, it can mitigate risks as well. First, production can be more reliable than purchasing on the open market, in terms of timing, price, and quality. Through contracting, and specifically timing requirements on performance of the contract, the buyer can better plan in order to optimize processing and delivery.[83] By setting a price through the contract, it can protect the buyer from market fluctuations.[84] Also, through quality standards in the contract and greater involvement at

[76]UNIDROIT, FAO & IFAD, UNIDROIT/FAO/IFAD Legal Guide on Contract Farming 1-2 (2015), *citing* Da Silva (2005).

[77]Eaton and Shepherd (2001).

[78]UNIDROIT, FAO & IFAD (2015), p. 8; *see also* Eaton and Shepherd (2001), p. 11.

[79]Eaton and Shepherd (2001), p. 11; *see also* UNIDROIT at 10.

[80]*Id.* at 11–12; *see also* UNIDROIT, FAO & IFAD (2015), p. 9.

[81]*Id.* at 12.

[82]*Id.* at 8 and 14.

[83]UNIDROIT, FAO & IFAD (2015), p. 7; *see also* Eaton and Shepherd (2001), p. 20.

[84]*Id.*

the farm level, more consistent quality can be obtained.[85] Second, the buyer has greater control over the inputs, methods, and outputs of farming. Through the contract, the buyer can specify required and prohibited inputs, if desired; for example, restricting the use of certain pesticides, or only using inputs provided by the buyer. The buyer can require or prohibit practices in farming; for example, prohibiting the use of child labour. The buyer can require conformity to regulatory or voluntary standards, related to food safety, or social or environmental issues. Traceability and compliance with certification schemes are increasingly playing a role in agriculture, and contract-farming provides a mechanism for buyers to facilitate this with farmers.[86] Finally, contract-farming allows companies to mitigate risks associated with land ownership in developing countries. Direct investment in land in developing countries, either through acquisition or long-term leases, carries with it risks and liabilities.[87] In some countries, there may be restrictions for foreign investors. Many companies are increasingly sensitive to social and political backlash from large-scale land acquisition and related impacts on local communities.[88]

While contract-farming offers certain potential benefits to farmers and buyers alike, it is not without drawbacks and risks. The power disparity between the contracting parties is extreme—the contract is often between individual smallholder farmers or a community-based organization representing smallholder farmers, resource-poor and often illiterate, and large Western international agribusiness corporations with a wealth of resources and sophisticated legal counsel. Contract disputes may leave few options for the farmers, especially in countries with weak legal systems.

For farmers, contract-farming can increase risks, particularly if a new variety of seeds, plants, or new technology is introduced.[89] Inefficient or corrupt management, where quotas or quality standards are manipulated, can result in not all contracted crops being purchased from the farmer.[90] Buyers can be unreliable, or engage in monopolistic or oligopolistic behaviour.[91] Monopsony creates the risk of hold-up, whereby the buyer changes the terms of the contract, knowing the farmer has few or no alternatives. This risk is particularly acute with tree crops, where farmers cannot easily change crops.[92] When credit is provided through the contract, farmers may face indebtedness or overreliance on advances.[93] Production problems, poor inputs or technical advice, changes in market conditions, and the buyer failing to honour the contract, all increase the likelihood of indebtedness for farmers under contract-

---

[85] Eaton and Shepherd (2001) at 21.

[86] UNIDROIT, FAO & IFAD (2015), p. 7.

[87] *Id.* at 8; *see also* Eaton and Shepherd (2001), pp. 18–20.

[88] *Id.* at 8; *see also* Eaton and Shepherd (2001), pp. 18–20.

[89] Eaton and Shepherd (2001), p. 15.

[90] *Id.* at 16–17.

[91] *Id.* at 17.

[92] *Id.*

[93] *Id.* at 18.

farming.[94] Finally, and of greatest concern, contract-farming encourages farm specialization in cash crops, and may come at the expense of food security.[95]

Likewise, contract-farming is not without risk for buyers. Land tenure can pose a major obstacle, as the farmer of the land to be cultivated may not have legal title to the land. Tenure insecurity, and the type of tenure under which the land is farmed, both have the potential to disincentivise investment in the land.[96] Further, land use disputes can arise between land users and land owners. Either scenario can jeopardize a buyer's contract-farming investment.[97] Farmers may also violate the terms of the contract, by diverting inputs supplied on credit to other purposes, or outright selling them, or by selling crops outside of the contract to a buyer who is not the contracting party.[98] Depending on the structure of the contract-farming arrangement, contract-farming may make it more difficult for buyers to monitor what is happening at the farm level, as opposed to more vertically-integrated business models.

It is also worth noting that contract-farming is not without controversy. At one end of the spectrum are those who see contract-farming "as a 'win-win' efficient arrangement in light of market failure" and at the other end of the spectrum, those who see it as "another means for global agribusiness to exploit peasants and labour".[99] The contract-farming literature tends to fall into three schools: development practitioners conducting evaluation studies, usually where donor money has been spent; academics and practitioners who are highly critical of agribusiness and concerned with food self-sufficiency; and a business-oriented approach, more concerned with the challenges of transnational corporate management than farmers' welfare or other social issues.[100] As one author points out, the significance of contract-farming in academic debates tends to relate to broader debates about capitalism and the role of smallholder farmers.[101]

No systematic empirical study, across countries and over time, has been carried out on contract-farming in Africa.[102] However, there have been studies carried out, focused on different countries or regions, crops, periods of time, and with different methodologies. A group of scholars conducted a systematic literature review in 2015 of contract-farming studies.[103] They looked at 23 studies, carried out in years ranging from 1984 to 2014; conducted in a wide selection of countries, but mostly

---

[94] *Id.*

[95] Oya (2012), p. 9.

[96] For an excellent analysis of these issues and their impact on Ghana's cocoa industry, *see* Asamoah and Owusu-Ansah (2015) and Asamoah et al. (2017).

[97] Eaton and Shepherd (2001), p. 22.

[98] *Id.* at 23–25.

[99] Oya (2012), p. 5.

[100] *Id.*

[101] *Id.* at 10.

[102] *Id.* at 3. While the article was published in 2012, the author of this paper is not aware of any systematic empirical studies being carried out between 2012 and the present (May 2018).

[103] Nguyen et al. (2015).

developing countries; and covering such agricultural products as rice, vegetables, soybeans, tea, dairy, poultry, and hogs.[104] They found that almost all of the selected studies analysing the impact of contract-farming on income argue that farmers experienced some increase in their income.[105]

Ultimately, contract-farming presents a method by which many companies in the cocoa industry can accomplish their stated goals. Its main benefit, from a business perspective, may be that it allows the buyer to set terms that align with its cultural values and protect it from lawsuits. However, these terms will only be as good as the resources provided to ensure they are feasible for the farmer, and the monitoring that accompanies them.

4 Contract-Farming of Cocoa in Africa: Studies and Businesses

There are few academic studies of contract-farming specifically focused on cocoa in Africa. While certainly much can be gleaned from studies of contract-farming of other crops and from other parts of the world, the context-specific nature of the methodology used by most contract-farming studies makes generalizations problematic. This paper focuses on three recent studies of cocoa contract-farming in Africa. Likewise, despite the large flow of cocoa from Africa, there are a limited number of chocolate businesses engaged in cocoa contract-farming. This paper looks at three such businesses. Both the studies and the businesses demonstrate the potential that contract-farming offers African cocoa farmers and the sustainability of the cocoa industry.

4.1 Studies of Cocoa Contract-Farming

There have been three recent studies of contract-farming in African cocoa markets: one from 2011 in Uganda, one from 2013 in Ghana, and one from 2014 in Tanzania. The 2011 study, conducted in rural Uganda, followed a contract-farming scheme centred around certified organic farming by Esco Ltd., a leading cocoa exporter in the region.[106] The study relied on repeated household surveys, comparing over time smallholders eligible for organic certification with smallholders ineligible for organic certification.[107] Farming in the region is largely "organic by default," meaning farming practices already meet organic standards, so implementation of

---

[104] *Id.* at 533–535.

[105] *Id.* at 535.

[106] Jones and Gibbon (2011).

[107] *Id.* at 1595–1599.

certifiable organic farming requires little change in practice for farmers.[108] Esco has a two-tiered business model: one for cocoa generally, and one for certified organic cocoa.[109] For cocoa that is not certified as organic, farmers can sell to Esco on a spot-marketing basis, so long as the cocoa meets minimum quality standards. Contracts are not used. However, for certified organic cocoa, Esco engages in contract-farming. Esco provides training and subsidized inputs (such as cocoa seedlings) to farmers, and in turn, farmers are required to follow organic farming standards and to sell to Esco.[110]

The study found that 5 years after the certification scheme and contract-farming initially started, farmers were increasingly producing high quality certified organic cocoa, and this cocoa received a premium price that was 16–18% higher than non-certified cocoa's price.[111] Specifically, the study found that households that were determined to be eligible for the scheme saw an "average effect" on net household income of 100% after 5 years.[112] There were also spillover effects: techniques for higher-quality cocoa were adopted throughout the cocoa farming community.[113] The study's authors acknowledge that as for the results of the study, "institutional, temporal and market specifications make generalization problematic".[114] The authors also note that two aspects of particular market conditions were conducive to the success of the scheme. First, Esco is a regional buyer focused on cocoa, with significant enough resources to implement an organic farming scheme, yet with its regional focus, is small enough (compared to Cargill, ADM, or Berry Callebaut) for such an in-depth investment to be crucial to its profitability.[115] Second, the remoteness of the region studied meant that the cocoa trees were free from serious plant health problems.[116]

Another study of cocoa farming, from 2013, focused on challenges in Ghana's cocoa value chain.[117] Ghana is the second largest producer of cocoa in the world (after Cote d'Ivoire).[118] In turn, cocoa is Ghana's second largest export product and approximately two million farmers depend on cocoa production as their main source of income.[119] Ghana's marketing board, COCOBOD, acts as an intermediary between farmers and registered traders, including setting prices.[120] The study's

[108] *Id.* at 1597.

[109] *Id.* at 1598–1600.

[110] *Id.* at 1599.

[111] *Id.* at 1599.

[112] *Id.* at 1614.

[113] *Id.* at 1613.

[114] *Id.* at 1614.

[115] *Id.* at 1615.

[116] *Id.*

[117] Roldan et al. (Fall 2013).

[118] *Id.* at 123.

[119] *Id.* at 124.

[120] *Id.* at 123.

authors conducted a value chain analysis to determine what processes might be improved and what might be done to raise farmers' income.[121] The study relied on surveys of 300 smallholder farmers, sampled from 20 different villages.[122] The authors also interviewed other key stakeholders, including COCOBOD and chocolate processors in Switzerland.[123]

The issue of contract-farming and its impact on cocoa farmers in Ghana was analysed. Of the sample size of smallholder farmers, 17.33% of those surveyed were working under contract.[124] The study found "a high correlation between the awareness of terms and conditions in contract-farming and the information flow about cocoa markets among farmers working under contract".[125] The study also found that for those engaged in contract-farming, there was a negative correlation with job security, meaning the farmers were not sure if the contract would be renewed for the next season.[126] The authors attributed this issue to a lack of trust between farmers and buyers, as well as difficulty of farmers in understanding the terms and conditions of written contracts, due to illiteracy.[127] Overall, the authors determined that "contract farming has a positive effect on cocoa communities because of the benefits provided to their farms," and they recommended COCOBOD and traders adopt practices conducive to contract-farming.[128]

The third study, published in 2014, examines whether contract-farming improved livelihoods of smallholder cocoa farmers in Tanzania.[129] The study relied on surveys of 271 smallholder farmers, sampled from across two districts.[130] The study found that farmers engaged in contract-farming experienced an increase in: access to farmer training, access to credit, production quantity, production acreage, and timely purchase and payment.[131] The study's findings suggest that contract-farming contributed to improving smallholder farmers' livelihoods.

These studies offer a good starting point, but the conclusions that can be drawn from them are limited by their methodologies. Each of the studies rely on cross-sectional sample surveys. The 2011 Uganda study and 2014 Tanzania study are impact assessments, which are typical of contract-farming studies.[132] They rely on an assessment of those who participate in contract-farming, compared with similarly situated farmers who do not participate in contract-farming. The first issue with

---

121 *Id.*

122 *Id.* at 124–125.

123 *Id.*

124 *Id.* at 131.

125 *Id.* at 133.

126 *Id.* at 131.

127 *Id.* at 131.

128 *Id.* at 133.

129 Kalimangasi et al. (2014).

130 *Id.* at 1.

131 *Id.*

132 Da Silva and Rankin (2013).

impact assessments is that the variables that are used to determine farm income are not stable over time, so depending on when and for how long the assessment takes place, the results will vary.[133] The results will also vary based on the entry-exit dynamics of farmers in contract-farming schemes.[134] Farmers who fail to see an increase in income are less likely to continue participating in contract-farming. Alternatively, the 2013 Ghana study focused on qualitative aspects of cocoa farming rather than quantitative analysis; specifically, farmers' perceptions. This approach is especially context-specific. While each of these studies provide useful insights into the experience of African cocoa farmers participating in contract-farming, broader interpretations of the results require caution.

4.2 Chocolate Companies That Use Contract-Farming

It is also worth looking at chocolate companies that have made equity throughout the cocoa global value chain part of their business model. Three chocolate companies provide illustration of business models that use contract-farming to operate in a way that provides a higher price point for smallholder cocoa farmers. Theo Chocolate uses a contract-farming business model to source cocoa from Democratic Republic of Congo. Divine Chocolate uses a joint venture model, which includes contracting, in Ghana. Finally, Madécasse is a chocolate company in Madagascar with a highly vertically integrated business model. Each company has a different business model, but each also uses contracting as a means to ensure a more equitable relationship with the farmers from which they source cocoa.

Theo Chocolate, based in Seattle, sources cocoa directly from farmers organizations in western Democratic Republic of Congo.[135] Rather than using the cocoa commodity market price, Theo directly negotiates a baseline price with the farmers' organizations on an annual basis, with basic quality specifications for the cocoa beans.[136] Theo uses forward-contracting: the negotiations take place and the price is fixed a year in advance.[137] On top of the baseline price and basic quality specifications, Theo offers farmers premiums for meeting higher quality standards for the

[133] *Id.*

[134] *Id.*

[135] What Makes Theo Different?, Theo Chocolate, https://www.theochocolate.com/blog/what-makes-theo-different/ (last visited May 26, 2018); and Congolese Cocoa, Theo Chocolate, https://www.theochocolate.com/blog/congolese-cocoa/ (last visited May 26, 2018). Theo works through exporter Esco Ltd., the same company that was previously discussed in the 2011 Uganda study.

[136] Interview with Emily Benson, Supply Chain Manager, Theo Chocolate, in Seattle, Washington (March 28, 2018).

[137] *Id.*

cocoa beans.[138] Theo works with the farmers to provide training workshops to better help farmers understand and account for their costs of production and profit margins.[139] Theo also uses third-party certification schemes, including organic and Fairtrade. The Fairtrade certification used, "Fair for Life" by Ecocert, goes beyond the traditional Fairtrade certification, to require both traceability and Fairtrade principles along the entire value chain. It additionally certifies that no forced labour or child labour take place on the farms where the cocoa is sourced.[140]

Divine Chocolate, which distributes both in the US and the United Kingdom, sources cocoa directly from a single farmers cooperative in Ghana.[141] When it launched in the UK in 1998, it was the first Fairtrade chocolate bar aimed at the mass market.[142] It is currently the only Fairtrade chocolate company co-owned by farmers.[143] Divine's business model is a joint venture: it is designed to be integrated with the cocoa farmers. A single farmers' cooperative, Kuapa Kokoo, founded the chocolate company, and the cooperative owns stock in the company.[144] Kuapa Kokoo's mission is "to empower farmers in their efforts to gain a dignified livelihood, to increase women's participation in all of Kuapa's activities, and to develop environmentally friendly cultivation of cocoa."[145] Kuapa Kokoo has approximately 85,000 members across 1400 villages.[146] In addition to the cooperative's stock ownership, Kuapa Kokoo has two seats on Divine's Board of Directors.[147] Notably, Divine is a certified Benefit Corporation, which permits business decision-making based on considerations aside from maximizing shareholder profits.[148]

Divine uses third-party certification schemes, including Fairtrade.[149] Divine follows the traditional Fairtrade model of guaranteed minimum pricing, purchasing

[138]Theo Chocolate Cocoa Pricing Specifications, Theo Chocolate, https://www.theochocolate.com/wp-content/uploads/2017/06/Theo-2017-Pricing-Matrix.pdf (last visited May 26, 2018). It is worth noting that in their dedication to transparency, they post the prices on their website.

[139]Interview with Emily Benson, Supply Chain Manager, Theo Chocolate, in Seattle, Washington (March 28, 2018).

[140]Our Certifications, Theo Chocolate, https://www.theochocolate.com/blog/our-certifications/ (last visited May 26, 2018). *See also* Fair for Life, Fair For Life, http://www.fairforlife.org/ (last visited May 26, 2018).

[141]The Divine Story, Divine Chocolate, http://www.divinechocolate.com/us/about-us/divine-story (last visited May 26, 2018).

[142]About Us, Divine Chocolate, http://www.divinechocolate.com/us/about-us (last visited May 26, 2018).

[143]Why Fairtrade, Divine Chocolate, http://www.divinechocolate.com/us/about-us/why-fairtrade (last visited May 26, 2018).

[144]The Divine Story, *supra* note 141.

[145]*Id.*

[146]*Id.*; *see also* Why Fairtrade, *supra* note 143.

[147]Frequently Asked Questions, Divine Chocolate, http://www.divinechocolate.com/us/about-us/frequently-asked-questions (last visited May 26, 2018).

[148]Divine Chocolate is a Certified B Corporation, Divine Chocolate, http://www.divinechocolate.com/us/about-us/b-corp (last visited May 26, 2018).

[149]Divine Chocolate, http://www.divinechocolate.com/ (last visited May 26, 2018).

from Kuapa Kokoo at $2000 per ton.[150] If the market value exceeds the Fairtrade minimum price, then the market value is paid.[151] The cooperative also receives $200 per ton sold, which is then used to invest in the cooperative's projects to improve farmers' livelihoods and towards investments in farm productivity. Additionally, 2% of Divine's revenue is invested in a non-governmental organization that funds projects that improve the livelihoods of Kapua Kokoo cooperative farmers.[152]

Madécasse, founded in 2008, is based in Madagascar.[153] Uniquely, they source the cocoa, process the cocoa, and produce the chocolate in Madagascar, rather than transporting the cocoa beans to Europe or the US for processing.[154] Madécasse is certified Direct Trade—not Fairtrade—meaning they have a vertically integrated supply chain and do not work through an export company.[155] Madécasse works directly with one landowner and two cooperatives, including smallholder farmers from five villages in north-western Madagascar.[156] They use fixed-term contracts that pay a fixed, above-market price.[157] For example, in December 2016, the Farm Gate Price of cocoa per kilogram for a Madécasse farmer was $3.12, whereas the price by the same measure for a famer in Cote d'Ivoire was $1.88 and for a farmer in Ghana was $1.91.[158] Madécasse thus provides farmers a higher price point and price stability through fixed-term contracts.[159]

While Theo, Divine, and Madécasse each have a different business model, there are certain aspects of their business model that they have in common. Each is using contract-farming to get around volatile market prices to achieve, first, a higher price point for cocoa farmers, and second, price stability and predictability for farmers. In each case, this is accomplished in conjunction with certification schemes, although each company's approach to certification schemes is different. In each company, there is direct interaction between the cocoa farmers and the chocolate company. At Theo, this direct interaction takes places through company visits to the region, contract negotiations, and training provided to farmers. For Divine and Madécasse, this direct interaction is fully integrated into their business models. Each company also works through farmers' organizations, which provide representation and resources to farmers and facilitate contract-farming.

[150]Why Fairtrade, *supra* note 143.

[151]*Id.*

[152]*Id.*

[153]Our Journey, Madécasse, https://madecasse.com/our-journey/ (last visited May 26, 2018).

[154]Made at the Source, Madécasse, https://madecasse.com/made-at-the-source/ (last visited May 26, 2018).

[155]Direct Trade, Madécasse, https://madecasse.com/direct-trade/ (last visited May 26, 2018).

[156]Madécasse, Madécasse 2017 Impact Report (2017), *available at* https://madecasse.com/wp-content/uploads/2016/09/Made%CC%81casse-2017-Impact-Report.pdf.

[157]*Id.*

[158]*Id.*

[159]*Id.*

5 Challenges and Prospects

The studies and businesses reviewed demonstrate the potential of contract-farming as a value chain model. This section further explores the possibilities of contract-farming: first, as compared to industry sustainability programmes, and second, with a more in-depth study of the issue of price in the cocoa market. Next, this section discusses challenges in implementing contract-farming as a means to improve smallholder farmers' livelihoods. Significant gaps in research and knowledge on how contract-farming impacts certain areas in practice could result in contract-farming having a negative impact on sustainable economic development, even if farmers obtain a higher price point for cocoa. Specifically, contract-farming can increase risks associated with land tenure insecurity, marginalization of women, and crop monoculture. Finally, this section discusses ways to mitigate these risks within the contract-farming framework.

5.1 Industry Sustainability Programmes Versus Higher Prices

It is important to distinguish the benefits to farmers seen in businesses such as Theo, Divine, and Madécasse, from the sustainability programmes that "Big Chocolate" companies have implemented. To take the Nestlé Cocoa Plan as an example, because it is the most ambitious and transparent of the "Big Chocolate" sustainability plans, they have built or refurbished 42 schools, implemented a child labour monitoring system through ICI, committed to distributing 12 million cocoa plants to farmers by 2020, and committed to sourcing increasing amounts of cocoa through the Nestlé Cocoa Plan each year.[160] In 2017, Nestlé sourced over 186,000 tonnes of cocoa through the Nestlé Cocoa Plan, meaning that the cocoa was traceable and considered sustainable.[161] This amounts to 42.9% of Nestlé's annual cocoa purchase.[162] By 2020, Nestlé has committed to source 230,000 tonnes of cocoa through the Nestlé Cocoa Plan, which would be approximately 50% of Nestlé's annual cocoa purchase.[163] In the last year, they have also started conducting gender training in the co-ops with which they work.[164]

[160]Our Commitments, Nestlé Cocoa Plan, http://www.nestlecocoaplan.com/our-commitments/ (last visited May 30, 2018).

[161]Nestlé Cocoa Plan, Nestlé, https://www.nestle.com/csv/raw-materials/nestle-cocoa-plan (last visited May 30, 2018).

[162]*Id.*

[163]*Id.*

[164]Our Commitments, Nestlé Cocoa Plan, http://www.nestlecocoaplan.com/our-commitments/ (last visited May 30, 2018).

While Nestlé's efforts are laudable, they do not address the scale of the problem, nor the root causes of the problem. Ultimately, Cocoa Plan is more of a corporate charity programme than a drive to achieve true sustainability. While building schools is likely to be welcome in communities, it is no substitute for paying farmers enough to cover school fees, and no substitute for paying farmers enough to create a local tax base sufficient for a community to fund school operations. While cocoa seedlings are likely to be welcomed by farmers, it is no substitute for more broadly giving farmers the inputs, tools, training, and surplus for investment that will keep cocoa farms productive over the long-term. Likewise, there is an element of neo-colonialism in Nestlé determining how investment in farms and communities should be spent, rather than allowing those farmers and communities to decide for themselves. In the end, Nestlé is only expecting to source 50% of its annual cocoa purchase in a traceable and "sustainable" way by 2020.

It is easy to pick on Nestlé, simply because of the "Big Chocolate" companies, they have made the most information about their sustainability efforts publicly available. Nestlé has the highest level of transparency of any of the "Big Chocolate" companies, publishing an annual corporate social responsibility report that totalled 113 pages in 2017,[165] and publishing their first annual "Tackling Child Labour" Report in 2017 as well.[166] Also to Nestlé's credit, they appear to be the only "Big Chocolate" company addressing gender issues. What is most notable, though, is that despite the shortcomings of the Nestlé Cocoa Plan, is still the most ambitious of the sustainability plans being implemented by "Big Chocolate" companies.

The gap between the scale of the problem and the scale of currently proposed solutions is well demonstrated in the Cocoa Barometer 2018 report. The number of children working in cocoa in West Africa is estimated to be over 2 million; however, the number of children the ICI hopes to help by 2020 is just 400,000, or 18%.[167] The number of cocoa farmers in Cote d'Ivoire and Ghana is estimated to be two million, but the number of farmers that CocoaAction aims to assist by 2020 is just 300,000, or 15%.[168] CocoaAction is not currently planning to assist cocoa farmers outside of Cote d'Ivoire or Ghana. Finally, Fairtrade estimates that a living income for a farmer in West Africa is $2.51 per day; however, current farmer income in West Africa is estimated to be $0.78 per day.[169]

What is more, much of the industry's efforts to help farmers focuses on yield and may do more to hurt farmers than help them, price-wise. While an increase in an individual smallholder farmers' yield can help that individual farmer make more

[165] *See* Nestlé, Nestlé In Society: Creating Shared Value And Meeting Our Commitments 2017 (2017), *available* at https://www.nestle.com/asset-library/documents/library/documents/corporate_social_responsibility/nestle-csv-full-report-2017-en.pdf.

[166] *See* Nestlé, Nestlé Cocoa Plan: Tackling Child Labour (2017), *available at* http://www.nestle.com/asset-library/documents/creating-shared-value/responsible-sourcing/nestle-cocoa-plan-child-labour-2017-report.pdf.

[167] ABVV/Horval et al. (2018), p. 6.

[168] *Id.*

[169] *Id.*

money for their crop in a given season, when there is a collective increase in yield, the increased supply of cocoa coupled with stable demand leads to a reduction in the market price for cocoa. The result is that farmers who are paid for their crop based on the market price will be paid less for each kilogram of cocoa. During the 2016/2017 growing season, this is exactly what happened. Cote d'Ivoire experienced a significant increase in cocoa production due to favourable weather, new cocoa trees planted in protected forests coming to maturity, and industry sustainability programmes' focus on increasing productivity.[170] As a result of the oversupply of cocoa, the market price plummeted, and farmers already struggling with poverty saw their income from cocoa decline further.[171]

The advantages offered by the business models used by Theo, Divine, and Madécasse, and by extension, contract-farming, is that they are able to provide farmers a higher price point, provide farmers greater price stability, and offer premiums for higher quality. The higher price allows farmers to have a higher standard of living; the price stability allows farmers to plan, budget, prioritize, and invest; and the premiums incentivize investment in cocoa quality. Rather than directing how investment money is spent in cocoa farming communities, the respective farmers' organizations and farmers are given the autonomy to invest premiums based on their own assessment of their needs. Divine and Madécasse go even further by integrating cocoa farmers into the operations of the chocolate companies. The end result is cocoa farmers and chocolate companies that are invested in one another for the long-term, not just the season. Notably, the average age of a Theo cocoa farmer is 35 years old,[172] rather than the industry average of 50 years old. The business models of Theo, Divine, and Madécasse, and by extension, contract-farming, offer a glimpse of a better way of doing business—one that improves livelihoods for cocoa farmers, and contributes to the sustainability of the industry.

5.2 *Price*

The studies and businesses examined in this paper demonstrate that contract-farming offers the potential to improve livelihoods for at least some farmers and create a different dynamic in the cocoa value chain. Specifically, they demonstrate that farmers can potentially obtain higher prices for their cocoa crop when contract-farming is used as part of the value chain. Table 1 allows for comparison of different prices for cocoa during the same time period. What this table does not directly demonstrate is the volatility in the cocoa market. The prices in Cote d'Ivoire and

[170] *Id.* at 8–9.

[171] *Id.* at 10.

[172] Interview with Emily Benson, Supply Chain Manager, Theo Chocolate, in Seattle, Washington (March 28, 2018).

Table 1 Cocoa market snapshot as of May 2018

	Market price (USD per tonne)	Estimated farm gate price (USD per kilogram)
Theo	$2800[a]—$4500[b]	$2.80—$4.50
Divine	$2000—Market price[c]	$2.00—Market price
Madécasse		$3.12[d]
ICCO daily price	$2558.55[e]	
New York futures	$2597[e]	
London futures	$2485[e]	
Cote d'Ivoire	$2450[f]	$1.22[f]
Ghana	$1618[g]	$1.61

[a]For beans meeting the lowest quality standard Theo will accept (small beans with low fermentation levels) (Theo Chocolate Cocoa Pricing Specifications, Theo Chocolate, https://www.theochocolate.com/wp-content/uploads/2017/06/Theo-2017-Pricing-Matrix.pdf (last visited May 26, 2018))
[b]For beans meeting high quality standards (large beans with high fermentation levels) (Theo Chocolate Cocoa Pricing Specifications, Theo Chocolate, https://www.theochocolate.com/wp-content/uploads/2017/06/Theo-2017-Pricing-Matrix.pdf (last visited May 26, 2018))
[c]Divine sets a price floor at $2000. If the market price is higher, Divine pays the market price (Why Fairtrade, Divine Chocolate, http://www.divinechocolate.com/us/about-us/why-fairtrade (last visited May 26, 2018))
[d]Farm Gate Price for December 2016 according to Madécasse's 2017 Impact Report (Madécasse, Madécasse 2017 Impact Report (2017), *available at* https://madecasse.com/wp-content/uploads/2016/09/Made%CC%81casse-2017-Impact-Report.pdf)
[e]As of May 25, 2018 (Daily Prices, ICCO, https://www.icco.org/statistics/cocoa-prices/daily-prices.html (last visited May 30, 2018)). The ICCO Daily Price is the average price for cocoa futures at the London and New York commodity exchanges
[f]Market Price and Minimum Price Guaranteed for Producers established for the 2018/2019 season by Cote d'Ivoire's marketing board, Conseil du Café-Cocoa. The Minimum Price Guaranteed for Producers is 700 FCFA per kilogram. The Market Price for April–June 2018 is 1356 FCFA per kilogram (Le Conseil du Café-Cocoa, http://www.conseilcafecacao.ci/index.php (last visited May 30, 2018))
[g]Producer Price established for the 2017/2018 season by Ghana's marketing board, COCOBOD. The Producer Price is 7600 GHS per tonne (*Government maintains cocoa producer price at GH¢ 7,600.00 per tonne*, Ghana News Agency (Oct. 13, 2017), *available at* http://www.ghananewsagency.org/print/123499)

Ghana are lower than current market prices, but reflect longer term trends in the cocoa market. The market price is currently higher than average for the last year.[173]

In comparing prices, particularly the Farm Gate Prices, it is important to keep in mind that the World Bank has set the extreme poverty line at $1.90 per day.[174] Anyone living on less than a $1.90 a day is considered by the World Bank to be living in extreme poverty. According to the ICCO, the average cocoa crop yield in

[173]*See* Monthly Review of the Market, ICCO, https://www.icco.org/statistics/monthly-review-of-the-market.html (last visited May 31, 2018).

[174]FAQs: Global Poverty Line Update, World Bank, http://www.worldbank.org/en/topic/poverty/brief/global-poverty-line-faq (last visited May 29, 2018).

Ghana is 300 kilograms per hectare.[175] At the above prices, a Ghanaian cocoa farmer being paid at the price established by COCOBOD would make $1.32 per day per hectare. In Cote d'Ivoire, the average crop yield is higher: 450 kilograms per hectare.[176] A Cote d'Ivoirian cocoa farmer being paid at the price established by the Conseil du Café-Cocoa would make $1.50 per day per hectare. Compare those numbers to a cocoa farmer contracting with Theo, producing an average yield (350 kilograms per hectare[177]), and producing all of their cocoa at the lowest quality level that Theo will accept: that farmer would make $2.68 per day per hectare. While smallholder cocoa farms often have more than one hectare, the typical farm household supports multiple individuals; thus, the farm's daily income per person may be below the World Bank's extreme poverty line.

Price is an important part of the picture; however, it is not the entire picture. While contract-farming is correlated with higher prices, what is less clear is how contract-farming has impacted and will impact the economic development of African cocoa producers and sustainability in the cocoa industry.

5.3 Gaps in Research and Knowledge

The conclusions that can be drawn from the current level of research on contract-farming is limited. While there are exceptions, the majority of the literature focuses on obtaining a higher price for farmers. Longitudinal studies are absent. Thus, based on the current level of research and academic knowledge, it is not possible to predict what could be the long-term impact of contract-farming on economic development beyond near-term price increases and technological transfers received by smallholder farmers.

This gap in knowledge is significant because there are a number of ways in which contract-farming could hurt sustainable economic development, even when smallholder farmers are obtaining a higher price for their crop. Contract-farming can increase risks associated with land tenure insecurity; increase marginalization of women; and increase crop monoculture and the risk of food insecurity. The effects of these institutions on economic development tend to be more difficult to measure, and their impact on economic development tends to occur over longer time spans.

When it comes to land tenure, the institutional landscape in Africa presents particular challenges. While land tenure varies greatly by country, levels of tenure insecurity are high across Sub-Saharan Africa. Many farmers do not have official land title, and often use the land according to informal or traditional tenure

[175] FAQ: How many smallholders are there worldwide producing cocoa?, ICCO, https://www.icco.org/faq/57-cocoa-production/123-how-many-smallholders-are-there-worldwide-producing-cocoa-what-proportion-of-cocoa-worldwide-is-produced-by-smallholders.html (last visited June 1, 2018).

[176] *Id.*

[177] 350 kilograms per hectare is the global average smallholder yield. *Id.*

systems.[178] This may place limits on their ability or their incentives to make changes to or invest in the land.[179] Farmers may owe rents to landlords, and thus see few of the economic benefits of contract-farming themselves.[180] Further, increased investment or expansion of areas where crops are cultivated can lead to land disputes, particularly where borders between farms are not well-defined. The dynamics of land tenure play a role in how contract-farming does or does not benefit smallholder farmers, and this creates opportunities for conflict over land as well as the risk of increasing levels of income inequality.

There are a number of different ways in which contract-farming and gender-related institutions interact in a way that is harmful to women and to economic development generally. First, women are less likely to be able to participate in contract-farming.[181] Buyers engaging in contract-farming may require land ownership or customary land rights, which women are less likely to have.[182] Buyers may also require participation in a cooperative or farmers' organization, to which women may be less likely to have access, or if they have access, may be excluded from decision-making roles.[183] Second, when smallholder farmer households are involved in contract-farming, women often lose out. Contracts are usually signed by the husband, as the head of the household, regardless of the actual distribution of labour within the household.[184] Contract-farming can lead to a shift in household resources from crops for consumption, which tend to be the women's decision-making domain, toward the contract crop, which tends to be the men's decision-making domain.[185] Thus, women often have an increased labour burden and are less involved in household decision-making, both regarding crops and the spending of household income.[186] As a result, contract-farming can cause an increase in conflict within the household.[187]

Concerns about how contract-farming impacts women are not just a matter of equality. It also affects farm productivity, as women are often the primary labourers on family farms.[188] When women see the benefits of higher crop income, they have a

---

[178]ABVV/Horval et al. (2018), p. 20.

[179]*Id.* For an excellent analysis of these issues and their impact on Ghana's cocoa industry, *see* Asamoah and Owusu-Ansah (2015) and Asamoah et al. (2017), *supra* note 96.

[180]Eaton and Shepherd (2001), p. 34.

[181]U.N. Special Rapporteur on the right to food, *Interim report of the special rapporteur on the right to food*, ¶, delivered to the General Assembly, U.N. Doc. A/66/262 (Aug. 4, 2011) and Schneider and Gugerty (2010).

[182]Schneider and Gugerty (2010), p. 4.

[183]U.N. Special Rapporteur on the right to food, U.N. Doc. A/66/262, at ¶ 15–21.

[184]*Id.*

[185]Schneider and Gugerty (2010), p. 3.

[186]*Id.*; *see also* U.N. Special Rapporteur on the right to food, U.N. Doc. A/66/262, at ¶ 15–21.

[187]*Id.*

[188]U.N. Special Rapporteur on the right to food, U.N. Doc. A/66/262, at ¶ 15–21.

greater incentive to increase production.[189] Additionally and more importantly, household food security and children's health, nutrition, and education all benefit from improved income for women, as compared to benefits seen from improved income for men.[190] The more decision-making power women have over household income, the more income is usually spent on children's needs.[191] If contract-farming reduces women's decision-making power over household income, this has serious implications for the well-being of families, and potentially undermines economic development.

Finally, contract-farming increases the likelihood of monoculture and food insecurity. The specialization in crops produced for the contract means producing crops to sell, usually for export, rather than for household consumption.[192] When farmers shift resources away from crops used to feed their families, toward the contract crop, they lose the safety net that those crops provided.[193] As a result, farmers may need to purchase more food on the market, and are more vulnerable to food price increases and volatility.[194] Differently fluctuating prices of the contract crop and food for household consumption could create a gap between what farmers are able to sell under the contract, and what they can afford to eat.[195] Contract-farming often involves entire communities, rather than just individual households; thus, increased contract-farming risks rendering communities more vulnerable, when a community might have otherwise been able to provide a cushion for hardships faced by individual households.[196] Essentially, contract-farming risks removing much of the food safety net for whole communities at a time. Further, if there is a bad harvest or other "act of God", guaranteeing farmers a minimum price for the contract crop will not be a sufficient safeguard.[197]

The issues of land tenure, gender dynamics, and monoculture may present serious challenges for the implementation of contract-farming to have a positive impact for smallholder cocoa farmers in Africa. However, there are opportunities within the contract-farming framework, if done well, to mitigate associated risks. National legislation by engaged governments can mitigate negative aspects of contract-farming.[198] The terms of contracts also create opportunities: they can create linkages with other bodies of law, creating accountability for corporations and also increasing the likelihood of sustainable economic development for smallholder farmers and their communities. Contracts might incorporate terms from human rights law,

[189] *Id.*

[190] *Id.*

[191] *Id.*; *see also* IFPRI, Women: The Key to Food Security (2000).

[192] *Id.*

[193] *Id.*

[194] *Id.*

[195] *Id.*

[196] *Id.*

[197] *Id.*

[198] *See* UNIDROIT, FAO & IFAD (2015), Ch. 1.

international labour standards, or the International Cocoa Organization agreements. Another promising approach for mitigation of risk might be found in the "Free, Prior and Informed Consent" (FPIC) approach, a process through which indigenous people are consulted prior to development or use of resources on the indigenous population's territory.[199] In short, contracts can create rights for farmers that they might not otherwise have. While there may still be extreme structural challenges for farmers to exercise these rights, contract-farming offers the benefit of creating an avenue for farmers to be informed and to exercise these rights.

6 Conclusions

The current direction of the cocoa industry is unsustainable. Most of the world's cocoa comes from equatorial Africa and is grown on smallholder family farms. At one end of the global value chain are the farmers, who face declining soil and tree fertility. Due to low and volatile prices, and lack of access to credit, farmers are unable to invest in their farms. In order to increase their yields, cocoa farmers have planted more trees, resulting in deforestation of protected land. Child labour is also prevalent in cocoa farming, as families cannot afford to pay school fees or hire labour. Cocoa farming is labour intensive and impoverishing. As a result, young people are leaving cocoa farming. At the other end of the global value chain, chocolate is a multi-billion dollar industry in which market share is dominated by just a few processing and manufacturing companies, including some of the largest companies in the world. Despite high demand, the dynamic of the market results in cocoa farmers being unable to negotiate higher prices.

There have been a number of initiatives to address the cocoa industry's issues, including formation of the International Cocoa Organization by the United Nations; national marketing boards in Cote d'Ivoire and Ghana; and industry-led initiatives, including the International Cocoa Initiative, to address child labour, and the World Cocoa Foundation, to address issues in the industry more generally. In the last decade, businesses have been taking a more active role, with cocoa processing and chocolate companies all having sustainability initiatives, which vary widely in scope and approach. Certification schemes, including organic and Fairtrade, have also been playing an increasingly prominent role in efforts to improve sustainability in the industry. Although these initiatives are on-going, they have thus far failed to alleviate the problems endemic to the cocoa industry.

[199]Currently, FPIC is enshrined as a right of indigenous communities by the United Nations Declaration on the Rights of Indigenous Peoples, but FPIC could also feasibly be implemented in communities regardless of their indigenous make-up. The only limitation is that it is focused on collectives, not individuals or households, so it would require working with farmer organizations. The FAO has developed a manual on the FPIC process: FAO, Free, Prior and Informed Consent (2016), *available at* http://www.fao.org/3/a-i6190e.pdf.

This paper has delved into the question of whether contract-farming might help solve some of the issues found in cocoa value chains in Africa. Contract-farming has been put forward as an institutional arrangement with the potential to solve many of the problems associated with agricultural value chains from a development standpoint. It offers potential advantages for both farmers and buyers alike, but presents risks as well. To this end, this paper examined studies of contract-farming of cocoa in Africa, and businesses in the chocolate industry that use the contract-farming model to source cocoa in Africa.

Studies of contract-farming schemes implemented in Uganda, Ghana, and Tanzania found that smallholder farmers benefitted. The Uganda study found that after 5 years, smallholder farmers participating in contract-farming produced higher quality cocoa, received a higher price for that cocoa, and had a greater household income, as compared to farmers who were not participating in the contract-farming scheme. The Ghana study found that cocoa farming communities benefitted from participation in contract-farming because of the benefits provided to farms, and that farmers who were more aware of the terms and conditions of their contracts also had better information flow about cocoa markets; however, the study also found uncertainty amongst farmers engaged in contract-farming about the continuation of contracts. The Tanzania study found that farmers participating in contract-farming experienced an increase in training, access to credit, higher yields, and overall contributed to an improvement in the smallholder farmers' livelihoods. While the results of these studies are promising, any generalized conclusions should be met with caution. The conclusions that can be drawn from them are limited by their methodologies.

Three chocolate businesses have used the contract-farming model as part of their approach to equitably sourcing cocoa: Theo Chocolate, which sources from Democratic Republic of Congo; Divine Chocolate, which sources from Ghana; and Madécasse, which sources from Madagascar. While each company has a different business model, each uses both contract-farming and certification schemes to pay cocoa farmers at a higher and more stable price point than what the market price, or the Ghanaian or Cote d'Ivoirian marketing boards, can provide. These businesses demonstrate that contract-farming, if done well, offers enormous potential.

Beyond recognizing that contract-farming has the potential to obtain a higher and more stable price for cocoa farmers, however, there is a need to recognize the limits of current research and knowledge. Contract-farming can negatively impact sustainable economic development, even if farmers are obtaining a higher and more stable price for their crop. Contract-farming can increase risks associated with land tenure insecurity, marginalization of women, and crop monoculture and the risk of food insecurity. The institutional landscape in Africa provides particular challenges for each of these issues. Nevertheless, there are ways to mitigate these risks within the contract-farming framework.

Ultimately, the problem in the cocoa value chain is largely one of market economics. The industry sustainability programme approach does not address the underlying market inequities that make such sustainability programmes necessary. Unless and until poverty, child labour, and environmental degradation are recognized and addressed as the result of the structure of the cocoa market and the low prices paid to smallholder cocoa farmers, cocoa farming will continue on its unsustainable path. Herein lies the true power and advantage of contract-farming: it provides a market approach to address a market problem.

References

About the International Cocoa Organization, International Cocoa Organization, https://www.icco.org/about-us/about-the-icco.html (last visited May 26, 2018)
About Us, COCOBOD, https://cocobod.gh/aboutus.php (last visited May 30, 2018)
About Us, Divine Chocolate, http://www.divinechocolate.com/us/about-us (last visited May 26, 2018)
About Us, International Cocoa Initiative, http://www.cocoainitiative.org/about-ici/about-us/ (last visited May 26, 2018)
ABVV/Horval et al (2018) Cocoa Barometer 2018 20, available at http://www.cocoabarometer.org/Cocoa_Barometer/Download_files/2018%20Cocoa%20Barometer%20180420.pdf
Asamoah M, Owusu-Ansah F (2015) Assessment of land tenure-related constraints to cocoa productivity in Ghana, available at http://www.worldcocoafoundation.org/wp-content/uploads/files_mf/1492612620CRIGLandTenureSurveyFinal41217.pdf
Asamoah M et al (2017) Report on land tenure & cocoa production in Ghana, available at http://www.worldcocoafoundation.org/wp-content/uploads/files_mf/1492612620CRIGLandTenureSurveyFinal41217.pdf
B-Corp, Divine Chocolate, http://www.divinechocolate.com/us/about-us/b-corp (last visited May 26, 2018)
Better Cocoa, Nestlé Cocoa Plan, http://www.nestlecocoaplan.com/better-cocoa/ (last visited May 26, 2018)
Cargill (2017) The 2016/2107 Cargill Cocoa Promise Global Summary Report, available at https://www.cargill.com/doc/1432099950824/cargill-cocoa-promise-report-2016-17.pdf
Cocoa Certifications, Cargill, https://www.cargill.com/sustainability/cocoa/cocoa-certifications (last visited May 28, 2018)
Cocoa, Fairtrade, https://www.fairtrade.org.uk/Farmers-and-Workers/Cocoa (last visited June 1, 2018)
Cocoa Life, Mondelez International, https://www.cocoalife.org/ (last visited May 28, 2018)
Cocoa: Caring for the future of cocoa, Mars, http://www.mars.com/global/sustainable-in-a-generation/our-approach-to-sustainability/raw-materials/cocoa (last visited May 28, 2018)
Congolese Cocoa, Theo Chocolate, https://www.theochocolate.com/blog/congolese-cocoa/ (last visited May 26, 2018)
Contract Farming Resource Centre, FAO, http://www.fao.org/in-action/contract-farming/en/ (last visited May 31, 2018)
Da Silva CA (2005) FAO, the growing role of contract farming in agri-food systems development: drivers, theory and practice 11–12
Da Silva CA, Rankin M (2013) Contract farming for inclusive market access 17. In: da Silva CA, Rankin M (eds) FAO
Daily Prices, ICCO, https://www.icco.org/statistics/cocoa-prices/daily-prices.html (last visited May 30, 2018)
Direct Trade, Madécasse, https://madecasse.com/direct-trade/ (last visited May 26, 2018)
Divine Chocolate, http://www.divinechocolate.com/ (last visited May 26, 2018)
Eaton C, Shepherd AW (2001) Contract farming: Partnerships for growth, 145 FAO Agricultural Services Bulletin 2 (Food and Agriculture Organization of the United Nations)
Fair for Life, Fair For Life, http://www.fairforlife.org/ (last visited May 26, 2018)

FAO (2016) Free, Prior And Informed Consent
FAQ: How many smallholders are there worldwide producing cocoa?, ICCO, https://www.icco.org/faq/57-cocoa-production/123-how-many-smallholders-are-there-worldwide-producing-cocoa-what-proportion-of-cocoa-worldwide-is-produced-by-smallholders.html (last visited June 1, 2018)
FAQs: Global Poverty Line Update, World Bank, http://www.worldbank.org/en/topic/poverty/brief/global-poverty-line-faq (last visited May 29, 2018)
Flick M, Ageing cocoa farmers pose risk for Ghana industry, Financial Times, https://www.ft.com/content/d9cb0d1c-26e7-11e5-bd83-71cb60e8f08c (last visited June 1, 2018)
Frequently Asked Questions, Divine Chocolate, http://www.divinechocolate.com/us/about-us/frequently-asked-questions (last visited May 26, 2018)
Gayi SK, Tsowou K (2015) United Nations conference on trade and development, cocoa industry: integrating small farmers into the global value chain 6 (UNCTAD/SUC/2015/4)
Government maintains cocoa producer price at GH¢7,600.00 per tonne, Ghana News Agency (Oct. 13, 2017), available at http://www.ghananewsagency.org/print/123499
Harkin-Engel Protocol, International Cocoa Initiative, http://www.cocoainitiative.org/knowledge-centre-post/harkin-engel-protocol/ (last visited May 26, 2018)
Hershey, 2016 Hershey CSR Report (2016). available at https://www.thehersheycompany.com/content/dam/corporate-us/documents/csr-reports/2016-hershey-csr-report-detail.pdf
Higonnet E, Bellantonio M, Hurowitz G (2017) Mighty Earth, chocolate's dark secret: how the cocoa industry destroys National Parks, available at http://www.mightyearth.org/wp-content/uploads/2017/09/chocolates_dark_secret_english_web.pdf
IFPRI (2000) Women: the key to food security
Industry Members, International Cocoa Initiative, http://www.cocoainitiative.org/about-ici/our-partners/industry-members/ (last visited May 26, 2018)
International Cocoa Agreement, 1972, art. 1, Oct. 21, 1972, 882 U.N.T.S. 12652
Interview with Emily Benson, Supply Chain Manager, Theo Chocolate, in Seattle, Washington (March 28, 2018)
Jones S, Gibbon P (2011) Developing agricultural markets in sub-Saharan Africa: organic cocoa in rural Uganda. J Dev Stud 47:1595–1618
Kalimangasi NN, Kihombo A, Kalimangasi N (2014) Contribution of contract cocoa production on improving livelihood of smallholder farmers. Int J Sci Res Publ 4:1–10
Kroeger A et al. Forest- and Climate-Smart Cocoa in Côte D'Ivoire and Ghana: Aligning Stakeholders to Support Smallholders in Deforestation-Free Cocoa 12 (World Bank)
Le Conseil du Café-Cocoa, http://www.conseilcafecacao.ci/index.php (last visited May 30, 2018)
Made at the Source, Madécasse, https://madecasse.com/made-at-the-source/ (last visited May 26, 2018)
Madécasse, Madécasse 2017 Impact Report (2017). available at https://madecasse.com/wp-content/uploads/2016/09/Made%CC%81casse-2017-Impact-Report.pdf
Membership of the International Cocoa Organization, International Cocoa Organization, https://www.icco.org/about-us/membership-of-the-icco.html (last visited May 26, 2018)
Midland Archer Daniels (2016) ADM 2016 Corporate Sustainability Report, available at https://www.adm.com/sustainability
Monthly Review of the Market, ICCO, https://www.icco.org/statistics/monthly-review-of-the-market.html (last visited May 31, 2018)
Nestlé Cocoa Plan, Nestlé, https://www.nestle.com/csv/raw-materials/nestle-cocoa-plan (last visited May 30, 2018)
Nestlé Cocoa Plan, Nestlé Cocoa Plan, http://www.nestlecocoaplan.com/ (last visited May 28, 2018)
Nestlé, Nestlé Cocoa Plan: Tackling Child Labour (2017). available at http://www.nestle.com/asset-library/documents/creating-shared-value/responsible-sourcing/nestle-cocoa-plan-child-labour-2017-report.pdf

Nestlé, Nestlé In Society: Creating Shared Value and Meeting Our Commitments 2017 (2017). available at https://www.nestle.com/asset-library/documents/library/documents/corporate_social_responsibility/nestle-csv-full-report-2017-en.pdf

Nguyen AT, Dzator J, Nadolny A (2015) Does contract farming improve productivity and income of farmers?: A review of theory and evidence. J Dev Areas 49:531–538

Nieburg O, Fair game: how effective is cocoa certification?, Confectionary News.com, Dec. 21, 2017., available at https://www.confectionerynews.com/Article/2017/12/20/Fair-trade-How-effective-is-cocoa-certification

Objectives and Functions of the Board, COCOBOD, https://cocobod.gh/Objectives_Functions_Board.php (last visited May 30, 2018)

Our Certifications, Theo Chocolate, https://www.theochocolate.com/blog/our-certifications/ (last visited May 26, 2018)

Our Commitments, Nestlé Cocoa Plan, http://www.nestlecocoaplan.com/our-commitments/ (last visited May 30, 2018)

Our Journey, Madécasse, https://madecasse.com/our-journey/ (last visited May 26, 2018)

Our Work: Community Level, International Cocoa Initiative, https://cocoainitiative.org/our-work/our-work/community-level/ (last visited May 26, 2018)

Oya C (2012) Contract farming in sub-Saharan Africa: a survey of approaches, debates and issues. J Agrarian Change 12:1–33, 2

Press Release, Barry Callebaut, "Forever Chocolate": Berry Callebaut targets 100% sustainable chocolate by 2025 (Nov. 28, 2016), available at https://www.barry-callebaut.com/news/2016/11/forever-chocolate-barry-callebaut-targets-100-sustainable-chocolate-2025

Roldan MB, Fromm I, Aidoo R (2013) From producers to export markets: the case of the cocoa value chain in Ghana. J Afr Dev 15:121Ÿ138

Schneider K, Gugerty MK (2010) Evans School policy analysis and research, gender & contract farming in Sub-Saharan Africa Literature Review 4

Statuts & Objectifs du Conseil du Café-Cacao, Le Conseil Du Café-Cocoa, http://www.conseilcafecacao.ci/index.php?option=com_content&view=article&id=112&Itemid=186 (last visited May 30, 2018)

Sustainable Cocoa: Evolving the Cargill Cocoa Promise, Cargill, https://www.cargill.com/sustainability/cocoa/sustainable-cocoa (last visited May 28, 2018)

The Divine Story, Divine Chocolate, http://www.divinechocolate.com/us/about-us/divine-story (last visited May 26, 2018)

The Rainforest Alliance and UTZ To Merge, Forming New, Stronger Organization, The Rainforest Alliance, Jun. 6, 2017, available at https://www.rainforest-alliance.org/articles/rainforest-alliance-utz-merger

Theo Chocolate Cocoa Pricing Specifications, Theo Chocolate, https://www.theochocolate.com/wp-content/uploads/2017/06/Theo-2017-Pricing-Matrix.pdf (last visited May 26, 2018)

Tulane University School of Public Health And Tropical Medicine, Final Report: Survey Research On Child Labor In West African Cocoa Growing Areas (2015). available at http://www.childlaborcocoa.org/images/Payson_Reports/Tulane%20University%20-%20Survey%20Research%20on%20Child%20Labor%20in%20the%20Cocoa%20Sector%20-%2030%20July%202015.pdf

U.N. Special Rapporteur on the right to food, Interim report of the special rapporteur on the right to food, delivered to the General Assembly, U.N. Doc. A/66/262 (Aug. 4, 2011)

UNIDROIT, FAO & IFAD, UNIDROIT/FAO/IFAD Legal Guide on Contract Farming 1-2 (2015)

Vigneri M, Kolavalli S (2017) FAO, Growth Through Pricing Policy: The Case of Cocoa in Ghana 5, available at http://www.fao.org/3/I8329EN/i8329en.pdf

Vision & Mission, World Cocoa Foundation, http://www.worldcocoafoundation.org/about-wcf/history-mission/ (last visited May 26, 2018)

Wessel M, Quist-Wessel PMF (2015) Cocoa production in West Africa, a review and analysis of recent developments. NJAS – Wageningen J Life Sci 74–75:3

What is Contract Farming?, Contract Farming Resource Centre, FAO, http://www.fao.org/in-action/contract-farming/background/en/ (last visited May 31, 2018)
What makes Theo different?, Theo Chocolate, https://www.theochocolate.com/blog/what-makes-theo-different/ (last visited May 26, 2018)
Why Fairtrade, Divine Chocolate, http://www.divinechocolate.com/us/about-us/why-fairtrade (last visited May 26, 2018)
World Bank (2008) World development report 2008: agriculture for development 127, 241
World Bank: Life expectancy at birth, men (years), https://data.worldbank.org/indicator/SP.DYN.LE00.MA.IN (last visited May 25, 2018)
World Bank: Life expectancy at birth, total (years), https://data.worldbank.org/indicator/SP.DYN.LE00.IN (last visited May 25, 2018)
World Cocoa Foundation (2016) CocoaAction annual report 2016: learning as we grow: putting cocoaaction into practice
Young AM (2007) The chocolate tree: a natural history of Cacao 40–42

Lindsey Callahan is a recent graduate of the University of Washington School of Law, Master of Law (LL.M.) in Sustainable International Development Law. She has a Juris Doctor (J.D.) degree from The George Washington University Law School, and a Bachelor of Arts (B.A.) degree from Johns Hopkins University. She has previously worked for the U.S. Agency for International Development, the United Nations International Criminal Tribunal for Rwanda, and the U.S. Air Force Judge Advocate General's Corps. She is currently a prosecutor in San Juan County, Washington.

Africa Post-Brexit in EU Development Cooperation Policy and UK Trade Policy: Investing in New Relationships?

Joseph A. McMahon

Abstract The departure of the United Kingdom (UK) from the European Union (EU) will see the introduction of new trade policy for the UK and changes to existing EU external policies, particularly its Development Cooperation Policy. The latter was due to be refreshed as the 2000 Cotonou Agreement comes to an end and the UK's departure will have a significant impact on the future shape of that policy as there may be fewer resources available for EU development activities and it will have to deal with the nascent UK trade policy which will focus on "old friends and new allies". Looking at future EU and UK relations with Africa, this contribution examines the future of the new relationships which both parties are seeking to forge with that continent in the years to come which seems to focus on greater investment as Africa itself moves towards greater regional integration. Whether these proposed ambitious plans will be realised remains uncertain as does the future scope of cooperation in the realm of development, which is referenced in the Political Declaration outlining the scope for an ambitious, broad, deep and flexible partnership between the EU and the UK to be negotiated by the end of 2020.

1 Introduction

On 23 June 2016, the people of the United Kingdom (UK) in response to the question, "should the United Kingdom remain a member of the European Union or leave the European Union?" voted to leave the European Union (EU).[1] This was a surprising result for many. Having secured the passage of the EU (Notification of Withdrawal) Bill, the UK Government finally triggered Article 50 of the Treaty on

[1]The results for the whole of the United Kingdom were 51.9% in favour of leaving and 48.1% in favour of remaining. For further details see, for example, http://www.bbc.co.uk/news/politics/eu_referendum/results.

J. A. McMahon (✉)
Sutherland School of Law, University College Dublin, Dublin, Ireland
e-mail: joseph.mcmahon@ucd.ie

Z. Yihdego et al. (eds.), *Ethiopian Yearbook of International Law 2018*, Ethiopian Yearbook of International Law 2018, https://doi.org/10.1007/978-3-030-24078-3_8

European Union (TEU) on 29 March 2017 indicating their intention to leave the EU, thus setting 29 March 2019 as the date for Brexit.[2] The letter expressed the Government's intention "to approach our discussions with ambition, giving citizens and businesses in the United Kingdom and the European Union – and indeed from third countries around the world – as much certainty as possible, as early as possible."[3] It is not surprising that the letter concentrates on the negotiation of the withdrawal agreement and the creation of a "deep and special relationship" in economic (and security) cooperation between the UK and the EU post-Brexit. With respect to this cooperation, the response of the European Council to the letter noted that this could only be concluded once the UK has become a third country.[4]

On 17 January 2017, in a speech at Lancaster House, the British Prime Minister set out her Government's plan for the UK post-Brexit which included building a truly Global Britain, i.e. "A country that reaches out to old friends and new allies alike. A great, global, trading nation. And one of the firmest advocates for free trade anywhere in the world."[5] This would begin with a free trade agreement between the UK and EU which would be "bold and ambitious" but there would also be new trade agreements with countries that would allow the UK to "rediscover its role as a great, global, trading nation." The countries mentioned by the Prime Minister included those who could be regarded as "old friends" such as Australia, India and New Zealand who are all members of the Commonwealth and those that could be seen as new allies such as Brazil, China and the Gulf States. New agreements with all these countries will have to accommodate the relationships established by the EU with these countries which up until now have included the UK as an EU Member State. So, the creation of a Global Britain will be accompanied by changes to the EU's Common Commercial Policy and Development Cooperation Policy both of which were developed whilst the UK was a Member State.

The EU's Development Cooperation Policy is clearly set out in Article 208 of the Treaty on the Functioning of the EU (TFEU) which gives it the primary objective of "the reduction and, in the long term, the eradication of poverty."[6] The policy is to be complementary to (and reinforce) the policies of the Member States and both the EU

[2]See https://www.gov.uk/government/publications/prime-ministers-letter-to-donald-tusk-triggering-article-50. The events and facts referred to in this article are up-to-date until 23 February, 2019. At the time of undertaking final proofs and authorising printing of this volume in August 2019 the UK newly appointed PM, Brois Johnson, has begun meeting European leaders making a case for a new Brexist agreement between the UK and the EU.

[3]Ibid, the fourth proposed negotiating principle also references third countries. It reads, in part; "Investors, businesses and citizens in both the UK and across the remaining 27 member states – and those from third countries around the world – want to be able to plan."

[4]Document XT 21001/17, *Draft guidelines following the United Kingdom's notification under Article 50 TEU* (31 March 2017), para 4.

[5]See https://www.gov.uk/government/speeches/the-governments-negotiating-objectives-for-exiting-the-eu-pm-speech.

[6]When Development Cooperation was first introduced in the Maastricht Treaty the objectives were: "To fight against poverty in developing countries; to enhance the social and sustainable development of developing countries, particularly the least favoured among them; and to further the integration of developing countries into the world economy."

and the Member States policies are to "comply with the commitments and take account of the objectives they have approved in the context of the United Nations and other competent international organisations."[7] For the EU there is an additional requirement, i.e. policy coherence for development which requires it to "take account of the objectives of development cooperation in the policies that it implements which are likely to affect developing countries." This concept of consistency can also be found in Article 21 of the Treaty on European Union (TEU) which applies it across all the external activities of the EU, for example, the Common Foreign and Security Policy and the Development Cooperation Policy.[8] This article also reinforces that the EU is to define and pursue common policies and actions ("and shall work for a high degree of cooperation in all fields of international relations") so as to "foster the sustainable economic, social and environmental development of developing countries, with the primary aim of eradicating poverty."[9] The TFEU provisions on Development Cooperation apply to all developing countries, with Articles 212 and 213 TFEU (on economic, financial and technical cooperation) applying to third countries who are not developing countries.[10] In this brief outline of the scope of the EU's Development Cooperation Policy, one final point is worth noting and it is that Article 209 omits the reference to the special status of the ACP-EC Convention.[11]

The questions addressed by this contribution relate not only to the EU's Development Cooperation Policy post-Brexit but also to the scope of the UK's Trade Policy as it leaves the EU. In answering these questions, the discussion begins with an examination of the implementation of the EU's Development Cooperation Policy focussing on the relationship developed with the African, Caribbean and Pacific (ACP) countries before looking at the scope of the Generalised System of Preferences ahead of a brief outline of the impact of Brexit on developing countries. Focussing in particular on Africa, the following sections will examine the changes that may be made to EU's Development Cooperation Policy before an examination

[7]See also Article 210(1) which provides, *inter alia* "In order to promote the complementarity and efficiency of their action, the Union and the Member States shall coordinate their policies on development cooperation and shall consult each other on their aid programmes, including in international organisations and during international conferences" and Article 211 which provides "Within their respective spheres of competence, the Union and the Member States shall cooperate with third countries and with the competent international organisations."

[8]Article 21(3) TEU. The principle of consistency was added by the Amsterdam Treaty to the principles of complementarity, coordination and coherence set out in the Maastricht Treaty.

[9]Article 21(2)(d) TEU. Also, of interest here is paragraph (e) which encourages "the integration of all countries into the world economy, including through the progressive abolition of restrictions on international trade."

[10]Article 212 references the provisions on Development Cooperation (Article 208-211 TFEU) to indicate that economic, financial and technical cooperation should not prejudice provisions these provisions.

[11]Article 179 of the Maastricht Treaty provided that "The provisions of this Article shall not affect cooperation with the, African, Caribbean and Pacific countries in the framework of the ACP-EC Convention."

of the Trade Policy that could emerge for Global Britain. The final part of this contribution offers some tentative conclusions.

2 From Rome Through Yaoundé and Lomé to Cotonou

There is little doubt that at the heart of the EU's Development Cooperation Policy lies the relationship with the ACP countries. The original Treaty of Rome provided that one of the activities of what was to be the European Economic Community (EEC) was to "increase trade and promote jointly economic and social development" in the Overseas Countries and Territories (OCT).[12] Part IV of the Treaty and an Implementing Convention on the Association of the OCT established a trade and investment relationship between the EEC and the OCT.[13] The Implementing Convention was set to expire after five years and during this period a number of the OCT had become independent, necessitating a new relationship—the Yaoundé Convention of 1963 which was renewed in 1969—with the OCT becoming the Associated African States and Madagascar (AASM). Despite an offer being made to Commonwealth African countries to take part in this new relationship or to conclude separate agreements with the EEC, it was to be the UK accession to the EEC that would signal a major change in the relationship.[14]

Ahead of the 1973 accession of the UK the Commission published its first Memorandum on a Community Policy for Development Cooperation advocating a policy going beyond commercial policy instruments to one commensurate with its responsibilities as a major economic actor.[15] The Development Cooperation policy that would emerge in the 1970s would have both regional and global dimensions. Perhaps the best example of the regional dimension is the successor to the Yaoundé Convention, the 1975 Lomé Convention between the EU, on the one hand, and on the other, the AASM and various developing Commonwealth countries who would become known as the ACP. The Preamble to this Convention promised a "new

[12]Article 3(k) Treaty of Rome establishing the EEC. These countries were defined in Article 131 as "non-European countries and territories which have special relations with Belgium, France and the Netherlands."

[13]Zartman characterised the relationship as "designed to share among the European six, at least to some small extent, the burdens and benefits of the colonial past and to provide some limited benefits for the African colonies. It was a means of protecting colonial markets and assuring supplies of primary products for the six instead of the metropole alone and of opening the colonies to greater trade and investment." "Europe and Africa: Decolonization of Dependency?" (1975–1976) 54 *Foreign Affairs* 325, 327.

[14]See for example, Zartman (1971), Ch 3 for discussion of the negotiations with Commonwealth Africa. See also Twitchett (1978). It should be noted that in 1969 an agreement was concluded between the EEC and the three members for the East African Community (Kenya, Tanzania and Uganda) – the Arusha Convention—which offered these countries benefits similar to those in the Yaoundé II Convention.

[15][1971] EC Bull Supp 5/71. See also follow-up communication, [1972] EC Bull Supp 2/72.

model for relations between developed and developing states" and the scope of this relationship expanded (as did the number of parties) with each successor Convention.[16] The relationship established by these Conventions was rethought in the late 1990s resulting in a new agreement in 2000—the Cotonou Partnership Agreement—which was amended in 2005 and 2010.[17] The trade and economic cooperation provisions of this Agreement reflected the end of the preferences received by these countries as from 2007 and encouraged the creation of Economic Partnership Agreements (EPAs) between the EU and various regional groupings of the 79 ACP countries.

Looking at the current status of these EPAs, one was concluded with the Caribbean region (CARIFORUM) in 2008 and the institutions it created have been meeting since 2010.[18] In the Pacific region, an EPA was signed with Papua New Guinea and Fiji in 2009, with Samoa submitting a request in February 2018 to accede to this EPA; a similar request is expected from the Solomon Islands.[19] Turning to Africa, in which there were to be five EPAs, negotiations with the West African regional grouping (ECOWAS) were concluded in 2014 but three West African countries, Nigeria, Mauritania and the Gambia did not sign the EPA.[20] "Stepping stone" EPAs with Côte d'Ivoire and Ghana have been provisionally applied since 2016.[21] In the Central African region, only one country has signed an EPA—Cameroon; although signed in 2009, it has been provisionally applied only since 2014.[22] Greater progress has been made in the remaining three regions. An EPA with Madagascar, Mauritius, Seychelles and Zimbabwe who are members of ESA (Eastern and Southern Africa) was signed in 2009 and has been provisionally applied since 2012.[23] An EPA with the South African Development Community (SADC), comprising Botswana, Lesotho, Mozambique, Namibia, South Africa and

[16][1976] OJ L 25 for the text of the first Convention which was signed by 46 ACP States. The second Convention was signed by 58 States, the third by 65 and the 70 ACP States signed the 1995 mid-term review of the Lomé IV Convention of 1990.

[17]See [2000] OJ L 317/3, [2005] OJ L 209/27 and [2010] OJ L 287/3 respectively. The agreement has also been amended on a number of occasions by decisions of the ACP-EC Council of Minister, see for example, Decision 1/2003 ([2003] OJ L 141/25) and most recently, Decision 1/2018 ([2018] OJ L 148/7).

[18][2008] OJ L 289/3 as amended by Decision 1/2012 of the Joint CARIFORUM-EU Council, [2012] OJ L 335/2. The ACP members are Antigua and Barbuda, The Bahamas, Barbados, Belize, Dominica, Grenada, Guyana, Jamaica, Saint Lucia, Saint Vincent and the Grenadines, Saint Kitts and Nevis, Suriname, Trinidad and Tobago, and the Dominican Republic.

[19][2009] OJ L 272/2. The other Pacific countries are the Cook Islands, Kiribati, Marshall Islands, Federal State of Micronesia, Nauru, Niue, Palau, Tonga, Tuvalu, and Vanuatu.

[20]See http://trade.ec.europa.eu/doclib/docs/2009/september/tradoc_144912.pdf for an overview of EPAs as of June 2018.

[21][2009] OJ L 59/3 and [2016] OJ L 287/3, respectively.

[22][2009] OJ L 57/2. The other countries in this region are Central African Republic, Chad, Congo, Democratic Republic of Congo, Equatorial Guinea, Gabon and São Tomé & Principe.

[23][2012] OJ L 111/3. Comoros signed the EPA in 2017. The other countries in this region are Djibouti, Eritrea, Ethiopia, Malawi, Sudan and Zambia.

Swaziland, was signed in 2016 and has been provisionally applied since then.[24] Finally, the EPA with the East African Community (Burundi, Kenya, Rwanda, Tanzania and Uganda.) was concluded in 2014 but only Kenya and Rwanda have signed the agreement to date; the other States have to sign and ratify the agreement for it to enter into force.[25]

The patchwork coverage of EPAs could lead to the conclusion that this instrument has not been a success. However, this would ignore the impact of the more global dimension of the EU's Development Cooperation policy which emerged in the 1970s—the Generalised System of Preferences (GSP). The GSP currently in operation is provided for in Regulation 978/2012 which creates a general arrangement, a special incentive arrangement for sustainable development and good governance (known as GSP+) and a special arrangement for the least-developed countries (known as Everything But Arms or EBA) "in order to foster the sustainable economic, social and environmental development of developing countries, with the primary aim of eradicating poverty."[26] The EBA grants least-developed countries, as recognised and classified by the United Nations, duty-free access to the EU for all products except arms. Thirty-four of the forty-eight countries on the list of least-developed countries are African which goes a long way to explain why EPAs have a patchwork coverage in Africa, but this does not mean that least-developed African countries do not enter into EPAs, especially given that they do not lose their EBA status by entering into such an agreement.[27]

Just four weeks after the UK referendum, the Overseas Development Institute (ODI) published an assessment of the impact of Brexit on developing countries.[28] It suggests a short-term negative effect on imports, and, in the event of a negative impact on immigration, there would be lower remittances. Brexit would also impact on the latter's development finance, especially if the UK were to withdraw from the European Investment Bank. It also suggested that in the short-term there were positive effects through improved terms of trade for those least-developed countries receiving increased prices for their commodity exports. Over the longer term, the trade effects would depend on the relationship established between the UK and the

[24][2016] OJ L 250/3. Angola has the option of joining this grouping.

[25]See the Annexes to COM (2016) 63 for details of the Agreement. South Sudan joined the EAC in 2016.

[26][2012] OJ L 303/31, Recital 3. The Regulation has been amended on a number of occasions, for example Commission Delegated Regulation 2017/217, [2017] OJ L 34/7 which removes Samoa from the list of EBA beneficiaries as from 1 January 2019.

[27]Ibid, Annex IV. See http://trade.ec.europa.eu/doclib/docs/2017/july/tradoc_155840.pdf for the current list of EBA beneficiaries. Article 19 lists five grounds allowing for the withdrawal of preferences, these include, for example, serious and systematic violation of principles laid down in various human rights and labour rights conventions.

[28]Mendez-Parra, M, P Papadavid and D Willem te Velde, *Brexit and development How will developing countries be affected?* (2016) available at https://www.odi.org/sites/odi.org.uk/files/resource-documents/10685.pdf.

EU and the UK's relationship with the rest of the world; at the moment, both of these are uncertain.

A more recent paper by Matthews assessed the implications of Brexit for developing countries' agri-food trade concluding that these will depend on the existing trade relationship with the EU, whether it is primarily an exporter (or importer) of products that are competitive with the temperate zone agricultural commodities traded between the UK and the remaining Member States of the EU and whether it is mainly an exporter of tropical commodities.[29] Overall, the paper tentatively concludes that Brexit will lead to both trade destruction and trade diversion with the principal beneficiaries being those developing countries who export competitive agricultural products (i.e. temperate zone products) on most-favoured-nation terms.[30] It is a tentative conclusion as, like the ODI paper, the future trade relationship between the UK and the EU is uncertain. Moreover, there will be changes as the UK introduces its own agricultural policy and develops its own trade policy just as there will be changes to the EU's Common Agricultural Policy (CAP) and its Development Cooperation Policy. The latter is a consequence of the need to replace the Cotonou Agreement which expires in 2020. So, there are a range of possible future scenarios for the UK, the EU and developing countries.

3 Future EU Development Cooperation Policy

In November 2017 a Commission Communication on the future direction of the CAP concluded with a discussion of its global dimension, an important consideration given the commitment made earlier in the Communication to the United Nations Sustainable Development Goals (SDGs).[31] The 2017 European Consensus on Development recognises the role that agriculture can play in promoting sustainable development noting that it[32]:

> ... remains a key driver for poverty eradication and sustainable development and is indispensable to ending hunger and ensuring food security. Two thirds of the world's poor depend on agriculture for their livelihoods and a number of developing countries remain highly dependent on trade in a few commodities. Support to smallholders, including family farmers and pastoralists, remains of central importance, contributing substantially to food security and to the fight against soil erosion and biodiversity loss, while providing jobs

Despite this recognition and the commitment to the SDGs, there is no discussion of the need to align the CAP's objectives and those of the EU's Development Cooperation policy; rather the primary focus is on promoting the EU's

---

[29]Available at http://www.tcd.ie/Economics/TEP/2018/tep0318.pdf.

[30]Ibid, p. 20.

[31]COM (2017) 713, *The Future of Food and Farming*, p. 25.

[32]Signed 7 June 2017. See https://ec.europa.eu/europeaid/sites/devco/files/european-consensus-on-development-final-20170626_en.pdf, para 55.

environmental and climate objectives. These objectives are to be realised through a new delivery model—National Strategic Plans—allowing the Member States to tailor their interventions under the CAP to realise its objectives with a greater role being given to them in the design of the compliance and control framework.[33]

In June 2018 the Commission published legislative proposals to implement its reform agenda, including that for National Strategic Plans.[34] Articles 5 and 6 of this proposed Regulation sets out general and specific objectives with the latter providing a clear environmental focus in paragraphs (d) to (f). Title V of the proposed Regulation deals with intervention strategies, quantitative targets and milestones to achieve these specific objectives.[35] The intervention strategy in each National Strategic Plan will outline how Member States intend to use direct payments, sectoral support and rural development measures. In the proposal for changes to the Regulation on the common organisation of markets, the Commission proposes the deletion of existing provisions allowing export refunds to be granted, thus implementing the 2015 WTO Ministerial Decision on Export Competition at the Nairobi Ministerial Conference.[36] Adoption of the proposals will depend on the views of the co-legislators, the European Parliament and the Council of Ministers.

In their input into the process, the European Parliament's Committee on Development called on the Parliament's Agriculture and Rural Development Committee to incorporate several suggestions into its proposed resolution on CAP reform, including a call that[37]:

> ... while recalling the original CAP objectives as set out in Article 39 TFEU, for another chapter in the CAP post-2020 legislation regarding its responsibility in development policy issues, to include better integration of environmental objectives and the SDGs, since the ban on export subsidies means that economic distortions persist, enabling the EU agricultural sector to export agricultural commodities below average production costs.

It also suggested a "shift away from indirect and untargeted subsidies such as area payments; asks for subsidies to be disbursed only if they contribute to public goods such as local jobs, biological diversity, animal welfare, clean air and water, and

[33] Above n 31, p. 10 at which the Commission note: "The CAP objectives would fulfil the EU Treaty obligations but also the already agreed objectives and targets on for instance the environment, climate change (COP 21), and a number of the SDGs."

[34] COM (2018) 392, National Strategic Plans, Proposal for a Regulation.

[35] Ibid, Articles 91 and 92. See also Article 98(2) which details a system of conditionality as comprising for each Good Agricultural and Environmental Condition standards a description of the way the EU standard is to be implemented and a description of the overall contribution to the specific objectives in Article 6(1) (d) to (f).

[36] COM (2018) 394. As for other elements of that Decision on export credits, export credit guarantees and insurance programmes, agricultural exporting state trading enterprises and international food aid, it should be noted that measures in these areas adopted by Member States must respect both EU law and the WTO Ministerial Decision (WT/MIN(15)/45); https://www.wto.org/english/thewto_e/minist_e/mc10_e/1980_e.htm.

[37] PE619.225v02-00 (AD\1151893EN.docx), Rapporteur M Noichl, para 10.

healthy, living soils."[38] Among the views expressed by the Council of Ministers, the continuation of voluntary coupled support was supported with some Member States suggesting its extension to other sectors; other Member States expressed caution about such a move given its possible impact on undistorted competition.[39] The proposals represent a real simplification of the CAP as there are to be fewer rules at the EU level as it seeks to address areas of common concern across all Member States, whilst also increasing the role and responsibilities of the Member States who have been provided with a degree to flexibility to design programmes that are better targeted to the real needs of their farmers.

Rudloff and Brüntrup have concluded that: "The damaging effects of today's CAP on development only remain in a few areas, such as voluntary coupled payments, the reduction of the milk quota, and through complex interactions with other policy areas."[40] In creating their National Strategic Plans, the impact of the CAP on development will continue to decline if Member States continue to move away from voluntary coupled support, but as noted above, some Member States are arguing for its continuation and even its extension to other sectors. A recent study has highlighted that such support, along with continuing high tariffs in certain sectors, is of concern with respect to food security in developing countries.[41] It concluded[42]:

> The future CAP should focus on the agricultural sector's sustainability and pay special attention to efforts made in contributing to the attainment of SDGs. The CAP must not be considered in isolation but coordinated with trade, environmental and development policies. Only by a cross-sector policy approach will it be possible to respond to the challenge of developing a more sustainable and climate-resilient agriculture. In addition, continuous innovation in the agricultural sector is crucial to address the challenges of agriculture in areas such as climate change, resource scarcity and long-term sustainability

The reform will promote greater policy coherence between agriculture and the environment but there is still work to be done on policy coherence between agriculture and development.

The 2016 Commission Communication on the renewal of the relationship with the ACP States reflected on the state of play with respect to EPAs, leading it to conclude that it: "is unsatisfactory when it comes to increasing economic diversification, increasing value addition and reducing dependency on a narrow range of

---

[38]Ibid, para 19.

[39]Council Document 6277/18, pp. 3–4. See also July 2018 Council meeting, Council Document 10200/18.

[40]"Fair Play: The Recent Common Agricultural Policy and Its Limited Effect on Development" available at https://www.swp-berlin.org/fileadmin/contents/products/comments/2018C21_rff_bruentrup.pdf, p. 4.

[41]Blanco, M *The impact of the Common Agricultural Policy on developing countries* (2018) available at http://www.europarl.europa.eu/RegData/etudes/STUD/2018/603862/EXPO_STU%282018%29603862_EN.pdf p. 21.

[42]Ibid, p. 31. See also Matthews, A *The development-related impacts of EU agricultural subsidies* (2017b) available at http://www.tcd.ie/Economics/TEP/2017/tep1617.pdf.

products, as well as redistribution of benefits leading to growing inequalities."[43] It continued: "As reflected by the SDGs, creating inclusive sustainable growth and decent jobs is critical for the stability and prosperity for partners. It is important as well for the provision of positive spill-over effects towards the EU. Therefore, the partnership should particularly focus on key drivers for inclusive sustainable growth."[44] Among the drivers for growth to be promoted in the new partnership would be a stronger role for the private sector and the need for increased investment with specific attention being paid to a sustainable and environmentally responsible agri-food sector. In June 2018, the Commission received Council authorisation to start negotiations with the ACP with the EU Commissioner for International Cooperation and Development commenting: "We are ready to embark upon a modern and dynamic partnership with our partners in Africa, the Caribbean and the Pacific. This new partnership will be a powerful tool to jointly tackle global challenges – from fighting poverty and inequality to peace and security, from climate change to sustainable growth for all."[45]

There is little doubt that there will be a successor to the Cotonou Partnership Agreement drawing on past experiences but one question here is the nature of the relationship to be established. The reason for this question arises, in part, from the recent speech of the Commission President, Jean-Claude Juncker, on the State of the European Union in which he stated[46]:

> Africa does not need charity, it needs true and fair partnership. And we, Europeans need this partnership just as much. Today, we are proposing a new Alliance for Sustainable Investment and Jobs between Europe and Africa. This Alliance, as we envision it, would help create up to 10 million jobs in Africa in the next 5 years alone. I believe we should develop the numerous EU-African trade agreements into a continent-to-continent free trade agreement, as an economic partnership between equals.

Does this suggest that the replacement for the Cotonou Partnership Agreement will establish bespoke arrangements for the EU and Africa, the EU and the Caribbean and the EU and the Pacific? This would continue the regionalisation initiated by the 2000 Agreement. Such regionalisation is in fact proposed in the June 2018 negotiating directives for a Partnership Agreement between the EU (and the Member States) and the ACP States which proposes that the Agreement would consist of a Foundation applicable to all ACP States setting out general objectives, principles

---

[43]JOIN (2016) 52 *A renewed partnership with the countries of Africa, the Caribbean and the Pacific*, p. 6. See also SWD (2016) 250 *Evaluation of the Cotonou Partnership Agreement.*

[44]Ibid, p. 9. See also pp. 16–17 on EU priorities for economic opportunities for economic development.

[45]Press Release available at https://ec.europa.eu/europeaid/news-and-events/european-commission-ready-start-negotiations-new-ambitious-partnership-79-countries_en.

[46]See https://ec.europa.eu/commission/sites/beta-political/files/soteu2018-speech_en_0.pdf. See also COM (2018) 643 *a new Africa – Europe Alliance for Sustainable Investment and Jobs: Taking our partnership for investment and jobs to the next level.*

and priorities followed by three regional partnerships.[47] With respect to Africa it is recognised that the regional partnership will "build on, reinforce and upgrade the Joint Africa-EU Strategy."[48]

Initiated in 2007, the Joint Africa-EU Strategy may be seen as a move away from the traditional relationship to create a new partnership for sustainable development.[49] Under the Strategy, support would be offered to the AU's Comprehensive Africa Agricultural Development Programme (CAADP) which would include an emphasis on improved governance of agriculture and support for capacity-building for those organisations, public and private, involved in agriculture.[50] In 2014 the AU adopted the Malabo Declaration setting a set of strategic goals for the AU, which included *inter alia* recommitments by the AU to the principles and values of the CAADP process, to enhancing investment finance in agriculture, to ending hunger in Africa by 2025 and to halve poverty by the year 2025.[51] At the second AU-EU Agriculture Ministerial Conference in July 2017 in Rome, the EU Agriculture Commissioner, Phil Hogan, indicated that he would be working with the AU Commissioner to implement the Malabo Declaration alongside an intensification of relations in agriculture.[52] That intensification would go beyond existing cooperation through development assistance and preferential trade arrangements to a consolidation of a third action—fostering responsible investment in African agriculture that would be leveraged by the launch of a European External Investment Plan (EEIP).

The results of the Rome Conference fed into the Africa-EU Summit in November 2017 which welcomed the launch of the EEIP "to crowd in investments from financial institutions and the private sector" which would focus on those sectors with the highest potential for sustainable job creation which included agriculture and agro-business.[53] This section of the Declaration also offered support for AU-EU

[47]Available at http://data.consilium.europa.eu/doc/document/ST-8094-2018-ADD-1/en/pdf. The Agreement would continue to be one concluded by the EU and the Member States despite the endorsement by the Council in May 2018 that in future the EU should negotiate free trade agreements (an area of exclusive competence) and separate investment agreements between the EU and the Member States on the one hand and third countries on the other. See http://data.consilium.europa.eu/doc/document/ST-8622-2018-INIT/en/pdf, Council Doc 8622/18.

[48]Ibid, p. 26.

[49]See https://www.africa-eu-partnership.org//sites/default/files/documents/eas2007_joint_strategy_en.pdf.

[50]Ibid, para 73. See also paragraph 9 which set the overall objectives for the agriculture and food security partnership; paragraphs 44 and 47 on SPS and TBT standards and paragraphs 64 and 65 on food security, land degradation and desertification. These objectives can also be found in the EU's negotiating directives, above n 47, pp. 37 and 46.

[51]See https://au.int/sites/default/files/documents/31247-doc-malabo_declaration_2014_11_26.pdf.

[52]See https://ec.europa.eu/commission/commissioners/2014-2019/hogan/announcements/speech-commissioner-phil-hogan-opening-2nd-au-eu-agriculture-ministerial-conference-fao-offices-rome_en.

[53]See http://www.consilium.europa.eu/media/31991/33454-pr-final_declaration_au_eu_summit.pdf, para 6.

trade arrangements which are to be "complementary and supportive to the African Union trade and structural transformation agenda especially now as it gears towards implementing a Continental Free Trade Area."[54] In a February 2018 speech, the EU Agriculture Commissioner stated: "We are re-thinking our traditional development cooperation models and, beyond our development assistance and trade relations, we are now focusing on targeting policy support, fostering investments in rural areas and supporting agro-industries in Africa, with the involvement of the private sector."[55]

As for the way forward, a Task Force was established that would offer recommendations to enhance the role of the EU agri-food and agro-industrial sector in promoting African sustainable development and would identify means to accelerate EU private investment to support sustainable African agriculture. The first meeting of the Task Force took place in May 2018 and its final report was issued in March 2019 with its central recommendation being that "Africa and the EU should implement an innovative partnership for the inclusive and sustainable development of Africa's agri-food sector and rural economy".[56] A range of short- to medium-term actions are proposed that would constitute the agri-food and rural agenda for the new Alliance for Sustainable Investment and Jobs.[57] That Alliance, as the Commission President suggested, will include a continent-to-continent free trade agreement encompassing not just the five African EPAs and the beneficiaries of the EBA but also the agreements with the countries of North Africa who are members of the AU. There is, therefore, real choices to be made both by the EU and by the ACP on the nature of the post-2020 relationship.[58]

[54]Ibid, para 64. One of the objectives listed in the negotiating objectives for the regional partnership with Africa (above n 47) is to support preparations for Africa's Continental Free Trade Area.

[55]Joint DEVE/AGRI Hearing on "The Impact of the CAP on Developing Countries"—27th February 2018, Brussels. See https://ec.europa.eu/commission/commissioners/2014-2019/hogan/announcements/speech-joint-deveagri-hearing-impact-cap-developing-countries-27th-february-2018-brussels_en.

[56]Available at https://ec.europa.eu/info/sites/info/files/food-farming-fisheries/farming/documents/report-tfra_mar2019_en.pdf.

[57]Ibid, Chapter 7. See also associated Press Release "Africa-Europe Alliance: European Commission committed to a sustainable African agri-food sector" available at http://europa.eu/rapid/press-release_IP-19-1569_en.htm.

[58]See for example, Medinilla, A and J Bossuyt *Charting the course to 2020: Fundamental Choices for the negotiation of a future ACP-EU Partnership*, (2018) available at http://ecdpm.org/wp-content/uploads/Charting-the-course-to-2020-Fundamental-choices-for-the-negotiation-of-a-future-ACP-EU-partnership-Medinillla-Bossuyt-ECDPM.pdf and Keijzer, N and A Medinilla, *Can the EU prioritise both the African Union and the Africa, Caribbean and Pacific group?* (2017) available at http://ecdpm.org/wp-content/uploads/ETTG-Brief-Keijzer-Medinilla-November-2017.pdf.

4 Future UK Trade Policy

In September 2017 the UK Government published a position paper entitled *Foreign policy, defence and development: a future partnership paper* in which it reaffirmed its support for the objectives listed in Article 21 TEU.[59] The paper points to the UK's Official Development Assistance (ODA) as evidence of its global leadership in development—in 2016 it was one of only five Member States to reach the 0.7% UN target for ODA.[60] The position paper goes on to highlight the central importance of trade to development and the UK's commitment, shared with the EU, to eradicate extreme poverty.[61] As for the future relationship between the UK and the EU in the area of development cooperation, the paper concludes[62]:

> Continued close working with European partners will form an important part of the UK's future international development strategy, not least as working collaboratively with other countries helps drive impact and coherence across the system. Such close collaboration would be on a case-by-case basis and be subject to UK's standards on full transparency, accountability, risk and assurance, results and value for money.

This collaborative relationship would not only support existing objectives (e.g. the fight against extreme poverty) but also the success of UN's SDGs through shared "approaches to building global prosperity in the most challenging contexts to reinforce our collective ability to tackle the causes of instability and insecurity."[63] On development issues, this proposed relationship would be unlike any that the EU has with a third country.

The UK's development efforts, to end extreme poverty and deliver the SDGs, are led by the Department for International Development (DfID).[64] The May 2018 Departmental Plan in relation to the elimination of extreme poverty promises a contribution to a number of the SDGs but with the exception of an increase in funding of UK-led medical and technical research into global health threats, no specific measure is identified.[65] A similar picture emerges with respect to promoting economic development although there is a promise that post-Brexit, the UK would "secure duty-free quota-free access for the world's Least Developed Countries to UK markets, be the world's foremost champion of free trade and continue to support the

[59]https://assets.publishing.service.gov.uk/government/uploads/system/uploads/attachment_data/file/643924/Foreign_policy__defence_and_development_paper.pdf, para 7.

[60]Ibid, para 53.

[61]Ibid, paras 55 and 56. See also paras 57 to 59 give examples of UK leadership on development and paragraphs 60 and 61 for its contribution on external migration.

[62]Ibid, para 79.

[63]Ibid, para 81. There would also be continued coordination on external migration (para 82).

[64]See https://www.gov.uk/government/organisations/department-for-international-development/about for details of DfID's objectives.

[65]See https://www.gov.uk/government/publications/department-for-international-development-single-departmental-plan/department-for-international-development-single-departmental-plan-december-2018#tackle-extreme-poverty-and-help-the-worlds-most-vulnerable, Objective 4.

overseas territories."[66] These criticisms of the Departmental Plan may be unfair given that in January 2017 DfID adopted a document entitled *Economic Development Strategy: prosperity, poverty and meeting global challenges* to help realise the Prime Minister's ambition for a Global Britain that would use trade as means to reduce poverty in developing countries.[67] The Strategy recognises the unique opportunity provided by Brexit to "build up a comprehensive package bringing together UK trade policy, aid that unlocks barriers to trade and investment promotion to reduce poverty." As for the elements of this package, the Strategy points to the importance for developing countries of the proper implementation of the 2013 WTO Trade Facilitation Agreement and the 2015 WTO Ministerial Decision on export competition.

Agriculture is identified as one of the priority sectors in the Strategy by promising an increasingly commercial approach in this sector that would help "farmers and their families to have opportunities and jobs outside of their farms and supporting SMEs in rural areas" and support "subsistence farmers, without other economic opportunities, to avoid hunger, malnutrition and extreme poverty."[68] It goes on to identify a number of aid projects and investments to which DfID has lent support, for example, those that integrate climate change into agribusiness.[69] The latter includes the Adaptation for Smallholder Agriculture Programme, a multi-donor ten year programme with funding of £150 million to help smallholder farmers adapt to climate change by promoting various approaches to climate smart agriculture.[70] Another multi-donor example is the Global Agriculture and Food Security Programme to which DfID has contributed £136 million, the majority of which is focussed on African countries, to support both public and private sector investment to improve the income and food security of poor people.[71]

The UK Secretary of State for International Development, Penny Mordaunt, may have had this latter project in mind, when on 8 October 2018 she delivered a speech on the future of ODA post-Brexit.[72] Having established coherence of ODA across the UK Government, she wanted to use that budget to increase private sector

[66]Ibid, Objective 3.

[67]See https://assets.publishing.service.gov.uk/government/uploads/system/uploads/attachment_data/file/587374/DFID-Economic-Development-Strategy-2017.pdf.

[68]Ibid, p. 17.

[69]Ibid, Boxes 7, 8 and 9. See also *Examples of DFID's Global Flagship Programmes on Inclusive and Sustainable Commercial Agriculture* available at https://www.gov.uk/guidance/examples-of-dfids-global-flagship-programmes-on-inclusive-and-sustainable-commercial-agriculture.

[70]This is a project led by the International Fund for Agricultural Development, for further details see https://www.ifad.org/web/guest/asap.

[71]For further details, see http://www.gafspfund.org/.

[72]Available at https://www.gov.uk/government/speeches/the-future-of-uk-aid-post-brexit. What is proposed is "a new national conversation to find out more about how the British people might want their savings and pension to be used to support the Global Goals and end poverty" and the development of indicators on how the social and environmental impact of investment is measured and flagged to the public.

investment in sustainable development to build a more inclusive global economy and to make up the financing gap necessary to realise the SDGs. She estimated that financing gap to be $2.5 trillion per year and as aid from traditional donor governments would be unable to fill this gap, private investment was needed.[73] What she proposed is a new partnership with the City of London, who manage over £8 trillion worth of assets, to design a new financing mechanism to mobilise more investment for poorer countries. The Secretary of State referenced the recent visit by the Prime Minister to Africa and her promise to hold a UK-Investment Summit in 2019 which would help to realise the goal that the UK would become the largest foreign direct investor of the Group of Seven (G7) in Africa by 2022.[74] The Secretary of State concluded that investment would build new markets which would be the focus of new trading relationships, arguing that more trade would lead to less aid.[75]

Responsibility for developing these new trading relationships for Global Britain rests with the Department of International Trade who have launched consultations on free trade agreements with old friends (e.g. Australia, New Zealand and the United States) and new allies (e.g. the Comprehensive and Progressive Agreement for Trans-Pacific Partnership (CPTPP) a trade agreement between Australia, Brunei, Canada, Chile, Japan, Malaysia, Mexico, New Zealand, Peru, Singapore, and Vietnam).[76] The consultations will be conducted, assuming that there is a withdrawal agreement with the EU, during its implementation period and any free trade agreements can only come into force as from the date when the UK formally leaves the EU. These agreements will aim to reduce barriers to market access (tariffs and regulatory measures) in both trade and investment giving consumers access to a greater range of products whilst maintaining standards protecting consumers, workers, animals, the environment and public services. The latter will involve the UK exercising its rights under two WTO Agreements, the Agreement on the application of Sanitary and Phytosanitary Measures (SPS Agreement) and the Agreement on Technical Barriers to Trade (TBT Agreement). Whilst the UK was a Member State, the EU also exercised rights under both agreements in areas of its competence.

As for other agreements it must be noted here that as the UK will no longer be an EU Member State, the agreements concluded with third countries will cease to apply to it. As a result, the Department of International Trade has been busy consulting with countries on the continuation of existing trade relationships which in the last few months have included Costa Rica, Panama, Peru, South Korea, Taiwan and the

[73] Ibid. She estimated that aid totalled $150 billion of which one third was devoted to Africa.

[74] See https://www.gov.uk/government/news/pm-announces-ambition-for-uk-to-be-largest-g7-investor-in-africa-by-2022 for details.

[75] Above n 72, she argued that a 1% increase in their share of global trade would equate to an additional £130 billion to deliver the SDGs.

[76] See https://www.gov.uk/government/publications?departments%5B%5D=department-for-international-trade&publication_filter_option=consultations for details of the consultations.

Ukraine.[77] During her visit to Kenya, Nigeria and South Africa in August 2018, the Prime Minister proposed innovation partnerships with these countries developing cooperation in the tech sector alongside a new DfID programme promoting investment in this area in the hope of encouraging future trade.[78] In September 2018 UK trade officials met with those of the ESA to discuss a UK-ESA EPA which would ensure the continuation of trade relations under the existing EPA with the EU, either from 30 March 2019 (if there is no UK-EU agreement on a withdrawal agreement) or 1 January 2021 (i.e. the proposed end of the implementation period under a withdrawal agreement).[79] Discussions have also taken place between the South African Customs Union (SACU) and Mozambique to allow for the continuation of the SADC-EPA once the UK leaves the EU and having reiterated their support for the WTO, they reaffirmed "the centrality of development in the WTO's work and the need to continue to fight WTO non-compliant measures that lead to protectionism and unilateralism."[80]

Turning to the WTO, in a letter to the WTO, the UK and EU's WTO Permanent Representatives informed the Members of the UK's intention to withdraw from the EU and as a result, existing quantitative commitments made by the EU on goods would have to be adjusted to reflect this.[81] As of the date of withdrawal, the UK will have new schedules of commitments in goods (under the General Agreement on Tariffs and Trade) and services (under the General Agreement on Trade in Services) which would as far as possible replicate its existing obligations under the current EU commitments. Adjustments will be necessary in two areas. The first of these would be tariff-rate quotas in agricultural products and these would be made through an apportionment of existing EU commitments based on trade flows under each tariff-rate quota. The second area for adjustment would be in relation to the EU's commitment level for domestic agricultural support which using objective methodology would be apportioned between the EU and the UK. The letter also noted that

---

[77] See https://www.gov.uk/government/announcements?departments%5B%5D=department-for-international-trade for announcements with respect to these countries.

[78] See https://www.gov.uk/government/news/ambitious-new-innovation-partnerships-with-african-countries. There was also the announcement by the Department for International Trade of the appointment of a dedicated Trade Commissioner to Africa who will lead a team providing expert in-country investment and export advice for UK and African companies.

[79] See https://www.gov.uk/government/news/joint-statement-on-uk-and-eastern-and-southern-africa-epa and the agreement was signed on 31 January 2019, see https://www.gov.uk/government/news/uk-signs-eastern-and-southern-africa-trade-continuity-agreement. See more generally, Razzaque M and B Vickers *Post-Brexit UK-ACP Trading Arrangements: Some Reflections* available at http://thecommonwealth.org/sites/default/files/news-items/documents/5jln9q109bmr-en.pdf.

[80] See https://www.gov.uk/government/news/joint-statement-on-uk-sacu-and-mozambique-epa. See also https://www.gov.uk/government/news/uk-southern-african-trade-boosting-uk-and-african-economies for a joint South Africa-UK statement that a trade agreement will be ready to enter into force as soon as the EU deal no longer applies to the UK.

[81] See https://ec.europa.eu/commission/publications/joint-letter-eu-and-uk-permanent-representatives-wto_en.

the UK would continue existing preferential arrangements for developing and least-developed countries on its withdrawal from the EU.

Some WTO members were not happy with the proposed approach to the division of tariff-rate quotas as even before the letter was delivered, a letter from the Geneva representatives of Argentina, Brazil, Canada, New Zealand, Thailand, the United States and Uruguay suggested that the proposed division of tariff rate quotas based on historical averages was unacceptable as it would not fully honour existing tariff quota commitments. The proposed technical rectification was deemed unacceptable with these seven countries arguing that negotiations were needed between the UK and the EU on the one hand, and "the countries which are holders of Country-Allocated Tariff Rate Quotas into the European Union market, users of Most Favoured Nation Tariff Rate Quotas as well as holders of initial negotiating rights and principal and substantial interests in several concessions,"[82] on the other hand. The methodology adopted by the EU and the UK involved establishing the UK usage share for each individual tariff-rate quota over the period 2013–2015 this was then subtracted from the figure for the EU tariff-rate quota which then became the figure for the EU minus the UK. The Commission has proposed changes to 123 of the existing 180 tariff-rate quotas for agricultural products and changes to ten of the nineteen existing tariff-rate quotas for other products.[83]

The Commission has acknowledged the concerns raised by WTO Members by recognising that negotiations will be needed with affected WTO Members under Article XXVIII GATT (i.e. those having principal or substantial supplying interest or holding an initial negotiating rights) to modify the EU Schedule but has noted that these negotiations may not be concluded by the time the UK leaves the EU.[84] For its part, in July 2018, the UK submitted its draft Schedule setting out its WTO market access commitments for goods once it leaves the EU.[85] Other WTO Members must review the Schedule within three months after which the WTO Director-General will certify the Schedule unless a Member objects. If one or more Members object, there will be informal consultations and if these fail to resolve the matter, there will be

[82]See link available in news story "Brexit: UK, EU Propose Cooperative Approach to WTO Commitments" *Bridges Vol 21 No 33* (21 October 2017) available at https://www.ictsd.org/bridges-news/bridges/news/brexit-uk-eu-propose-cooperative-approach-to-wto-commitments. Australia has also joined the list of countries criticising the arrangement, see *Australia knocks UK Brexit Trade Plan*, (25 November 2017) available at http://www.bbc.co.uk/news/uk-politics-42121442.

[83]COM (2018) 312 Proposal for a Regulation of the European Parliament and of the Council on the apportionment of tariff rate quotas included in the WTO schedule of the Union following the withdrawal of the United Kingdom from the Union.

[84]Ibid, Recitals 4 and 5 of the Preamble to the proposed Regulation.

[85]See https://www.wto.org/english/news_e/news18_e/mark_24jul18_e.htm. The UK has also submitted a request to join the Government Procurement Agreement along with a market access offer, see https://www.wto.org/english/news_e/news18_e/gpro_27jun18_e.htm. See also "WTO Negotiators Look to Lay Groundwork on Post-Brexit Food Import Quotas" Bridges, Vol. 22, No. 34 (18 October 2018) available at https://www.ictsd.org/sites/default/files/review/bridgesweekly22-34c.pdf.

formal negotiations under Article XXVIII GATT and if these fail, recourse can be had to the Dispute Settlement Understanding.

A solution is thus emerging for the first adjustment problem. As for the second adjustment problem—domestic agricultural support commitments—it appears that this may not be a significant problem given the different approaches being taken by the devolved administrations within the UK to future agricultural policy. The recently published Agriculture Bill provides that the agricultural policy for England will focus on a new environmental land management system which will replace existing EU direct payments over a 7-year transitional period.[86] This new system will offer public money (e.g. multi-annual payments) for public goods (i.e. managing and mitigating the effects of climate change and fulfilling the Government's promise to leave the environment in a better state than they found it). There will also be publicly-funded schemes for farmers to deliver animal welfare enhancements beyond a regulatory baseline for those enhancements valued by the public but not sufficiently provided by the market. Both schemes may fall within Annex 2 of the Agreement on Agriculture (the Green Box) exempting certain policies from commitments to reduce domestic agricultural support. Even if these schemes do not fall within the Green Box, it has been estimated that the UK would be able to offer adequate support using Article 6(4) of the Agreement—the *de minimis* provision.[87]

Given that the UK remains a net-food importer, it may be that Brexit will be an opportunity to reduce the level of tariffs on agricultural products thus making it an attractive partner for the free trade agreements it hopes to conclude with new friends and old allies. With respect to the latter, the final question here is, what role, if any, will the Commonwealth play post-Brexit? Whilst the Commonwealth is not a trade organisation, it must also be noted that, of this group of 53 developed and developing countries, 41 are ACP countries. The Communiqué for the 2018 Commonwealth Heads of Government meeting, *Towards a Common Future*, after noting the risks of protectionism in the multilateral trading system, set the goal of boosting intra-Commonwealth trade to US$2 trillion by 2030.[88] This is an ambitious target given that the Strategic Plan adopted by the Commonwealth Secretariat in June 2017 for the period 2017–2021 estimated that intra-Commonwealth trade was expected to reach US$1 trillion by 2020.[89] As for the impact of Brexit, a 2016 assessment published by the Commonwealth Secretariat argued for the maintenance of existing

[86]See https://publications.parliament.uk/pa/bills/cbill/2017-2019/0266/cbill_2017-20190266_en_1.htm. See also https://www.gov.uk/government/news/landmark-agriculture-bill-to-deliver-a-green-brexit.

[87]See Matthews, A *Establishing the UK's non-exempt limit on agricultural support after Brexit* (2017a) available at http://capreform.eu/establishing-the-uks-non-exempt-limit-on-agricultural-support-after-brexit/. Article 6(5) of the Agreement could also be used to allow for the continuation of product-specific support, which currently operates only in Scotland.

[88]See https://www.chogm2018.org.uk/sites/default/files/CHOGM%202018%20Communique.pdf paras 16 and 17.

[89]The Strategic Plan was for the period 2017–2021, see http://thecommonwealth.org/sites/default/files/inline/CommonwealthSecretariatStrategic_Plan_17_21.pdf, para 32.

market access arrangements in both the post-Brexit UK and EU markets and continued development aid from both.[90] Pointing out that a Commonwealth-wide agreement will not be possible as two of its members will still be Member States of the EU (Cyprus and Malta), it concluded that post-Brexit there needed to be continuing cooperation between the UK and the EU to mitigate post-Brexit risks and uncertainties for Commonwealth developing countries.[91] The scope of such cooperation, depends on the agreement to be concluded between the UK and the EU on their post-Brexit relationship and the shape of this agreement (and whether it included provisions on development cooperation) remains uncertain at the moment.

5 Conclusions

Since their launch the Brexit negotiations have focussed on a range of issues, such as the free movement of goods and services, the rights of EU nationals in the UK post-Brexit (and vice versa) and how to avoid a hard border between Northern Ireland and Ireland. It was not expected that development cooperation would feature heavily in the negotiations and this has been the case. Indeed, the European Council guidelines for the Brexit negotiations adopted in April 2017 do not even mention development cooperation although they do indicate that "The EU stands ready to establish partnerships in areas unrelated to trade, in particular the fight against terrorism and international crime, as well as security, defence and foreign policy."[92] Yet Brexit will have a major impact on the EU's Development Cooperation Policy post-Brexit as the UK develops its trade policy. It could be argued that the timing of Brexit is particularly unfortunate (or fortunate, depending on your point of view) for the EU's Development Cooperation Policy as it will coincide with the negotiations for a replacement for the Cotonou Partnership Agreement with the ACP and the renewal of the Multiannual Financial Framework (MFF) within the EU. A host of questions have been raised, the answers to which are not yet clear.

Brexit will have an impact on trade not only between the UK and the EU but also between developing countries and the UK (and the EU). The extent of that impact will depend on the agreement established between the UK and the EU to govern their relationship, but it is not yet certain whether agreement can be reached and if it can, what it will provide. The UK wishes to depart from the customs union and the single

---

[90]See Razzaque, M, B Vickers and P Goel *Brexit and Commonwealth Trade* (2016) available at http://thecommonwealth.org/sites/default/files/news-items/documents/BrexitandCommonwealthTrade.pdf and Stevens C and J Keenan *Trade Implications of Brexit for Commonwealth Developing Countries* (2016) available at http://thecommonwealth.org/sites/default/files/news-items/documents/TradeImplicationsBrexit_0.pdf.

[91]Ibid, (Razzaque et al) *SDGs and a Lost Decade of Trade Gains: What Commonwealth Role Post-Brexit?* p. 15.

[92]See https://www.consilium.europa.eu/en/press/press-releases/2017/04/29/euco-brexit-guidelines/, para 22.

market whilst maintaining regulatory convergence through a common rule-book for goods (but not services), whilst the EU maintains that there can be no "cherry-picking" between the four freedoms (goods, persons, services and capital).[93] Adherence to a common rule book could restrict the scope of future UK Trade Policy as it seeks to conclude free trade agreements with new friends and old allies as it would limit the scope of regulatory divergence between the UK and the EU. As for the tariff concessions inherent in free trade agreements, the UK Goods Schedule is awaiting certification in the WTO and it is likely to allow it a degree of freedom to reduce tariffs, especially on agricultural products given the UK's status as a net-food importer. This will offer other countries an opportunity to export these products to the UK which may not have been possible under the EU's Common Customs Tariff as a result of the CAP. This should be of benefit to certain developing countries. As the UK leaves the EU, and all the agreements concluded by the EU with third countries, it is preparing to take the opportunity to maintain these links by negotiating similar arrangements. However, it may also need to be more ambitious if it is to realise the objectives of Global Britain.

Such ambition was demonstrated in the recent trip to Africa by the Prime Minister with the conclusion of a number of innovation partnerships and more recently by the Secretary of State for International Development in her speech on ODA. The objective is to make the UK the hub for major investment in Africa which may have the side-effect of increasing trade between Africa and the UK as the African Continental Free Trade is progressively realised. A similar ambition with respect to Africa is also evident in the Commission President's State of the Union speech, particularly the call for a new Alliance for Sustainable Investment and Jobs between Europe and Africa. Whether this will be located within a more bespoke arrangement between Africa and the EU in the context of the renegotiation of the Cotonou Partnership Agreement is an open question. The negotiating guidelines suggest the final Agreement will be concluded by the EU and the Member States with African countries, despite the endorsement by the Council in May 2018 that in future the EU should negotiate free trade agreements (an area of exclusive competence) and separate investment agreements between the EU and the Member States on the one hand and third countries on the other.[94] Even if it is not to be part of the renegotiation, the Alliance will include AU members currently outside the ACP and this may involve changes to the European Neighbourhood Policy.

To be successful, the two investment proposals of the UK and the EU should be complementary generating sufficient resources to promote development. This could be realised if agreement could be reached on development cooperation (and development aid) as part of the deep and special relationship which the UK hopes will be

[93]Ibid, para 1 for the Council position. For details of the Chequers Plan, see https://assets.publishing.service.gov.uk/government/uploads/system/uploads/attachment_data/file/723460/CHEQUERS_STATEMENT_-_FINAL.PDF.

[94]Above n 47 and see also http://data.consilium.europa.eu/doc/document/ST-8622-2018-INIT/en/pdf, Council Doc 8622/18.

established with the EU post-Brexit. It should be noted here that the UK makes a significant contribution to the EU's development cooperation funding instruments and the European Development Fund.[95] A 2018 study for the European Parliament's Committee on Development offered three scenarios for future UK involvement in EU aid policy in two of which there would be no cooperation between the UK and the EU (nationalist and realist scenarios).[96] Only in the third scenarios (cosmopolitan) would the UK maintain its commitment to EU aid programmes but could divert funds to multilateral organisations.[97] The scenario that finally emerges must consider the recent Commission proposal for a new Neighbourhood, Development and International Cooperation Instrument (NDICI) in the next MFF which would replace a number of the existing Regulations establishing various funding instruments and incorporate the EDF into the EU Budget.[98] The proposed funding for NDICI is €89.2 billion for the 2021–2027 period, an increase of 11% compared to the resources allocated to the instruments it replaces. Adoption of the proposal is not certain; the European Parliament has long asked for the EDF to be incorporated within the EU budget whilst within the Council, several Member States wish to maintain the current status of the EDF and keep it open to third country participation.[99] The UK will be a third country in the next MFF.

Brexit has been a long road which has taken many a winding turn, but it is not yet clear where exactly it is leading with respect to the future of the EU's Development Cooperation Policy and the nascent Trade Policy of the UK. Brexit represents an opportunity for both the UK and the EU to bring their development efforts to a new level whether this be through a formal agreement or on a case-by-case basis. For the EU decisions will need to be taken on the renegotiation of the Cotonou Partnership agreement and the scope of the next MFF but whilst these decisions are reasonably imminent, it is not possible to offer definitive guidance on what they will be. For the UK who wishes to rediscover its role as a great, global trading nation and an

---

[95]It has been estimated that the UK contributes just less than 11% to the EU Budget and around 15% to the EDF. See D'Alfonso, A *European Development Fund - Joint development cooperation and the EU budget: out or in?* (2014) available at http://www.europarl.europa.eu/EPRS/EPRS-IDA-542140-European-Development-Fund-FINAL.pdf, p. 14. The overall contribution is about £1.5billion, above n 72.

[96]Olivié I and A Pérez, *Possible impacts of Brexit on EU development and humanitarian policies* (2017) available at http://www.europarl.europa.eu/RegData/etudes/STUD/2017/578042/EXPO_STU(2017)578042_EN.pdf.

[97]Ibid, p. 23.

[98]COM (2018) 460. The Regulations include those establishing the Instrument contributing to Peace and Stability (Regulation 230/2014, [2014] OJ L 77/1), the Development Cooperation Instrument (Regulation 233/2014, [2014] OJ L 77/44) and the European Fund for Sustainable Development (Regulation 2017/1601, [2017] OJ L 249/1).

[99]See http://www.europarl.europa.eu/sides/getDoc.do?type=TA&language=EN&reference=P8-TA-2018-0226 for the European Parliament Resolution of 30 May 2018 on the 2021-2027 Multiannual Financial Framework and own resources and http://data.consilium.europa.eu/doc/document/ST-11871-2018-INIT/en/pdf for a note by the Council President of 18 September 2018 on the state of play concerning the MFF proposals.

advocate for free trade, it is important that it remembers the values it cherishes such as compassion and concern for the welfare of others, which suggests that its trade policy should not be a zero-sum game.

On 25 November 2018 agreement was reached at the European Council meeting on the Withdrawal Agreement and the Political Declaration outlining the future relationship. However, problems have arisen with the approval of the Withdrawal Agreement by the UK Parliament and it is still not certain that that Agreement will be approved or that the UK will leave the EU on 29 March 2019. Development cooperation is addressed in the Political Declaration which sets the parameters for "an ambitious, broad, deep and flexible partnership" between the UK and the EU to be negotiated before the end of the transition period i.e. 31 December 2020.[100] Analysis of the Declaration suggests that what is envisaged within an overarching institutional framework is an Association Agreement covering various areas of cooperation but whether development cooperation will sit inside or outside this framework is an open question. Given that the UK will have an independent trade policy and its own foreign policy objectives, it seems likely that it will sit outside the framework.[101] So, with decisions on future EU funding programmes due to be made in 2020, it is not yet certain whether the UK will participate in such programmes and if it does not on-going consultations will be needed to ensure coherence (and consistency) between the EU's and the UK's development cooperation policies.

References

Blanco M (2018) The impact of the Common Agricultural Policy on developing countries (February 2018). Available at http://www.europarl.europa.eu/RegData/etudes/STUD/2018/603862/EXPO_STU%282018%29603862_EN.pdf

D'Alfonso A (2014) A European Development Fund - Joint development cooperation and the EU budget: out or in? European Parliament Research Service (November 2014). Available at http://www.europarl.europa.eu/EPRS/EPRS-IDA-542140-European-Development-Fund-FINAL.pdf.

Keijzer N, Medinilla A (2017) Can the EU prioritise both the African Union and the Africa, Caribbean and Pacific group? Available at http://ecdpm.org/wp-content/uploads/ETTG-Brief-Keijzer-Medinilla-November-2017.pdf

Matthews A (2017a) Establishing the UK's non-exempt limit on agricultural support after Brexit (January 29, 2017). Available at http://capreform.eu/establishing-the-uks-non-exempt-limit-on-agricultural-support-after-brexit/

---

[100]See https://assets.publishing.service.gov.uk/government/uploads/system/uploads/attachment_data/file/759021/25_November_Political_Declaration_setting_out_the_framework_for_the_future_relationship_between_the_European_Union_and_the_United_Kingdom__.pdf, para 3.

[101]Ibid, paras 98, 108 and 109 which references a dialogue between the UK and the EU on strategies for the programming and delivery of development and coordination between their delegation in third countries. Such cooperation will offer continued support for the UN's Sustainable Development Goals and the European Consensus on Development (para 93).

Matthews A (2017b) The development-related impacts of EU agricultural subsidies (TEP Working Paper No. 1617, June 2017). Available at https://www.tcd.ie/Economics/TEP/2017/tep1617.pdf

Matthews A (2018) Implications of Brexit for food and agriculture in developing countries (TEP Working Paper No. 0318, March 2018). Available at https://www.tcd.ie/Economics/TEP/2018/tep0318.pdf

Medinilla A, Bossuyt J (2018) Charting the course to 2020: Fundamental Choices for the negotiation of a future ACP-EU Partnership. Available at http://ecdpm.org/wp-content/uploads/Charting-the-course-to-2020-Fundamental-choices-for-the-negotiation-of-a-future-ACP-EU-partnership-Medinillla-Bossuyt-ECDPM.pdf

Mendez-Parra M Papadavid P, Willem te Veld D (2016) Brexit and development How will developing countries be affected? ODI Briefing (July 2016). Available at https://www.odi.org/sites/odi.org.uk/files/resource-documents/10685.pdf

Olivié I, Pérez A (2017) Possible impacts of Brexit on EU development and humanitarian policies. Directorate-General for External Policies, Policy Department, April 2017. Available at http://www.europarl.europa.eu/RegData/etudes/STUD/2017/578042/EXPO_STU(2017)578042_EN.pdf

Razzaque M, Vickers B. Post-Brexit UK-ACP Trading Arrangements: Some Reflections. The Commonwealth, Issue 137. Available at http://thecommonwealth.org/sites/default/files/news-items/documents/5jln9q109bmr-en.pdf

Razzaque, M, Vickers B, Goel P (2016) Brexit and Commonwealth Trade. Commonwealth Trade Policy Briefing, November 2016. Available at http://thecommonwealth.org/sites/default/files/news-items/documents/BrexitandCommonwealthTrade.pdf

Rudloff B, Brüntrup M (2018) "Fair Play: The Recent Common Agricultural Policy and Its Limited Effect on Development". (SWP Comment, May 2018). Available at https://www.swp-berlin.org/fileadmin/contents/products/comments/2018C21_rff_bruentrup.pdf

Stevens C, Keenan J (2016) Trade Implications of Brexit for Commonwealth Developing Countries. The Commonwealth, Issue 133, 2016. Available at http://thecommonwealth.org/sites/default/files/news-items/documents/TradeImplicationsBrexit_0.pdf

Twitchett CC (1978) Europe and Africa from Association to Partnership. Saxon House

Zartman IW (1971) The politics of trade negotiations between Africa and the EEC. Princeton University Press

Zartman IW (1975–1976) Europe and Africa: decolonization of dependency? Foreign Affairs 54:325

Joseph A. McMahon is full Professor of Commercial Law at Sutherland School of Law, University College Dublin, Ireland. He would like to thank the Editors for the encouragement and suggestions for this article. Responsibility for all remaining faults with the article rests with the author. The events and facts referred to in this article are up-to-date until 23 February, 2019.

The Obligation of Due Diligence and Cyber-Attacks: Bridging the Gap Between Universal and Differential Approaches for States

Enenu O. Okwori

Abstract States are obliged under international law to exercise due diligence in preventing their territories from being used to perpetrate harmful conducts that will interfere with the rights of other states. Prevailing scholarship advocates that this obligation extends to harmful cyber activities perpetrated from within the territory of a state or where they are routed through a state. This obligation would implicitly attenuate the menace posed by cyber-attacks. There are specific elements capable of triggering this obligation however; exercising the obligation itself cannot exceed the factual capabilities of states—their legal, financial and technological wherewithal. More so, the obligation is largely understood to be one of conduct rather than result, simply expecting nothing more or less than best efforts from states, as there are no standards of adherence. This laxity has crippled the potency of the obligation and increased the likelihood of more states evading responsibility for their failure to observe it like developing states whose territories are being used to perpetrate harmful cyber-attacks and yet lack sufficient capacity to prevent them. It is opined that adopting concrete measures, encouraging monitoring obligations and upholding calls for mutual assistance that will strengthen cooperation between developed and developing states, will allow for a fair and universal application in all states despite varying circumstances.

1 Introduction

The evolution of globalization ushered in an increased need for interconnectedness among states, one largely met by Information and Communication Technology (ICT). Though this development has birthed economic and political advancement and to some extent, security for states, it has had its accompanying challenges.[1] From rise in cyber-crimes such as cyber theft, computer-related forgery and fraud,

[1]Herzog (2011), p. 50.

E. O. Okwori (✉)
School of Law, University of Aberdeen, Aberdeen, UK

Z. Yihdego et al. (eds.), *Ethiopian Yearbook of International Law 2018*, Ethiopian Yearbook of International Law 2018, https://doi.org/10.1007/978-3-030-24078-3_9

child pornography[2] to more recent threats of cyber-terrorism.[3] The list is inexhaustive. Computer Network Attacks (CNAs) have been defined as 'actions taken through the use of computer networks to disrupt, deny, degrade, or destroy information resident in computers and computer networks, or the computers and networks themselves'.[4] Majority of the cyber-attacks manifested through various forms like malware, ransomware, viruses, and more often, Distributed Denial of Service (DDoS) attacks, have erupted from states and non-state actors alike.[5]

A 2017 report showed an alarming increase in world-wide ransomware—a malicious software that threatens victims for ransom, reaching about 1242 detections daily.[6] An earlier report purported that the detections already increased from 18% to 66% between January and November 2016.[7] Presently, developing countries like those on the African continent face about 13–15% external malware attacks while about 47% of malware attacks are generated from within Africa against other countries.[8] It has been estimated that Africa's cyber security market may be worth two billion (USD) by 2020. Yet it is still incapable of establishing effective cyber security solutions viable in preventing these attacks.[9] The African Union (AU) Commissioner for Infrastructure and Energy, in reiterating the magnitude of the threat that cyber-attacks pose, commented that 'cybercrime is a global scourge'.[10] The former US Homeland Security Advisor has also remarked that states are '... in the midst of a revolution of the cyber threat—one that is growing more persistent, more diverse, more frequent and more dangerous every day'.[11]

---

[2]These are some of the offences listed as cybercrimes under the Council of Europe's Convention on Cybercrime. Although, the convention has not provided a definition of cybercrime. See the Council of Europe Convention on Cybercrime, opened for signature 23 November 2001, CETS No 185 (entered into force 1 July 2004), (Budapest Convention).

[3]There has been no occurrence of cyber-terrorism but with the rise in cyber operations globally and states already taking initiatives to address cyber-attacks by terrorists, it seems cyber-terrorism may be inevitable. Fidler (2016), p. 478; ASEAN Convention on Counter Terrorism, opened for signature 13 January 2007, (entered into force 27 May 2011), (ASEAN Convention) art. 6(j).

[4]NATO Standardization Agency (2018). This definition is still controversial, as CNAs have been described as a type of cyber-attack and not cyber-attack itself. The US Department of Defense who initiated this definition in 2001, recently modified it by identifying it as cyberspace attacks which are 'actions taken in cyberspace that create noticeable denial effects (i.e., degradation, disruption, or destruction) in cyberspace or manipulation that leads to denial that appears in a physical domain and is considered a form of fires'—US Department of Defense (2018).

[5]Moore (2017). These non-state actors include organized criminal groups, terrorist and insurgent organizations. An example of such is the famous Lazarus Hacktivist group.

[6]Symantec Corporation (2017). This report is from a commercial cyber security corporation and may not represent exhaustive facts of all security threats globally.

[7]Malwarebytes Labs (2017).

[8]African Union Commission (AUC) and Symantec Report (2016), p. 22.

[9]Serianu (2017), p. 37.

[10]Abou-Zeid (2018).

[11]Monaco (2016).

Despondent as the situation seems, these attacks may be preventable, at least within the ambit of state control. States hold sovereign powers of enforcement over their territories and areas they exercise governmental control. Hence, they may be in a better position to handle such. Moreover, cyber-attacks are usually perpetrated using cyber infrastructures located on the territories of states.[12] These infrastructures include data and information storage systems, management and computing systems, networks and network grids. It also includes people located on the territories of states to improve state productivity and ensure interconnectedness.[13] The primary challenges of undertaking this however is a matter of assessing whether there exists an obligation incumbent upon states to prevent cyber-attacks in the first place and whether states possess the necessary capacity to do so.

States are obliged under international law to prevent their territories from knowingly being used for acts that are contrary to the rights of other states.[14] The standard of conduct that states are expected to adhere to in complying with this grand obligation is due diligence.[15] It is that level of care and vigilance a responsible state should observe under the circumstances, using the best resources at its disposal,[16] in order to fulfil an international obligation. Recent discussions have analysed the plausibility of applying this obligation to cyberspace operations, pushing the limits of international law as we know it, to embrace the changing tides of technological advancement.[17] However, there are no specified and stringent rules for states to follow duly since it requires no more and no less than each state's best efforts according to their capacity,[18] hence presenting disproportionate standards of application among states. The due diligence obligation thus projects some amount of unpredictability and is still subject to momentous debates due to its vagueness.[19]

This article argues that states have an obligation to prevent their territories from being used to perpetrate harmful cyber-attacks against other states albeit the obligation is not without accompanying challenges. The underlying problem of overdependence on state capacity to accomplish the obligation has fuelled varying standards of application in both developed and developing states, notwithstanding its supposed universality.[20] Hence, this article seeks to explore the innate debates surrounding the application of the obligation to cyber-attacks with a view to

[12]Herzog (2011), p. 52.

[13]Stewart et al. (2018).

[14]ICJ, *Corfu Channel (United Kingdom of Great Britain and Northern Ireland v Albania)*, Judgment (1949) ICJ Rep 1.

[15]Kulesza (2016).

[16]Bannelier-Christakis (2014), p. 5.

[17]Korzak (2011), p. 147.

[18]ICJ, *Application of the Convention on the Prevention and Punishment of the Crime of Genocide (Bosnia v Serbia)*, Judgement (2007) ICJ Rep 1, para. 430.

[19]Jensen and Watts (2017), p. 1566; Takano (2018), pp. 1–2; Kulesza (2016).

[20]Moslemi and Babaeimehr (2015), pp. 688–689.

proffering recommendations on how it can best be solidified as a universally accepted principle of state practice and general international law that transcends state sovereignty and jurisdiction.

The following section briefly describes the due diligence obligation by tracing its evolution under international law from its invocation in international law cases of an environmental nature to its adoption in other fields of law, some with modifications. Section 3 further evaluates its application in cyberspace activities—the stance that states indeed owe a due diligence obligation to prevent their territories from being used to perpetrate harmful cyber-attacks that will affect the rights of other states. Section 4 then appraises the core elements of the due diligence obligation—determining factors on when a state is said to owe the obligation and whether or not it has effectively carried it out. An examination of the two facets of international obligations—obligations of result and obligations of conduct, in the light of the due diligence obligation is set out in Sect. 5. Because the due diligence obligation is seen as an obligation of conduct, it is overly dependent on state capacity. This is also analysed, considering the perception of the differing levels in development among developed and developing countries. Section 6 then explores the debate on whether the due diligence obligation extends to states that only serve as conduits for harmful cyber-attacks, in order words, transit states. Based on the weaknesses deduced from the applicability of the obligation in cyberspace, Sect. 7 offers recommendations on strengthening the core areas of the due diligence obligation which imbibes mutual assistance and cooperation to achieve a more resolute standard for all states and Sect. 8 provides a brief conclusion.

2 The Obligation of Due Diligence in International Law

The historical grasp of the due diligence obligation can first be traced to the *Alabama Arbitration* of 1872,[21] where the US alleged that Great Britain breached its due diligence obligation by failing to prevent a war vessel, the *Alabama,* from being equipped and armed on its territory for the purposes of war against US.[22] However, two *locus classicus* cases embodying the concept of transboundary harm and responsibility of states for injurious acts to aliens on their territories brought the principle to the fore. The arbitral tribunal in the *Trail Smelter* arbitration[23] drawing from principles of customary international law on respect for territorial sovereignty, pronounced that 'states are not to use or allow their territories to be used in ways that

[21] Arbitral Tribunal, *Alabama Claims of the United States of America against Great Britain,* Award (1871) Reports of International Arbitral Awards 29.

[22] Blomeyer-Bartenstein (1987), pp. 138–139.

[23] Arbitral Tribunal, *Trail Smelter Arbitration (United States v Canada)*, Award (1941) Reports of International Arbitral Awards 3, p. 1905.

are capable of causing injuries to properties or persons in other states',[24] and the same position was affirmed in the *Corfu Channel* case.[25] This principle was later mirrored in Principle 21 of the Stockholm Declaration of 1972[26] and the Rio Declaration of 1992.[27]

These pronouncements, largely referred to as the 'obligation to prevent' or the 'no harm' principle, stemmed from 'certain general and well recognized principles' of international law[28] particularly international environmental law, requiring states to take reasonable care in ensuring that activities done on their territories do not hamper the rights of other states.[29] The ICJ's recognition of the obligation to prevent harm as part of the body of international environmental law[30] without a doubt solidified its hold as an integral part of state international obligations.

The 'no harm' obligation expected of states requires states to exert minimum efforts in preventing harm, hence the interchangeable reference to this 'no harm' principle as the principle of due diligence.[31] As outlined in the *Pulp Mills* case which involved joint utilization of transboundary water sources, the obligation to prevent is an obligation of state parties to act with due diligence regarding all activities that occur within their jurisdiction.[32] More so, the obligation is derived from state sovereignty, the state's ability to effectively control its territory.[33]

Thus, the failure of a state to exercise its due diligence obligation is practically a:

> Failure to use for the prevention of an act which the government was bound to endeavour to prevent, such care as governments ordinarily employ in their domestic concerns, and may reasonably be expected to exert in matters of international interest and obligation.[34]

---

[24]Ibid.

[25]ICJ, *Corfu Channel (United Kingdom of Great Britain and Northern Ireland v Albania),* Judgment (1949) ICJ Rep 1.

[26]UNGA (1972), principle 21.

[27]UNGA (1992), principle 2.

[28]Ibid.

[29]Koivurova (2008), para. 16.

[30]ICJ, *Legality of the threat or use of nuclear weapons,* Advisory Opinion (1996) ICJ Rep 226, Para. 29 (*Nuclear Weapons* Case).

[31]Koivurova (2008), para 15; In some instruments, like the Convention on the Law of the Non-Navigational Uses of International Watercourses. Opened for Signature, 21 May 1997, 36 ILM 700 (entered into force 17 August 2014) (Watercourses Convention), art. 7 for example, the 'no harm' obligation is referred to as 'no significant harm'. This may be because the exercise of due diligence requires that the harm or damage be 'significant' or substantial enough in order to trigger the obligation. This element shall be discussed further in Sect. 4 of this work.

[32]ICJ, *Pulp Mills on the River Uruguay (Argentina v Uruguay),* Judgement (2010) ICJ Rep 79, para. 197 (*Pulp Mills Case*).

[33]Permanent Court of Arbitration, *Island of Palmas,* Award (1928) 2 RIAA 829

[34]Arbitral Tribunal, *Alabama Claims of the United States of America against Great Britain,* Award (1871) Reports of International Arbitral Awards.

The due diligence obligation is best appreciated as a standard.[35] That standard could be flexible and also relative,[36] hence the compelling arguments that it may be interpreted broadly or restrictively depending on the particular facts or circumstances that require it, in order to hold states accountable for their questionable conducts or omissions where non-state actors are concerned.[37] The obligation assesses the elements of the reasonable conduct of a state accepted generally under the relevant international law instrument, depending on the resources available at the state's disposal.[38]

The breach of a due diligence obligation is usually by omission but could also be by commission. A breach would lie where a state has failed to exercise the requisite care and vigilance needed, using the resources at its disposal, to prevent significant harm from its territory.[39] A state could also be held in breach where it in fact took steps to prevent such, but the measures taken were inadequate and ineffective when other practically feasible measures were available[40] and the damage itself is significant.

Though the pioneering cases on the obligation to prevent harm emanated from issues of an environmental nature, the evolving nature of global challenges with a corresponding growth in legal jurisprudence has allowed for diverse applications and interpretations of the principle in other fields like corporate law,[41] international humanitarian law (IHL) and human rights law,[42] international law relating to the treatment of foreign representatives of other states[43] as well as the law relating to the use of force.[44]

For IHL, it generally seeks to regulate the conduct of war among states, especially limiting the effects of armed conflicts on specified categories of persons outlined in

---

[35] Rao (1999).

[36] Kulesza (2016), p. 264.

[37] Barnidge (2006), pp. 81–82.

[38] Okowa (2000), p. 79. The issue of available resources will be dealt with in Sect. 5.

[39] Bastin (2017), pp. 50–51; ICJ, *Case Concerning United States Diplomatic and Consular Staff in Tehran (United States of America v Iran),* Judgement (1980) ICJ Rep 3, para. 68 (*Hostages Case*).

[40] Schmitt and Vihul (2017), p. 43; Pisillo-Mazzeschi (1992), p. 20.

[41] Lawrence (2017).

[42] Aust (2015), p. 71.

[43] Pisillo-Mazzeschi (1992), p. 22.

[44] Dorr (2015), p. 92; UNGA (1970).

its set of rules[45] by preventing and prosecuting grave violations of IHL.[46] Every form of interaction between a state and these categories of persons is usually subject to some form of state control[47] and this control informs the standard of care required by states towards fulfilling their obligations under IHL.[48] Article 36 of Additional Protocol I for instance requires states to determine whether the acquisition or development of a new weapon or procedure of warfare would be prohibited under the Protocol or other applicable rules of international law, before putting such to use,[49] so as not to 'risk causing "wide-spread, long-term and severe" damage to the environment'.[50]

Corporate law and human rights tend to run parallel where due diligence is concerned.[51] The obligation of due diligence obtainable under international corporate law is two-fold: the first deals with the processes involved in identifying and then mitigating risks and losses in commercial transactions and the second entails 'the standard of conduct required to discharge an obligation'.[52] It stands that companies give priority to the first aspect over the second,[53] but it is impossible for them to know or prove that they respect human rights if they do not observe human rights due diligence.[54]

The UN Guiding Principles on Business and Human Rights are aimed at effectively strengthening corporate responsibility with respect to human rights which cannot be exercised without due diligence.[55] Opinions are however divided on

[45]Geneva Convention for the Amelioration of the Condition of the Wounded and Sick in Armed Forces in the Field. Opened for signature 12 August 1949, 75 UNTS 31 (entered into force 21 October 1950) (First Geneva Convention); Geneva Convention for the Amelioration of the Condition of the Wounded, Sick and Shipwrecked Members of the Armed Forces at Sea. Opened for signature 12 August 1949, 75 UNTS 85 (entered into force 21 October 1950) (Second Geneva Convention); Geneva Convention relative to the Treatment of Prisoners of War. Opened for signature 12 August 1949, 75 UNTS 135 (entered into force 21 October 1950) Third Geneva Convention); Geneva Convention Relative to the Protection of Civilian Persons in Time of War. Opened for signature 12 August 1949, 75 UNTS 287 (entered into force 21 October 1950) (Fourth Geneva Convention); Protocol Additional to the Geneva Conventions of 12 August 1949 and relating to the Protection of Victims of International Armed Conflicts. Opened for signature 12 December 1977, 1125 UNTS 3 (entered into force 7 December 1978) (Additional Protocol I); Protocol Additional to the Geneva Conventions of 12 August 1949 and relating to the Protection of Victims of Non-International Armed Conflicts. Opened for signature 12 December 1977, 1125 UNTS 609 (entered into force 7 December 1978) (Additional Protocol II).

[46]International Committee of the Red Cross (2004).

[47]ILA Study Group (2014), p. 11.

[48]ILA Study Group (2016), p. 15.

[49]Additional Protocol I (1978), art. 36; Vincze (2017), p. 30.

[50]Desgagne (2000), p. 125.

[51]Bonnitcha and McCorquodale (2017), p. 899.

[52]Ibid.

[53]Ibid, p. 900.

[54]Ruggie and Sherman (2017), p. 924.

[55]UN Human Rights Council (2011).

whether or not the UN Guiding Principles have effectively clarified where these two aspects of the obligation in relation to corporate law start and end.[56] It is opined that the required degree of due diligence varies from field to field in international law and are usually given content by an existing primary rule.[57] As such, the due diligence required will depend on the requisite interest in need of it in each case.[58] Thus, where the interest involved is risk related, the due diligence standard to be applied will be towards mitigating losses. In the event of an interface with human rights protection, it will be a case for exercising the due diligence necessary to prevent the breach of an international obligation, even though a contrary study opines that the obligation to respect human rights expected from companies is not directly derived from international law but rather 'social expectations and moral considerations'.[59]

The recognition of any legal principle at state level qualifies it for consideration as a principle of international law.[60] The due diligence principle is largely recognized by states as constituting part of their domestic legal systems rather mere moral or religious norms.[61] It has been propounded that a 'general' or 'fundamental' principle in international law has to pass certain criteria: firstly, it must be specifically important to the theory and practice of international law. Then, it must allow for a 'natural application' to various rules existing under international law and finally, it must be accepted as an integral or non-negligible part of the ever-evolving international law regime.[62] The due diligence principle stands as a necessity for ensuring state responsibility for harmful conducts emanating from their territories[63] and having been applied in different spheres of international law,[64] it has thus undoubtedly been accepted as a principle of international law.[65]

---

[56]Bonnitcha and McCorquodale (2017), pp. 900–901.

[57]Grans (2018), p. 735.

[58]Ibid.

[59]Grabosch and Scheper (2015). This analysis constitutes the foundation upon which corporate social responsibility for businesses are built.

[60]Kulesza (2016), p. 27.

[61]Ibid.

[62]Ibid, p. 24.

[63]ILA Study Group (2014), p. 3; Arbitral Tribunal, *Alabama Claims of the United States of America against Great Britain,* Award (1871) Reports of International Arbitral Awards 29.

[64]As discussed above with regards to international human rights and humanitarian law, and corporate law.

[65]UNGA (1992); ICJ, *Corfu Channel (United Kingdom of Great Britain and Northern Ireland v Albania),* Judgment (1949) ICJ Rep 1, p. 22; ICJ, *Armed Activities on the Territory of the Congo* (DRC V Uganda), Merits (2005) ICJ Rep 168, para. 162 (*Armed Activities Case*); UNGA (1970), principle 1.

3 Applying the Due Diligence Obligation in Cyberspace

The decisions of international courts and writings of scholars have proved that general principles of international law are largely identified by logic and deductive legal reasoning from international legal regimes and treaties.[66] Hence, where a general principle of international law like due diligence,[67] is established and concretized, even though it originated from a specific aspect of international law, it may be applied to other relevant situations in the absence of any state practice or *opinio juris* expressly excluding it.[68] The internet has gradually become a spiralling global resource for states, 'a global digital network that is embedded in every aspect of our daily life'.[69] As such, importing the principle of prevention of harm does not seem implausible,[70] especially as there are no specific international regulations applicable to cyberspace operations *ad interim*. The due diligence obligation thus binds states in relation to international cyberspace activities.

In other words, there exists an obligation on states to ensure that they do not use or allow their territories, their computer hardware and all cyber infrastructures located on their territories or the ones under their control, to be used in a way that will cause serious adverse consequences and affect the rights of other states,[71] contiguous or not. A state is therefore expected to exercise the requisite diligence needed in order to prevent harmful cyber activities or risk thereof from occurring within its territory against another state and where it manifestly fails to take such reasonable measures, its responsibility under international law is engaged.

An argument has been raised against the application of the due diligence principle in cyberspace purports that cyberspace may be viewed as global commons (*res communis*), a space where states cannot necessarily exercise sovereignty or claim territoriality,[72] and so no international obligations accruing to states can lie. There appears to be little or no corroboration on this view as majority of scholarship argues that states exercise sovereignty in cyberspace.[73] They exercise control over actors within their territories and information that passes through their networks and computer systems.[74] Though cyberspace may appear borderless, its operations are effected through physical infrastructures that aid the transmission of data and

---

[66]Ziolkowski (2013), p. 167.

[67]ICJ, *Legality of the threat or use of nuclear weapons,* Advisory Opinion (1996) ICJ Rep 226, Para. 29 (*Nuclear Weapons* Case); Permanent Court of Arbitration, *Island of Palmas,* Award (1928) 2 RIAA 829.

[68]Khanna (2018), p. 141.

[69]Liaropoulos (2017), p. 25.

[70]Ziolkowski (2013), p. 167.

[71]Schmitt and Vihul (2017), r. 6; Ney and Zimmermann (2015), p. 62; Schmitt (2013), r. 5.

[72]British Institute of International and Comparative Law (BIICL) (2014), pp. 11–12; Ku (1990).

[73]Liaropoulos (2013); Khanna (2018), p. 140.

[74]Siroli (2018), p. 112; this is also evident in the various national laws that have been enacted by states in enhancing cyber security.

information.[75] Thus, it can be viewed as a 'shared global infrastructure' but it is definitely not a global commons.[76]

The UN GGE Reports[77] have to a certain degree, affirmed that the due diligence obligation applies in cyberspace. The 2013 report specifically expresses that 'State sovereignty and international norms and principles that flow from sovereignty apply to State conduct of ICT-related activities, and to their jurisdiction over ICT infrastructure within their territory'.[78] Further, it enjoins states to 'ensure that their territories are not used by non-State actors for unlawful use of ICTs'.[79] Although the language of the reports do not exhibit a binding authority on states when considering the UN GGE's use of the word 'should', it connotes an acknowledgement of the principle in relation to cyber activities. The UN General Assembly also affirmed these reports by adopting them unanimously.[80]

The group of governmental experts for the UN GGE Reports was chosen from the alleged major state players in the field of international security,[81] evidencing the support of states towards preventing harmful cyber operations. These representatives were selected from 15 countries including the United Kingdom, Russia and the United States, as representatives of the various member states. A careful consideration of this selection shows that these experts did not constitute a full representation cutting across all categories of members of the United Nations. Developing countries for example were obviously not represented in that capacity, notwithstanding that the challenge to ICT and security is of a global nature, affecting states collectively.[82]

Further, the recommendations ensuing from the discussions are expected to exert some form of impact on all states, whether developed or developing. Inadvertently, the exclusion may impact the response of developing states on taking the recommendations seriously, having been denied the opportunity of providing input peculiar to their developmental circumstances. The UN GGE 2015 however, saw an extension of the group of governmental experts to 20, which now included some developing states, including two African countries (Ghana and Kenya), allowing for better applicability.[83]

[75] Liaropoulos (2017), p. 28.

[76] Cornish (2015), p. 158.

[77] UNGGE (2013, 2015).

[78] UNGGE (2013).

[79] Ibid, para. 23.

[80] UNGA (2013, 2015).

[81] UNGGE (2013), p. 5.

[82] There are several instances of cyber-attacks that have tampered with various African economies like Nigeria, Ethiopia, Liberia and Kenya. South Africa alone has been hit with spades of several cyber-attacks since 1994. Niekerk (2017), p. 115.

[83] UNGGE (2015), p. 5.

4 Decisive Elements in Cyber Diligence

4.1 Knowledge and Foreseeability

The due diligence obligation entails that where a state is aware (that is, has actual knowledge) of an impending harm or attack detrimental to another state, it has a duty to terminate it immediately.[84] A state's organ may detect or be hinted on harmful cyber operations occurring on its territory against another state[85] and in such cases, the state is deemed to have actual knowledge, thus triggering its due diligence obligation.[86] With conventional armed attacks, knowledge is easily established and states response is quicker but with cyber-attacks, there is difficulty in ascertaining when an attack is being planned or is likely to occur, especially when state capacity is insufficient to detect such threat in time or tackle such sophisticated composition. Cyber-attacks could be routed through subliminal networks and so may not be detected early enough[87] until it has inevitably rendered havoc on target computer systems.

The obligation is tested in a situation where a state could not have been aware of the potential risk or harm that such conduct would cause to the territory of another state, and hence could not have reasonably prevented such harm from occurring.[88] It seems appropriate under such circumstances, taking into consideration the capacity of the state, to apply the 'should have known' test especially where the situation warrants that constructive knowledge is imputed. For example, where cyber facilities owned and controlled by the state have repeatedly been breached for the purpose of causing harm to another state, such state 'should have known' that a similar attack is likely to occur again.[89] Also, cyber-attacks with working patterns that are common knowledge like a Distributed Denial of Service (DDoS) attack that uses up more bandwidth than normal limits,[90] would be considered obvious to cyber security monitoring. The question whether there exists a duty to monitor is quite debatable as major opinions purport that it is extreme and demanding such duty from states will be stepping beyond the scope of what state capacity can handle and the due diligence obligation entails.[91] In spite of this, it is unlikely for a state to know and suppress a cyber threat without measures (technical and administrative) in place to detect such in the first place.

[84] ICJ, *Application of the Convention on the Prevention and Punishment of the Crime of Genocide (Bosnia v Serbia),* Judgement (2007) ICJ Rep 1, para. 431; Kulesza (2016).

[85] Schmitt and Vihul (2017), p. 40.

[86] Ibid.

[87] Sklerov (2009), p. 80.

[88] Birnie et al. (2009), p. 153.

[89] Schmitt and Vihul (2017), pp. 41, 46.

[90] Ibid, p. 41.

[91] Takano (2018), p. 8; Schmitt and Vihul (2017), pp. 44–45.

Foreseeability of the significant harm or risk thereof, is akin to state's knowledge of a cyber-attack. Under international environmental law, states are expected to apply precautionary measures in accordance with their capabilities to limit environmental degradation.[92] Foreseeability may thus be subjective depending on state capacity, the degree of the harm involved and the probability of it occurring. The tribunal in the *Trail Smelter* arbitration,[93] explained that the obligation to prevent lies when harm is 'likely' to occur portraying that a state need not affirm that the harm will have severe effects before exercising due diligence. On the other hand, the ICJ[94] firmly identified that the obligation will lie where there is a 'known' risk to another state implying that a state only needs take preventive measures when it confirms that there would be significant harm on another state.[95]

Foreseeability here sits between the state's response to risk of harm that they 'must have known' ('known' risk as proclaimed in the *Corfu* case) and 'should have known' ('likelihood' of risk as proposed in the *Trail Smelter* arbitration) would occur.[96] The 'must have known' standard is possibly more acceptable and easier to prove,[97] because it will be difficult to argue with knowledge that clear and certain.[98] Nonetheless, assessing state's knowledge (actual or constructive) will likely be decided on a case-by-case basis and before the relevant courts. Irrespective of the kind of knowledge a state possesses, it 'owes at all times a duty to protect other states against injurious acts . . . from within its jurisdiction'.[99]

4.2 Assessing the Origin and Perpetrator of the Cyber-Attack: Duty to Investigate and Act Accordingly

Determining the source of a cyber-attack can be daunting. Unlike armed attacks where tracing the perpetrators is much easier seeing as they work with physical weapons and actually operate mostly from a defined location as in the case of terrorists,[100] identifying specifically the perpetrator and exact location of a cyber-attack is more complicated. This is likely because cyber-attacks can manage through

[92]UNGA (1992).

[93]Arbitral Tribunal, *Trail Smelter Arbitration (United States v Canada)*, Award (1941) Reports of International Arbitral Awards 3.

[94]ICJ, *Corfu Channel (United Kingdom of Great Britain and Northern Ireland v Albania)*, Judgment (1949) ICJ Rep 1.

[95]See generally Sect. 4.3.

[96]Jensen (2014), p. 76.

[97]Ibid.

[98]Ibid, pp. 76–77.

[99]Arbitral Tribunal, *Trail Smelter Arbitration (United States v Canada)*, Award (1941) Reports of International Arbitral Awards 3, p. 1963.

[100]Kayode (2014).

encrypted networks across several servers, and often target several outlets at the same time like deploying a botnet leading to a DDoS.[101] The Stuxnet worm for example, was a sophisticated malware discovered in several computer systems, although passive in some and planted with the aim of sabotaging centrifuges located at a power plant in Iran.[102] An analysis of the attack depicted that the worm targeted vulnerable systems and infected their software to access and use data on the programmable controllers of the Natanz nuclear facilities where the centrifuges were stored, causing severe damage.[103]

The capacity of a state to trace the location of the computer used in executing the cyber-attack is necessary for fulfilling its due diligence obligation.[104] Recent technological developments hint that cyber-tracing is gradually becoming possible.[105] Internet Protocol (IP) address assigned to the device used can aid in identifying the location of the device.[106] IP addresses are made up of binary numbers that are necessary to enable communication across the network used as well as identify the location of the network computers.[107] The origin of the attack may become difficult to trace if mounted through several routes using Botnets or spoofing software.[108] This can make it difficult to pinpoint the exact origin of the cyber-attack in order to initiate preventive measures.

Identifying the perpetrators of a cyber-attack is as important as tracing the location of the attack. Without knowledge of the attacker, a state may encounter difficulty in formulating rapid responses to stopping the attack, as they may be unable to determine the magnitude or likely effects in time. Hence, where states lack capacity to trace perpetrators, they can cooperate with private network providers having the necessary resources[109]; as such an issue may be deemed a matter of national and international security. Two private computer security companies, Symantec and Kaspersky Lab, were instrumental in tracing the WannaCry cyber-attacks—attacks that rendered access to several patient's information impossible on NHS database, to North Korea, particularly to hacktivists known as Lazarus Group,[110] infamously known for one of the largest cyber thefts in history.[111]

[101]NCSC (2015).

[102]Kushner (2013).

[103]Baezner and Robin (2017).

[104]Couzigou (2018), p. 4.

[105]An example is the DarkTrace enterprise system. https://www.darktrace.com/technology/. Accessed 22 February 2018.

[106]Buchan (2016), p. 430.

[107]Pfeiffer (2016).

[108]Shackelford (2014), p. 146.

[109]Carr (2016).

[110]Graham (2017).

[111]Kaspersky Lab (2017).

4.3 Risk of Significant Transboundary Harm

Generally, a state is not obliged to exercise due diligence for a conduct that poses no risk of any significant harm to another state's territory.[112] A scholarly view has argued that such harm need not register physical effects solely, as any damage that induces state responsibility, suffices.[113] Indeed damage may not be restricted to physical effects alone however, only 'significant' damage is capable of triggering the due diligence obligation of the origin state.

'Significant' or 'substantial' harm signifies the degree of seriousness of the harm.[114] This is the most overarching description of the term as there is no precise definition obtainable under general international law. This ascribed definition is also an offshoot of international environmental law like the obligation to prevent transboundary harm. It would have proven quite a herculean task imputing a more precise definition under environmental law considering that environmental conditions are inevitable and invasive.[115] Such interferences could be social, brought about by natural occurrences or even economic with effects that can cause decline in the value of commodities.[116] Hence, there was need to specify significant harm with regards to environmental law as harm caused by human conduct, which would include forms of pollution causing injuries to persons and destruction of properties.[117] The reference made to certain state activities as having 'serious consequence' or capable of inflicting 'serious damage' stand out as the likely threshold of what 'significant' transboundary harm entails.[118]

Analogically teasing this position from environmental law, harmful cyber operations that exert serious consequences on cyber infrastructures, whether public or private, can trigger the due diligence obligation.[119] Not all cyber-attacks can be classified as exerting 'serious' harm and those with less 'serious consequences' are unlikely to trigger the due diligence obligation. For instance, a cyber-attack that tampers with an official website relating to sporting activities may not be categorized as having 'serious adverse consequences', but rather negligible disruptions.[120] A hacktivist group commandeered some social media sites under the US central

---

[112]Kolb (2015), p. 121.

[113]Ibid.

[114]ILC (2001a), art. 3. This is the persuasive meaning ascribed to the word 'substantial' even though the Draft Articles are not binding upon states.

[115]Schachter (1991), p. 464.

[116]Ibid.

[117]Ibid, p. 465.

[118]Arbitral Tribunal, *Trail Smelter Arbitration (United States v Canada)*, Award (1941) Reports of International Arbitral Awards 3, p. 1965; Arbitral Tribunal, *Lake Lanoux Arbitration (France v Spain)*, Award (1957) RIAA 281.

[119]Schmitt (2018).

[120]Schmitt and Vihul (2017), p. 37.

command in 2015, creating a temporal minor disruption to which the US acknowledged as mere 'cyber vandalism'.[121]

The terms 'substantial' or 'significant' are used interchangeably when assessing degree of damage that has been sustained by an affected state. In the *Pulp Mills* case,[122] the ICJ held that there was no conclusive evidence to show that Uruguay did not act with the necessary level of due diligence towards the construction of Pulp Mills and that there was no proof that the discharge emitted from the mills had a significant damage on the river or its environs. It is necessary that the threshold of harm stands at 'substantial' or 'serious' so states are not unduly burdened in observing cyber diligence for all degrees of harm emanating from their territories.

4.4 Contradiction with the Rights of Another State

Where a state commits an internationally wrongful act, breaching an international obligation owed to another state, such breach engages the responsibility of the offending state.[123] The element of 'contradiction with the rights of another state' is primarily linked to the element of substantiality, in that the cyber-attack has to be of significant gravity in order to constitute an internationally wrongful act. This is what triggers the origin state's international obligation to prevent the harmful cyber-attack emanating from its territory, as it will have serious consequences on the target state.[124] When the origin state fails to act with the due diligence necessary to prevent the significant cyber-attack, it is said to have breached its international obligation to prevent transboundary harm, in this case, a harmful cyber operation and its responsibility will hence, be engaged.

For instance, if an unauthorized attack is launched from state A infiltrating certain computer systems in state B to access security information, state A would not be said to have committed any internationally wrongful act which would constitute a breach of its international obligation to prevent. This is because the act of infiltrating another state's network system to access information is viewed as cyber espionage, which is not unlawful neither is it expressly prohibited under international law.[125] Hence, requiring state A to exercise due diligence in preventing such attack would be an unnecessary burden, even if the perpetrators are likely non-state actors operating from within state A's territory.

---

[121]Alexander and Finkle (2015).

[122]ICJ, *Pulp Mills on the River Uruguay (Argentina v Uruguay)*, Judgement (2010) ICJ Rep 79, para. 197 (*Pulp Mills Case*).

[123]ILC (ARSIWA 2001b); ICJ, *Case Concerning the Gabčikovo-Nagymaros Project (Hungary v Slovakia)*, Judgement (1997) ICJ Rep 7, para. 47.

[124]Chircop (2018), pp. 650–651.

[125]Ziolkowski (2013), p. 430.

In a similar vein, where State A possesses classified documents belonging to State B and decides to release them publicly through State C's network servers with State C's knowledge, a controversial question arises on whether State C owes a due diligence obligation to stop the publication of these documents. Major opinions assert that State C does not owe a due diligence obligation because there is no contradiction with any legal right in this case, as there exists no 'right to keep your secrets secret' under international law. Hence, State C owes no due diligence obligation even if the resultant effect of publishing the documents may pose serious adverse consequences on State B.[126]

In essence, a state's due diligence obligation to prevent harmful cyber operations emanating from its territory may not be triggered unless the attack violates or poses a risk of violating the rights enjoyed by the target state under international law,[127] even if the attack is significant. But then, there exists the possibility for supposed 'low-intensity' cyber-attacks becoming more frequent and untamed since states may be less inclined to exercise any due diligence at all for harmful cyber operations that are not in contradiction with the rights of other states.[128] More so, this creates a justifiable argument in favour of developing states who lack the necessary resources to prevent all cyber-attacks emanating from their territories seeing as the due diligence obligation is to a large extent, observed as an obligation of conduct.

5 Cyber Diligence: Obligation of Result or Conduct

In understanding the scope of the due diligence obligation of states in cyberspace and deciphering when a breach has occurred,[129] it is necessary to ascertain whether it is an obligation of result or conduct. There is yet to be an international treaty on cyber operations or cyber-attacks. A treaty of this nature would have laid down the guidelines and parameters surrounding the due diligence obligation expected of states under the relevant circumstances, among other issues. Nonetheless, the available constituents of the obligation obtainable under international law presently have informed its application in cyberspace.[130]

[126]Schmitt (2018).

[127]Ibid.

[128]Chircop (2018), p. 651.

[129]ILC (ARSIWA 2001b), art. 12, commentary 11.

[130]Dupuy (1999), p. 375.

5.1 Obligation of Result

Under international law, an obligation of result is one that requires the achievement of a particular result,[131] placing the burden of attaining the specific result on the person who owes such an obligation.[132] It ensures taking practical measures that may give full effect to the obligation to achieve a precise result. For example, payment is made for an item by a buyer, the seller has an obligation to deliver the sold item to the buyer upon receipt of the consideration.[133] The European Court of Human Rights (ECtHR) in the *Colozza* case[134] addressed the concept of an obligation of result in relation to article 6(1) of the European Convention on Human Rights (ECHR) on the right to a fair trial. It expressed that states are to ensure their legal systems are compliant with article 6(1) of the ECHR, but the means by which states ensure this, is discretional. The court is not concerned about those means, but in rather determining whether or not the result intended by the ECHR has in fact been achieved.

The ILC[135] further explained that the ECtHR compared 'the result required (the opportunity for a trial in the accused's presence) with the result practically achieved (the lack of that opportunity in the particular case)' in deciphering whether article 6 (1) was breached. But more importantly, the ECtHR looked critically at what more the state could have done to ensure the effectiveness of the applicant's right.[136] Another similar example of an obligation of result is the maximum emission thresholds stipulated under certain environmental law norms, but the same norms leave the process of meeting the set goals to the states.[137]

Unlike the examples given above,[138] there are no deliberate requirements ensuring states exercise their due diligence obligation in cyberspace, although some states have undertaken initiatives at the national level to boost their cyber security.[139] In addition to the fact that states are not mandated to adopt legal and administrative measures *sensu stricto,* unless there is an international treaty expressly stating so,[140]

[131]Shany (2005), p. 917.

[132]Dupuy (1999), p. 375.

[133]*Ibid,* p. 375.

[134]EHRR, *Colozza v Italy* (7 EHRR 1985) VII 516, 525.

[135]ILC (ARSIWA 2001b), art 12, Commentary 11.

[136]*Ibid.*

[137]Shany (2005), p. 917.

[138]*See,* footnotes 104–108.

[139]An example is the US Cyber Command (USCYBERCOM), a former sub-unified command under US Strategic Command (USSTRATCOM), which was elevated to a Unified Combatant Command of its own in August 2017 in 'recognition of the growing centrality of cyberspace to U.S. national security and an acknowledgement of the changing nature of warfare.' U.S. CYBER COMMAND. https://www.cybercom.mil/About/History/. Accessed 1 October 2018.

[140]Schmitt and Vihul (2017), p. 48.

proponents of the obligation contend that it is a form of soft law, proffering 'programs rather than prescriptions, guidelines rather than strict obligations.[141]

5.2 *Obligation of Conduct*

An obligation of conduct is an obligation to endeavour[142] to achieve a given result. An example is a doctor-patient relationship, where a doctor is to do all that is reasonable and within his power to help an ailing patient, but in no way has a strict obligation to ensure the patient is cured.[143] In more practical applications, the ECtHR in interpreting the provisions of article 11 of the ECHR explained that it is a state's duty to adopt reasonable measures towards upholding lawful and peaceful demonstrations, but it cannot absolutely guarantee this. The obligation a state enters under article 11 of the ECHR 'is an obligation as to measures to be taken and not as to results to be achieved'.[144] The ICJ in the *Bosnia Genocide* case has equally concluded that 'a state cannot be under an obligation to succeed' no matter the circumstances, but they are to 'employ all means reasonably available to them' in order to prevent harm (genocide).[145] Generally, with obligations of conduct, focus is placed on the conduct of the state (its ability and capability applied) towards preventing the harm rather than the end result (whether or not the harm was prevented).

This is the same obligation applied to harmful cyber operations. States do not guarantee that the cyber-attack will be prevented[146] but they exert their best efforts with the available resources at their disposal, to prevent the cyber-attack from happening.[147] In other words, the obligation to prevent harmful cyber-attacks would only be breached by a state if it manifestly fails to act with due diligence in preventing substantial harm.[148] Hence, the reason why the due diligence obligation is largely upheld as an obligation of conduct and not result.[149]

---

[141]Dupuy (1991), pp. 421, 428.

[142]Buchan (2016), p. 434.

[143]Dupuy (1999), p. 375.

[144]ECtHR, *Case of Plattform "Arzte für das Leben" v Austria*, Judgment (App no 10126/82), 21 June 1988, para. 34.

[145]ICJ, *Application of the Convention on the Prevention and Punishment of the Crime of Genocide (Bosnia v Serbia),* Judgement (2007) ICJ Rep 1, para. 400.

[146]Bastin (2017), p. 50.

[147]ICJ, *Application of the Convention on the Prevention and Punishment of the Crime of Genocide (Bosnia v Serbia),* Judgement (2007) ICJ Rep 1, para. 430.

[148]Koivurova (2008), para 15.

[149]Kulesza (2014), p. 79.

5.3 State Capacity

The feasibility of preventing a cyber-attack originating from a state's territory or areas it exercises governmental control depends on its technical, intellectual, financial and institutional capabilities.[150] While they rely on their capacity, domestic legal restrictions in any form will not be an excuse for non-compliance.[151] For instance, if a state needs a court order to implement the legal measures necessary to abort a cyber-attack, its failure to obtain that order will not release the state from liability for the wrongfulness of not terminating the cyber-attack when it could.[152] However, where this failure is in compliance with international law, especially human rights law, the argument of holding such state liable for its failure to exert measures in terminating the cyber-attack is invalidated.[153]

The obligation of due diligence is observed 'in many contexts on the basis of common but differentiated responsibilities'.[154] 'Common' here connotes the universality of the principle and it is differentiated because of the varying development levels of states. The second generation of human rights[155] for instance affirms the obligation placed on states to universally promote respect for human rights but also recognizes that states possess different levels of development and so prescribes a duty of progressive realization of the rights enshrined in the Covenant through cooperation and assistance.[156]

State capacity entails relevant measures,[157] as well as financial and technological[158] capacity—'proficiency' and 'wherewithal' to prevent and tackle cyber-attacks.[159] Exercising due diligence would appear easier for developed states compared to developing ones like most countries in Africa with unstable economies saddled with numerous challenges like poverty, unemployment, health issues like AIDS and Ebola, fuel crisis, and even ethnic and other religious and political instabilities.[160] Challenges to preventing criminal activities in cyberspace in Botswana for example, have been linked to lack of access to data, inconsistent legal frameworks, and issues of communication with the international

[150]Buchan (2016), p. 437; Arbitration Tribunal, *Pantechniki SA Contractors & Engineers (Greece) v Republic of Albania,* Award (2009) ARB/07/21 IIC 383, para. 81.

[151]Arbitral Tribunal, *Alabama Claims of the United States of America against Great Britain,* Award (1871) Reports of International Arbitral Awards 29; Couzigou (2018), p. 14; Kolb (2015), p. 117.

[152]Schmitt and Vihul (2017), r. 7.

[153]Ibid.

[154]ILA Study Group (2014).

[155]International Covenant on Economic, Social and Cultural Rights. Opened for signature 16 December 1966, 993 UNTS 3 (entered into Force 3 January 1976) (ICESCR), Preamble.

[156]*Ibid*, art. 2(1).

[157]Couzigou (2018), p. 14.

[158]*Ibid*, p. 11.

[159]Schmitt (2015–2016), p. 75.

[160]Cassim (2011), p. 127.

community.[161] The due diligence expected to be observed by the UK for instance, in controlling its cyber structures and preventing cyber-attacks would consequently be higher than that of a state like Botswana.[162] The UK already has cogent systems in place to tackle harmful cyber operations and has recently adopted the National Security Capability Review to keep abreast with addressing cyber threats.[163] In fact in further asserting its cyber security strategies, the UK prime minister mentioned 'economic levers...cutting-edge military resources...wider diplomatic and cultural influence on the world's stage', as its capabilities in defending cyber security.[164]

Developed countries are more likely to face significant cyber threats and most often, are targets of cyber-attacks compared to developing countries.[165] Notwithstanding, cyber-attackers do change tactics and re-routing malicious cyber actions through less advanced states in order to reduce the likelihood of the host state suppressing the threat is possible.[166]

Much consideration is given to the specifications of states' network structures, with major security obligations integrated into their technical operations and implemented through security policies, as cyber threats constitute national and international challenges.[167] This would enable state accountability for breach of their international obligation to prevent cyber-attacks where they manifestly fail to keep their structures safe, take necessary actions for cyber threats or even fail to cooperate in solving them.[168]

Most importantly, a state will not be held in breach of its due diligence obligation where pouring its resources into preventing a harmful cyber-attack would place an undue burden or strain on the state.[169] The due diligence expected cannot exceed the capabilities of the state involved.[170] Hence, a state is expected to take only reasonable measures using the available resources 'within its power' to curb a cyber threat.[171] The ICJ concluded in the *Armed Activities* case that due to the difficult territory the armed activists operated in and the inability of the Congolese

---

[161]Country Situation Report (2018).

[162]Dorr (2015), p. 95.

[163]The National Cyber Security Centre is one of its cyber security parastatals; Cabinet Office (2018).

[164]Ibid, p. 2.

[165]Examples of the Sony hack on Sony Pictures in the United States; WannaCry attacks affected most western states including UK and the US.

[166]Buchan (2016), p. 451; Kolb (2015), p. 127. A proper discussion on transit states and due diligence obligation is detailed in Sect. 6.

[167]Kulesza (2016), p. 300.

[168]Bendiek (2016), p. 8.

[169]The European Court of Human Rights stressed this view in the case of ECtHR, *Osman v UK*, Judgment (App No 23452/94), 28 October 1988, para. 116.

[170]Buchan (2016), p. 445.

[171]ICJ, *Application of the Convention on the Prevention and Punishment of the Crime of Genocide (Bosnia v Serbia),* Judgement (2007) ICJ Rep 1, para. 430.

government to control that area effectively, it was not in breach of its due diligence obligation for failing to prevent the said armed group from using armed force against Uganda.[172] Though this decision favoured Uganda at the time, it is not expected that it should remain at that stage of insufficient resources, being unable to tackle such challenge should it re-occur. States are expected to take appropriate steps towards progressively realizing their international obligations.[173]

The interpretation and application of state capacity raise several concerns, among which is determining the extent a state is to go to keep abreast with technological advancements like pooling cyber specialists to monitor cyber trends and discover shifts in network systems.[174] The feasibility of tracking cyber attackers, apprehending and prosecuting same with limited state resources that should equally go to other prioritized national issues will pose a cause for concern. The French government was able to trace a cyber-attack perpetrated against a French station to Russian hackers within a short time as it had available resources at its disposal.[175] If this situation occurred in a developing country, the chances of discovering the cyber-attack may be minimal, when the level of resources required for investigation and monitoring is taken into consideration.

A feasible solution for state incapacity before or during cyber security incidents would be to seek assistance from other technologically-advantaged and financially-stable states. In principle, however, there are no requirements for states to seek or render assistance in suppressing harmful conduct[176] and in the absence of an international treaty on cyberspace operations and cyber-attacks specifying same yet, states exercise free-will in such situations.[177] Still, states may be required to inform the target state of an impending attack in the event of its inability to suppress it in time. The ICJ concluded in the *Corfu Channel* case that Albania had an obligation to inform the British warships about the mines present on parts of its territory.[178]

The due diligence principle in all ramifications, may not hold developed and developing states to the same standard of due diligence.[179] This capacity stance is quite logical, but states may incessantly rely on this to justify their failures in exerting the necessary efforts to prevent cyber-attacks.[180] However, this should not be the case as 'every State has the duty to fulfil in good faith its obligations

[172]ICJ, *Armed Activities on the Territory of the Congo* (DRC V Uganda), Merits (2005) ICJ Rep 168, para. 301.

[173]As similarly stipulated for fulfilling human rights obligations. ICESCR (1976), art 2.

[174]Kolb (2015), p. 127.

[175]Fidler (2016), p. 479.

[176]Couzigou (2018), p. 13.

[177]Walter (2015), p. 83.

[178]ICJ, *Corfu Channel (United Kingdom of Great Britain and Northern Ireland v Albania)*, Judgment (1949) ICJ Rep 1, p. 22; Couzigou (2018), p. 12.

[179]Koivurova (2008), para 19.

[180]Trapp (2011), p. 71.

under the generally recognized principles and rules of international law'.[181] In any case, the obligation owed may even vary over time. In the event that the capabilities of a developing state improve, the due diligence expected is likely to increase as well.[182]

The recognition of the due diligence obligation as an obligation of conduct inadvertently creates a vacuum in its exercise by states individually. Asides the challenge of rendering the due diligence obligation unpredictable since it is subject to disparate state responses, the problem of effectively deciphering state capacity in the absence of any underlying common standards applicable to all states on an equal basis is quite daunting. In addition, there is lack of clarity on whether a due diligence obligation is owed by a state whose territory was merely used as a route for a cyber-attack in transit. This, along with the uncertainty of the due diligence obligation, simply leaves room for further speculation.

6 Cyber Diligence and Transit States

Generally, the notion of a transit state elicits thoughts on time and space, referring to the territory of a third state that is being crossed within a period of time.[183] It is also a state 'through whose territory traffic in transit passes'.[184] In cyberspace, such state would not be the final destination of the intended attack, but its cyber infrastructures could be used as routes to channel attacks towards another state. Most cyber-attacks are routed through one or more transit states before getting to the target state by making use of Botnets and different spoofing techniques in order to make the origin of the attack harder to trace.[185]

The due diligence obligation owed by such state would be to the extent of its knowledge of the attack being transmitted through its territory.[186] Where actual knowledge is not established, constructive knowledge could also be imputed where the network infrastructures of such transit state have previously or repeatedly been hacked into for similar purposes.[187] Hence, where the transit state is aware or 'should have known' of its cyber infrastructures being used to perpetrate a cyber-attack against another state, it has an obligation to take reasonable measures to prevent such operation.[188] Knowledge is not imputed merely because a harmful attack passed

[181] UNGA (1970), Principle 7.

[182] Herdegen (2015), pp. 181–182.

[183] Reinisch and Beham (2015), p. 103.

[184] UNCLOS (1994), art. 124.

[185] Shackelford et al. (2016), p. 20.

[186] Ibid.

[187] Ibid.

[188] The ICJ stated in the *Nicaragua Case* that Nicaragua had an obligation to prevent its territory from being used to traffic equipment to be used by insurgents in El Salvador—ICJ, *Case concerning*

through a state or the state has exclusive control over its area.[189] The target state will mostly find it difficult proving knowledge of the transit state, hence they may be allowed a liberal approach—making 'inferences of facts' and circumstantial evidence, as long as 'they leave no room for reasonable doubt'.[190]

It remains debatable which state actually owes the due diligence obligation in a situation where the infrastructures used do not belong to the state they are located in. For example, non-state actors in state A infiltrate telecommunication grids in state B to perpetrate a cyber-attack against state C. The ownership and control of the grids is actually vested in state A even though the grids are located in state B. International law on state responsibility suggests that state A has the obligation of exercising the necessary due diligence required to prevent the cyber-attack as it owns and exclusively controls the grids.[191] A state owes an obligation of due diligence in matters of all cyber infrastructures located within its territory and other areas it exercises effective control, even if the structures are within the territory of another state.[192]

When a transit state's due diligence obligation is triggered, it is likely to take into consideration the extent to which its cyber infrastructures were used in effecting the cyber-attack,[193] before taking steps to suppress it. It may take into consideration the nature of the cyber operation involved, the kind of information passing through and the various actors involved in sending information through the same cyber infrastructures.[194] Nonetheless, weighing these factors can establish incommensurate burdens of exercising due diligence between bigger states and smaller states.[195]

In addition, transit states may not have the wherewithal to carry out the necessary investigation especially where they are developing countries with minimal resources and there is the tendency for the cyber-attack to have already occurred before a transit state has a grasp of its passage.[196] Cyber-attacks in transit travel at a fast pace[197] and may only be stopped where the network systems used have been subject to some form of state monitoring. This then raises another issue on whether monitoring obligations if any, extend to states whose territories merely served as routes for cyber-attacks passing through to a target state. Since there are no specific requirements for states to monitor their cyber infrastructure and network systems

Military and Paramilitary Activities in and against Nicaragua (Nicaragua v United States of America), Merits (1986) ICJ Rep 115, para. 157 (*Nicaragua Case*).

[189]ICJ, *Corfu Channel (United Kingdom of Great Britain and Northern Ireland v Albania),* Judgment (1949) ICJ Rep 1, p. 18.

[190]Ibid.

[191]Schmitt (2013), r. 5.

[192]Schmitt and Vihul (2017), p. 33.

[193]Shackelford et al. (2016), p. 21.

[194]Jensen (2014), p. 77.

[195]Shackelford (2016), p. 21.

[196]Bannelier-Christakis (2014), p. 6.

[197]Buchan (2016), p. 441.

under current international law,[198] neither origin nor transit states are mandated to do so. Thus, any due diligence obligation accruing may be evaded consequently.[199]

Some experts have opined that customary international law may not have evolved enough to include cyber operations launched beyond a state's territory.[200] In other words, extending the due diligence obligation in cyberspace to transit states seems farfetched and should only be restricted to origin states. With technological advancement, state capacity is undoubtedly improving and so is the application of legal principles. Hence, where a transit state detects harmful cyber operations being transmitted through its territory, whether through its own cyber infrastructures or those belonging to another state, nothing prevents it from terminating the attack where feasible or warning the target state of the impending attack.[201] The ICJ in the *Corfu Channel* case affirmed that Albania indeed had an obligation to inform the British warships of mines present in the channel, even though the mines were not laid by Albania.[202]

Having explored the principle of due diligence and its application to harmful cyber operations, the question of putting to rest the raised arguments on the absence of concrete requirements for effective implementation of the obligation as well as the overarching dependence on state capacity, comes to fore. More importantly, is the question of whether a resolute standard of due diligence in relation to cyber-attacks can be achieved for all states notwithstanding their levels in development?

7 The Need to Strengthen Relevant Existing Endeavours and Rules Surrounding the Due Diligence Obligation in Cyberspace

There are no hard or fast rules when it comes to applying the due diligence principle to cyber-attacks and this probably affects its effectiveness. A recognized international instrument on cyber operations may lay all intervening discrepancies to rest. Nevertheless, its absence should not be a barrier to effective responses in curtailing harmful cyber conducts. Setting internationally agreed minimum standards, ones recognized and applicable to all states irrespective of circumstances, will ensure a precise content and offer universal predictability.[203]

[198]This obligation constitutes soft law and there seems to exist some persuasive scholarly opinions purporting that this obligation does not exist in cyberspace. Schmitt (2015–2016), p. 75.

[199]Ziolkowski (2013), p. 209.

[200]Schmitt (2015–2016), pp. 72–73.

[201]Dorr (2015), p. 98.

[202]Footnote 169.

[203]Birnie et al. (2009), p. 149.

7.1 Ensuring the Adoption and Implementation of Concrete Legislative and Administrative Measures on Cyber-Attacks by States

Adopting the relevant legislative and administrative framework is the first step in adequately ensuring due diligence as this will provide a fair and effective universal premise for all states to act upon detection of a cyber threat. This proposition if adopted, would constitute the substantive aspect of the obligation of due diligence as an obligation of result.[204] The current wide margin of appreciation afforded states, in terms of the laws they adopt and the extent to which implementation is executed based on several convenient factors,[205] is a major cause for concern. This lee-way should rather be applied only to how states manage their resources and procedures in combating cyber-attacks while the necessary adoption of legislative and administrative frameworks should be complied with strictly.

Ideally, the obligation of preventing cyber harm should have two dimensions: the first would be for all states to have legal and administrative frameworks to be complied with strictly to ensure that international obligations of prevention and protection are upheld. The Watercourses Draft Articles[206] for example, expressed that a state may be held responsible for significant harm where it failed: to adopt necessary legislation, enforce them, prevent/stop an illegal conduct or even punish persons responsible for such conduct. States exercise control over operations carried out on international watercourses and watercourse states are equally required to exercise due diligence in the utilization of international watercourses in ways that will not cause significant harm to other watercourse states.[207] Thus, adopting a similar structure for cyber diligence is not far-fetched. Then, the utilisation of such available frameworks diligently, to the best of their available resources and as situations warranting such arise,[208] will constitute the second aspect of the obligation of preventing cyber harm.

A related treaty that mandates state parties to adopt measures is the Convention on Cybercrime.[209] The Convention, with its Protocol, has been ratified by over

[204]Ney and Zimmermann (2015), p. 63.

[205]ICJ, *Application of the Convention on the Prevention and Punishment of the Crime of Genocide (Bosnia v Serbia),* Judgement (2007) ICJ Rep 1, para. 430; Liu (2017), p. 203. Reference was made by example to variances in how France, Germany, and the UK may approach the issue of suppressing criminal acts—Lauterpacht (1928), p. 128; Shany (2005), p. 917.

[206]ILC (1994), p. 103. This Draft has now been developed into the Watercourses Convention (1997); Koivurova (2008), para 23–26.

[207]ILC (1994), pp. 102–103. Though the Watercourses Convention has now eliminated the words' due diligence' which was formerly inserted in the Draft Articles, the wordings of article 7 of the Convention still encapsulate the concept of due diligence obligation.

[208]Pisillo-Mazzeschi (1992), p. 26.

[209]Budapest Convention, art. 14; other regional treaties exist for Africa and Asia—Shackelford et al. (2016), p. 6.

twenty European countries while some other states were granted observer-status.[210] Despite its international acclamation, there have been criticisms on the laid-back language of the treaty with regards to privacy rights, its lack of representation as well as requiring an unjustifiable expansion of investigative mechanisms for effective implementation.[211] Furthermore, it covers cybercrimes that would constitute crimes under various national criminal laws of member states,[212] but it does not consider the notion of cyber-attacks as a whole like ransomware attacks affecting state infrastructures, denial of service attacks or even the likelihood of cyber-terrorism. The latter may however be because cyber-terrorism does not necessarily constitute a cybercrime within the context of the Convention. Nonetheless, the Convention is the most comprehensive instrument on some aspects of cyberspace operations so far and has laid the foundation for a more effective treaty on broader cyber challenges with a more international reach.[213]

In contrast, the Malabo Convention[214] is another regional treaty adopted by developing countries under the auspices of the African Union (AU) in 2014. The Convention focuses on the promotion of cyber security and data protection for all electronic transactions and is geared towards the prevention of cybercrimes with a better hands-on approach on capacity building when compared with the Budapest Convention. This is perhaps because developing states are more in need of capacity building measures to boost their inadequate knowledge on cyber security operations than developed states who possess advanced systems with highly skilled personnel for their cyber operations. On the other hand, both Conventions uphold the tenets of state cooperation and mutual assistance as a necessity for the effective fulfilment of the provisions contained therein.[215]

Some rights have also been embedded within the provisions of the Malabo Convention like the rights to information, access and erasure of data where necessary.[216] This treaty is however yet to be enforced as it requires ratification by 15 member states of the AU[217] and so far, only three states have ratified the treaty.[218] Furthermore, while the treaty is invested in adopting measures, legislative and

---

[210]The states include the US, Japan, Canada and Mexico. Marion (2010), p. 702.

[211]Clough (2012), p. 366.

[212]Budapest Convention, art 2-11.

[213]Shackelford et al. (2016), p. 7.

[214]African Union Convention on Cyber Security and Personal Data Protection, Opened for signature 27 June 2014, (not yet entered into force) (Malabo Convention).

[215]Budapest Convention, arts 23, 25–34; Malabo Convention, art. 28. The ASEAN Convention although not directly related to cyber operations enjoins member states to observe the due diligence obligation towards countering terrorism (cyberterrorism) through cooperation—ASEAN Convention, art. 6.

[216]Ibid, arts 16–19.

[217]Ibid, art 36.

[218]These states are Guinea, Mauritius and Senegal. https://au.int/sites/default/files/treaties/29560-sl-african_union_convention_on_cyber_security_and_personal_data_protection_1.pdf. Accessed 14 January 2019.

otherwise, geared towards cyber security on all domestic fronts; it has side-lined any due diligence obligations that may flow from its member states towards other states regarding harmful cyber activities. Thus, despite agitations geared towards African states ratifying the agreement and embracing these cyber reforms,[219] it would be lacking in depth without express obligations safeguarding the rights and interests of other states.

Ensuring that states exercise their due diligence obligation by taking all necessary and available measures to prevent cyber-attacks originating from their territories would advertently advance the security of global networks.[220] Due diligence requires nothing more or less than 'reasonable' best efforts that a reasonable government will observe in similar situations.[221] A state must not standby and do nothing at all.[222] In the *Tehran Hostages* case,[223] ICJ found Iran to be in violation of certain conventions and general rules under international law as Iran neither did anything to prevent the hostage attack, stop it before its completion nor engage with the militants to desist from the act and release the hostages.

Notwithstanding, adopting measures is not where the tussle lies, but in actual implementation. Several states ratify international treaties and make legislation that is mostly enforced in theory than in practice.[224] Again, some developing countries lack judges, lawyers or law enforcement personnel who are versed in this area hence the likelihood of discrepancies or lapses in regulations and judgements. As at 2001, there were judges in Moldova and Bulgaria who assumed that cyber-crime dealt simply with theft of computers.[225] Of course, such thinking would be considered preposterous in recent times. In India, a cybercrime allegedly occurs every ten minutes, based on a report that collated cybercrimes from January to June 2017 in that area. Compared to this rating, convictions have been low, and this has been blamed on the improper enforcement of the IT Act 2008 by relevant personnel.[226] It is a prerogative of every state to exert some amount of vigilance when it comes to enforcement.[227]

---

[219] AU urges Member States to Ratify Malabo Convention. https://www.ena.et/en/2018/10/17/au-urges-member-states-to-ratify-malabo-convention/. Accessed 14 January 2019.

[220] Liu (2017), p. 195.

[221] Askin (2017).

[222] ICJ, *Application of the Convention on the Prevention and Punishment of the Crime of Genocide (Bosnia v Serbia),* Judgement (2007) ICJ Rep 1, para. 438.

[223] ICJ, *Case Concerning United States Diplomatic and Consular Staff in Tehran (United States of America v Iran),* Judgement (1980) ICJ Rep 3, para. 68 (*Hostages Case*).

[224] There is a general issue of non-compliance when it comes to rules of international law and this is not peculiar to developing states alone. Some scholarly opinion also suggest that the concept of compliance may in fact be different from implementation and effectiveness. Pollack (2015), pp. 880–881.

[225] Kshetri (2010), p. 1064.

[226] Iqbal and Beigh (2017).

[227] ICJ, *Pulp Mills on the River Uruguay (Argentina v Uruguay),* Judgement (2010) ICJ Rep 79, para. 197 (*Pulp Mills Case*).

7.2 *Seeking International Cooperation and Assistance Based on the Principle of Good Neighbourliness*

A state's responsibility for breach of its due diligence obligation is triggered when it manifestly fails to utilise 'all' measures reasonably available to it in preventing a cyber-attack emanating from its territory.[228] Where a state has effectively implemented such legislative measures and administrative capabilities in attempting to curb a cyber threat and the harm still occurs, the state would not be held in breach.[229] Nevertheless, the likelihood of achieving a different result—the harm not occurring, would be greater if such state sought assistance from another state, even the target state, where its own capabilities seemed inadequate. The ICJ in the *Bosnia Genocide* case opined that:

> ... the possibility remains that the combined efforts of several States, each complying with its obligation to prevent, might have achieved the result — averting the commission of genocide — which the efforts of only one State were insufficient to produce.[230]

Seeking assistance should be a priority for states with regards to harmful activities they are unable to contain themselves,[231] especially those that pose risk of significant harm to other states. This has further been reiterated by a UN Resolution which is focused on combating crimes related to misuse of information technologies and preventing crimes in 'dangerous new forms' with 'transnational dimensions'.[232] The resolution affirms the necessity for international cooperation and mutual assistance among states.

Some states may be reluctant to seek assistance so they do not appear to be incapable of handling their affairs without any external interference and this is lawful and respected under international law. Nonetheless, their inability to curb cyber threats emanating from their territories, which they had knowledge of, may trigger countermeasures from victim states where the attack actually occurs, especially where significant effects are recorded.[233] States may not regard the principle of sovereignty when threatened or under attack.[234] Seeking and providing assistance is discretional,[235] but considering the dire consequences of cyber-attacks, states should

---

[228]ICJ, *Application of the Convention on the Prevention and Punishment of the Crime of Genocide (Bosnia v Serbia),* Judgement (2007) ICJ Rep 1, para. 430.

[229]Kulesza (2016), p. 32.

[230]Ibid.

[231]Couzigou (2018), p. 13.

[232]UNGA (2001).

[233]Akande and Vermeer (2015).

[234]The US in the *Nicaragua* Case attempted to justify its aiding the *Contras'* incursion into Nicaraguan territory based on collective self-defense. Gunaratne (2012).

[235]Walter (2015), p. 83.

by no means hold back on seeking international assistance where they are manifestly incapable of suppressing the threat.[236]

The principle of good neighbourliness, emanating from notions of state sovereignty and equality, enjoins states to cooperate with and have mutual respect for each other as a course to maintaining international peace and security.[237] This principle is a source of some persuasive instruments such as the UN Declaration on friendly relations,[238] even though it does not prescribe legal obligations in itself. The foundation of this principle is rooted in the consciousness of states 'using their properties in such a way as not to injure other's'.[239] Hence, developed states should be willing to render assistance to states incapable of implementing effective measures towards preventing cyber-attacks due to lack of sufficient capacity. Assistance rendered could be in form of knowledge and technology transfer or even capacity building.[240] Incapacitated states should also maximise such assistance in preventing cyber-attacks.

The need to strengthen the resilience of all cyber infrastructures and upgrade the cyber competencies of stakeholders, including the cultivation of a vibrant atmosphere for ICT security research have been set out as the panacea for the ravaging cyber insecurity in developing countries in Africa.[241] Without a doubt, this applies to other developing countries combating cyber-attacks within and without. Due diligence entails imputing continuous efforts and is definitely not a one-off investment.[242]

7.3 *Obligation to Monitor*

International law should evolve to incorporate monitoring of cyber infrastructures as a minimum standard in exercising cyber-diligence obligation. It requires only reasonable means in order to detect perturbing changes in a state's network or cyber routes. Although some assertions purport that due to difficulty in distinguishing serious cyber-attacks from less severe ones, more attention should be given to obligations that build state cooperation during cyber incidents and afterwards than obligations that prevent.[243] Nonetheless, the cost of prevention, albeit broad, in terms of managing state resources may be more feasible compared

[236] Alkousaa (2017).

[237] Basheska (2015), p. 24.

[238] UNGA (1970).

[239] Embodied in the Latin maxim, *Sic utere tuo ut alienum non laedas.*

[240] Kolb (2015), p. 127; Buchan (2016), p. 445; The US and ECOWAS have partnered to build cyber diligence in West Africa—Vazzana (2017).

[241] Serianu (2016).

[242] Dörr (2015), p. 97.

[243] Walter (2015), p. 86.

to the resources that will be invested in reconditioning after a cyber-attack occurs. The National Audit Office's report[244] showed that the WannaCry attack on NHS systems could have been averted had basic best practices been followed but the NHS is now to spend about £150m on boosting cyber security.[245] Moreover, the underpinning focus of the due diligence obligation is preventing harm rather than proffering solutions after harm has occurred.

The obligation to monitor a state's cyber infrastructure is yet to gain maximum acceptance among states due to differences in state capacity, asides the extensive costs involved.[246] Still, 'governments regardless of social, economic, political or any other differences, all are equal members of the international community and have equal rights and duties'.[247] The ILC has reiterated that though capacity varies, the degree of care expected is that of a 'good government' and monitoring, alongside vigilance and utilising structures, is a natural responsibility of any good government.[248]

'The highest level of due diligence that could reasonably be required of a state would be an affirmative obligation to monitor a nation's networks for cyber-attacks and to mitigate any such threat.'[249] However, such must be done with due regard for human and intellectual property rights. There may be pitfalls for states trampling on rights of privacy, freedom of expression and information, under the guise of monitoring cyber activities.[250] The recent Ethiopian cybercrime legislation for example mandates a 'duty to report' on all service providers and organs of government involved in the use of computer networks.[251] With this obligation, these private network providers may engage in pre-emptive monitoring on networks used by service users in order to avoid facing penalties consequently. They may engage the use of 'algorithmic bots' in monitoring systems and this may unavoidably breach certain privacy and freedom of expression rights.[252] The establishment of efficient trust systems has been underscored as a necessity for upholding privacy and data protection rights.[253] In instances where people feel that their privacy is not secure, they can hold back relevant information that may be pivotal to preventing a cyber-attack.

---

[244]National Audit Office (2018).

[245]Dearden (2018).

[246]Jensen (2014), p. 80.

[247]Moslemi and Babaeimehr (2015), pp. 688–689.

[248]ILC (2001a), art 3, para 17.

[249]Shackelford et al. (2016), p. 21.

[250]Bannelier-Christakis (2014), p. 8; Dorr (2015), p. 95.

[251]Computer Crime Proclamation, Federal Negarit Gazeta, Proclamation No 958/2016 (ET), art 27.

[252]Yilma (2016), p. 453.

[253]Yoon (2018).

The ICJ expressly declared that states are to act only 'within the limits permitted by international law'.[254] The need for states to consider upgrades to their security infrastructures to meet rising cyber challenges cannot be overemphasized.[255]

8 Conclusion

For over two decades, cyber-attacks have continuously posed a growing concern and threat to international peace and security. Several measures have been advanced with a view to mitigating these threats; however, ones involving state obligations and responsibility have been given less attention. The obligation to prevent significant harm also known as the due diligence principle is hinged on the necessity to hold states responsible for preventing significant harm originating from their territories.[256] It focuses on the necessary care and vigilance a state is to exercise in order to prevent a significant harm from occurring that will affect the rights of other states. While the adoption of this obligation in other fields of international law like human rights, humanitarian law and corporate law may have been seamless, the extension of this principle to emerging challenges like cyber-attacks has met with some hitches.

There are certain decisive elements capable of triggering the obligation: a state's knowledge of the cyber-attack, their ability to assess the origin of the cyber-attack in order to prevent it, the fact that such an attack poses a risk of significant transboundary harm and that it contradicts with the rights of other states. Asides these triggers, there are no specified requirements for states to follow that will ensure the exercise of the obligation, therefore, making the due diligence obligation ambiguous and liable to subjective interpretations. This view is further strengthened by the absence of a binding international treaty on cyber-attacks.

Furthermore, international obligations are categorized as either obligations of conduct or obligations of result. The due diligence obligation has largely been upheld and exercised as one of conduct seeing as it expects only best efforts from states to exercise care in preventing cyber-attacks perpetrated from their territories. The exercise of this obligation thus lends more credence to the capacity of states in exercising this obligation in cyberspace. Due to differing levels of development among developed and developing countries, this obligation can be easily observed by developed states who possess sufficient technological and financial capacity to exercise necessary measures, but this may not be the case for developing states. Hence, there may be a possibility for developing states to avoid any responsibility for manifestly failing to fulfil the obligation.

[254]ICJ, *Application of the Convention on the Prevention and Punishment of the Crime of Genocide (Bosnia v Serbia),* Judgement (2007) ICJ Rep 1, para. 430.

[255]Fidler (2016), p. 478.

[256]Bendiek (2016), p. 31.

These challenges to the effective application of the due diligence obligation in cyberspace has necessitated the proposition for imposing a more defined baseline approach. There is a need for enforcing the adoption of necessary legislative and administrative measures for all states, as a requirement nationally. This will create an obligation of result ensuring that states take specific steps within their available resources to prevent cyber-attacks. Then, states should fully respect their duties of cooperation and mutual assistance as enshrined in the principle of friendly relations and good neighbourliness applicable to all states under customary international law. Ensuring this will provide developing states with the help that they lack in effectively fulfilling their due diligence obligation. Finally, if the obligation to monitor state cyber infrastructures and networks is given due consideration and enforced under international law, states can initiate preventive measures timely to avoid significant harm. Recognising these minimum rules will effectively create a fair and predictable standard of due diligence applicable to all states notwithstanding their disparate capacities.[257]

References

Abou-Zeid A (2018) Policies and legislation, international cooperation and capacity building. African Forum on Cybercrime, Addis-Ababa. Accessed 8 Sept 2018

African Union Commission (AUC) and Symantec (2016) Report, cyber crime and cyber security trends in Africa (November 2016) 22. https://www.symantec.com/content/dam/symantec/docs/reports/cyber-security-trends-report-africa-interactive-en.pdf

Akande D, Vermeer Z (2015) The airstrikes against Islamic State in Iraq and the alleged prohibition on military assistance to governments in civil wars. EJIL: Talk! (2 February 2015). https://www.ejiltalk.org/the-airstrikes-against-islamic-state-in-iraq-and-the-alleged-prohibition-on-military-assistance-to-governments-in-civil-wars/. Accessed 8 Jan 2018

Alexander J, Finkle J (2015) Apparent Islamic State backers hack US military Twitter feed. Reuters (12 January 2015). https://www.reuters.com/article/us-cybersecurity-centcom-hack/apparent-islamic-state-backers-hack-u-s-military-twitter-feed-idUSKBN0KL1UZ20150112. Accessed 9 May 2018

Alkousaa R (2017) Iraq seeks international help to investigate Islamic State crimes. Reuters (16 August 2017). https://www.reuters.com/article/us-mideast-crisis-iraq-un/iraq-seeks-international-help-to-investigate-islamic-state-crimes-idUSKCN1AW2E7. Accessed 4 June 2018

Arbitral Tribunal, *Alabama Claims of the United States of America against Great Britain,* Award (1871) Reports of International Arbitral Awards 29

Arbitral Tribunal, *Lake Lanoux Arbitration (France v Spain),* Award (1957) RIAA 281

Arbitral Tribunal, *Trail Smelter Arbitration (United States v Canada)*, Award (1941) Reports of International Arbitral Awards 3

Arbitration Tribunal, *Pantechniki SA Contractors & Engineers (Greece) v Republic of Albania,* Award (2009) ARB/07/21 IIC 383

Armed Activities on the Territory of the Congo (DRC V Uganda), Merits (2005) ICJ Rep 168 (*Armed Activities Case*)

[257]Takano (2018), p. 11.

Askin E (2017) Due diligence obligation in times of crisis: a reflection by the example of international arms transfers EJIL: Talk! (1 March 2017). https://www.ejiltalk.org/due-diligence-obligation-in-times-of-crisis-a-reflection-by-the-example-of-international-arms-transfers/. Accessed 3 Feb 2018

Aust HP (2015) The UN human rights due diligence policy: an effective mechanism against complicity of peacekeeping forces? JCSL 20:61–73

Baezner M, Robin P (2017) Hotspot analysis: Stuxnet. Centre for Security Studies, ETH Zurich. http://www.css.ethz.ch/content/dam/ethz/special-interest/gess/cis/center-for-securities-studies/pdfs/Cyber-Reports-2017-04.pdf

Bannelier-Christakis K (2014) Cyber diligence: a low-intensity due diligence principle for low-intensity cyber operations? BYIL 14:1–15

Barnidge R (2006) The due diligence principle under international law. ICLR 8:81–121

Basheska E (2015) The position of the good neighbourliness principle in international and EU law. In: Kochenov D, Basheska E (eds) Good neighbourliness in the European legal context: studies in EU external relations, vol 9. Brill/Nijhoff

Bastin L (2017) State responsibility for omissions: establishing a breach of the full protection and security obligation by omissions. Dissertation, University of Oxford, Oxford

Bendiek A (2016) Due diligence in cyberspace: guidelines for international and European cyber policy and cybersecurity policy. SWP Research Paper 3/20. https://www.swp-berlin.org/fileadmin/contents/products/research_papers/2016RP07_bdk.pdf. Accessed 3 Jan 2018

Birnie P et al (2009) International law and the environment, 3rd edn. Oxford University Press, Oxford

Blomeyer-Bartenstein H (1987) Due diligence. In: Bernhardt R et al (Advisory Board) Encyclopedia of public international law, vol 10. Elsevier Science Publishers B V

Bonnitcha J, McCorquodale R (2017) The concept of 'due diligence' in the UN guiding principles on business and human rights. EJIL 28:899–919

British Institute of International and Comparative Law (BIICL) (2014) Report, state responsibility for cyber operations: international law issues (9 October 2014), pp 11–12. https://www.biicl.org/documents/380_biicl_report_-_state_responsibility_for_cyber_operations_-_9_october_2014.pdf?showdocument=1

Buchan R (2016) Cyber space, non-state actors and the obligation to prevent transboundary harm. JCSL 21:429–453

Cabinet Office (2018) National Security Capability Review. National Security Review Web. https://assets.publishing.service.gov.uk/government/uploads/system/uploads/attachment_data/file/705347/6.4391_CO_National-Security-Review_web.pdf. Assessed 23 Oct 2018

Carr M (2016) Public-private partnerships in national cyber-security strategies. Int Aff 92:43–62

Cassim (2011) Addressing the growing spectre of cyber crime in Africa: evaluating measures adopted by South Africa and other regional role players. Int Law J South Afr 44:123–138

Chircop L (2018) A due diligence standard of attribution in cyberspace. ICLQ 67:643–668

Clough J (2012) The Council of Europe Convention on Cybercrime: defining 'crime' in a digital world. Crim Law Forum 23:363–391

Computer Crime Proclamation, Federal Negarit Gazeta, Proclamation No 958/2016 (ET)

Convention on Cybercrime (Council of Europe) (23 November 2001) CETS No 185 (Budapest Convention)

Convention on the Law of the Non-Navigational Uses of International Watercourses. Opened for Signature, 21 May 1997, 36 ILM 700 (entered into force 17 August 2014) (Watercourses Convention)

Cornish P (2015) Governing cyberspace through constructive ambiguity. Survival 57:153–176

Country Situation Report: *Botswana,* Report on International Cooperation against Cybercrime in Africa - Challenges and Opportunities (2018) African Forum on Cybercrime, Addis Ababa. https://rm.coe.int/3148-afc2018-ws2-internatcoop-botswana/16808e6898 (23 October 2018)

Couzigou I (2018) Securing cyber space: the obligation of states to prevent harmful international cyber operations. IRLCT 32:1–21

DarkTrace enterprise system. https://www.darktrace.com/technology/. Accessed 22 Feb 2018
Dearden L (2018) NHS to spend £150m on Cyber Security to bolster defences after WannaCry attack. The Independent (28 April 2018). https://www.independent.co.uk/news/health/cyber-attacks-nhs-wannacry-security-investment-microsoft-a8327091.html. Accessed 30 Apr 2018
Desgagne R (2000) The prevention of environmental damage in the time of armed conflict: proportionality and precautionary measures. Yearb Int Humanitarian Law 3:109–129
Dorr O (2015) Obligations of the state of origin of a cyber security incident. GYIL 58:87–99
Dupuy P (1991) Soft law and the international law of the environment. Mich J Int Law 12:420–435
Dupuy P (1999) Reviewing the difficulties of codification: on Ago's classification of obligations of means and obligations of result in relation to state responsibility. EJIL 10:371–385
ECtHR, *Case of Plattform "Arzte für das Leben" v Austria*, Judgment (App no 10126/82), 21 June 1988
ECtHR, *Osman v UK,* Judgment (App No 23452/94), 28 October 1988
EHRR, *Colozza v Italy* (7 EHRR 1985) VII 516
Fidler D (2016) Cyberspace, terrorism and international law. JCSL 21:475
Geneva Convention for the Amelioration of the Condition of the Wounded and Sick in Armed Forces in the Field. Opened for signature 12 August 1949, 75 UNTS 31 (entered into force 21 October 1950) (First Geneva Convention)
Geneva Convention for the Amelioration of the Condition of the Wounded, Sick and Shipwrecked Members of the Armed Forces at Sea. Opened for signature 12 August 1949, 75 UNTS 85 (entered into force 21 October 1950) (Second Geneva Convention)
Geneva Convention Relative to the Protection of Civilian Persons in Time of War. Opened for signature 12 August 1949, 75 UNTS 287 (entered into force 21 October 1950) (Fourth Geneva Convention)
Geneva Convention relative to the Treatment of Prisoners of War. Opened for signature 12 August 1949, 75 UNTS 135 (entered into force 21 October 1950) Third Geneva Convention)
Grabosch R, Scheper C (2015) Corporate obligations with regard to human rights due diligence: policy and legal approaches. https://library.fes.de/pdf-files/iez/12167.pdf. Accessed 28 Nov 2018
Graham (2017) NHS cyber-attack: everything you need to know about 'biggest Ransomware' offensive in history. The Telegraph (20 May 2017). https://www.telegraph.co.uk/news/2017/05/13/nhs-cyber-attack-everything-need-know-biggest-ransomware-offensive/. Accessed 26 Mar 2018
Grans L (2018) The concept of due diligence and the obligation to prevent honour-related violence: beyond deterrence. Int J Hum Right 22:733–755
Gunaratne R (2012) Nicaragua v the United States: use of force and self-defense (1 of 3). https://ruwanthikagunaratne.wordpress.com/2012/11/15/nicaragua-vs-us-case-summary/. Accessed 4 June 2018
Herdegen M (2015) Possible legal framework and regulatory models for cyberspace: due diligence obligation and institutional models for enhanced inter-state cooperation. GYIL 58:169–185
Herzog S (2011) Revisiting the Estonian cyber-attacks: digital threats and multinational responses. J Strateg Sec 4:49–60
https://au.int/sites/default/files/treaties/29560-sl-african_union_convention_on_cyber_security_and_personal_data_protection_1.pdf. Accessed 14 Jan 2019
https://www.ena.et/en/2018/10/17/au-urges-member-states-to-ratify-malabo-convention/. Accessed 14 Jan 2019
ICJ, *Application of the Convention on the Prevention and Punishment of the Crime of Genocide (Bosnia v Serbia),* Judgement (2007) ICJ Rep 1, para. 430
ICJ, *Case concerning Military and Paramilitary Activities in and against Nicaragua (Nicaragua v United States of America),* Merits (1986) ICJ Rep 115 (*Nicaragua Case*)
ICJ, *Case Concerning the Gabčikovo-Nagymaros Project (Hungary v Slovakia),* Judgement (1997) ICJ Rep 7

ICJ, *Case Concerning United States Diplomatic and Consular Staff in Tehran (United States of America v Iran),* Judgement (1980) ICJ Rep 3(*Hostages Case*)
ICJ, *Corfu Channel (United Kingdom of Great Britain and Northern Ireland v Albania),* Judgment (1949) ICJ Rep 1
ICJ, *Corfu Channel Case (UK V Albania),* Merits (1949) ICJ Rep 4
ICJ, *Legality of the threat or use of nuclear weapons,* Advisory Opinion (1996) ICJ Rep 226 (*Nuclear Weapons* Case)
ICJ, *Pulp Mills on the River Uruguay (Argentina v Uruguay),* Judgement (2010) ICJ Rep 79 (*Pulp Mills Case*)
ILA Study Group (2014) Report, due diligence in international law (7 March 2014), p 11. http://www.ila-hq.org/index.php/study-groups?study-groupsID=63
ILA Study Group (2016) Report, due diligence in international law (July 2016), p 15. http://www.ila-hq.org/index.php/study-groups
ILC (1994) Draft articles on the law of the non-navigational uses of international watercourses and commentaries thereto and resolution on transboundary confined groundwater (8 March 1994). UN Doc A/49/52
ILC (2001a) Draft articles on prevention of transboundary harm from hazardous activities, with commentaries (30 Nov 2001). UN Doc A/54/10
ILC (2001b) Draft articles on responsibility of states for internationally wrongful acts, with commentaries. UN Doc A/56/10 (ARSIWA 2001)
International Committee of the Red Cross (2004) What is International Humanitarian Law? https://www.icrc.org/en/doc/assets/files/other/what_is_ihl.pdf. Accessed 4 February 2019
International Covenant on Economic, Social and Cultural Rights. Opened for signature, 16 December 1966, 993 UNTS 3 (entered into Force 3 January 1976) (ICESCR)
Iqbal J, Beigh M (2017) Cybercrime in India: trends and challenges. ICAIETM 2017, Hyderabad
Jensen ET (2014) State obligations in cyber operations. Baltic Yearb Int Law 14:71–92
Jensen ET, Watts S (2017) A cyber duty of due diligence: gentle civilizer or crude destabilizer? TLR 95:1555–1577
Kaspersky Lab (2017) Chasing Lazarus: a hunt for the infamous hackers to prevent large bank robberies. https://www.kaspersky.com/about/press-releases/2017_chasing-lazarus-a-hunt-for-the-infamous-hackers-to-prevent-large-bank-robberies. Accessed 30 Apr 2018
Kayode (2014) Inside Nigeria's Sambisa forest, the *Boko Haram* hideout where kidnapped school girls are believed to be held. The Guardian. https://www.theguardian.com/world/2014/apr/29/nigeria-sambisa-forest-boko-haram-hideout-kidnapped-school-girls-believed-to-be-held. Accessed 21 Feb 2018
Khanna P (2018) State sovereignty and self-defence in cyberspace. BRICS Law J 5:139–154
Koivurova T (2008) Due diligence. In: Wolfrum R (ed) Max Planck encyclopedia of public international law. Oxford University Press, Oxford
Kolb R (2015) Reflections on due diligence duties and cyberspace. GYIL 58:113–128
Korzak E (2011) Computer network attacks, self-defence and international law. In: Hehir A et al (eds) International law, security and ethics: policy challenges in the post-9/11 world. Routledge, London
Kshetri N (2010) Diffusion and effects of cyber-crime in developing countries. Third World Q 31:1057–1079
Ku C (1990) The concept of res communis in international law. Hist Eur Ideas 12:459–477
Kulesza J (2014) Due diligence in cyber space. In: Portela IM, Almeida F (eds) Organizational, legal and technological dimensions of information system administration. Information Science Reference
Kulesza J (2016) Due diligence in international law. Brill Nijhoff, Leiden/Boston
Kushner (2013) The real story of Stuxnet. IEEE Spectrum (26 February 2013). https://spectrum.ieee.org/telecom/security/the-real-story-of-stuxnet. Accessed 22 Feb 2018
Lauterpacht H (1928) Revolutionary activities by private persons against foreign states. AJIL 22:105–130

Lawrence GM (2017) Due diligence in business transactions, Revised edn. Law Journal Press
Liaropoulos A (2013) Exercising state sovereignty in cyberspace: an international cyber-order under construction? J Inf Warf 12:19–26
Liaropoulos A (2017) Cyberspace governance and state sovereignty. In: Bitros GC, Kyriazis NC (eds) Democracy and an open-economy world order. Springer International Publishing
Liu YI (2017) State responsibility and cyber-attacks: defining due diligence obligations. Indonesian J Int Comp Law 4:191–260
Malwarebytes Labs (2017) Report, State of Malware Report (5 December 2018). https://www.malwarebytes.com/pdf/white-papers/stateofmalware.pdf
Marion N (2010) The Council of Europe's Cyber Crime Treaty: an exercise in symbolic legislation. IJCC 4:699–712
Monaco L (2016) Remarks. International Conference on Cyber Security, New York
Moore (2017) ISIS hacking group threatens global cyber-attack starting with the US tomorrow. Mail Online (7 December 2017). http://www.dailymail.co.uk/news/article-5155331/ISIS-hacking-group-threatens-global-cyber-attack-TOMORROW.html. Accessed 11 May 2018
Moslemi B, Babaeimehr A (2015) Principle of sovereign equality of states in the light of the doctrine of responsibility to protect. IJHCS:687–697
National Audit Office (2018) Investigation: WannaCry Cyber Attack and the NHS. https://www.nao.org.uk/report/investigation-wannacry-cyber-attack-and-the-nhs/. Accessed 26 Mar 2018
NATO Standardization Agency (2018) NATO glossary of terms and definitions AAP-6. http://nso.nato.int/nso/zzlinks/terminology_public__non-classified%20nato%20glossaries.html. Accessed 5 Sept 2018
NCSC (2015) How cyber-attacks work. https://www.ncsc.gov.uk/articles/how-cyber-attacks-work. Accessed 22 Feb 2018
Ney M, Zimmermann A (2015) Cyber-security beyond the military perspective: international law, 'cyberspace' and the concept of due diligence. GYIL 58:51–66
Niekerk V (2017) An analysis of cyber-incidents in South Africa. AJIC 20:113–132
Okowa PN (2000) State responsibility for transboundary air pollution in international law. Oxford University Press, Oxford
Permanent Court of Arbitration, *Island of Palmas,* Award (1928) 2 RIAA 829
Pfeiffer N (2016) What is an IP Address? The Cisco Learning Network (15 March 2016). https://learningnetwork.cisco.com/docs/DOC-30059. Accessed 7 Dec 2018
Pisillo-Mazzeschi R (1992) The due diligence rule and the nature of international responsibility of states. German Yearb Int Law 35:9–51
Pollack M (2015) Who supports international law and why? The United States, the European Union and the international legal order. Int J Constit Law 13:873–900
Protocol Additional to the Geneva Conventions of 12 August 1949 and relating to the Protection of Victims of International Armed Conflicts. Opened for signature 12 December 1977, 1125 UNTS 3 (entered into force 7 December 1978) (Additional Protocol I)
Protocol Additional to the Geneva Conventions of 12 August 1949 and relating to the Protection of Victims of Non-International Armed Conflicts. Opened for signature 12 December 1977, 1125 UNTS 609 (entered into force 7 December 1978) (Additional Protocol II)
Protocol on Environmental Protection to the Antarctic Treaty of 1991. Opened for signature 4 October 1991, 30 ILM 1455 (entered into force January 1998) (Madrid Environmental Protection Protocol)
Rao PS (1999) International liability for injurious consequences arising out of acts not prohibited by international law (Prevention of Transboundary Damage from Hazardous Activities. Second Report of the Special Rapporteur for the ILC on the topic of International Liability (5 May 1999). UN Doc A/CN.4/501
Reinisch A, Beham M (2015) Mitigating risks: inter-state due diligence obligations in case of harmful cyber incidents and malicious cyber activity-obligations of transit state. GYIL 58:101–112

Ruggie J, Sherman J (2017) The concept of 'due diligence' in the UN guiding principles on business and human rights: a reply to Jonathan Bonnitcha and Robert McCorquodale. EJIL 28:921–928
Schachter O (1991) The emergence of international environmental law. JIA 44:463–464
Schmitt MN (ed) (2013) Tallinn manual on the international law applicable to cyber warfare. Cambridge University Press, Cambridge
Schmitt MN (2015–2016) In defence of due diligence in cyber space. YLJF 125:68–81
Schmitt MN (2018) Due diligence in cyberspace: the Tallinn manual approach. 10th International Conference on Cyber Conflict, Tallinn
Schmitt MN, Vihul L (eds) (2017) Tallinn manual 2.0 on the international law applicable to cyber operations. Cambridge University Press, Cambridge
Serianu (2016) Report, Africa Cyber Security Report: achieving cyber security resilience- enhancing visibility and increasing awareness (2016). https://www.serianu.com/downloads/AfricaCyberSecurityReport2016.pdf
Serianu (2017) Report, Africa Cyber Security Report: Demystifying Africa's Cyber Security Poverty Line (2017). 37. https://www.serianu.com/downloads/AfricaCyberSecurityReport2017.pdf
Shackelford (2014) Managing cyber attacks in international law, business and relations: in search of cyber peace. Cambridge University Press, Cambridge
Shackelford S et al (2016) Unpacking the international law on cybersecurity due diligence: lessons from the public and private sectors. CJIL 17:1–49
Shany Y (2005) Towards a general margin of appreciation doctrine in international law? EJIL 16:907–940
Siroli G (2018) Considerations on the cyber domain as the new worldwide battlefield. Int Spectator 53:111–123
Sklerov M (2009) Solving the dilemma of state responses to cyberattacks: a justification for the use of active defenses against states who neglect their duty to prevent. MLR 201:1–85
Stewart C et al (2018) What is cyberinfrastructure? 38th annual ACM SIGUCCS fall conference, Virginia
Symantec Corporation (2017) Internet Security Threat Report. https://www.symantec.com/security-center/threat-report. Accessed 1 May 2018 (Symantec Report)
Takano A (2018) Due diligence obligations and transboundary environmental harm: cybersecurity applications. LAWS 7:1–12
Trapp K (2011) State responsibility for international terrorism-problems and prospects. Oxford University Press, Oxford
U.S. Cyber Command. https://www.cybercom.mil/About/History/. Accessed 1 Oct 2018
UN Agreement for the Implementation of the Provisions of the United Nations Convention on the Law of the Sea of 10 December 1982 relating to the Conservation and Management of Straddling Fish Stocks and Highly Migratory Fish Stocks of 1995. Opened for signature 4 August 1995, 2167 UNTS 3 (entered into force 11 December 2001)
UN Group of Governmental Experts (UNGGE) (2013) Report on Developments in the Field of Information and Telecommunications in the Context of International Security. (24 June 2013) UN Doc A/68/98
UN Group of Governmental Experts (UNGGE) (2015) Report on Developments in the Field of Information and Telecommunications in the Context of International Security. (22 July 2015) UN Doc A/70/174
UN Human Rights Council (2011) Guiding Principles on Business and Human Rights: Implementing the United Nations "Protect, Respect and Remedy" Framework (June 2011). UN Doc HR/PUB/11/4 (Guiding Principles on Business and Human Rights)
UNGA (1970) Declaration on Principles of International law concerning Friendly Relations and Co-operation among States in accordance with the Charter of the United Nations (24 Oct 1970). UN Doc A/RES/25/2625
UNGA (1972) Declaration of the United Nations Conference on the Human Environment (16 June 1972). UN Doc A/RES/2994 (Stockholm Declaration)

UNGA (1992) Declaration on Environment and Development (12 Aug 1992). UN Doc A/CONF.151/26 (Rio Declaration)
UNGA (2001) Combating the Criminal Misuse of Information Technologies (19 Dec 2001). UN Doc A/55/63
UNGA (2013) Developments in the Field of Information and Telecommunications in the Context of International Security (27 December 2013). UN Doc A/68/243
UNGA (2015) Developments in the Field of Information and Telecommunications in the Context of International Security (23 December 2015). UN Doc A/70/237
United Nations Convention on the Law of the Sea, Opened for signing 10 December 1982, 1833 UNTS 396 (entered into force 16 November 1994) (UNCLOS)
US Department of Defense (2018) Dictionary of Military and Associated Terms JP 3-12 (January 2019). https://www.jcs.mil/Portals/36/Documents/Doctrine/pubs/dictionary.pdf. Accessed 03 Feb 2019
Vazzana J (2017) U.S. Department of State and ECOWAS partner to promote cyber due diligence in West Africa. Global Forum on Cyber Expertise (21 November 2017). https://www.thegfce.com/news/news/2017/11/21/u.s.-department-of-state-and-ecowas-partner-to-promote-cyber-due-diligence-in-west-africa. Accessed 18 Oct 2018
Vincze V (2017) The role of customary principles of international humanitarian law in environmental protection. Pecs J Int Eur Law 2:19–39
Walter C (2015) Obligations of states before, during and after a cyber security incident. GYIL 58:67–86
Yilma K (2016) Comment: some remarks on Ethiopia's new cybercrime legislation. Mizan Law Rev 10:448–458. https://www.ajol.info/index.php/mlr/article/view/153608. Accessed 4 Feb 2019
Yoon KM (2018) Protecting human rights. African Forum on Cybercrime, Addis Ababa, p 13. https://au.int/sites/default/files/newsevents/workingdocuments/34851-wd-keong_safeguards.pdf. Accessed 15 Jan 2019
Ziolkowski K (ed) (2013) Peacetime regime for state activities in cyber space: international law, international relations and diplomacy. NATO CCD COE Publication, Tallinn

Enenu O. Okwori is a PhD candidate at the school of law, University of Aberdeen, United Kingdom.

Part III
Book Review

L. Chenwi and T. Soboka Bulta (eds.): Extraterritorial Human Rights Obligations from an African Perspective

Intersentia, Cambridge, 2018

Cedric Ryngaert

Abstract In an era in which doubt has been cast over the international legal discipline's internationalist credentials, scholarship which addresses alternative perceptions and conceptions of international law in the non-West deserves our full attention. In this context, we welcome Lilian Chenwi and Takele Soboka Bulto's collection on 'Extraterritorial Human Rights Obligations from an African Perspective', which highlights the destructive human rights impacts of states' acts, decisions, and omissions outside their territory, and makes a convincing doctrinal case that extraterritorial obligations (ETOs) can legally be based on the African Charter on Human and People's Rights (ACHPR). This is a carefully edited collection which forms a coherent whole. The individual contributions are well-written and contain a wealth of doctrinal insights and empirical information. The editors and contributors deserve particular credit for highlighting the ETO potential of the ACHPR, the refined reasoning of the African Commission (largely unknown outside Africa), and the extant and potential interactions between the African human rights system and other regional or universal systems. The voices of the new generation of African (and Africa-minded) scholars who have contributed to this volume deserve a wide audience.

In an era in which doubt has been cast over the international legal discipline's internationalist credentials,[1] scholarship which addresses alternative perceptions and conceptions of international law in the non-West deserves our full attention. In this context, we welcome Lilian Chenwi and Takele Soboka Bulto's collection on 'Extraterritorial Human Rights Obligations from an African Perspective', which highlights the destructive human rights impacts of states' acts, decisions, and

[1]See for a critique: Roberts (2017).

C. Ryngaert (✉)
Public International Law, Utrecht University, Utrecht, The Netherlands
e-mail: C.M.J.Ryngaert@uu.nl

Z. Yihdego et al. (eds.), *Ethiopian Yearbook of International Law 2018*, Ethiopian Yearbook of International Law 2018, https://doi.org/10.1007/978-3-030-24078-3_10

omissions outside their territory, and makes a convincing doctrinal case that extraterritorial obligations (ETOs) can legally be based on the African Charter on Human and People's Rights (ACHPR).

The collection starts out with a sizable chapter by the editors on extraterritoriality in the African system from a comparative perspective, followed by a number of case-studies running the entire gamut of ETOs. These case-studies range from ETOs in the area of economic and social rights (*e.g.*, the right to education, the right to water, the right to food) to ETOs in the context of international security (*e.g.*, extraordinary renditions in the fight against terrorism and military ventures abroad). Most chapters are written by African scholars and practitioners, who are based in Africa. This surely lends additional force and legitimacy to the arguments presented.

All scholars interested in ETOs—this reviewer is one of them—will, in principle, have little difficulty connecting with the African perspective set out in this book. Just like the International Covenant on Economic and Social Rights (ICESCR), the ACHPR lacks a (limiting) jurisdiction clause, which, in the context of duties of cooperation, can ground extraterritorial obligations (p. 21). Also, the African Commission uses the familiar tripartite typology of human rights obligations (the obligation to respect, the obligation to protect and the obligation to fulfil/promote).[2] Moreover, *per* Article 60 and 61 ACHPR, the African Commission can rely on cases and materials that have been developed elsewhere.[3] This enables the Commission—as well as States Parties to the Convention—to productively draw on the rich case-law and scholarly endeavours regarding ETOs.

This begs the question, however, whether there is, or can be something specifically *African* about ETOs. Or are ETOs instead conceptualised *elsewhere* and only *applied* in the African context, bearing in mind that the African Commission has not yet explicitly engaged with ETOs? In their opening substantive chapter, the editors imply that African culture provides particularly fertile ground for ETOs. This raises the prospect that African states could provide an innovative contribution to the larger debate on ETOs. This is not entirely seen through in the collection, however. Possibly, general concluding observations by the editors could have had added value in this respect. But what about these intriguing notions grounding the relevance of cooperative ETOs: that Africans are 'community, or group oriented rather than individualistic' (p. 17), and have a 'sense of cooperation and collective responsibility' (p. 18)? This link between the duty of cooperation and extraterritorial obligations has earlier been drawn in respect of Article 2(1) ICESCR, which provides that '[e]ach State Party to the present Covenant undertakes to take steps, individually and through international assistance and co-operation, especially economic and technical, to the maximum of its available resources, with a view to

[2]ACHPR, *SERAC v Nigeria*, Communication No 155/96 (2001) AHRLR 60, paras. 45–47.

[3]These articles provide that the Commission shall draw inspiration from other instruments (provided that African Charter parties are also parties to these instruments), and 'shall also take into consideration, as subsidiary measures to determine the principles of law', *inter alia*, 'legal precedents and doctrine'.

achieving progressively the full realisation of the rights recognised in the present Covenant.'[4] Arguably, the penchant of Africans—possibly unlike other people—for cooperation further strengthens the case for ETOs. However, doubts could be cast over the anthropological reality of the characterisation of Africans as 'group oriented': such a characterisation has an essentialist flavour and may fail to account for the variety of the African approaches to life, including ones that emphasise the individual.[5] Yet more importantly, to make the case for ETOs, it does not suffice to highlight group orientation. Instead, it should be established that solidarity extends *beyond the immediate group* to which one belongs. If the perspective is limited to Africa, this means that Africans belong to one single community, and on that ground have obligations towards fellow Africans, regardless of ethnicity, language, and geographical location. It is not certain whether, sociologically speaking, such pan-African solidarity truly exists, in spite of the valiant efforts of the pan-African movement,[6] one of the products of which is obviously the African Union. Furthermore it is unclear whether, in a general sense, Africans necessarily identify more with, and share more characteristics with fellow Africans than they do with non-Africans.[7] Ultimately, however, even if pan-African solidarity were indeed to exist, and, accordingly, Africans would have heightened ETOs towards fellow Africans (individuals, communities, states), this would not say much about—or even worse, would detract from—*genuine* ETOs. Genuine ETOs are not regionally restricted. Instead, they have a cosmopolitan, non-ethnic, and non-national/-regional dimension. This means 'we' have obligations towards 'distant others' regardless of whether the latter belong to our group or have a shared history and geography, so as to realise 'global justice'.[8] In this reading of ETOs, Africans also have obligations towards those based *outside* Africa. This is a perspective which is not fully developed in the book—for obvious reasons, given current world power relations. Still, Bulto interestingly tackles aspects of this problem when discussing extraordinary

[4]The emphasis in this provision on international cooperation, in conjunction with the aforementioned absence of a limiting jurisdictional clause, has indeed been construed as grounding ETOs. See more at length: Langford et al. (2013).

[5]Compare Agulanna (2010), p. 296 (arguing that 'while in the Nazi and Stalinist societies the life of the individual only added instrumental value in the sense that people were seen as tools to be used and discarded, in Africa, the life of the individual is seen as possessing great value and worth'—although proceeding to state that 'in Africa that the individual can only be defined by reference to the environing community').

[6]See, *e.g.*, one of the early doubters: Emerson (1962), pp. 275–290, and for a recent discussion: Kasanda (2016), pp. 179–195.

[7]Verve Search, a London-based agency, has developed an interesting quiz for the BBC on the discrepancy between one's nation of birth and one's true home ('When it comes to your personality, your nation of birth may not be your true home. Where in the world are people most like you?'). See http://www.bbc.com/future/story/20180409-whats-your-secret-nationality (last consulted on 16 July 2018). The author, who is Belgian by birth, lives in the Netherlands, and has never lived in Africa, participated in the quiz and was quite surprised to find out that his true home is ... Ethiopia!.

[8]See, *e.g.*, Langford et al. (2013).

rendition of non-Africans by an African state to the CIA, which then goes on to torture them.

In more important practical terms, the cosmopolitan nature of ETOs implies that not only African states, but also *non-African states—i.e.* Western states as well as emerging powers such as China and the Gulf countries—have obligations toward Africans. In an economic context, this requires non-African states to ensure that their trade and investment relationships with African states do not result in human rights violations. In fact, quite a number of contributors address the adverse impact of non-African states and 'their' companies (*i.e.*, companies incorporated in those states) on the enjoyment of human rights in Africa. Coomans, for instance, calls on foreign (especially French and UK) public and private actors to apply a human rights impact assessment when they plan to support and offer private educational services in Africa. In three separate contributions, Lambek, Debucquois, Jegede and Mbazira denounce land deals (*e.g.*, for biofuels purposes), or even plain land-grabbing involving non-African states, insofar as these deals lead to evictions and adversely affect Africans' enjoyment of the right to food. Moyo, for his part, highlights how subsidiaries of multinational corporations domiciled in the Global North contribute to violations of the right to water, thereby engaging the international responsibility of their home states. As Viljoen notes in his foreword (p. ix), such violations cannot be captured by African human rights instruments, as they are committed by states which are not parties to these instruments. To tackle these violations, faith should be put into global (UN) instruments or non-African regional instruments, such as the European Convention on Human Rights. Fortunately, bodies monitoring compliance with these instruments have already drawn attention to their extraterritorial application, even if practice leaves a lot to be desired. Most recently—and most relevantly in the context of corporate activities in Africa—the UN Committee on Economic, Social and Cultural Rights has adopted a General Comment (No. 24) on State obligations in the context of business activities, including extraterritorial obligations.[9]

Highlighting the Global North/Global South divide is however not to minimise the relevance of extraterritorial obligations resting on *African states themselves*, especially in an *intra*-African context. The African Commission (which supervises those African states' compliance with the ACHPR) has not tackled the concept of extraterritorial obligations head-on. Still, it has engaged with it, albeit somewhat obliquely, in a number of cases, as discussed notably by Chenwi and Bulto. In the *Burundi Embargo* case, the Commission held that states, when taking economic sanctions, must ensure basic rights,[10] while in the *DRC Invasion* case, it held a number of states neighbouring the DRC responsible for violations of individual and group rights committed during those states' occupation of parts of DRC territory.[11] Other contributions, on the basis of rich empirical information, draw attention to

[9]Committee on Economic, Social and Cultural Rights (2017). See Part C on extraterritorial obligations.

[10]ACHPR, Communication No. 157/96, (2003) AHRLR 111.

[11]ACHPR, *Democratic Republic of Congo v Burundi, Rwanda and Uganda*, Communication No. 227/1999, (2004) AHRLR 19.

contemporary intra-African situations in which ETOs (should) apply. Acirokop, for instance, finds that Uganda incurs extraterritorial obligations for its military's failure to respect and protect civilians in areas in the Central African Republic (CAR) where the Lord's Resistance Army is active. Drawing on the *Al Skeini* judgment of the European Court of Human Rights,[12] she argues that Uganda, which leads a Regional Task Force in the CAR, exercises public powers there. Other contributions foreground the responsibility of South Africa, one of Africa's economic powerhouses, in respect of its corporations' business deals which adversely impact human rights across the African continent.

Taking this last scenario of corporate abuses—of which Africa is, and has been so much at the receiving end—it is striking that the contributors writing in this field (the majority of them in fact) accept at face value the validity of the 2011 Maastricht Principles on Extraterritorial Obligations of States in the Area of Economic, Social and Cultural Rights, a scholarly expert opinion 'restating' human rights law on extraterritorial obligations.[13] Pursuant to the Maastricht Principles, a state has obligations to respect, protect and fulfil economic, social and cultural rights, not only in situations over which it exercises authority or effective control, but also in 'situations over which State acts or omissions bring about foreseeable effects on the enjoyment of economic, social and cultural rights, whether within or outside its territory', and 'situations in which the State, acting separately or jointly, whether through its executive, legislative or judicial branches, is in a position to exercise decisive influence or to take measures to realize economic, social and cultural rights extraterritorially'.[14] On this basis, states are arguably under an obligation to 'take necessary measures to ensure that non-State actors which they are in a position to regulate ... such as private individuals and organisations, and transnational corporations and other business enterprises, do not nullify or impair the enjoyment of economic, social and cultural rights.'[15] As a matter of policy, this may perhaps be defensible. However, it is questionable whether extraterritorial state obligations in respect of corporate abuse exist as a matter of law. In a recent article, Claire Methven O'Brien has rather convincingly argued that, 'on the weight of evidence ... at present, there cannot be said to exist any positive legal basis ... for recent claims by scholars that the responsibility of home states under human rights treaties extends to the prevention of abuses by [transnational corporations] beyond national borders'.[16] Methven O'Brien did however not seek to evaluate whether home state duty to regulate transnational corporations would be normatively desirable or optimal.[17]

[12]ECtHR, *Al-Skeini and Others v The United Kingdom,* Judgment, (2011) App. No. 55721/07).

[13]International Commission of Jurists (2011), p. 3. On closer inspection, this acceptance may not be that surprising, as the first editor of the collection was one of the expert signatories of the Maastricht Principles.

[14]Maastricht Principles, para. 9.

[15]Maastricht Principles, para. 24.

[16]Methven O'Brien (2018), pp. 47–73, 72.

[17]*Id.*

Clearly, the contributors to this volume are of the view that such a duty is indeed called for. Given the deleterious human rights effects of transnational corporate activity which they have—sometimes first-hand—witnessed in Africa, their activist scholarship, and the attendant blurring of the lines between the *lex lata* and the *lex ferenda*, this may be understandable, and even commendable.

At a more theoretical level, this book appears to form part of the Third World Approaches to International Law (TWAIL) movement,[18] even if it does not explicitly adhere to any school or legal movement. It is recalled that TWAIL seeks to critique and to change norms of international law that are viewed as serving Western interests to the detriment of the Global South. If a change of law is not immediately available, TWAIL scholars would call for a reinterpretation of the law with a view to serving the interests of the world's downtrodden. In the context of ETOs, this means in the first place abandoning jurisdictional barriers based on territory, casting doubt on the public/private divide, and construing sovereignty as giving rise to duties rather than only rights: states have ETOs 'relating to the acts and omissions of a State, within or beyond its territory, that have effects on the enjoyment of human rights outside of that State's territory'.[19] To the editors' and authors' credit, this volume does however not seek to blame the West—the continent's former colonial masters—for the ills befalling the African continent. Rather, what transpires from a number of contributions is that African states themselves are in typical scenarios *also* to blame for the human rights violations taking place on their territory, at least for violations of economic and social rights, *e.g.*, when leasing land to foreign investors in questionable circumstances. At the end of the day, ETOs are to be conceived of as *subsidiary* obligations resting on bystander states. ETOs should not replace the primary responsibility of the states on whose territory the violations take place.[20]

Concluding, this is a carefully edited collection which forms a coherent whole. The individual contributions are well-written and contain a wealth of doctrinal insights and empirical information. The editors and contributors deserve particular credit for highlighting the ETO potential of the ACHPR, the refined reasoning of the African Commission (largely unknown outside Africa), and the extant and potential interactions between the African human rights system and other regional or universal systems. The voices of the new generation of African (and Africa-minded) scholars who have contributed to this volume deserve a wide audience.

[18]See on TWAIL, *e.g.*, Gathii (2011), pp. 26–48.

[19]Maastricht Principles, para. 8(a).

[20]Obviously, to the extent that foreign states exercise effective territorial or personal control to the exclusion of the territorial state, *e.g.*, in situations of occupation, these foreign states will have primary human rights obligations.

References

Agulanna C (2010) Community and human well-being in an African culture. Trames 14(64/59), 3:282–298

Committee on Economic, Social and Cultural Rights (2017) General Comment No. 24 on State Obligations under the International Covenant on Economic, Social and Cultural Rights in the Context of Business Activities (10 August 2017). UN Doc. E/C.12/GC/24

Emerson R (1962) Pan-Africanism. Int Organ 16(2):275–290

Gathii JT (2011) TWAIL: a brief history of its origins, its decentralized network and a tentative bibliography. Trade Law Dev 3(1):26–48

International Commission of Jurists (2011) Maastricht principles on extraterritorial obligations of states in the area of economic, social and cultural rights. FIAN International, Heidelberg

Kasanda A (2016) Exploring Pan-Africanism's theories: from race-based solidarity to political unity and beyond. J Afr Cult Stud 28(2):179–195

Langford M et al (2013) Global justice, state duties: the extraterritorial scope of economic, social, and cultural rights in international law. CUP, Cambridge

Methven O'Brien C (2018) The home state duty to regulate the human rights impacts of TNCs abroad: a rebuttal. Bus Human Rights J 3(47–73):72

Roberts A (2017) Is international law international? OUP, Oxford

What's your secret nationality? (2018) BBC (10 July 2018). http://www.bbc.com/future/story/20180409-whats-your-secret-nationality. Accessed 16 July 2018

Cedric Ryngaert (PhD Leuven 2007) is Chair of Public International Law at Utrecht University (Netherlands) and Head of the Department of International and European Law of the University's Law School.

James Nyawo: *Selective Enforcement and International Criminal Law: The International Criminal Court and Africa*

Intersentia 2017, 288 Pages

Chris Maina Peter

Those campaigning against the ICC, just because it is prosecuting one of them, want to take the continent back to 1970s. They are seeking a licence to kill and maim and oppress their people without consequences.

—Archbishop Emeritus Desmond Tutu

Whenever serious violations of human rights have occurred, the tendency of the international community has been to treat such occurrences as separate accidents and hence to establish *ad hoc* mechanisms to deal with them. This explains the establishment of institutions such as the Nuremberg, Tokyo, Yugoslavia and Rwanda Tribunals, to mention but a few. Due to their *ad hoc* nature, these institutions had a life span only as long as the adjudication of the case they were assigned to see.

The adoption of the Rome Statute in 1998 completely changed history, as it established, for the first time, a permanent institution to address serious human rights violations i.e. genocide, crimes against humanity, war crimes, and later aggression. Four years later in 2002 the Statute entered into force and the International Criminal Court (ICC) was born. This new institution was a game changer. It provided no immunity to any person notwithstanding their office. Article 27(1) was explicit in that the Statute would apply to "all persons without any distinction based on official capacity. In particular, official capacity as a Head of State or Government, a member of a Government or parliament, an elected representative or a government official shall in no case exempt a person from criminal responsibility under this Statute, nor shall it, in and of itself, constitute a ground for reduction of sentence." This was a threat to all in power.

C. M. Peter (✉)
United Nations International Law Commission (ILC), Geneva, Switzerland

School of Law, University of Dar es Salaam, Dar es Salaam, Tanzania
e-mail: peter1404@gmail.com

Z. Yihdego et al. (eds.), *Ethiopian Yearbook of International Law 2018*, Ethiopian Yearbook of International Law 2018, https://doi.org/10.1007/978-3-030-24078-3_11

It is these 17 years of existence of the Court and its performance which is being examined in the book under review. The question being whether the ICC is a fair institution or whether it selectively exercises its jurisdiction.

The book is divided into eight chapters. Following the introduction, which maps the contents of the book, chapter two deals with the establishment of the ICC, and in particular the role of the African continent in its establishment and its early support. In chapter three, the focus of the book then shifts to the Office of the Prosecutor of the Court and the politics involved in choosing where to direct prosecutions. The referrals by the United Nations Security Council to the Court and the selection of situations are considered in chapter four. Chapter five criticises the achievements attained thus far and assesses the selective enforcement by the Court from an admissibility perspective. The new attitude of African states towards the court is addressed in chapter six, noting a shift from co-operation with the Court to non-co-operation due, allegedly, to the focus of the Court's activities mainly on the African continent. The lack of a common position by Africa on the Court and proposals to "correct" the Rome Statute through amendment—particularly on the deferrals—is examined in chapter seven of the book. The book, in chapter eight, ends with lessons that Africa has learned from its interaction with the ICC over the last 20 years.

The book has a helpful index. The bibliography, however, is not up to date as it does not include some current literature on this topic. However, this might be as a result of a time lapse between submission of the manuscript and the actual publication time of the book.

The book's key themes revolve primarily around four areas. The first explores Africa's initial support of the Rome Statute. Africa played a leading role in the negotiations that led to the adoption of the Rome Statute in 1998. It is therefore not surprising that Africa, with 34 out of 55 members of the African Union, forms the strongest block in the State Parties to the Rome Statute. This was mainly due to impunity which was entrenching itself on the continent. The new court was therefore seen as an alternative to address this dire situation.

It was due to this belief that some of the early cases in the Court were in fact filed by African States. This includes the case brought against the Lord's Resistance Army in Uganda. Following a reference by the Government of Uganda, a Warrant for the Arrest of Joseph Kony was issued on 8 July 2005 and amended on 27 September 2005 by Pre-Trial Chamber II. Other cases were brought by the Democratic Republic of the Congo, Central African Republic and Mali. This was an indication of the confidence of leaders on the continent in the new court.

However, this love affair between Africa and the Court did not last long. Soon it became clear that the new court, under the guidance of its first Prosecutor Luis Moreno Ocampo, was concentrating all its efforts on the African continent. This observation is not without substance. The ICC has received complaints relating to alleged crimes from a number of countries across the globe. However, for unknown reasons, the Office of the Prosecutor only opened investigations into situations in Africa. These include cases in the Democratic Republic of the Congo, Uganda, the Central African Republic, Darfur, Sudan, the Republic of Kenya, the Libyan Arab Jamahiriya, the Republic of Côte d'Ivoire and Mali. In addition, by Power of Attorney from the Union of the Comoros, a law firm referred the situation on the

Comorian-flagged *MV Mavi Marmara* vessel to the Court, prompting the Prosecutor to initiate a preliminary examination.

The second important area of the book discusses the issue of targeting African rulers. African States watched the work of the ICC silently and with uneasiness. It was the targeting of rulers in office that 'broke the camel's back'. It began with the issuance of a warrant of arrest against the President of Sudan, Omar Hassan Ahmed Al-Bashir, who was being sought in connection with serious crimes allegedly committed in the Western Region of Darfur (*Prosecutor v. Omar Hassan Ahmad Al-Bashir* (ICC-02/05-01/09-1). Interestingly, Sudan is not party to the Rome Statute. Taking a case against Al-Bashir was an initiative of the UN Security Council.

The second-high profile case was that of Kenya. Following the general election of December 2007 there were serious ethnic clashes in which about 1200 people lost their lives and many more were injured. Property worth millions of shillings was destroyed and a number of citizens were internally displaced. Following the violence, a thorough investigation was conducted by Hon. Mr. Justice Philip Waki, a senior member of the Kenyan judiciary. The investigation identified six persons as the ringleaders of the whole ethnic fracas. Their names were placed in an envelope which was given to the mediator of this crisis, former UN Secretary General, the late Kofi Annan. On his part Annan recommended to the government of Kenya to undertake serious accountability measures against all those implicated in the post-election violence. The recommendation was ignored as the government of Kenya was unwilling to conduct an effective or credible prosecution.

Eventually, Kofi Annan handed over the envelope with the names of the suspects to the ICC. These included high-profile politicians Uhuru Muigai Kenyatta and William Samoei Ruto, who were later elected president and deputy president of Kenya respectively. They were charged in *The Prosecutor v. Francis Kirimi Muthaura and Uhuru Muigai Kenyatta*, ICC-01/09-02/11; and *The Prosecutor v. William Samoei Ruto and Joshua Arap Sang*, ICC-01/09-01/11 respectively. These two cases from Sudan and Kenya indicated that the ICC was serious. The author of the book notes that these and other cases from the continent also galvanised African rulers and the elite in general against the Court. This thinking was confirmed by other cases including those of concerning the Libyan Arab Jamahiriya, the Republic of Côte d'Ivoire and others. The selective prosecution of African leaders provoked a thinking that Africans had to stand as in solidarity against the Court. Hence, assistance had to be sought at both regional and sub-regional levels.

The third area of focus has been on Africa's threat to leave the ICC. The issue of the pursuit of African leaders by the ICC was placed on the agenda of the African Union. The African leaders felt that if nothing was done, the court would come for the next head of state or government and the process would be an unstoppable flood towards The Hague. The AU, invoking Article 16 of the Rome Statute, requested deferral of both the investigation and prosecution of African rulers in office.

This request was flatly rejected. This was an embarrassment for the African leaders, hence solidarity amongst members of the AU was required to protect the continent. The campaign was spear-headed by Kenya and strongly supported by

Rwanda (which is not a party to the Rome Statute) for African States to leave the ICC *en masse*. There was a lot of support for this course of action in the speeches of the various heads of state and government.

This was mainly due to the fact that the operation of the Court had become a major disappointment to many African States. The main complaint was that the new Court was unfairly targeting the continent. The Court was turning a blind eye to violations of human rights and particularly the commission of serious crimes in other areas of the world by the powerful in Europe and the Americas. With this double-standard, an alternative to the ICC had to be sought. Africa should be in a position to deal with its own problems of an international nature at home on the continent.

This complaint is the main question being evaluated in this book. Is this a justified complaint and does it have basis?

In an effort to curb the threat posed to them by the ICC, African leaders and the African Union prepared a Protocol which aimed at organising for the exodus of African countries from the Rome Statute and the ICC. This Protocol amends the Protocol on the Statute of the African Court of Justice and Human Rights to give the African Court jurisdiction over serious violations of human rights (Exp/Min/IV/Rev.7 of 15 May 2012). It was prepared by experts and approved by Ministers of Justice/Attorneys General and endorsed by the Heads of State and Government of the African Union. This document was adopted in June 2014 at Malabo, Equatorial Guinea, hence the name—the Malabo Protocol 2014. The author provides his views on this legal instrument underlining the belief that "the majority of African ruling elite are not ready to be held accountable for their actions, whether domestically, regionally or internationally." This is actually the aim and purpose of the Malabo Protocol, 2014.

In brief, the Protocol amends the Statute of the African Court of Justice and Human and Peoples' Rights to add a criminal jurisdiction. Draft Article 28A gives the Court powers to try persons charged with any one of the 14 crimes enumerated in the Protocol. These are Genocide, Crimes against Humanity, War Crimes, the Crime of Unconstitutional Change of Government, Piracy, Terrorism, Mercenarism, Corruption, Money Laundering, Trafficking in Persons, Trafficking in Drugs, Trafficking in Hazardous Wastes, Illicit Exploitation of Natural Resources, and the Crime of Aggression. Then, from Articles 28B to 28M these crimes are elaborated at length. An interesting fact is that the main offences provided here in the Protocol are those currently being handled by the ICC. It was, therefore, created to serve as a political point that Africa can handle its own affairs and it does not need the ICC.

At sub-regional level, there was action too. In a similar manner as the African Union, the members of the East African Community decided to give their own court, the East African Court of Justice (EACJ) jurisdiction over serious crimes, similar to those handled by the ICC. This was a strange decision because the same governments have for years denied this court a human rights jurisdiction despite the fact that such jurisdiction is envisaged under the 1999 treaty establishing the East African Community.

The fourth area that the book addresses is the failure of unity and short-term interests of African states. As the author notes, it is not easy to understand the behaviour and actions of the member states of the African Union. It would seem that none of their actions related to the work of the International Criminal Court were intended to have a logical conclusion.

To appreciate the absurdity of the situation, one needs to soberly examine the development of the dispute settlement system in the African Union. In 2000 the Constitutive Act of the African Union set to establish an African Court of Justice, which, unfortunately, was never established. In the meantime, Africa had a functioning African Court of Human and Peoples' Rights established in 1998 through a Protocol to the African Charter on Human and Peoples' Rights of 1981. This Court is operational and sits in Arusha Tanzania. In 2008, the African Union decided to merge the two courts i.e. the African Court of Justice and the African Court on Human and Peoples' Rights to create the African Court of Justice and Human Rights. This was done through a 2008 protocol. The Malabo Protocol is built on this 2008 merger protocol, which as a result is titled Protocol on Amendments to the Protocol on the Statute of the African Court of Justice and Human Rights. It is therefore a protocol amending another protocol.

The question then is what is the legal status of the Protocol that merges the two courts and on which Malabo Protocol is based? As of November 2018, the Protocol establishing the African Court of Justice and Human Rights of 2008 was signed by 31 of the 55 members of the African Union. While a total of 15 ratifications is required to bring the Protocol in to force, only 6 AU member countries ratified it. It, therefore, has not yet entered into force although 10 years have lapsed since its adoption. This raises a serious legal question. Can a protocol be based on another protocol which has not yet entered in force? Whatever the answer is, the Malabo Protocol is put on a very shaky ground as it is built on a "legal document" which is not yet in force and thus, of questionable legal value.

What is equally worrying is the fact that the legal status of the Malabo Protocol itself is highly questionable. The Protocol was adopted on 27 June 2014 about 5 years ago. However, only 11 states out of the 55 AU members have signed it and none have ratified it. Yet, this is the legal instrument intended to replace the Rome Statute and establish a mechanism to address serious crimes, thus removing the ICC from the continent once and for all. This is a very unfortunate legal situation which casts doubts on the seriousness of the continent. It is one thing to complain and another to undertake serious measures.

The author argues that things may be as they are due to the political dynamics that led to the ICC's establishment, particularly the withdrawal of some of the powerful countries after they failed to extract concessions in Rome. Based on this, one valuable recommendation the author makes is for African countries to address serious crimes committed in their territories instead of looking for ways to avoid the ICC. The ICC is not a court of first instance. It becomes relevant only where the State involved is either incapable or unwilling to act. Therefore, if African states are willing and capable of handling these serious crimes, they will never cross ways with the ICC. Even where they are incapable, they could be assisted.

The author also suggests that the ICC Prosecutor should be fair and look beyond Africa. There are serious crimes being committed across the globe. Africa should not be an easy pick for the Court. The Office of the Prosecutor should be open- minded in order to remove the existing belief, which is not entirely unfounded, that it is being manipulated by the strong western States through the UN Security Council.

It is the belief of the reviewer that the book makes a valuable contribution to knowledge. The book is easy to read and scientifically written with very well-thought and balanced commentary on the performance of the Court. It raises many fundamental issues including the legitimacy of the wide powers enjoyed by institutions like the United Nations Security Council to refer matters to the Court, while some of its permanent members are in fact not parties to the Rome Statute and do not contribute to the budget for running the Court. The book also exposes the absurdity of the attempts by African states to replace the ICC in Africa through the Malabo Protocol which they have abandoned before its implementation. It ends by suggesting a balance between politics and justice in addressing international criminal law.

This book makes a considerable contribution to enhancing our understanding of not only international criminal justice but also the performance of the first permanent international criminal institution in its first decade plus of existence. It should therefore be on the shelves of academics, students, judges, politicians and common citizens in Africa and beyond.

Chris Maina Peter is a Professor of Law, School of Law, University of Dar es Salaam, Tanzania and currently a Member, United Nations International Law Commission (ILC), Geneva, Switzerland. Professor Peter has written and edited several books and articles in scholarly journals. His most recent publications include: “Fighting Impunity: African States and the International Criminal Court,” in ANKUMAH, Evelyn (ed.), *The International Criminal Court and Africa: One Decade On*, Cambridge: Intersentia Ltd., 2016, p. 1. He is also the Managing Editor of the *Zanzibar Yearbook of Law* (ZYBL) published by Zanzibar Legal Services Centre (ZLSC) in Zanzibar, Tanzania.

Part IV
UN and Other Bilateral Documents

Peace Agreements Between Ethiopia and Eritrea: Ending Two Decades of Hostilities—An Introductory Note

Melaku Geboye Desta

Abstract Following the appointment of Abiy Ahmed as Prime Minister of Ethiopia in April 2018, a number of encouraging political developments have unfolded in Ethiopia and the Horn of Africa region. This short note introduces the peace accord concluded between Ethiopia and Eritrea soon after Prime Minister Abiy came to power and its broader ramifications for the Horn region.

1 Introduction

In a *Joint Declaration of Peace and Friendship* that was signed on 9 July 2018 in Asmara, Eritrea, and a subsequent *Agreement on Peace, Friendship and Comprehensive Cooperation Between the Federal Democratic Republic of Ethiopia and the State of Eritrea* signed on 16 September 2018 in Jeddah, Saudi Arabia, the leaders of Ethiopia and Eritrea brought two decades of stalemate in their bilateral relations to an end. Following the conclusion of these agreements, a number of significant developments swept across the sub-region, including (i) opening up of the borders between Ethiopia and Eritrea and resumption of flights between Addis Ababa and Asmara; (ii) restoration of Eritrea's bilateral relations with neighbouring Djibouti, as well as with Somalia; and (iii) the lifting by the United Nations Security Council of sanctions on Eritrea.

M. G. Desta (✉)
Leicester De Montfort School of Law, Faculty of Business and Law, De Montfort University, Leicester, UK

United Nations Economic Commission for Africa, Addis Ababa, Ethiopia
e-mail: melaku.desta@dmu.ac.uk

Z. Yihdego et al. (eds.), *Ethiopian Yearbook of International Law 2018*, Ethiopian Yearbook of International Law 2018, https://doi.org/10.1007/978-3-030-24078-3_12

2 Background

Eritrea, formerly Ethiopia's northern most and coastal province on the Red Sea, declared its independence on 24 May 1993 following a referendum organised to that effect. The referendum itself was organised after the Ethiopian People's Revolutionary Democratic Front (EPRDF), on the one hand, and the Eritrean People's Liberation Front (EPLF), the ruling parties in the respective countries to this day, fought side by side to remove the military regime in the then united Ethiopia led by Colonel Mengistu Hailemariam. The two groups were close allies in every sense of the term; it was the breakdown in the relations between these former comrades-in-arms that effectively brought the two countries to war in 1998. By the time the war came to an end through the signing of the Algiers Agreement by the two parties on 12 December 2000, its human and economic cost was enormous for both sides.[1]

Under the Algiers Agreement, the warring parties agreed to, inter alia, submit themselves to two independent commissions—a Border Commission to be made up of five independent arbitrators to decide on the delimitation and demarcation of the contested border areas, and a Claims Commission, also to be made up of five independent arbitrators, to consider claims for compensation from both parties and award damages. The Border Commission issued its final award on delimitation of the border on 13 April 2002, which was complete with geographical coordinates of where the actual lines of demarcation would lie.[2]

However, and contrary to the explicit commitment contained in the Algiers Agreement to accept the decision of the Border Commission as final and to ensure the delimitation decision is followed up with "expeditious demarcation", the delimitation decision was never translated into actual demarcation of the physical border due to Ethiopia's insistence on further negotiations. The resulting stalemate of a "no war, no peace" situation—or "state of frozen hostility", as Martin Plaut put it[3]—that continued for over 16 years came to an end only after Abiy Ahmed was sworn in as Prime Minister of Ethiopia on 2 April 2018. The two important agreements signed by the leaders of the two countries in succession are reproduced in this Yearbook: the *Joint Declaration of Peace and Friendship* that was signed on 9 July 2018, and the *Agreement on Peace, Friendship and Comprehensive Cooperation Between the Federal Democratic Republic of Ethiopia and the State of Eritrea* signed in Jeddah, Saudi Arabia 16 September 2018.

The conclusion of these agreements was immediately followed up with several concrete actions on the ground, including official opening of the borders and

---

[1]According to estimates by the International Crisis Group (ICG), the war "took some 100,000 lives between 1998 and 2000". See *Ethiopia and Eritrea: War or Peace? ICG Africa Report N°68* (Nairobi/Brussels, 24 September 2003) available at https://d2071andvip0wj.cloudfront.net/68-ethiopia-and-eritrea-war-or-peace.pdf.

[2]Yiallourides and Yihdego (this volume), pp. 35–62.

[3]See Martin Plaut, "Ethiopia and Eritrea: Returning to War?", *International Journal of Ethiopian Studies*, Vol. 2, No. 1/2 (Summer/Fall 2005–2006), pp. 179–194, at 184.

reunification of families for the first time in almost two decades. These commendable developments, although not without difficulties, were given due recognition by the African Union (AU)[4] as well as the United Nations (UN).[5] On 14 November 2018, the United Nations Security Council unanimously voted to lift sanctions on Eritrea, which had been in place since 2009.[6]

3 Highlights of the Two Agreements

The *Joint Declaration of Peace and Friendship* was signed in Asmara on 9 July 2018 at the conclusion of the first ever visit of an Ethiopian Prime Minister to Eritrea since the war.[7] The *Joint Declaration* underlined the shared history, geography and interests of the two countries, declared an end to the state of war that had been in place for almost two decades, and ushered in the dawn of a “new era of peace and friendship”. These emphatic statements were followed up with aspirational commitments to “endeavor to forge intimate political, economic, social, cultural and security cooperation that serves and advances the vital interests of their peoples”. Finally, through the *Joint Declaration,* the two leaders agreed to resume diplomatic and trade relations, to reopen transport and communications links, and to implement the 2002 Border Commission decision. Equally importantly, the two leaders also appreciated the adverse impact of their hostile bilateral relations on the larger Horn of Africa region and committed themselves to, inter alia, make up for lost time and to work towards regional peace.

The *Agreement on Peace, Friendship and Comprehensive Cooperation* was signed at the port city of Jeddah in the Kingdom of Saudi Arabia on 16 September 2018.[8] The *Jeddah Agreement* effectively subsumed the substantive content of the *Joint Declaration* from Asmara, but also went a step further in at least four ways. Firstly, the Jeddah Agreement supplemented the commitment to resume economic ties with specific and concrete undertakings to develop “joint investment projects,

[4]See AU Assembly Decision on the *Report of the Peace and Security Council on Its Activities and the State of Peace and Security in Africa* (Assembly/AU /Dec.695(XXXI) 31st Ordinary Session, 1 - 2 July 2018) Nouakchott, Mauritania, para. 9.

[5]See *Secretary-General Welcomes Steps by Ethiopia, Eritrea to Normalize Relations*, UN Press Release SG/SM/19098, 21 June 2018, available at https://www.un.org/press/en/2018/sgsm19098.doc.htm.

[6]See Security Council Resolution 2444 (2018) adopted at its 8398th, held on 14 November 2018, available at https://www.un.org/press/en/2018/sc13576.doc.htm. The resolution is reproduced in this volume of the Yearbook see Nicole Hirt's Commentary and Resolution 2444 (this volume) pp. 269–284.

[7]See http://www.shabait.com/news/local-news/26639-joint-declaration-of-peace-and-friendship-between-eritrea-and-ethiopia.

[8]See http://www.shabait.com/news/local-news/27076-agreement-on-peace-friendship-and-comprehensive-cooperation-between-the-federal-democratic-republic-of-ethiopia-and-the-state-of-eritrea.

including the establishment of joint special economic zones". Secondly, in the *Jeddah Agreement* the two countries provided for an institutional mechanism to underpin implementation of their commitments in the form of a High-Level Joint Committee and possible sub-committees as may become necessary. Thirdly, the two parties joined their hosts, the Government of the Kingdom of Saudi Arabia, and issued the *Jeddah Joint Statement* (also reproduced below) with the same date. Finally, the signing of the *Jeddah Agreement* was witnessed by important regional and global leaders, including Rwanda President and then African Union Chairperson Paul Kagame, UN Secretary-General Antonio Guterres, and African Union Commission Chairperson Musa Faki.

4 Regional Significance

The resumption of peace between Ethiopia and Eritrea started paying regional dividends almost immediately. In pursuit of their commitment of 9 July 2018 to work towards regional peace, the leaders of Ethiopia and Eritrea took steps to engage their counterparts in Djibouti and Somalia, two countries with whom Eritrea had severed diplomatic relations for over a decade. The fruits of these exercises came fast. On 5 September 2018, the President of Somalia arrived in Asmara for a tripartite summit with his Ethiopian and Eritrean counterparts, while the presidents of Eritrea and Djibouti held their first face-to-face meeting in over a decade in Jeddah on 17 September 2018. On 13 December 2018, the president of Eritrea arrived in Mogadishu for an official visit. The bilateral peace between Ethiopia and Eritrea has thus led to the restoration of peaceful relations amongst all countries of the Horn of Africa region within just a few months.

5 Conclusion

Ethiopia and Eritrea are united by geography, history, religion, tradition and kinship. At a time when the entire continent of Africa is integrating fast, it probably was only natural and inevitable that these two countries would come together again. Of course, we also know, especially in inter-state relations, that even the inevitable needs the right leadership on both sides before it becomes real. The appointment of Abiy Ahmed as Prime Minister of Ethiopia in April 2018 was the game changer in this respect. Within 6 months of his appointment, Eritrea has resumed peaceful relations with all three countries of the Horn. The resulting peace has created enormous opportunities for both sides to right past wrongs, open a new chapter in their relations for mutual benefit, and put in place mechanisms against backsliding. NO doubt several hurdles will come up on the way towards normalisation of relations, but we have seen that, with the right leadership, nothing is permanently out of reach. However, we also need to realise that leaders come and go, while the two countries and peoples will be there together for ever. A sustainable peace must rest on something more than good leaders; it must be underpinned by enduring principles and strong institutions. History has shown again and again that bilateral relations based on fair and clear rules applied fairly and transparently hold the best promise for a prosperous future in the relations between any two neighbours. This timeless wisdom also applies to the future of these two natural partners—and indeed to the entire Horn region.

Ethiopia-Eritrea Peace Process: Recent Agreements and Joint Statements

July 9, 2018 (from http://www.shabait.com/news/local-news/26639-joint-declaration-of-peace-and-friendship-between-eritrea-and-ethiopia)

Joint Declaration of Peace and Friendship between Eritrea and Ethiopia

Conscious that the peoples of Ethiopia and Eritrea share close bonds of geography, history, culture, language and religion as well as fundamental common interests;

Recognizing that over the past decades, they were denied the opportunity to build a bright future for their peoples on the basis of their common heritage;

Determined to close this very costly chapter, which also had a detrimental role in the Horn of Africa, and to make up for lost opportunities and create even bigger golden opportunities for their peoples;

The governments of Ethiopia and Eritrea have reached the following joint agreement which reflects the desires and aspirations of their peoples:

1. The state of war between Ethiopia and Eritrea has come to an end. A new era of peace and friendship has been opened.
2. The two governments will endeavor to forge intimate political, economic, social, cultural and security cooperation that serves and advances the vital interests of their peoples;
3. Transport, trade and communications links between the two countries will resume; diplomatic ties and activities will restart;
4. The decision on the boundary between the two countries will be implemented.
5. Both countries will jointly endeavor to ensure regional peace, development and cooperation.

Both governments express their gratitude to all friends of Eritrea and Ethiopia and call on them to redouble their solidarity and support.

Done in Asmara, July 9, 2018

For the State of Eritrea	For the Federal Democratic Republic of Ethiopia
President Isaias Afwerki	Prime Minister Dr. Abiy Ahmed Ali

Agreement on Peace, Friendship and Comprehensive Cooperation Between the Federal Democratic Republic of Ethiopia and the State of Eritrea (Source: http://www.shabait.com/news/local-news/27076-agreement-on-peace-friendship-and-comprehensive-cooperation-between-the-federal-democratic-republic-of-ethiopia-and-the-state-of-eritrea)

The Federal Democratic Republic of Ethiopia and the State of Eritrea, hereinafter referred to as the Two Parties;

Considering the close bonds of geography, history, culture and religion between the two countries and their peoples;

Respecting each other's independence, sovereignty and territorial integrity;

Desiring to achieve lasting peace and cement their historical ties to achieve their lofty objectives; Determined to establish comprehensive cooperation on the basis of complementarity and synergy; Determined further to contribute actively to regional and global peace and security;

Reaffirming the Joint Declaration on Peace and Friendship that they signed on July 9, 2018 in Asmara; Reiterating their commitment to the principles and purposes of the Charter of the United Nations;

The Two Parties agree as follows:

Article One

The state of war between the two countries has ended and a new era of peace, friendship and comprehensive cooperation has started.

Article Two

The two countries will promote comprehensive cooperation in the political, security, defense, economic, trade, investment, cultural and social fields on the basis of complementarity and synergy.

Article Three

The two countries will develop Joint Investment Projects, including the establishment of Joint Special Economic Zones.

Article Four

The two countries will implement the Eritrea-Ethiopia Boundary Commission decision.

Article Five

The two countries will promote regional and global peace, security and cooperation.

Article Six

The two countries will combat terrorism as well as trafficking in people, arms and drugs in accordance with international covenants and conventions.

Article Seven

The two countries will establish a High-Level Joint Committee, as well as Sub-committees as required, to guide and oversee the implementation of this Agreement.

This Agreement is made at Jeddah, Kingdom of Saudi Arabia on this day of September 16, 2018 in two original copies in Amharic, Tigrinya, Arabic and English languages; in case of discrepancy in interpretation, the English version shall prevail.

For The Federal Democratic Republic of Ethiopia	Abiy Ahmed Ali, Prime Minister
For The State of Eritrea	Isaias Afwerki, President

****

Jeddah Joint Statement, 16 September 2018 (Source: http://addisstandard.com/full-text-of-the-ethio-eritrea-agreement-signed-in-jeddah/)

A Joint Statement on Jeddah Reconciliation and Cooperation Agreement between the Federal Democratic Republic of Ethiopia, and the State of Eritrea

In light of well-established relations between the Kingdom of Saudi Arabia, the Federal Democratic Republic of Ethiopia, and the State of Eritrea, and given the Kingdom of Saudi Arabia's firm interest to ensure peace, security, and stability between the two countries, a meeting was convened this day of Sunday, 16 September 2018 (corresponding to 6/1/1440H) between the Custodian of the Two Holy Mosques, King Salman bin Abdulaziz Al Saud, the King of the Kingdom of Saudi Arabia, His Excellency the President of the State of Eritrea, President Isaias Afewerki, and His Excellency the Prime Minister of the Federal Democratic Republic of Ethiopia, Abiy Ahmed, at Al-Salam Palace in Jeddah, Saudi Arabia. The meeting was attended by the African Union Chairperson, His Excellency the President of the Republic of Rwanda, President Paul Kagame, His Excellency the United Nations Secretary-General, and the Chairpersons of the African Union Commission (AUC), the Intergovernmental Authority on Development (IGAD), and the Common Market for Eastern and Southern Africa (COMESA).

The two leaders expressed their appreciation for the tremendous and continued efforts of the Custodian of the Two Holy Mosques, King Salman bin Abdulaziz Al Saud, the King of the Kingdom of Saudi Arabia, and HRH Prince Mohammed bin Salman bin Abdulaziz Al Saud, the Crown Prince, First Deputy Prime Minister and

Minister of Defence over the past few months to achieve a reconciliation between the two nations and end a 20-year conflict [between them].

Those efforts resulted in restoration of normal relations between the countries, on the basis of the close bonds of geography, history, culture and religion between the two nations and their peoples. With the Grace of God, tireless reconciliation efforts have culminated in the restoration of the brotherly relations between the two countries, thus forming the foundation for a new phase that will- God willing- bring significant developments in the relations between the two nations in all fields.

The Custodian of the Two Holy Mosques welcomed the signing of Jeddah Agreement between the two countries, expressing hope that this Agreement would strengthen the ties of friendship and cooperation between them, thus achieving peace and security for the two countries and reflect positively on the security and stability of the whole region.

References

Algiers Agreement of December 2000

AU Assembly Decision on the *Report of the Peace and Security Council on Its Activities and the State of Peace and Security in Africa* (Assembly/AU /Dec.695(XXXI) 31st Ordinary Session, 1 - 2 July 2018) Nouakchott, Mauritania, para. 9

Ethiopia and Eritrea: War or Peace? ICG Africa Report N°68 (Nairobi/Brussels, 24 September 2003). Available at https://d2071andvip0wj.cloudfront.net/68-ethiopia-and-eritrea-war-or-peace.pdf

Hirt N (this volume) Commentary: UN Security Council Resolution 2444 (2018) and the lifting of sanctions against Eritrea: a commentary on domestic and regional perspectives. In: Yihdego Z, Desta MG, Hailu MB (eds) Ethiopian Yearbook of International Law 2018: in pursuit of peace and prosperity. Springer, Cham, pp 269–284

http://www.shabait.com/news/local-news/26639-joint-declaration-of-peace-and-friendship-between-eritrea-and-ethiopia

http://www.shabait.com/news/local-news/27076-agreement-on-peace-friendship-and-comprehensive-cooperation-between-the-federal-democratic-republic-of-ethiopia-and-the-state-of-eritrea

Plaut M (Summer/Fall 2005–2006) Ethiopia and Eritrea: returning to War? Int J Ethiopian Stud 2 (1/2):179–194

Secretary-General Welcomes Steps by Ethiopia, Eritrea to Normalize Relations, UN Press Release SG/SM/19098, 21 June 2018., available at https://www.un.org/press/en/2018/sgsm19098.doc.htm

Security Council Resolution 2444 (2018) Adopted at its 8398th, held on 14 November 2018, available at https://www.un.org/press/en/2018/sc13576.doc.htm (Reproduced in this volume of the Yearbook in pp 269–284)

Yiallourides C, Yihdego Z (this volume) Disputed territories and the law on the use of force: lessons from the Eritrea-Ethiopia case. In: Yihdego Z, Desta MG, Hailu MB (eds) Ethiopian Yearbook of International Law 2018: in pursuit of peace and prosperity. Springer, Cham, pp 35–62

Melaku Geboye Desta is Professor of International Economic Law at Leicester De Montfort University School of Law, Leicester, UK, and co-edits the Ethiopian Yearbook of International Law.

Commentary: UN Security Council Resolution 2444 (2018) and the Lifting of Sanctions Against Eritrea: A Commentary on Domestic and Regional Perspectives

Nicole Hirt

Abstract In 2009 the UN Security Council imposed sanctions on Eritrea in response to the country's alleged support of the Al-Shabaab militias in Somalia. This must be seen against the background of the unresolved conflict between Eritrea and Ethiopia, the latter having been the mastermind behind the sanctions, although they were officially promoted by the AU and the Intergovernmental Agency for Development (IGAD). The sanctions imposed through resolution 1907 (2009) were targeted sanctions, and de facto the only implemented component was an arms embargo. The Eritrean government called the sanctions "unjust and illegal" and used them to garner support among the Eritrean diaspora, calling for a "resolute national rebuff". In 2011 the sanctions were tightened, scrutinizing the Eritrean two percent diaspora tax and its possible use to destabilize the Horn of Africa region. However, the government did not comply with the UNSC's demands and continued to collect financial resources from diaspora Eritreans. In 2018, Ethiopia's Prime Minister Abiy Ahmed initiated a political rapprochement and a peace agreement between the former foes, and as a result, the sanctions imposed on Eritrea were lifted during the same year, again on the initiative of the Ethiopian government.

1 The Background and Nature of the Sanctions

On 23 December 2009, the UN Security Council passed resolution 1907 (2009), imposing sanctions on Eritrea in response to the country's alleged support for extremist Al-Shabaab militias in Somalia and its refusal to cooperate with Djibouti to find a solution to the border conflict between both countries and to withdraw

N. Hirt (✉)
GIGA German Institute of Global and Area Studies, Institute of African Affairs, Hamburg, Germany
e-mail: nicole.hirt@giga-hamburg.de

Z. Yihdego et al. (eds.), *Ethiopian Yearbook of International Law 2018*, Ethiopian Yearbook of International Law 2018, https://doi.org/10.1007/978-3-030-24078-3_13

troops from the contested areas.[1] It was the first time in African history that two regional organisations, namely the Horn of Africa's regional organisation Intergovernmental Agency for Development (IGAD) and the African Union (AU) had demanded sanctions against one of their member states. This development must be seen against the background of the unresolved conflict between Ethiopia and Eritrea. The two nations had fought a devastating border war that claimed up to 100,000 lives from 1998 to 2000,[2] and remained in an uneasy "no war no peace" relation when Ethiopia refused to implement an international border verdict issued in 2002 by the Eritrea-Ethiopia Boundary Commission (EEBC). The Ethiopian government accepted the ruling 'in principle', but demanded a dialogue about certain aspects of the ruling, which Eritrea denied, pointing out that the EEBC's decision was final and binding. The period following 9/11 2001 was marked by an extension of the "War against Terror" to the Horn of Arica, where Ethiopia became the major ally of the Bush administration against militant Islamism, much to the dismay of Eritrea, which had sought closer ties to the United States in previous years.[3] In 2006 Ethiopia invaded Somalia with the support of the US to back the Provisional Government of Somalia (PGS) against the United Islamic Courts (UIC) which had taken control over Mogadishu with the justification that it was acting in self-defence against Islamist forces that threatened peace and stability in the region. Eritrea sided with the UIC, arguing that the UIC had brought stability to the country, while the PGS was dominated by warlords. It also withdrew from IGAD and AU in protest of both organisation's support for Ethiopia's military operations. This act of self-isolation should have severe consequences for Eritrea: Ethiopia, which pursued a strategy of weakening its arch-enemy, used its influence in the regional bodies and was the acting force behind their proposal to impose sanctions on Eritrea that were supposed to weaken its military capacities decisively. Djibouti, which had been involved in an armed border conflict with Eritrea in 2008 also strongly supported a sanction regime against its neighbour. Accordingly, with the support of the United States, but also of the United Kingdom and even Russia, the Security Council imposed sanctions in response to Eritrea's alleged support to the Islamist Al-Shabaab militias that had emerged in Somalia after the UIC had been ousted from power.[4]

The sanctions imposed through resolution 1907 (2009) were targeted sanctions, namely an arms embargo, and in theory they provided for asset freezes and travel bans against leading figures of the Eritrean ruling elite. However, only the first component was implemented by the international community. The aim was to deprive Eritrea of its military capability to threaten the stability of the Horn of Africa by supporting Al-Shabaab and other militant groups, mainly some armed Ethiopian opposition groups hosted by the Eritrean government.[5] Two years later, the UN

[1]See UNSC (2009).

[2]See Gilkes and Plaut (2000), pp. 1–6; Negash and Tronvoll (2000).

[3]See Hirt (2008), pp. 222–235.

[4]See Hirt (2009), pp. 321–322.

[5]See UNSC (2017).

Security Council tightened the sanctions by passing resolution 2023 (2011),[6] which scrutinizes the Eritrean two percent diaspora tax. It demands that the country stop collecting the tax by coercion and demands Member States to make sure that funds derived from the tax are not going to be used to destabilize the Horn of Africa. It also demands that Eritrea stops to directly or indirectly destabilize states in the region and resolve border conflicts with its neighbours peacefully.

In the same year, the Security Council established the Monitoring Group on Somalia and Eritrea (SEMG) through resolution 2002 (2011).[7] Its mandate was to monitor the upkeeping of the arms embargo and to observe if Eritrea was compliant with the demands of the sanction regimes. In its first report dated 27 June 2012,[8] it stated that Eritrea had not directly support the al-Shabaab militias in Somalia but had failed to comply with the sanctions resolutions in different aspects by supporting armed Ethiopian opposition groups, namely the Ogaden National Liberation Front and the Oromo Liberation Front. It also stated that the Eritrean government continued to collect taxes and donations from the diaspora through coercive means and that there was no transparency regarding the purposes on which these revenues were spent.

2 National and Regional Implications

Not entirely without reason, the Eritrean government felt being treated unfairly, since Ethiopia had not faced any criticism for violating Somali's sovereignty in 2006 and reacted harshly to the "unjust and illegal sanctions" as it branded them. It also argued that the sanction regime was masterminded by the US and was part of an ongoing conspiracy against the Eritrean nation.[9] Regionally, the sanctions did not cause any major shifts, since Eritrea had already isolated itself by withdrawing from IGAD and the AU, and its conscripted army was in no condition to wage another war; accordingly, the arms embargo did not yield significant results. On the other hand, the Eritrean regime used the sanctions to boost diaspora engagement by calling for a "resolute national rebuff". Eritrea has a very large diaspora comprising about one third up to one half of its population, mostly from the refugees of the independence struggle and second-generation diaspora Eritreans spread across all continents. They have been obliged to pay two percent of their income as diaspora tax, and now the transnational government organisations urged them to make additional contributions to counter anti-Eritrean conspiracies such as the sanctions. Although opposition groups in the diaspora lobbied against the tax and the demand for further contributions and the 2011 sanction regime prohibited the collection of the tax by

[6]See UNSC (2011a).

[7]See UNSC (2011b).

[8]See Monitoring Group on Somalia and Eritrea (2012).

[9]See Hirt (2009), p. 322.

coercion, the government did not defer to the international community's demands and used informal ways to collect the diaspora tax and other contributions.[10] It is therefore inaccurate to claim that the sanctions caused economic hardships for the population, as the narrative of the government goes. Even the political and military elite were hardly affected, since no asset freezes and travel bans were implemented.

3 Effects of the Targeted Sanctions

The impact of the sanctions has never been very significant, contrary to what the Eritrean government tried to make its diaspora and the international community believe. The government had purchased large quantities of arms during the border war with Ethiopia, and its destructive interior policies of societal militarization through an open-ended military and national service led to the deterioration of the economy. A large portion of the adult population was forced to serve for years without noteworthy renumeration, and the morale of the Eritrean Defence Forces was low. There were no economic sanctions in place, and the government could easily bypass the restrictions concerning the collection of the two percent diaspora tax through its transnational institutions. Currently, the government can no longer build on the threat scenario it has built up to mobilise the diaspora for its own purposes. Since the tale of the "Ethiopian threat" has been u-turned into a narrative of peace and friendship, demands for internal reforms have grown louder among diaspora Eritreans who are asking for a time-limitation of the national service, the release of political prisoners and the implementation of the constitution. However, at the moment, it seems that the lifting of the sanctions has not changed much inside Eritrea. At the same time, government will now be able to import arms without scrutiny, which might lead to new risks if other destabilizing events will occur within the volatile Horn of Africa region.

4 Key Elements of Resolution 2444 (2018)

After sixteen years of political stalemate and a prevailing 'no war, no peace' situation between Eritrea and Ethiopia, the newly elected Ethiopian Prime Minster Abiy Ahmed took a surprising move and pledged to accept the border decision of the EEBC that awarded the town of Badme to Eritrea in June 2018. He invited President Isaias Afewerki to Addis Ababa, and in July both leaders signed a Joint Declaration of Peace and Friendship in Asmara.[11] His initiative was backed by Saudi Arabia and the UAE who have partnered with Eritrea in their war against the Houthis in Yemen

[10]See Hirt (2014), p. 129.

[11]See Eritrean Ministry of Information (2018).

and using the Eritrean port of Assab as a military base. There are also forces in the US government who want "to bring Eritrea in from the cold",[12] among them is President Trump's current security adviser John Bolton. Besides making peace with Eritrea, Abiy managed to bring the presidents of Eritrea and Djibouti together, and during a meeting in Jeddah both pledged to settle their border dispute peacefully. This having been achieved, there were no more reasons for upholding the sanctions, and Ethiopia now lobbied at the UNSC to terminate them. Accordingly, resolution 2444 (2018), which lifts the sanctions on Eritrea, was adopted unanimously in November 2018.[13] It argues that there has been no Eritrean support for Al-Shabaab for years, and there has been a rapprochement between Eritrea and Djibouti, although the border issue has yet to be resolved and some Djiboutian POWs are still missing. UNSC Resolution 2444 has others aspects that focus on Somalia which were not the focus of this commentary.

[12]This thread of argument was first brought up by Hank Cohen, former Assistant Secretary of State for Africa, see Cohen (2013).

[13]See UNSC (2018).

Resolution 2444 (2018)

Adopted by the Security Council at Its 8398th Meeting, on 14 November 2018

The Security Council,

Recalling all its previous resolutions and statements of its President on the situation in Somalia and Eritrea, in particular resolutions 733 (1992), 1844 (2008), 1907 (2009), 2023 (2011), 2036 (2012), 2093 (2013), 2111 (2013), 2124 (2013), 2125 (2013), 2142 (2014), 2182 (2014), 2244 (2015), 2317 (2016) and 2385 (2017),

Taking note of the final reports of the Somalia and Eritrea Monitoring Group (the SEMG) on Somalia (S/2018/1002) and Eritrea (S/2018/1003) and their conclusions on the situations in Somalia and Eritrea,

Reaffirming its respect for the sovereignty, territorial integrity, political independence and unity of Somalia, Djibouti and Eritrea, and underscoring the importance of working to prevent destabilising effects of regional crises and disputes from spilling over into Somalia,

Condemning Al-Shabaab attacks in Somalia and beyond, *expressing concern* that Al-Shabaab continues to pose a serious threat to the peace and stability of Somalia and the region, and *further expressing concern* at the presence of affiliates linked to Islamic State in Iraq and the Levant (ISIL, also known as Da'esh) and the security implications of the situation in Yemen for Somalia,

Reaffirming the need to combat by all means, in accordance with the Charter of the United Nations and international law, including applicable international human rights law, international refugee law, and international humanitarian law, threats to international peace and security caused by terrorist acts,

Underlining its support for the efforts of the Somali authorities to deliver stability and security in Somalia and to reduce the threats to peace and security posed by Al-Shabaab and affiliates linked to ISIL (also known as Da'esh),

Condemning any flows of weapons and ammunition supplies to and through Somalia in violation of the arms embargo on Somalia, including when they result in supplies to Al-Shabaab and affiliates linked to ISIL (also known as Da'esh) and when they undermine the sovereignty and territorial integrity of Somalia, as a serious threat to peace and stability in the region, and *expressing concern* at reports of increased illegal flows of weapons and ammunition supplies from Yemen to Somalia,

Welcoming the cooperation between the Federal Government of Somalia (FGS), the Federal Member States (FMSs), and the SEMG, and *underlining* the importance of these relationships improving further and strengthening in the future,

Welcoming the development of a conditions-based transition plan with clear target dates for the progressive transfer of security responsibilities from the African Union Mission in Somalia (AMISOM) to the Somali security institutions and forces, *calling for* its swift and coordinated implementation with full participation from all stakeholders, and *recalling* the critical importance of accelerating the implementation of the National Security Architecture agreement between the FGS and the FMSs, including decisions to define the composition and roles of Somalia's security forces and to integrate and provide federal support to regional forces, in order to provide the foundation for a successful transition to Somali-led security,

Taking note of the efforts of the FGS to improve its notifications to the Committee pursuant to resolutions 751 (1992) and 1907 (2009) concerning Somalia and Eritrea ("the Committee"), *urging* further progress in this regard, and *recalling* that improved arms and ammunition management in Somalia is a fundamental component of greater peace and stability for the region,

Commending the efforts of the FGS to restore key economic and financial institutions, increase domestic revenue and implement financial governance and structural reforms, *welcoming* the continued progress on building a track record of reforms under the International Monetary Fund Staff-Monitored Programme, together with progress on the anti-corruption bill, and *highlighting* the importance of continual progress in these areas,

Welcoming the FGS's efforts to implement the Anti-Money Laundering and Countering the Financing of Terrorism Act (2015) and the National Communications Act (2017), *underlining* the importance of compliance with the counter-terrorism and national security provisions in this legislation, and *further welcoming* the establishment of a Financial Reporting Centre to serve as Somalia's financial intelligence unit,

Underlining the importance of financial propriety in contributing to stability and prosperity, *welcoming* the efforts of the FGS to address corruption, and *stressing* the need for a zero tolerance approach to corruption to promote transparency and increase mutual accountability in Somalia,

Expressing serious concern at reports of illegal, unreported and unregulated fishing in waters where Somalia has jurisdiction, *underlining* the importance of refraining from illegal, unreported and unregulated fishing, *welcoming* further reporting on the matter, and *encouraging* the FGS, with the support of the international community, to ensure that fishing licenses are issued in a responsible manner and in line with the appropriate Somali legal framework,

Expressing serious concern at the ongoing difficulties in delivering humanitarian aid in Somalia, and *condemning* in the strongest terms any party obstructing the safe delivery of humanitarian assistance, any misappropriation or diversion of any humanitarian funds or supplies, and acts of violence against and harassment of humanitarian workers,

Recalling that the FGS has the primary responsibility to protect its population, and *recognising* the FGS's responsibility, working with the FMSs, to build the capacity of its own national security forces, as a matter of priority,

Welcoming the FGS's efforts to address sexual- and gender-based violence, *encouraging* strengthened reporting mechanisms to facilitate prosecutions, and *further encouraging* the FGS to continue to implement its National Action Plan on Ending Sexual Violence in Conflict through training, accountability, victim support and oversight of the security sector,

Commending efforts towards peace, stability and reconciliation in the region, including the signing of the Joint Declaration of Peace and Friendship between Eritrea and Ethiopia on 9 July 2018, the signing of the Joint Declaration on Comprehensive Cooperation between Ethiopia, Somalia and Eritrea on 5 September 2018, and the signing of the Agreement on Peace, Friendship and Comprehensive Cooperation between Eritrea and Ethiopia on 16 September 2018,

Taking note of the decision of the Secretary-General to appoint a new Special Envoy for the Horn of Africa who will, inter alia, work with the Intergovernmental Authority on Development (IGAD) and other relevant subregional and regional organisations in consolidating recent gains in peace and security in the region, and carry out good offices on behalf of the Secretary-General,

Regretting that the SEMG has not been able to visit Eritrea since 2011 and fully discharge its mandate, and *welcoming* the meeting on 5 October 2018 between the representative of the Government of Eritrea and the Coordinator of the SEMG,

Welcoming that in recent months several armed groups in the region have declared that they will cease hostilities and engage peacefully in efforts to pursue reconciliation in the region,

Expressing concern at ongoing reports of Djiboutian combatants missing in action since the clashes in 2008, *calling on* Eritrea and Djibouti to continue to engage in resolving the issues of combatants, and *urging* Eritrea to share any further available detailed information pertaining to the combatants,

Taking note of increased engagement between Eritrea and Djibouti, *strongly encouraging* further efforts towards normalisation of relations and good neighbourhood between Djibouti and Eritrea, including cooperation in accordance with international law to resolve any disputes regarding their shared border, and *reaffirming* its readiness to continue to assist the parties in the peaceful settlement of any prolonged disputes,

Determining that the situation in Somalia continues to constitute a threat to international peace and security in the region,

Acting under Chapter VII of the Charter of the United Nations,

Lifting of Arms Embargoes, Travel Bans, Asset Freezes and Targeted Sanctions on Eritrea

1. *Recalls* paragraphs 16 and 17 of resolution 1907 (2009) and *recognises* that during the course of its current and four previous mandates the SEMG has not found conclusive evidence that Eritrea supports Al-Shabaab;

2. *Welcomes* the meeting on 25 September 2018 between the representative of the Government of Eritrea and the Chair of the Committee, and *further welcomes* the meeting on 5 October 2018 between the representative of the Government of Eritrea and the Coordinator of the SEMG, with the participation of the Chair of the Committee;

3. *Welcomes* the meeting between the President of Djibouti and the President of Eritrea in Jeddah on 17 September 2018, *underlines* the importance of continuing efforts towards the normalisation of relations between Eritrea and Djibouti for regional peace, stability and reconciliation, and *encourages* Member States, international, regional and subregional organisations and other parties to continue to support these efforts including through their good offices;

4. *Decides* to lift from the date of adoption of this resolution the arms embargoes, travel bans, asset freezes and targeted sanctions imposed on Eritrea by the Security Council in its resolutions 1907 (2009) 2023 (2011), 2060 (2012) and 2111 (2013);

5. *Expresses its satisfaction* that funds derived from the mining sector of Eritrea are not contributing to violations of resolutions 1844 (2008), 1862 (2009), 1907 (2009) or 2023 (2011), and *decides* that from the date of adoption of this resolution, States are no longer required to undertake the measures set out in paragraph 13 of resolution 2023 (2011);

6. *Urges* Eritrea and Djibouti to engage on the issue of the Djiboutian combatants missing in action including through the mediation of any relevant party of their own choosing, and *further urges* Eritrea to make available any further detailed information;

7. *Urges* the two parties to continue efforts to settle their border dispute peacefully in a manner consistent with international law by conciliation, arbitration or judicial settlement, or by any other means of pacific dispute settlement identified in Article 33 of the Charter upon which they agree;

8. *Affirms* that it will continue to follow developments towards the normalisation of relations between Eritrea and Djibouti and will support the two countries in the resolution of these matters in good faith;

Committee

9. *Decides* that the mandate of the Committee pursuant to resolutions 751 (1992) and 1907 (2009) concerning Somalia and Eritrea, hereafter to be known as the Committee pursuant to resolution 751 (1992) concerning Somalia ("the Committee"), shall

include the tasks as set out in paragraph 11 of resolution 751 (1992), paragraph 11 of resolution 1844 (2008), and paragraph 23 of resolution 2036 (2012), and *requests* that the Committee amends its guidelines, its implementation assistance notices and its website accordingly;

Somalia and Eritrea Monitoring Group

10. *Decides* to terminate the mandate of the Somalia and Eritrea Monitoring Group (SEMG), with effect from 16 December 2018;

Panel of Experts on Somalia

11. *Decides* to establish, with effect from the date of adoption of this resolution, until 15 December 2019, the Panel of Experts on Somalia, *further decides* that the mandate of the Panel of Experts shall include the tasks as set out in paragraph 13 of resolution 2060 (2012) and updated in paragraph 41 of resolution 2093 (2013), paragraph 15 of resolution 2182 (2014), paragraph 23 of resolution 2036 (2012) and paragraph 29 of this resolution as they relate to Somalia, and *expresses* its intention to review the mandate and take appropriate action regarding any extensions of the mandate of the Panel of Experts no later than 15 November 2019;

12. *Requests* the Secretary-General to take the necessary administrative measures as expeditiously as possible to establish the Panel of Experts, consisting of six members and to be based in Nairobi, in consultation with the Committee, until 15 December 2019, drawing, as appropriate, on the expertise of the members of the SEMG established pursuant to previous resolutions, and *further requests* the Panel of Experts to include the necessary gender expertise, in line with paragraph 6 of resolution 2242 (2015);

Somalia Arms Embargo

13. *Reaffirms* the arms embargo on Somalia, imposed by paragraph 5 of resolution 733 (1992) and further elaborated upon in paragraphs 1 and 2 of resolution 1425 (2002) and modified by paragraphs 33 to 38 of resolution 2093 (2013) and paragraphs 4 to 17 of resolution 2111 (2013), paragraph 14 of resolution 2125 (2013), paragraph 2 of resolution 2142 (2014), paragraph 2 of resolution 2244 (2015), paragraph 2 of resolution 2317 (2016) and paragraph 2 of resolution 2385 (2017) (hereafter referred to as "the arms embargo on Somalia");

14. *Decides* to renew the provisions set out in paragraph 2 of resolution 2142 (2014) until 15 November 2019, and in that context *reiterates* that the arms embargo

on Somalia shall not apply to deliveries of weapons, ammunition or military equipment or the provision of advice, assistance or training, intended solely for the development of the Somali National Security Forces, to provide security for the Somali people, except in relation to deliveries of the items set out in the annex of resolution 2111 (2013);

15. *Reaffirms* its decision that the entry into Somali ports for temporary visits of vessels carrying arms and related materiel for defensive purposes does not amount to a delivery of such items in violation of the arms embargo on Somalia, provided that such items remain at all times aboard such vessels;

16. *Reiterates* its decision that weapons or military equipment sold or supplied solely for the development of the Somali National Security Forces may not be resold to, transferred to, or made available for use by, any individual or entity not in the service of the Somali National Security Forces, and *underlines* the responsibility of the FGS and the FMSs to ensure the safe and effective management, storage and security of their stockpiles;

17. *Welcomes* in this regard the improvements made by the FGS in weapons registration, recording and marking procedures and *encourages* further improvements, *expresses concern* at reports of continued weapons diversion from within the FGS and FMSs, *notes* that further improved weapons and ammunition management is vital in order to prevent the diversion of weapons and ammunition, and *reiterates* that the Security Council is committed to monitoring and assessing improvements in order to review the arms embargo when all conditions as set out in Security Council resolutions are met;

18. *Calls upon* the FGS to facilitate access for the Panel of Experts, on the basis of written requests to the FGS by the Panel of Experts submitted at least ten days in advance, to all FGS armouries in Mogadishu, all FGS imported weapons and ammunition prior to distribution, all FGS military storage facilities in Somalia National Army (SNA) sectors and all captured weaponry in FGS custody, and to allow photographs of weapons and ammunition in FGS custody and access to all FGS logbooks and distribution records, in order to enable the Security Council to monitor and assess progress in this area;

19. *Welcomes* the ongoing efforts of the FGS to develop detailed Standard Operating Procedures for weapons and ammunition management including an issue and receipt system to track all weapons post distribution, *further welcomes* the development of a mechanism to distribute weapons and ammunition to regional forces, consistent with the requirements of this resolution including paragraph 16, *encourages* that such a mechanism be expanded to include other military equipment and supplies, consistent with the requirements of this resolution including paragraph 16, and *urges* the FGS to finalise and implement these procedures as soon as possible;

20. *Welcomes* the establishment of the Joint Verification Team (JVT) and *urges* Member States to support improved weapons and ammunition management to improve the capacity of the FGS to manage weapons and ammunition;

21. *Takes notes of* FGS reporting to the Security Council pursuant to paragraph 9 of resolution 2182 (2014) and as requested in paragraph 7 of resolution 2244

(2015), *calls on* the FGS and FMSs to accelerate the implementation of the National Security Architecture agreement, the Security Pact, and the transition plan in order to provide Somali-led security and protection to the people of Somalia, and *requests* the FGS to report to the Security Council in accordance with paragraph 9 of resolution 2182 (2014) and as requested in paragraph 7 of resolution 2244 (2015), by 15 March 2019 and then by 15 September 2019, on the structure, composition, strength and disposition of its Security Forces, including the status of regional and militia forces, and to include as annexes the reports of the JVT requested in paragraph 7 of resolution 2182 (2014);

22. *Recalls* that the FGS has the primary responsibility to notify the Committee of any deliveries of weapons, ammunition or military equipment or the provision of advice, assistance or training to its Security Forces, pursuant to paragraphs 3 to 8 of resolution 2142 (2014), and *calls upon* the FGS to improve its notifications to the Committee;

23. *Calls upon* the FGS to continue to improve the timeliness and content of notifications regarding the completion of deliveries, as set out in paragraph 6 of resolution 2142 (2014);

24. *Requests* the FGS to incorporate the notifications regarding the destination unit in the Somali National Security Forces upon distribution of imported arms and ammunition, detailed in paragraph 7 of resolution 2142 (2014), into the regular FGS reporting to the Security Council requested in paragraph 20;

25. *Stresses* Member States' obligations pursuant to the notification procedures set out in paragraph 11 (a) of resolution 2111 (2013), *urges* Member States to strictly follow the notification procedures for providing assistance to develop Somali security sector institutions, and *encourages* Member States to consider Implementation Assistance Notice No.2 of the Committee as a guide;

26. *Recalls* paragraph 2 of resolution 2142 (2014) and *notes* that support for the development of the Somali National Security Forces may include, inter alia, building infrastructure and provision of salaries and stipends solely provided to the Somali National Security Forces;

27. *Urges* increased cooperation by the FGS, FMSs and AMISOM, as set out in paragraph 6 of resolution 2182 (2014), to document and register all military equipment captured as part of offensive operations or in the course of carrying out their mandates;

28. *Calls upon* the FGS and FMSs to enhance civilian oversight of their security forces, to continue to adopt and implement appropriate vetting procedures of all defence and security personnel, including human rights vetting, and to investigate and as appropriate prosecute individuals responsible for violations of international law, including international humanitarian law and human rights law, and in this context *recalls* the importance of the Secretary-General's Human Rights and Due Diligence Policy in relation to the support provided by the United Nations to Somali security forces;

29. *Decides* that the Panel of Experts will continue the investigations started by the SEMG related to the export to Somalia of chemicals that may be used as oxidisers in the manufacture of improvised explosive devices, such as the precursors

ammonium nitrate, potassium chlorate, potassium nitrate and sodium chlorate with a view to considering further action, and *calls on* Members States and the FGS to cooperate with the Panel of Experts in this regard;

30. *Underlines* the importance of timely and predictable payment of salaries to the Somali security forces and *calls on* the FGS to continue to implement systems to improve the timeliness and accountability of payments and supply of provisions to the Somali security forces, and *welcomes* the progress made to date on biometric registration;

31. *Recalls* the need to build the capacities of the Somali National Security Forces, in particular the provision of equipment, training and mentoring, in order to develop credible, professional and representative security forces to enable the gradual handing over of security responsibilities from AMISOM to the Somali security forces in line with the transition plan, and *encourages* further donor support and coordination as set out in the Security Pact;

32. *Requests* the Secretary-General to conduct a technical assessment regarding the arms embargo, with options and recommendations for improving implementation, by 15 May 2019;

Threats to Peace and Security in Somalia

33. *Condemns* Al-Shabaab's increased revenue from natural resources including the taxing of the illicit sugar trade, agricultural production and livestock, *further expresses concern* at the group's involvement in the illicit charcoal trade, and *welcomes* the Panel of Experts' reporting on these issues;

34. *Requests* the FGS to cooperate with the Panel of Experts to facilitate interviews of suspected members of Al-Shabaab and ISIL (also known as D'aesh) held in FGS custody, in order to assist the Panel of Experts with its investigations;

35. *Welcomes* the efforts that the FGS has made to improve its financial management procedures including the successful completion of two International Monetary Fund (IMF) Staff-Monitoring programmes and the commitments to further reform made under the third Staff-Monitored programme, *encourages* the FGS and FMSs to maintain the pace of reform to increase transparency, accountability, comprehensiveness and predictability in revenue collection and budget allocations, and *expresses concern* at the generation and distribution of counterfeit Somali currency;

36. *Expresses concern* at the continued reports of corruption and diversion of public resources, including reports of alleged financial impropriety involving members of the FGS, FMSs, Federal Parliament and Somali opposition groups which pose a risk to state-building efforts, and in this context *strongly welcomes* the steps taken by the FGS to address cases of corruption and to develop anti-corruption legislation;

37. *Underlines* that individuals engaged in acts that threaten the peace and reconciliation process in Somalia may be listed for targeted measures;

38. *Recognises* that addressing outstanding constitutional issues around power and resource sharing between the FGS and FMSs is crucial for Somalia's stability, *calls* upon the FGS and the FMSs to work constructively together to address these issues in an inclusive manner, and *encourages* the FGS and FMSs to implement the outstanding elements of the National Security Architecture agreement, including decisions around the make-up, distribution and command and control of the security forces and resource-sharing;

39. *Reaffirms* Somalia's sovereignty over its natural resources;

40. *Reiterates its serious concern* that the petroleum sector in Somalia could be a driver for increased conflict, *welcomes* the political agreement on petroleum and mineral resource-sharing reached by the FGS and the FMSs in June 2018, and *underlines* the vital importance of the FGS and FMSs putting in place, without undue delay, resource-sharing arrangements and credible legal frameworks to ensure that the petroleum sector in Somalia does not become a source of increased tension;

Somalia Charcoal Ban

41. *Reaffirms* its decision regarding the ban on the import and export of Somali charcoal, as set out in paragraph 22 of resolution 2036 (2012) ("the charcoal ban"), *welcomes* efforts of Member States to prevent the import of charcoal of Somali origin, *reiterates* that the FGS and FMSs shall take the necessary measures to prevent the export of charcoal from Somalia, *urges* Member States to continue their efforts to ensure full implementation of the ban, and *further reiterates* that individuals and entities engaged in acts which violate the charcoal ban may be listed for targeted measures;

42. *Reiterates* its requests in paragraph 18 of resolution 2111 (2013) and paragraph 16 of resolution 2431 (2018) that AMISOM support and assist the FGS and FMSs in implementing the total ban on the export of charcoal from Somalia, and *calls upon* AMISOM to facilitate regular access for the Panel of Experts to charcoal exporting ports;

43. *Welcomes* the efforts of the Combined Maritime Forces (CMF) to disrupt the export and import of charcoal to and from Somalia, and *further welcomes* the cooperation between the Panel of Experts and CMF in keeping the Committee informed on the charcoal trade;

44. *Expresses concern* that the charcoal trade provides significant funding for Al-Shabaab, and in that context reiterates paragraphs 11 to 21 of resolution 2182 (2014), and *further decides* to renew the provisions set out in paragraph 15 of resolution 2182 (2014) until 15 November 2019;

45. *Condemns* the ongoing export of charcoal from Somalia, in violation of the total ban on the export of charcoal, *calls* on Member States to share information with the Panel of Experts, *requests* the Panel of Experts to continue to focus on this in their next report and propose further measures, taking account of human rights

concerns, and *expresses* its intention to consider further measures if violations continue;

46. *Encourages* the United Nations Office on Drugs and Crime to continue its work with the FGS, within its current mandate, under the Indian Ocean Forum on Maritime Crime to bring together relevant Member States and international organisations to develop strategies to disrupt the trade in Somali charcoal;

Humanitarian Access in Somalia

47. *Expresses grave concern* at the ongoing humanitarian situation in Somalia and its impact on the people of Somalia, *commends* the efforts of the United Nations humanitarian agencies and other humanitarian actors to deliver life-saving assistance to vulnerable populations, *condemns* in the strongest terms attacks against humanitarian actors and any misuse of donor assistance and the obstruction of the delivery of humanitarian aid, *reiterates* its demand that all parties allow and facilitate full, safe and unhindered access for the timely delivery of aid to persons in need across Somalia, and *encourages* the FGS to improve the regulatory environment for aid donors;

48. *Decides* that until 15 November 2019 and without prejudice to humanitarian assistance programmes conducted elsewhere, the measures imposed by paragraph 3 of resolution 1844 (2008) shall not apply to the payment of funds, other financial assets or economic resources necessary to ensure the timely delivery of urgently needed humanitarian assistance in Somalia, by the United Nations, its specialised agencies or programmes, humanitarian organisations having observer status with the United Nations General Assembly that provide humanitarian assistance, and their implementing partners including bilaterally or multilaterally funded non-governmental organisations participating in the United Nations Humanitarian Response Plan for Somalia;

49. *Requests* the Emergency Relief Coordinator to report to the Security Council by 15 October 2019 on the delivery of humanitarian assistance in Somalia and on any impediments to the delivery of humanitarian assistance in Somalia, and *requests* relevant United Nations agencies and humanitarian organisations having observer status with the United Nations General Assembly and their implementing partners that provide humanitarian assistance in Somalia to increase their cooperation and willingness to share information with the United Nations;

Targeted Sanctions in Somalia

50. *Recalls* its decisions in resolution 1844 (2008) which imposed targeted sanctions and resolutions 2002 (2011) and 2093 (2013) which expanded the listing criteria, *notes* one of the listing criteria under resolution 1844 (2008) is engaging in or

providing support for acts that threaten the peace, security or stability of Somalia, and *decides* that such acts may also include but are not limited to planning, directing or committing acts involving sexual and gender-based violence;

51. *Reiterates* its willingness to adopt targeted measures against individuals and entities on the basis of the above-mentioned criteria;

52. *Recalls* paragraph 2 (c) of resolution 2060 (2012) and emphasises that certain misappropriation of financial resources is a criterion for designation and applies to misappropriation at all levels;

53. *Reiterates* its request for Member States to assist the Panel of Experts in its investigations, and *further requests* the FGS, FMSs and AMISOM to share information with the Panel of Experts regarding Al-Shabaab activities;

Reporting

54. *Requests* the Panel of Experts to provide monthly updates to the Committee pursuant to resolution 751 (1992), and a comprehensive midterm update, as well as to submit, for the Security Council's consideration, through the Committee, a final report by 15 October 2019;

55. *Requests* the Committee, in accordance with its mandate and in consultation with the Panel of Experts and other relevant United Nations entities, to consider the recommendations contained in the reports of the Panel of Experts and recommend to the Security Council ways to improve the implementation of and compliance with the Somalia arms embargo, the measures regarding the import and export of charcoal from Somalia, as well as implementation of the measures imposed by paragraphs 1, 3 and 7 of resolutions 1844 (2008) in response to continuing violations;

56. *Requests* the Committee to consider, where and when appropriate, visits to selected countries by the Chair and/or Committee members to enhance the full and effective implementation of the measures above, with a view to encouraging States to comply fully with this resolution;

57. *Requests* the Secretary General to keep the Security Council informed of developments towards the normalisation of relations between Eritrea and Djibouti and to report to the Security Council no later than 15 February 2019 and every six months thereafter, and *expresses its intention* to keep this request under review in light of developments;

58. *Decides* to remain seized of the matter.

References

Cohen H (2013) Time to bring Eritrea in from the cold. African Arguments, 16 December 2013. https://africanarguments.org/2013/12/16/time-to-bring-eritrea-in-from-the-cold-by-hank-cohen/

Eritrean Ministry of Information (2018) Joint Declaration of Peace and Friendship between Eritrea and Ethiopia. http://www.shabait.com/news/local-news/26639-joint-declaration-of-peace-and-friendship-between-eritrea-and-ethiopia. Accessed 18 Jan 2019

Gilkes P, Plaut M (2000) The war between Ethiopia and Eritrea. Foreign Policy Focus 5:1–6

Hirt N (2008) Eritrea, the USA and the "War on Terrorism": internal challenges and the international dimension. In: Bruchhaus E-M, Sommer M (eds) Hot spot horn of Africa revisited: approaches to make sense of conflict. Lit Verlag, Berlin

Hirt N (2009) Eritrea. In: Mehler A, Melber H, Van Walraven K (eds) Africa yearbook: politics, economy and society south of the Sahara. Brill, Leiden

Hirt N (2014) The Eritrean diaspora and its impact on regime stability: responses to UN sanctions. Afr Aff 114(454):129

Monitoring Group on Somalia and Eritrea (2012) Letter dated 27 June 2012 from the members of the Monitoring Group on Somalia and Eritrea addressed to the Chairman of the Security Council Committee pursuant to resolutions 751 (1992) and 1907 (2009) concerning Somalia and Eritrea. http://www.marsecreview.com/wp-content/uploads/2012/09/UN_REPORT_2012.pdf

Negash T, Tronvoll K (2000) Brothers at war: making sense of the Eritrean-Ethiopian war. James Currey, Oxford

UNSC (2009) Resolution 1907 (2009). http://www.un.org/ga/search/view_doc.asp?symbol=S/RES/1907(2009). Accessed 18 Jan 2019

UNSC (2011a) Resolution 2023 (2011). https://www.securitycouncilreport.org/atf/cf/%7B65BFCF9B-6D27-4E9C-8CD3-CF6E4FF96FF9%7D/Somalia%20S%20RES%202023.pdf. Accessed 18 Jan 2019

UNSC (2011b) Resolution 2002 (2011). http://undocs.org/S/RES/2002(2011). Accessed 18 Jan 2019

UNSC (2017) Letter dated 2 November 2017 from the Chair of the Security Council Committee pursuant to resolutions 751 (1992) and 1907 (2009) concerning Somalia and Eritrea addressed to the President of the Security Council (S/2017/925) at https://www.securitycouncilreport.org/atf/cf/%7B65BFCF9B-6D27-4E9C-8CD3-CF6E4FF96FF9%7D/s_2017_925.pdf

UNSC (2018) Resolution 2444 (2018). https://www.securitycouncilreport.org/un-documents/document/sres2444.php. Accessed 18 Jan 2019

MIX
Papier aus verantwortungsvollen Quellen
Paper from responsible sources
FSC® C105338

If you have any concerns about our products,
you can contact us on
ProductSafety@springernature.com

In case Publisher is established outside the EU,
the EU authorized representative is:
Springer Nature Customer Service Center GmbH
Europaplatz 3, 69115 Heidelberg, Germany

Printed by Libri Plureos GmbH
in Hamburg, Germany